Teaching

Elementary School

Mathematics

Teaching Elementary School Mathematics

Robert G. Underhill

University of Houston

721393

Charles E. Merrill Publishing Company

A Bell & Howell Company
Columbus, Ohio

International Standard Book Number: 0–675–09138–1

Library of Congress Catalog Card Number: 70–186447

2 3 4 5 6 7 8 9 10—76 75 74 73 72

Printed in the United States of America

Preface

This text was written for people who wish to understand or who have a need to become familiar with the content and instruction of elementary school mathematics. The reader will attain a good grasp of the structure of elementary school mathematics, knowledge of specific methods and materials of instruction, knowledge of general instructional and evaluation strategies, and a greater awareness of the influence of his actions on the development of attitudes and understandings of young learners.

Several format features and topics set this text apart from others which are designed for the same purpose. Several such areas will be briefly described.

Programmed Content-Methods Sections

Nine chapters contain twelve programmed sections in which the reader explores content and methods simultaneously. Many pictures and diagrams are used to explain how sequences of mathematical steps relate to manipulations of teaching aids.

Behavioral Obectives. Each programmed section has behaviorally stated objectives. The reader is told what he should be able to do after completing each section of programmed materials.

Self-Tests. At the conclusion of each programmed section, the reader can respond to the items on a self-test. Each self-test is designed to evaluate the reader's performance on the behaviorally stated objectives. Answers to all questions in the programmed materials and self-tests are readily available to the reader for immediate reinforcement.

Learner Involvement. Materials available in most dormitory rooms and dwellings are used as manipulative aids in helping the reader understand mathematics instruction. The programmed materials are *not* the usual paper-and-pencil type.

Methods Core

The first six chapters of this text briefly summarize major methodological concepts. Those chapters are referred to repeatedly in later chapters and form a methods framework to which all instructional decisons can be related. Chapters 1 through 6 present the basic ideas and later chapters present numerous examples which exemplify, elaborate and illustrate them. The reader will probably refer to the first six chapters many times as he seeks to relate the broad ideas to the specific applications.

Psychology. Some basic ideas of Piaget, Bruner and Gagné are presented to focus the reader's attention on important concepts of child development, types of learning, content structure and readiness. Succeeding chapters relate mathematics learnings to these basic ideas.

Individualization. After the term is defined, a model is presented which is applicable to self-contained classrooms and team-teaching. Several learner needs are considered. Succeeding chapters consider aspects of specific implementation of the model.

Modes of Instruction. Pure discovery, guided discovery and expository instruction are defined. The strengths, weaknesses and appropriate uses of each are explored, and many specific examples of guided discovery strategies are discussed throughout the remainder of the book.

Diagnosis. A somewhat different approach is taken to construction of diagnostic instruments which has evolved from Bruner's emphasis on structure and types of learning and upon Piaget's emphasis on learner involvement in concept-related manipulations. The reader is given a model and, in succeeding chapters, is given many helpful content structure sequences, sample objectives and sample questions.

Slow Learners. Several implications are drawn from memory research which may be helpful to the reader. Materials and bibliographies for slow and fast learners are included.

Numerations Materials

Chapter 9 contains notation which is unique. The notation is an outgrowth of the author's work with first-graders and has been highly successful in developing place value concepts with a wide ability range of first-graders and with many classes of undergraduate and graduate level teacher education majors. The college students' responses have been very enthusiastic.

Suggested Resources

In addition to numerous application and discussion sections on teaching aids, each chapter in Part 2 contains a list of *teacher education resources* such as films, filmstrips and references to specific pages of selected elementary school mathematics textbooks. Each chapter also has a list of discussion and/or project questions which are designed to stimulate discussion and encourage the reader to maintain a high level of awareness of the concepts in the methodological core (chapters 1–6). Finally, most chapters contain references to other sources for the reader who desires further examples and/or points of view.

Overview

This book discusses transfer; it then attempts to use the ideas of transfer. Major ideas are presented and reinforced throughout the book in a variety of applicable situations. This book discusses individual needs; it then attempts to meet individual needs through use of programmed materials. This book discusses learner involvement; it then involves the learner in using instructional materials while practicing the skills being taught. This book discusses behavioral objectives, pre-tests, and post-tests; it then incorporates these items in the programmed sections.

Chapters in Part 1 (the methods core) have purposefully been kept short. They are the theoretical, general expositions. Chapters in Part 2 encompass great detail relative to the general treatments in Part 1. The reader will undoubtedly refer to chapters 1 through 6 many times while studying Part 2. Frequent references to Part 1 are noted in later chapters. Only through this integration can all the material be presented in one volume.

Robert G. Underhill

University of Houston

January, 1972

Acknowledgments

Many people have made significant contributions towards the development and completion of this manuscript. The greatest contribution and sacrifice has been made by my wife, Ethel Marie Fowler Underhill, without whose work and support this book might not have become a reality. She typed all the programmed materials during two of the four revisions, prepared them for the final manuscript and typed the entire draft. Her typing and artwork were masterpieces of painstaking detail. Also, her moral support, patience and tolerance have been of inestimable value to me as she assumed nearly all of the responsibilities of maintaining a house, caring for three pre-schoolers and keeping me sane!

Special thanks are also given to Dr. Lorren Stull of The Ohio State University whose reviews were far beyond the call of duty in the attention paid to detail and nuance of meaning and interpretation. Thanks, too, to Mrs. Jerriene Underwood for her personal attention and the attention of her staff in the preparation of the final manuscript.

I am especially grateful to Mrs. Judith Lubina for her review of memory research, to all my students who have provided examples, and to my colleague, Dr. Charles W. Smith, who has served as a source of many excellent ideas.

One cannot help but reflect momentarily about past associates who have influenced the course of idea development and direction in one's career. I am mindful of the many fine staff members at Michigan State University in the College of Education and the Mathematics Department, especially my friend and advisor, Dr. W. Robert Houston. Teaching as an art and mathematics as a source of esthetic appreciation were impressed upon me by my dear friend William K. Viertel of Canton, New York.

Finally, I thank Mr. Steve Branch and my production editor, Miss Chrystyne Cotting.

R.G.U.

To my wife, Ethel Marie,
with love and appreciation.

Contents

PART I

Methodological Core

Psychology and Mathematics Instruction

Your instruction can be enhanced if you are familiar with some general ideas of developmental and learning theories of psychology. Translation of those theories into some meaningful components of a theory of mathematics instruction is the primary goal of this chapter. Some particularly relevant ideas from the work of Piaget are summarized and major implications drawn. Further, Jerome Bruner's contributions towards a viable theory of instruction are cited. Particular attention is devoted to the relationship between Bruner's work and Piaget's theory and possible contributions for the improvement of mathematical learning experiences for children.

Some Key Ideas from Piaget's Developmental Psychology

Since Piaget's initial training was in biology, he tends to view the development of intelligence within the framework of a rather broad biological model. Aspects of general growth and self-preservation are translated into a model for intellectual development. A broad but brief overview of his development theory follows.[1]

---

[1] This section is based primarily on John H. Flavell's book, *The Developmental Psychology of Jean Piaget* (Princeton, New Jersey: Van Nostrand Reinhold Co., 1963). On p. vii of the foreword Piaget states that "it *is* a fine book, and hence there is no reluctance about praising its virtues and expressing my deepest appreciation to its author."

An organism attempts to maintain itself in a state of equilibrium. It takes in food to sustain a state of life; it is active and restful; its existence is characterized by *organization* and *adaptive* behavior. *Adaptation* is an evolutionary chain of actions in which the organism changes its life forms and seeks to modify its environment.

An organism's need for nourishment can be used as an illustration. Assuming that the organism has a built-in need for continued existence, stability of its state-of-being is an end in itself. During the life of the organism, food is taken in (assimilated) and changed into a usable form. At the same time, the food, because of its shape or other physical characteristics, brings about in the organism a corresponding adjustment to the ingested substance; the substance is accommodated. *Adaptation* refers to the dual relations between the food and the organism and has two components: *assimilation* and *accommodation*. Objects which cannot be assimilated or accommodated cannot serve as food. Objects which are taken in but which cannot be broken down by digestive enzymes, such as a rock, can be assimilated but not accommodated, and objects which are too large or which the organism refuses to ingest have an accommodation potential but are not assimilated. In both cases adaptive behavior is incomplete.

Piaget relates these biological phenomena to the learning process. He views the biological components of *organization* and *adaptation* as integral parts of the growth of intelligence. In his view, an individual always exists in an organized, i.e., systematic, orderly, self-predictable, state which is maintained as a stable system through adaptive behavior. However, the state of equilibrium varies in degrees of stability. The following outline indicates the various possibilities.

I. No Adaptation
    A. No Assimilation
        1. Biological: A large rock cannot be ingested.
        2. Intellectual: Meaningless and/or irrelevant material is not "taken in."
    B. No Accommodation
        1. Biological: A small rock can be ingested but the organism cannot digest it.
        2. Intellectual: Rote material is taken in but is not useful knowledge. People memorize formulas but cannot use them.
II. Partial Adaptation
    A. Partial Assimilation
        1. Biological: A person eats the meat but leaves the bone.
        2. Intellectual: Information (perception) is altered to agree with previous beliefs (distortion).
    B. Partial Accommodation
        1. Biological: When lettuce is ingested, nutrients are extracted but cellulose is not broken down.
        2. Intellectual: Pieces of information are logically inconsistent but the person is not aware of the inconsistency.

III. Total Adaptation—Total Assimilation and Accommodation
  1. Biological: Certain sugars and proteins
  2. Intellectual: No distortion of reality

Adaptation sometimes occurs and sometimes it does not. When assimilation does not occur, the organism does not adapt, and when accommodation does not occur, the organism does not adapt.

Thus, there exist parallels in biological and intellectual adaptive behaviors. A primary difference is in the value judgment associated with incomplete adaptation. When biological adaptation in the food example is incomplete, one would merely conclude that the ingested substance was not the most appropriate one for nourishment; the attitude is rather neutral.

On the other hand, incomplete intellectual adaptation has implications for teaching and learning. When assimilation is inappropriate, the organism has altered information or "reality" to fit existing cognitive structures. When the organism accommodates information inappropriately, he has introduced logical inconsistencies into his cognitive structures. Such inconsistencies are said to produce disequilibrium.

As you will see in the remainder of this section, a child's inappropriate adaptations are related to a series of stages in his intellectual development. Perception and thought are characterized and influenced by certain factors which determine the types of distortions occurring in the process of adaptation.

When a child adapts appropriately he maintains cognitive equilibrium, but when he adapts inappropriately he increases the amount of cognitive disequilibrium. Equilibrium equates with stability, and disequilibrium increases instability. Youngsters at each level of intellectual development are characterized by types and extent of instability. The transition from an unstable to a more stable condition is termed *equilibration*. Through the process of equilibration, the child acquires *new* structures and a *new* state of equilibrium.

Stages of Development

The process of equilibration is a central theme of Piaget's theory of cognitive development. Why do stages of equilibrium become unbalanced? According to Piaget, the following are factors influencing the process of equilibration:

  A. Maturation of the nervous system
  B. Experience
  C. Peer interaction

Also according to Piaget, intellectual development is a series of equilibrations, each one stemming from the one before it. Transition from one stage to another occurs as the child becomes aware, through the influence of these three factors, of inadequacies of one system and potentialities of the other.

During his many years of study of Swiss children, including his own, Piaget found that development can be broken down into three or four distinct stages, and each stage is made up of several sub-stages. Most literature refers to four stages:

I. Sensory Motor Stage (about birth to two years)
II. Preoperational Stage (about two to six or seven years)
III. Stage of Concrete Operations (about six or seven to eleven or twelve years)
IV. Stage of Formal or Logical Operations (begins at about eleven or twelve years)

Note that the ages are approximate. Note, too, that the sequence is *fixed* (invariant); children always pass through these stages *in this order*. The speed varies from child to child. In the brief description which follows, emphasis is placed on the characteristics which have special importance for elementary school instruction. These characteristics will be referred to repeatedly in later chapters.

I. Sensory Motor Intelligence. During the first two years of life the child is without language. Many motor sequences are learned which enable the child to master complex motor activities. He begins to exercise considerable control over objects in his environment. During the latter part of this stage he becomes aware of "self-other," and language begins to appear.

II. Preoperational Intelligence. During the pre-school years and most of nursery school, kindergarten and grade one, the child exhibits the following characteristics:

A. *Egocentrism.* He can see only his own point of view and, further, feels no impulse to try to see any other point of view. He does not adjust his speech to the listener, nor does he see any need to justify his behavior. He may, for example, use many pronouns without apparent referents and become rather irritated when you fail to understand his attempts to communicate. "He thinks but cannot think about his own thinking" (4:156). He cannot recount a train of reasoning.

He thinks everyone observes the world through a perspective which is identical to his own. My four-year-old daughter, Amy, looks out the window and says, "Look at the bird, Daddy." I am sitting in a position which does not permit me to see it. "Where, Amy? I don't see a bird." She points and says, "Right there." She is unable to comprehend that my field of vision differs from hers.

B. *Centration.* The preoperational child focuses on one attribute at a time without regard to others. If two sticks are placed side by side and the child says they are the same length, he will think one is longer if one is moved to the right or left.

C. *Transformations.* The child cannot easily retrace successive steps. He is tied to the observable present and has difficulty recounting a sequence of events or movements. When you ask a four-year-old, "How did you do that?" he will frequently reply with a shrug, "I just *did* it!"

D. *Equilibrium.* He is in an unstable state most of the time since he is so perceptually bound.

E. *Thought.* He thinks very concretely, replicating in his memory impressionistic perceptions and actions on concrete objects.

F. *Irreversibility.* He cannot retrace changes (transformations) back to their logical beginnings as exemplified in the length situation cited above.

G. *Cause and effect.* He is very lax in relating events causally; every event, idea, name, and relation is believed to have an explanation which is causal in nature.

III. Concrete Operational Intelligence. During the first or second year of school the child begins to develop a *system* of thought. The various components are brought into equilibrium, and the resultant operations form a logical system. He gradually overcomes the limitations formerly possessed. The child still has the following limitations:

A. He is tied to the concrete here-and-now. The starting point is always the *real* rather than the potential—given a problem, he cannot formulate all the possible alternatives at the outset and appraise them one at a time.

B. He is still bound to the concrete and must achieve conservation of attributes one at a time (area, time, mass, volume, etc.). He gradually learns that length, area and quantity are the same regardless of position. This important concept of conservation is explored in considerable detail in the preoperational, addition and subtraction, measurement and geometry chapters.

C. The operational systems do not form an integrated whole which allows management of complex tasks.

IV. Formal Operations. "The most important general property of formal-operational thought, the one from which Piaget derives all others, concerns the *real* versus the *possible*" (4:204). When approaching a new problem the child begins by formulating all the possibilities and then determining which ones in fact do hold true through experimentation and logical analysis. Reality is the "is" portion of the "might be" domain. In summary,

The preoperational child is the child of wonder; his cognition appears to us naive, impression-bound, and poorly organized. There is an essential lawlessness about his world without, of course, this fact in any way entering his awareness to inhibit the zest and flights of fancy with which he approaches new situations. Anything is possible because nothing is subject to lawful constraints. The child of concrete operations can be caricatured as a sober and bookkeeperish organizer of the real and a distruster of the subtle, the elusive, and the hypothetical. The adolescent has something of both: the 7-11-year-old's zeal for order and pattern coupled with a much more sophisticated version of the younger child's conceptual daring and uninhibitedness. Unlike the concrete-operational child, he can soar; but also unlike the preoperational child, it is a controlled and planned soaring, solidly grounded in a bedrock of careful analysis and painstaking accommodation to detail (4:211).

Implications

Since succeeding chapters will deal with specific implications, two more global methodological implications will be presented in this section: (1) the importance of concrete materials of instruction used *by the child,* and (2) group learning experiences.

Individualized Concrete Learning Experiences.   The concept of *action* is fundamental to Piaget's theory of intellectual development. Actions are developmental building blocks. In very early childhood (Stage I), actions are overt acts such as sucking, grasping and so on. As the child matures, actions become increasingly *internalized*. In Stages II and III, actions are very literal internalizations. The child repeats in his mind real motor actions on objects. He simply repeats in his head what he has done in a physical setting. These actions of the preoperational and concrete-operational child eventually become more sophisticated as the child develops cognitive systems of thought. Actions become parts of the systems of operations which move from concrete representation to highly abstract levels. Piaget likens all levels of actions to the actions of the infant. There is a thread of commonality between sensory-motor actions, concrete operational actions and actions which are manipulations of highly abstract structures.

Müeller-Willis who worked with Piaget and who also worked with the MINNEMAST Project summarizes it this way:

> Actions are fundamental and constitute the raw material of intelligence or cognition. With development, actions become progressively internalized. No structure is ever radically new; each is simply a generalization of an action drawn from the preceding structure. Thus, adult logical operations are sensori-motor actions which have undergone a succession of transformations (7:40).

Since the child learns new ideas through successive internalization of concrete actions, good instruction should begin with a development of generalizations through operations or actions upon physical entities. An appropriate instructional sequence is one which facilitates internalization and abstract manipulation through careful pacing on a concrete-to-abstract continuum.

> In trying to teach a child some general principle or rule, one should so far as is feasible parallel the developmental process of internalization of actions. That is, the child should first work with the principle in the most concrete and action-oriented context possible; he should be allowed to manipulate objects himself and "see" the principle operate in his own actions. Then, it should become progressively more internalized and schematic by reducing perceptual and motor supports, e.g., moving from objects to symbols of objects, from motor action to speech, etc. (4:84).

Hence, the concrete, physical world which the child comprehends should always be the starting point for new learning. If one thinks of a concrete-abstract continuum, the differences in attention given at any age level should be thought to differ by *degree* rather than kind. The young child encountering fractions for the first time should have a very large degree of concrete experiences, some semi-concrete experiences (pictorial) and very little abstract manipulation of symbols and operations.

Young Child

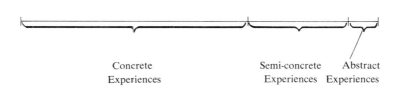

Concrete   Semi-concrete Abstract
Experiences   Experiences Experiences

On the other hand, the older child, assuming he has been taught fractional number concepts previously, can handle new learnings with less concrete work and more semi-concrete and abstract work.

Older Child

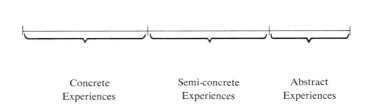

Concrete   Semi-concrete   Abstract
Experiences   Experiences   Experiences

The fact which cannot be over-emphasized, however, is that *all* children need concrete experiences throughout elementary school. Older children may need less than younger children, and intellectually astute children may need less than slow learners, but *all* should have some.

Group Learning Experiences. As noted earlier, the preoperational child is characterized by his egocentrism. This attribute makes him so tied to his own thoughts and behavior that he does not feel any compulsions to justify his logic, adjust his speech to the observer, note his logical inconsistencies and so on. Piaget feels that peer interaction over extended time plays an important role in loosening the child from the grip of egocentrism. In the words of Flavell:

> There remains the question of the mechanism by which the child ultimately frees himself from the grip of egocentrism, with its attendant ills of absolutism, lack of introspection, disinclination towards logical-causal justifi-

cation, and all the rest. It is not simply experience with objects and events in the real world; the child, says Piaget, can and does readily distort physical experience to fit his preexistent schemes. Rather, social interaction is the principal liberating factor, particularly social interaction with peers. In the course of his contacts (and especially, his conflicts and arguments) with other children, the child increasingly finds himself forced to reexamine his own percepts and concepts in the light of those of others, and by so doing, gradually rids himself of cognitive egocentrism . . . (4:279).

Paul Rosenbloom, first director of MINNEMAST, translates the idea succinctly in this manner:

Piaget has identified a preoperational stage when the child makes intuitive judgments but is unable to conceive of operations. During this stage, he is quite egocentric. He sees only his own point of view and the aspects that currently attract his attention. The transition to the next stage seems to occur when the child has to demonstrate what he thinks to someone else. And this happens as a result of social interaction with other children (7: 48–49).

The child is unable to develop and use either concrete or logical operations until he can rid himself of the egocentrism which enfolds him. Social interaction in learning experiences will help release him from its hold

A Summary of Bruner's Interpretation and Extension of Piaget's Theory

Developmental theory helps you place the child's learning abilities into an appropriate frame of reference. You have seen two very important implications of the theory for elementary school mathematics instruction. Now your knowledge of development will be supplemented with some aspects of *learning theory* and a brief summary of some additional teaching implications.

As Bruner says in *Toward a Theory of Instruction,* theories of learning and development are *descriptive* rather than *prescriptive* (2:40). A theory of instruction must necessarily account for development and learning. In this section aspects of Bruner's theory which have particular relation to Piaget's theory of development will be discussed. Other important aspects of Bruner's theory can be found in the following section and in the chapter on instructional modes.

Levels of Knowing

Just as Piaget has described the levels of development as sensory-motor, concrete operations and logical operations, Bruner describes in a corollary manner three levels or kinds of knowing. He calls these *enactive, iconic,* and *symbolic.* During the sensory-motor level of development the child *knows* at the motor level. He can perform many coordinated movements learned primarily through a stimulus-response, trial-and-error manner. Adults, too, know many things at this level. The very young child has no language with which to describe the skills, and neither can the adult, even though he has language, describe his motor knowledge. He cannot communicate to another human being how he walks. Such knowing is termed *enactive*.

During Piaget's second stage the child thinks with mental images of concrete objects. He pictures mentally the collection of two blocks and three blocks which make five blocks. Adults produce imaginary "maps" in their minds to go from one place to another. Visual memory and perceptual organization describe and dominate this type of knowing which is the *iconic* form.

Formal or logical operations do not require concrete referents. Formal operations allow the child to perform mental manipulations on abstract symbols such as occurs in highly organized and symbolized forms in mathematics. Such representations are in the *symbolic* form.

These three levels do not appear in sequence and then disappear; rather, they are used simultaneously for acquisition of new knowledge.

> In the end, the mature organism seems to have gone through a process of elaborating three systems of skills that correspond to the three major tool systems to which he must link himself for full expression of his capacities—tools for the hand, for the distance receptors, and for the process of reflection (2:28).

In essence, man passes through stages of development, and in each stage he develops new tools for dealing with his environment. Cumulatively, these skills enable him to extend his knowledge. New learnings appear to be developed sequentially through these three skills. In working with children, teachers can introduce new concepts at the concrete level. Through motor impressions the child can acquire the concept at an *intuitive* or *non-verbal* level. He cannot explain the meaning of place value, but he can group twelve popsicle sticks into a group of ten and two left over (enactive). Next the child can work with pictures of objects by circling a group of ten (iconic). Finally, he can work with symbols, $12 = 10 + 2$ (symbolic).

A Famous Pronouncement

". . . Any subject can be taught effectively in some intellectually honest form to any child at any stage of development" (1:33). These now famous words will here be placed into the context of the previous section.

The key to understanding is *intuitive* or *non-verbal learning*. Bruner's own words clarify the meaning of the statement:

> . . . The basic ideas that lie at the heart of all science and mathematics and the basic themes that give form to life and literature are as simple as

they are powerful. . . . It is only when such basic ideas are put in formalized terms as equations or elaborated verbal concepts that they are out of reach of the young child, if he has not first understood them intuitively and had a chance to try them out on his own (1:12–13).

Inhelder, who has worked closely with Piaget for many years, agrees with this point of view. She feels that methods of instruction should accommodate the natural thought processes of the child. He should be confronted with concrete experiences which challenge his existing levels of thought. She says,

> . . . It seems highly arbitrary and very likely incorrect to delay the teaching, for example, of Euclidean or metric geometry until the end of the primary grades. . . . Basic notions in these fields are perfectly accessible to children of seven to ten years of age, *provided that they are divorced from their mathematical expression and studied through materials that the child can handle himself* (1:43).

The teacher builds bridges. New concrete experiences build foundations upon which later, more sophisticated learning can occur. This train of thought is closely correlated with the concept of readiness which will be explored presently.

Summary

Children *know* mathematics at different levels. The most basic way of knowing is through motor activity (enactive). Children need intuitive investigations (the *child* will not verbalize the concept) of sophisticated concepts before encountering them through perceptual schema (iconic) or abstract representations (symbolic). A good beginning strategy for developing mathematical concepts in young children is to present concrete materials for manipulation without stress on pupil verbalization or abstract notation.

Readiness and the Spiraling Curriculum

"Is the child ready?" This is a question appropriately asked by teachers at every grade level. New learnings occur within a predetermined context of "givens." The child brings to the learning setting skills, information, experiences and attitudes which are related to his ability to assimilate and accommodate new material. How do these "givens" affect the child's readiness for new learning?

What is readiness and how are children's readiness levels accommodated in the instructional process? In this section, three different but overlapping points of view will be discussed from a theoretical standpoint. Reconciliation of the three points of view will be explored and the importance of the spiraling curriculum elaborated.

Three Points of View

Clark and Eads (3) have stated that the child should not be hurried by the teacher; the teacher should wait until the child's maturational development is adequate to master learning tasks. This point of view is similar to Piaget's (8) who feels there may be an "optimal time" for learning. As Müeller-Willis says,

> His [Piaget] experiments have led to the conclusion that it is not possible to accelerate the pace very much. The child must be biologically ready. Piaget does not say that education can do nothing, only that education is confined by the child's developmental sequence (7:41).

Research studies by several recognized psychologists have been notably *unsuccessful* in hurrying sequential development. The question of pacing remains unanswered, but for the present time, at least, there are known no specific techniques for classroom use to move a child along on the evolutionary scale of intellectual development.

Bruner's famous pronouncement captures his attitudes relative to readiness. He feels that a child is always ready for a concept *in some manner*. His concept of readiness is related to the three ways of knowing discussed previously. The child is ready in the enactive, iconic or symbolic mode: the teacher has the task and responsibility to determine the appropriate strategy, i.e., the one for which the child is *ready*. When children are not ready for an abstract treatment, means can be found by which they can begin to develop an intuitive notion of the concept or to deal with it in mental imagery.

> The "curriculum revolution" has made it plain even after only a decade that the idea of "readiness" is a mischievous half-truth. It is a half-truth largely because it turns out that one *teaches* readiness or provides opportunities for its nurture, one does not simply wait for it. Readiness, in these terms, consists of mastery of those simpler skills that permit one to reach higher skills. Readiness for Euclidean geometry can be gained by teaching intuitive geometry or by giving children an opportunity to build increasingly elaborate constructions with polygons (2:29).

As Shulman (9:43) points out, Bruner works into the concept the relation between learner and what is to be learned. The subject matter can be presented in a way which is consonant with the learner's level of intellectual functioning.

In Robert M. Gagné's *The Conditions of Learning* (5), a hierarchy of learning is theorized upon which readiness acquires a slightly different focus. Acquisition of a new skill or concept is contingent upon the learner's possession of all prerequisite subskills or subconcepts. Structure is the crucial element of Gagné's theory. Suppose you want to know if the child is ready to learn 2 + 3. Gagné proposes that you identify all of the subskills or subconcepts necessary to learn 2 + 3. If the child has the subconcepts, he is ready; if he does not, he is *not* ready. In his view, the child who is not ready to learn a given concept is one

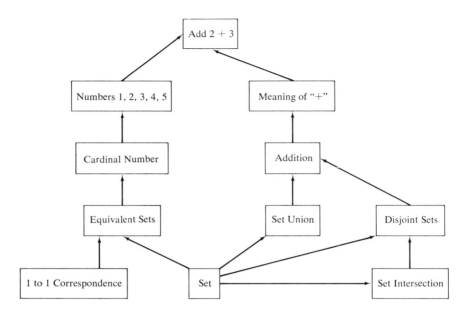

who is lacking prerequisite experiences. Determine the hierarchy of subskills, provide the child with the set of experiences needed to attain the subskills and he will be ready to learn the new concept. Gagné is not concerned with developmental aspects.

Reconciliation

If a structured, inflexible curriculum is meted to the child, the question of readiness must be answered affirmative for some children and negative for others. "Is the child ready to multiply 26×43 using the standard algorithm?" According to Piaget, the child is ready if he has attained a level of maturational development which enables him to deal with such abstractions. According to Bruner, the child is ready if he has already mastered this concept at the enactive and iconic levels. And according to Gagné, the child is ready if he has attained the subskills necessary to use the algorithm.

The child is *ready* or *not ready* in relation to an externally imposed curriculum and set of expectations. Perhaps teachers ask the wrong question. Instead of asking, "Is the child ready?" they should ask, "*For what* is the child ready?" Bruner and Piaget do not seem to be in basic disagreement. They both subscribe to the view that children learn in increasingly more sophisticated means. They are both saying, "Relate the instructional sequence to the developmental level of the child." Gagné's set of experiences fits nicely into this development. Children with experiences in the enactive level are gaining readiness for the iconic level and so on.

What is not reconciled is Gagné's disregard for developmental theory. Considerable research has failed to support the hypothesis that developmental stages can be accelerated. So far, it seems that children can be provided opportunities for manipulations of concrete materials and social interaction but they cannot be taught, for example, to conserve. Further research is needed to resolve this issue but teachers can still seek to provide experiences which facilitate growth.

The Spiraling Curriculum

The previous discussion leads logically to the concept of a spiraling curriculum. The elementary school mathematics curriculum can be thought of as a dual development of arithmetic and geometry. With each succeeding year, the concepts of arithmetic and geometry increase in sophistication and abstractness. Concepts are introduced intuitively and proceed through enactive, iconic and symbolic modes. The curriculum "repeatedly returns to each topic, always expanding it and showing more connections with other topics" (6:8). "Although more and more rigor is introduced for older topics as the course proceeds, at the same time new topics and advanced concepts are being introduced pre-mathematically" (6:14).

The teacher at each grade level builds upon the readiness experiences provided by teachers at lower grade levels and provides the readiness experiences upon which other teachers can later build. The spiraling curriculum is especially obvious in the development of fractions. The kindergarten or first-grade teacher begins with concrete materials. Children manipulate parts and become acquainted with halves, thirds and fourths. In the second and third grades, fractional parts of groups, non-unit fractions and equivalent fractions are explored. Then, moving on, children learn to add, subtract, multiply and divide fractions and to relate them to decimals and percents. The experiences become increasingly complex.

Summary

Readiness is a powerful concept. It helps the teacher accommodate the needs of learners by relating new experiences to old. If teachers at all levels actively seek to provide readiness experiences, they help children develop a sense of unity and interdependence in mathematics. Further, they facilitate learning by presenting instructional concepts in means which are consistent with the learner's level of cognitive development.

In this chapter a brief summary of Piaget's theory was presented and Bruner's work was related to it. A theoretical basis was presented to support the use of concrete materials and group learning experiences, and to call attention to the role of every teacher in accommodating needs of children relative to varying degrees of abstraction and in providing a continuous strand of mathematics readiness experiences.

This chapter contains more material than you can digest in one sitting. A second reading tomorrow or the next day is advisable. Even then, the ideas presented will not be integrated and entirely meaningful.

This book is written in such a way as to refer continually to this and other chapters of the methods core in Part 1. This chapter has attempted to present major ideas which help ensure that mathematics instruction will be developmentally and psychologically sound. The major ideas presented will take on increasingly expansive meaning as you continue to explore specific content and methodology.

Refer to this chapter often. You will gain many new insights as succeeding chapters present specific teaching strategies based upon the generalizations explored here.

Bibliography

1. Bruner, Jerome S. *The Process of Education*. New York: Vintage Books, 1963.

2. Bruner, Jerome S. *Toward a Theory of Instruction*. New York: W. W. Norton & Company, Inc., 1966.

3. Clark, John R., and Laura K. Eads. *Guiding Arithmetic Learning*. Yonkers-on-Hudson, New York: World Book Company, 1954.

4. Flavell, John H. *The Developmental Psychology of Jean Piaget*. Princeton, New Jersey: Van Nostrand Reinhold Company, Inc., 1963.

5. Gagné, Robert M. *The Conditons of Learning*. New York: Holt, Rinehart & Winston, 1965.

6. *Goals for School Mathematics—The Report of the Cambridge Conference on School Mathematics*. Boston: Educational Services Incorporated, 1963. Sponsored by the National Science Foundation.

7. *Improving Mathematics Education for Elementary School Teachers—A Conference Report,* edited by W. Robert Houston, Michigan State University, 1967. Sponsored by The Science and Mathematics Teaching Center and The National Science Foundation.

8. Jennings, Frank G. "Jean Piaget: Notes on Learning," *Saturday Review* (May 20, 1967), 82.

9. *Mathematics Education*. The Sixty-ninth Yearbook of the National Society for the Study of Education, edited by Edward G. Begle. Chicago: University of Chicago Press, 1970.

2

Individualization of Mathematics Instruction

Children deserve to be treated as unique individuals with special strengths and weaknesses. Some learn quickly; some learn slowly. Some need many manipulative experiences; some need few manipulative experiences.

All programs and procedures which claim to individualize instruction in mathematics seek to meet particular learner needs. Children are grouped on some basis to help teachers accommodate needs. Age is the variable which has traditionally been used; schools group children in grade levels by age. Several programs identify other variables for grouping children. These criteria frequently include mathematics achievement scores, intelligence test scores, reading achievement scores, and rate of learning.

There exists no satisfactory system which satisfies all learner needs and can be easily implemented and executed. In this chapter a model is presented which seems to be a step in the right direction. Its major strength is that it seeks to accommodate *several* learner needs.

Cognitive Needs. The child needs an instructional system which is flexible in the amount of time and the kinds of materials provided to master a *given concept*. Also, the child needs an instructional system which is flexible in the amount of time and kinds of materials needed to master *different concepts*. In other words, *intra*-concept flexibility and *inter*-concept flexibility are *both* needed in relation to skill and concept acquisition. In a given class some youngsters learn more quickly than others, and a given youngster varies in the rate in which he attains mastery of different concepts.

Social Needs.   As emphasized in the previous chapter, children learn through peer group interaction. The model to be proposed and the specific applications suggested repeatedly emphasize small-group work in which children are provided opportunities to explore, share and challenge perceptions with others of diverse ability. Homogeneous and heterogeneous grouping are both used.

Emotional Needs.   Children must form realistic concepts of themselves as individuals who are slow in acquiring some skills and fast in acquiring others. This is accomplished through utilization of flexible grouping, i.e., groups are formed on the basis of frequent diagnoses. Children are much less likely to be tagged as *slow* or *fast* if they are regrouped periodically on the basis of a particular need and when they are given frequent opportunities to identify with the broader class-range of ability during developmental work on new concepts. Further, children will have success experiences because appropriate use of the model ensures that children work with materials consonant with their levels of concept mastery.

A Model for Individualizing Mathematics Instruction

In this section a specific model will be presented which helps teachers individualize mathematics instruction in such a way as to strike a well-proportioned balance among the diverse needs of a heterogeneously grouped class of elementary school children. Most teachers will teach in self-contained classrooms, so the model will be presented with such a structure in mind. Since, however, many schools are using semi-departmentalization and team teaching, the model will be related to these arrangements at the end of the section.

The model will first be presented schematically with a capsulized summary, then each component will be presented in detail. Study this model carefully. Most of the chapters of Part Two of this book will relate to this model and explain in more specific terms how it can be implemented on various content areas of the elementary school mathematics curriculum.

The Model

The following diagram presents the model schematically. Study the flow and then read the detailed description which follows.

Instruction begins with well-conceived goals. The components of a concept or the subconcepts constitute a road map; they are the objectives which, in totality, cause you to say at the end of the instructional process, "This child has an adequate mastery of this concept."

Some children may already have mastered the concept. This is why you should preassess. If there are such students, rather than have them sit through

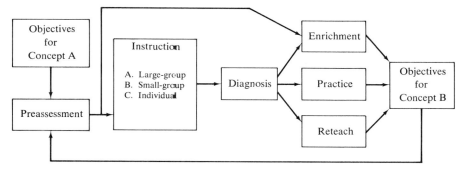

instruction which is inappropriate and boring, channel them into other learning activities (referred to as "Enrichment" above).

The large majority of students will be ready to enter the instructional phase of the model. After large-group, small-group or individual instruction has continued to an optimum point, administer a diagnostic test to regroup children on the basis of their mastery *of this concept*. Those who have attained mastery can move into the enrichment group; those who have grasped the concept but need additional reinforcement can move into a practice group; and those whose mastery is inadequate can move into a reteach group.

At the optimum time, the class can be brought back together to proceed as a unit to the next major concept. Each of these components will now be elaborated.

Objectives.   If you were going on a scenic tour, you would first decide where you were going. After you made this decision, you would make plans to travel by train, bus, or auto and decide how much money and time would be needed. You would also decide upon certain guideposts to be observed to see how you are progressing; you would probably check your watch, read a map, calculate the number of miles traveled and remaining, and so on.

Mathematics instruction can be related analogously to the trip just described. Trips correspond to major concepts, preparations correspond to planning of appropriate teaching-learning strategies, and guideposts correspond to subconcepts and/or levels of development. Once you have decided on the next major concept in the instructional program, pupil mastery of the concept is your one, major, encompassing goal.

When you travel, arrival at the destination, i.e., your physical presence, is the criterion measure. When you teach, a criterion measure is needed, too. How will you decide "yes" or "no" in relation to the child's mastery of the concept? A way which is emphasized throughout this book is through pupil-demonstration of some behavior which is deemed by you to reflect mastery. Since you judge people by their behavior, it seems quite reasonable to assess learnings by observing behaviors. You may expect the child to "*compute* sums of two two-digit numerals with regrouping," "*describe* a rectangle," "*write* the prime factors of a given number," "*draw* an array" and so on. The terminal behaviors help you plan your instructional program. When you know the behaviors which students must be able to demonstrate, the instructional program is centered about activities which teach those behaviors.

The signposts along the way help you decide the degree of progress which is being made and the extent to which the route is being followed. If you tell a friend you took a scenic route to a distant city, the friend may want to know the names of the towns, highway numbers, etc. Similarly, when the destination is "computing sums of two two-digit numerals," you will want to know the route followed. The child may be interested in arriving at the destination, i.e., compute and get correct answers. You desire more than that the child arrived at the terminal point. *You* want a scenic route, the traveling of which assures you not only that the child can compute and get correct answers but also that he *understands* the computational procedures followed. It therefore behooves you to build into the instructional program measures of guidepost behaviors.

Guidepost behaviors are related to levels of abstraction in this book: concrete, semi-concrete, and abstract. Since most terminal behaviors (final destinations) in the curriculum are abstract (computations), pupil progress towards acquisition of abstract skills can and should be carefully regulated by teaching and evaluating progress at the concrete and semi-concrete levels. An example: "The child will be able to compute sums of two two-digit numerals with regrouping of ones." This is an abstract computational procedure. The child may work it as follows:

$$
\begin{array}{llll}
\text{A.} \quad \begin{array}{r} 36 \\ +47 \\ \hline 83 \end{array} &
\text{B.} \quad \begin{array}{r} 36 \\ +47 \\ \hline 713 \end{array} &
\text{C.} \quad \begin{array}{r} 36 \\ +47 \\ \hline 73 \end{array} &
\text{D.} \quad \begin{array}{r} 36 \\ +47 \\ \hline 13 \\ 7 \\ \hline 20 \end{array}
\end{array}
$$

There are certainly other possibilities, but, clearly, only child A has acquired this skill. Success of the trip will not be assured but is greatly enhanced by making certain that students acquire related skills as they move toward this terminal behavior:

> *Concrete:* A. The child can use bundles of objects (groups of ten) or ones- and tens-strips of paper to find orally given sums.
> *Semi-Concrete:* Given a picture of objects in groups of tens and ones, the student will be able to write an equation and find the sum.

If the objectives encompass the three levels of abstractness, the learning possibilities *which produce understanding* are greatly enhanced. In succeeding chapters, major concepts and objectives at all three levels will be suggested, and you will be challenged to write additional ones. The major question you must ask is, "What can I ask children to do which will demonstrate to me that they have mastered this concept?" What behavior must the child demonstrate?

Preassessment.   Once objectives are defined, the destination is known. It is reasonable at that propitious moment to ascertain which youngsters, if any, already have the skills. As you can realize, some children may exhibit the terminal behavior without being able to exhibit the intermediate behaviors. Such may be the case if a child has learned to add with regrouping by memorizing a computational procedure utilized by an older sibling or a parent. Such a child must be placed in an instructional milieu which will teach him the meaning of the memorized algorithm.

Preassessment can be formal or informal. If you feel because of your familiarity with the backgrounds of students that there are none who have the skill, you may wish to ask the class if anyone thinks he can do it. Informal introduction of the new unit may elicit responses which can be followed up. Another informal way to evaluate current status is to provide concrete materials, pose a question, and see if anyone can answer the question without the materials. You can probe responses as the children work. Finally, you can prepare a short pretest on your objectives. Ask the same range of questions you plan to ask at the conclusion of instruction. Children who demonstrate mastery of your objectives can be channeled into other meaningful activities. Specific suggestions for children who demonstrate mastery are made in subsequent chapters.

Instructional Phase. Nearly all the students will move into the instructional phase of the sequence. Your unit objectives help you ascertain whether children should engage in large-group, small-group or individual learning activities.

Large-group instruction can be used when you wish to coordinate the actions of the entire class on concept development. Large-group instruction is particularly expedient for expository instruction (telling and/or demonstrating) presented in the next chapter. If you plan to use a large teaching aid while children are using scaled-down or alternate aids at their seats, large-group instruction can be utilized advantageously.

Small-group instruction is especially valuable when you wish to have children work together on aids to search for and to discover patterns exhibited, to carry out projects and to carry out laboratory-type learning experiences. Small-group learning experiences are especially valuable for the contribution they make to learning and concept development through peer-group interaction. Small groups help maintain a sense of class or peer-group identity since children can be grouped heterogeneously for most small-group work. Pure and guided discovery methods are excellent strategies.

There are also times when children can benefit from totally individualized work. Materials similar to IPI or some teacher-modification described in a later section of this chapter can be utilized. Such learning experiences can be especially meaningful when children use aids in their work and when they are allowed to interact with each other at will.

Since no single group size is best, no single group size should be used exclusively. No single strategy, expository, pure discovery or guided discovery, meets all the learners' needs. Each strategy has its strengths and weaknesses as explained in the next chapter. A good instructional program uses all three with a balance influenced by facilities, time, materials, and learner needs.

Diagnosis. When on the basis of observation you feel that many children have mastered the concept and will no longer benefit from continued work, a diagnostic test should be administered. The form and substance of the diagnostic test are dictated by the objectives you are seeking to attain. Since your objectives cover one or two major concepts, related subconcepts and levels of development, so, too, the diagnostic test will cover the same components.

If the objectives are properly spelled out, they will define the evaluation instrument. If the child is to be able to use the number line, the diagnostic test will include number line items; if the child is to be able to compute, the diagnostic test will include computations, and so on.

After the diagnostic test has been administered, the children can be grouped according to levels of concept development into three groups. One group consists of those who in your judgment have attained adequate mastery. These students can be channeled into enrichment activities. A second group consists of those who have attained the rudiments of the concept but who need additional practice for retention and transfer. These students will be channeled into a practice group. The third group consists of those students whose mastery is still questionable. These students have not profited adequately from the instructional sequence followed and should be rechanneled through a different set of learning experiences designed to teach the same concept.

Diagnostic Groups.   On the basis of mastery of the *concept(s) of this unit,* students are channeled into enrichment, practice, or reteach groups. While activities for these groups are suggested in succeeding chapters, an overview is presented here.

The basic types of enrichment are described in detail in the chapter on fast learners. Suffice it to say here that the nature of the model necessitates the use of lateral forms: mathematics experiences which are *not* a part of the regular curriculum. The model precludes use of vertical forms, i.e., moving ahead in the curriculum, because the model seeks to bring the class back together as a single learning unit when each new unit or major concept is presented. This is clearly impossible if some students are moving ahead in the book. The teacher needs to be resourceful in determining student interests and channeling students into mathematics-related learning experiences.

The practice group needs activities which have the desired skill built in. Practice can be provided through workbooks and practice sheets but these should not be overused; the child may rehearse the skill but build a poor attitude toward mathematics in the process! Extensive use of commercial and teacher-made games, puzzles, student-created stories, and similar activities which are fun and motivational are most desirable. Specific suggestions and bibliographies are made in the chapter on selection and use of aids.

The reteach group needs additional development activities. Different aids and methods should be used since the ones used in the instructional phase didn't work. Children in this group need many more concrete and semi-concrete experiences related to the concept(s) of the unit. Specific materials are suggested in the content chapters in Part 2 of this book.

The entire class is brought back together to proceed as a unit to the next major concept when you feel the reteach group has attained adequate mastery of the concept. Because of time pressures, you may deem it necessary to move on before *every* child has reached this minimum level of performance. For the children who have not reached this level, you should employ special diagnostic techniques to further facilitate their growth. Specific suggestions for such diagnosis are discussed in the chapter on slow learners.

A Brief Appraisal

The model described above attempts to meet many learner needs. Each child is reevaluated with a diagnostic instrument on each major concept in the curriculum. The child is placed in a group on the basis of specific needs demonstrated relative to a given concept rather than his level of intelligence, his reading ability, or his more general mathematics achievement scores. This flexibility gives credence to the fact that children who are slow acquiring one skill may be fast on another.

The manner in which diagnostic grouping is done also prevents unpleasant results of labeling which are characteristic of most plans utilizing some type of homogeneous grouping. Even though many children will tend to remain in one of the diagnostic groups most of the time, the nature of the model is such as to allow easy intergroup mobility on the basis of demonstrated needs in each instructional unit. This is an advantage of this model over homogeneous grouping and tracking plans.

Bringing the class back together for the beginning of each new unit helps each child identify with the *total peer group.* Each child feels a part of a *class* of youngsters. All children are provided opportunities for interaction and interchange with the entire spectrum of ability. This feature allows children to form more realistic self-concepts and become aware of individual strengths and weaknesses. This practice also allows the child who is slow in grasping a concept the opportunity to gain insights from a child who has grasped the concept. Further, the child who has attained insights is given the rewarding experience of sharing his knowledge and deepening his understanding by explaining his knowledge to peers.

The use of behaviorally stated objectives with the incorporation of levels of abstractness helps the teacher define goals, plan instruction, evaluate success of strategies and determine pupil progress. If large-group instruction was not satisfactory, the teacher gains feedback and can use different intraclass groupings and different aids. And, finally, the child has continuous feedback from peers, teacher, and diagnostic evaluations concerning his relative success.

Implementation

What can a teacher realistically do to implement this model given the many responsibilities which are already a part of the teaching task? One teacher in a self-contained classroom can implement the model gradually. The enrichment component of the model is the most frustrating aspect at this time since enrichment materials of the type called for are in short supply.

The most reasonable place to begin is to define your instructional program in behavioral terms taking into account the levels of abstractness as suggested in succeeding chapters. Lists of objectives are available through the Instructional Objectives Exchange.[1] Also, most teachers' manuals have stated objectives. You can formulate your objectives as you move along through the first year and then modify them each succeeding year.

Because of the shortage of enrichment materials, you could omit the pre-assessment the first year. After the instructional phase, you can diagnose and use two groups: reteach and practice.

In summary, during the first year you can define objectives, diagnose and regroup. You can begin to seek out enrichment materials and use them whenever possible. For children who should be in the enrichment group, you can provide challenging mathematics games, model construction kits, and related literature. Specific suggestions can be found in the chapter on slow and fast learners and in most other chapters of this book.

After the first year, you can devote more time to enrichment. At that time you can begin to implement the preassessment phase and use enrichment activities following preassessment and diagnosis for those children who have mastered the concepts. With many activities in the room occurring simultaneously, you may feel anxious and torn, but you can be assured that, if children are performing meaningful tasks based upon their needs, the lack of order and apparent confusion are signs of productive learning activity.

Modified Uses of the Model

In schools with more than one class at each grade level, teachers can use a teaming arrangement to implement the model. Such an organization will make less work for each teacher.

If there are two teachers, they can work with intact classes until diagnostic regrouping occurs. At that time, they can regroup children and teachers. One teacher can work with the reteach group and the other with the practice and enrichment groups or some other combination which is suitable in relation to the concepts and group sizes.

If there are three teachers, they can work with their own classes until diagnostic regrouping. Then one teacher each can work with the research, practice and enrichment groups, respectively. If preassessment results indicate many children should go on to enrichment, one teacher can begin enrichment activities immediately and the other two can carry out the instructional phase of the model.

Not only will the work load be proportionately reduced, but teachers will also have a choice in selecting the group they wish to teach during the diagnostic phase. If there are teachers who find slow or fast children especially enjoyable and challenging, they can work with them regularly. If, on the other hand, teachers like variety, they can rotate every second or third topic.

---

[1] The Instructional Objectives Exchange, P.O. Box 24095, Los Angeles, California 90024.

Other Current Methods for Accommodating Learner Needs

In addition to grouping procedures, several developments of the past few years hold promise for individualizing mathematics instruction through the use of special materials and technological developments. All of the ones described here are being used in schools across the nation. You may encounter one or more of them in your future teaching. Some are very costly, but costs are being reduced. Others, such as Unipacs, can be teacher-made and are very inexpensive. Six developments will be presented briefly. For further information on one or more of the topics, refer to the bibliography at the end of the chapter.

Mathematics Laboratories

A mathematics laboratory may consist of a specially equipped room in the building where mathematics classes meet on a regular basis or a corner of the regular classroom with tables and equipment, or a closetful of teaching aids for pupil manipulation. These laboratories vary greatly in design and equipment, but they agree in spirit and intent.

The laboratory movement has at its grass roots the intention of making mathematics learning exciting, interesting, and meaningful for children. Three of the main characteristics of this movement are (1) pupil-involvement in the discovery of mathematical relations and properties, (2) use of many manipulative aids, and (3) exploration of mathematical applications.

Many of the guided discovery activities described throughout this text are laboratory-type activities. If you wish to explore the laboratory setting in more detail, examine materials of the Nuffield Project and MINNEMAST and study Kidd, *et al.* (2).

Unipacs

A unipac is a set of materials for independent pupil study. A mathematics unipac includes behavioral objectives, pre- and post-tests, specific learning activities incorporating appropriate manipulative materials, and instructions to the teacher which include a brief summary of content, prerequisites, uses and materials needed. Example: *Addition with Regrouping* (5 or 6 lessons).

Individually Prescribed Instruction (IPI)

IPI was developed through the Learning Research and Development Center at the University of Pittsburgh. It utilizes behavioral objectives, diagnostic tests and lessons to channel each student through a mathematics curriculum which is in harmony with his rate of learning.

The main role of the teacher is that of prescriber. On the basis of diagnostic tests, the teacher, with suggestions, decides the next appropriate step for each child. The teacher also tutors and works with small groups. The system heavily utilizes teacher aides and is now available commercially.

Programmed Materials

Programmed materials use a type of sequencing to take a learner through a pattern of concept development. Such materials are usually characterized by carefully defined objectives and pre- and post-tests. Another strength is immediate reinforcement. Most programmed materials ask the learner frequent questions. After he responds, he can evaluate his success immediately.

Portions of many chapters in this book are programmed. The nature of these materials is fairly typical in style and sequence. Many programmed materials do *not,* however, provide for utilization of learning aids other than paper and pencil.

Computer Assisted Instruction (CAI)

Computers can teach. Many difficulties arise when a computer is used for concept *development* because the person who programs the computer must anticipate so many possible pupil responses and misunderstandings.

However, work has progressed quite well with computer utilization providing review or practice of skills after they have been developed. Students can, for example, practice basic facts at a computer console. The computer "remembers" which ones are hard or easy for each child and keeps a record of progress. Patrick Suppes of Stanford University is particularly well-known for his work on CAI.

Computer Managed Instruction (CMI)

The task of individualizing instruction is greatly impeded by the tremendous task of record-keeping. If children are engaged in many different activities, how can you keep track of where each one has been and ought to go?

The computer can be used as a record-keeper. The student does not learn from the computer; rather, the computer's memory is used to supplement the teacher's. The computer can be used to score tests, maintain progress records and make plans of study based on student progress.

Summary

There is no single way to individualize instruction. Variety is the spice of life. Children learn best in an environment which is flexible and interesting in the variety it provides. Teachers are also individuals. Teaching styles are different. Some teachers work well with individuals, others with small groups. Some teachers work well with slow children, others with fast children.

Whatever the methods, they should be grounded in sound principles of developmental and educational psychology. The single-method teacher and the routinized teacher will both have problems motivating and stimulating interest in learners.

Bibliography

1. Howes, Virgil M. *Individualizing Instruction in Science and Mathematics.* London: The Macmillan Company, 1970.

2. Kidd, Kenneth P., Shirley S. Myers, and David M. Cilley. *The Laboratory Approach to Mathematics.* Chicago: Science Research Associates, Inc., 1970.

3. Moench, Laurel. "Individualized Practice in Arithmetic—A Pilot Study," *Arithmetic Teacher* (October 1962), 9:321–29.

4. Rosenbloom, Paul C. "Science and the New Math," *The Instructor* (October 1956), 25, 87, 125.

5. Suydam, Marilyn N., and C. Alan Riedesel. *Interpretative Study of Research and Development in Elementary School Mathematics. Volume 3: Developmental Projects.* Washington, D.C.: U.S. Department of Health, Education and Welfare, 1969.

6. Swenson, Esther J. "Rate of Progress in Learning Arithmetic," *The Mathematics Teacher* (February 1955), 70–76.

7. Unkel, Esther. "Arithmetic Is a Joyous Experience for Elementary School Children in Great Britain," *Arithmetic Teacher* (February 1968), 15:133–37.

3

Modes of Instruction

According to DeVault and Kriewall (6:414), a workable theory of instruction must account for variables related to four sources: learners, teachers, instruction and content. In addition to the diverse learner needs discussed in the previous chapter, a viable theory must account for teacher differences such as personality, education, and roles; content variables such as sequence and structure; and instructional variables such as materials and equipment.

The previous chapter which dealt with individualization gave careful consideration to learner variables. The materials chapter and each chapter of Part 2 will consider instructional variables. This chapter will relate generally to teacher and content variables. Three modes of instruction are examined in this chapter: pure discovery, guided or directed discovery, and expository instruction. The examination includes appropriate uses, strengths and weaknesses of each. Such a discussion must necessarily be based upon certain assumptions relative to the purposes or broad objectives of mathematics instruction. Consideration must also be given to the relevant variables which influence a teaching decision, e.g., time, resources, space.

In the first section, a comprehensive overview of a good mathematics instructional program is presented and analyzed. Sections two, three and four relate each of the three modes to the overview, and the last section summarizes and relates the three modes of instruction.

Characteristics of a Good Mathematics Instructional Program

In *Toward a Theory of Instruction* (4:41), Jerome Bruner states that a theory of instruction should have four major features:

    A. A plan for motivating the learner
    B. A plan for helping the learner grasp the structure of a body of knowledge
    C. A plan for sequencing learning activities
    D. A plan which designates the types and distribution of rewards and punishments, i.e., reinforcement

These are the four major assumptions against which the modes of instruction will be evaluated.

Motivation

A positive predisposition toward learning greatly increases the likelihood that a concept will be learned. Instructional modes should be utilized which maximize this predisposition in some manner.

McDonald (10:144) describes two major motivational strategies. The first he calls an *arousal strategy*. The teacher who utilizes this approach presents the material in an unusual manner, arousing the learner's interest, attention, and curiosity. The second strategy associates the learning experience with other items in which the learner is already interested. In the latter, teachers use *incentives* to motivate students.

Incentives may be grades, teacher approval, peer approval or prizes, but the best educational incentives are those which are internalized. Bruner appeals for motivational strategies which satisfy curiosity and enable the student to derive esthetic satisfaction and a sense of accomplishment. Success experiences are critically important in developing and maintaining healthy pupil attitudes toward learning. The child who experiences considerable failure lowers his level of aspiration. Success builds confidence in one's ability. Increased confidence results in higher levels of aspiration.

Structure

An important instructional consideration is the structuring of mathematics in such a way that it is comprehensible to the child. ". . . Since the merit of a structure depends upon its power for *simplifying information,* for *generating new propositions,* and for *increasing the manipulability of a body of knowledge,* structure must always be related to the status and gifts of the learner." (4:41)

Bruner characterizes structure in three ways. First, knowledge can be mastered at one of the three levels noted in chapter one: *enactive, iconic,* or *symbolic*. Second, structure is characterized by *economy;* this relates to size of storage (memory) necessary for the learner to master mathematics. And, third, structure is characterized by *power;* this is the "generative value" or "usability" of the structure *by a given learner*.

Bruner (3) claims the following advantages for teaching structure:

A. Knowledge of structure makes mathematics easier to understand
B. Knowledge of structure facilitates memory of details
C. Knowledge of structure facilitates transfer[1]
D. Knowledge of structure shortens the distance between elementary and advanced concepts

Structure allows the learner to take command of the mathematics he possesses. "Good" structure should help the child simplify and interrelate details, create new ideas from ones already possessed and enhance his ability to use knowledge. As you can readily see, the *quality* of structure is closely related to the amount of transfer which it generates or facilitates.

Structure in mathematics refers to the "rack" of basic ideas upon which facts, skills and subskills may be hung. The structure is the framework which makes mathematics a meaningful and comprehensible whole and which makes visible the interrelatedness of many mathematical concepts.

For example, the chapter on developmental concepts of multiplication and division describes the important core idea of *set*. All four basic operations on whole numbers (addition, subtraction, multiplication and division) can be related to operations on sets. That chapter also notes the properties of operations such as commutativity, associativity, identity elements and closure and describes the sets upon which certain operations possess them.

The spiraling curriculum offers a way to conceptualize structure, also. Basic concepts can be expanded at each successive encounter and the level of abstraction can also be structured appropriately. The structure of mathematics is represented by the basic concepts, properties and definitions which give the curriculum continuity and cohesiveness.

Transfer refers to the facility of the child to *use* a generalization once it has been learned. If the child learns that addition is associative, $a + (b + c) = (a + b) + c$, can he use it to add $32 + 4$ as in $(30 + 2) + 4 = 30 + (2 + 4) = 30 + 6$? Will he see the property being used in algebra: $2a + (3a + b) = (2a + 3a) + b = 5a + b$? Can the child who encountered the distributive property, $a \times (b + c) = (a \times b) + (a \times c)$, transfer its use from *whole* numbers, $3 \times (10 + 2) = (3 \times 10) + (3 \times 2)$, to *literal* numbers, $a(a + 4) = a^2 + 4a$? Bruner feels from his work on cognitive structure that comprehension of structure facilitates transfer.

---

[1] McDonald defines *transfer* as the "use of a previously learned response in a new situation." Bruner calls this *specific transfer*. When Bruner refers to transfer, he means *transfer of principles and attitudes*.

Sequence

Ease of concept acquisition is influenced by the *sequence of learning activities* in the instructional program. A viable theory should help establish one or more workable sequences. As pointed out in the previous chapter, most mathematics proceeds through the enactive, iconic and symbolic levels. Several *content* sequences are given in succeeding chapters.

Reinforcement

Information is needed relative to the nature and frequency of rewards. Intrinsic rewards are most desirable since they generally reflect learning for the sake of learning. Learning should be an end in itself, i.e., self-rewarding. Success experiences are important in this process of internalization.

Special considerations arise in the use of rewards and feedback in problem-solving situations. Knowledge of results should come at the optimum moment when the learner is ready to decide if his solution is correct or whether or not his problem-solving strategy is workable.

Overview of Instructional Modes

The following definitions are presented to set a frame of reference. Each mode is described in detail in subsequent sections.

Pure Discovery. When a learner formulates his own questions or hypotheses, develops his own strategies for answering the questions or testing the hypotheses, collects data, and answers his own questions, he is engaging in *pure discovery*. Pre-schoolers engage in pure discovery extensively. As they explore the environment, natural curiosity and wonder lead them in the discovery process.

Guided Discovery. When a problem or question is posed *externally* and the child develops strategies, collects data and answers the questions with teacher help as needed, he is engaging in *guided* or *directed discovery*. When a child is presented with a set of data, formulates hypotheses and tests them with teacher guidance as needed, he is engaged in guided or directed discovery. Problems are posed and materials for their solution are made readily accessible, or a set of data is provided and the child is helped to "make sense of" or extract a generalization from the data.

Expository. When a problem is posed and answered *externally* and the child is expected to replicate the problem and solution or to work others which are similar, he is engaging in *expository instruction*. Lectures and explanations are expositorily presented. The learner is likened to a receptacle which is being filled. Nearly all secondary school and college instruction and much elementary school instruction is expository.

Pure Discovery

Scientists and mathematicians hypothesize relationships and then seek to prove or disprove them. Adults encounter impasses in their personal lives concerning relationships with people or with technology. They define problems, think of possible alternatives, and act. No one knows for sure how people learn to define and solve problems, but there is surely some value in practicing problem-solving behaviors. Pure discovery provides children with such opportunities. Examples:

1. Children are encountering Cuisenaire Rods for the first time. They are given rods for independent exploration. What are some things they *might* find out (discover) without teacher guidance?
    a. Cuisenaire Rods make tall towers.
    b. The orange rod is longer than the dark green rod.
    c. Red and blue placed end-to-end have the same length as blue and red placed end-to-end.
    d. The rods can be grouped into color families.
    e. The rods can be placed in a stair-step pattern, etc.

2. Third-graders are given several containers of standard size, i.e., cup, pint, quart, half-gallon. They take them to the sandbox to play. What *might* they find out (discover)?
    a. Some jars hold more sand than others.
    b. Some jars hold multiples of other jars.
    c. Two cup containers fill a pint container.
    d. A container cannot be *exactly* filled.
    e. A more *precise* or *descriptive* measure can be obtained by using smaller and smaller units, etc.

3. Fifth-graders are given many solid objects and asked if they can find any relationships among the objects. What are some facts they *might* discover?
    a. Some objects are smooth, and others are rough
    b. Some objects have flat portions; others do not.
    c. Some objects are slanted, and some are not.
    d. Some objects roll; others do not.
    e. Some objects have vertices; others do not, etc.

Characteristics. *Might* is emphasized in each of the preceding illustrations. Pure discovery learning experiences are very unstructured and open-ended. The child poses questions, selects a route towards resolution of the question, and decides on the validity or merit of his results. The learning is very internal and self-centered.

The child asks questions which are meaningful to him, uses strategies for resolution which are within his experience and grasp, and determines his own success. The learning is very intimate and personal; it has meaning and significance. There is no tangent; the child is right on target because he is allowed to seek his own meaning. The questions raised are the questions for which answers are desired.

If the teacher expects the child to discover something in particular, the experience is not a pure discovery experience. Pure discovery is characterized by randomness, trial-and-error and absence of externally imposed structure.

Objectives Attained.   This mode is excellent when you wish to provide children with unstructured opportunities to formulate and evaluate hypotheses. Pure discovery, because of its inherent freedom, permits much opportunity for creative expression by providing stimulating opportunities to explore, discover, compare, and evaluate. It is a good motivational experience since children can explore mathematical teaching aids for enjoyment without the pressure of "having to learn something."

Appropriate Uses.   The objectives of the previous paragraph can be attained through several occasions which occur throughout the K-6 curriculum:

> A. When new teaching materials are introduced, a free-play period or time of exploration can be provided. This has the dual impact of acquainting students with the materials while providing opportunities for new discoveries.
> B. Children can be given access to mathematics-related materials during recess and other play periods.
> C. After a structured presentation, pupil exploration may yield teacher insights relative to pupil transfer of ideas to new materials.
> D. Children can be given free-play exploration time prior to a more structured sequence of guided discovery or expository instruction.

Appraisal.   In relation to the four instructional criteria mentioned in section one, the following statements can be made:

> A. Pure discovery is a good motivator for most students. When the child is given opportunities to operate in an unstructured setting in which he can "go his own way," he is motivated to follow his own interests. He relates well to his own quest behavior and is *involved* in the learning experience. The appeal to the child's curiosity is a natural motivator.
> B. Pure discovery does not enhance the learner's knowledge of structure except in a very coincidental or random way. If the learner discovers structure, that is well and good, but the nature of the mode is such that there is no assurance this will happen. The experience can be structured to emphasize the concrete as a starting point, but the child can pursue as he sees fit.
> C. Sequence is similarly coincidental. The idea of sequence is rather antithetical to the unstructuredness of a pure discovery learning experience, except that it can begin with the concrete. The sequence of learning activities is determined by the *student* rather than the teacher.
> D. Since the child asks his own questions and answers them, success is

almost assured. Success is determined internally. The child receives immediate feedback which is almost certainly understandable, and he is relatively sure to answer his questions which means success is almost a certainty.

In summary, pure discovery has a place in elementary school mathematics instruction. It rates highly on motivation and success and contributes to the attainment of broad objectives relative to strategy formulation, hypothesizing and data-gathering.

Guided Discovery

Most instruction which carries the label "discovery" is some form of inductive learning, i.e., the child determines a generalization and the instances to which it applies. Children are discovering when they use problem-solving behavior. The steps can be roughly described as follows:

    A. Awareness—The child becomes aware of the problem. He interprets, rephrases and redefines it.
    B. Strategy Formulation—The child formulates a strategy.
    C. Data Collection—The child gathers information and reflects on relationships.
    D. Hypothesis Formulation—The child hypothesizes relationships.
    E. Hypothesis Testing—The child tests hypotheses and accepts or rejects them.

When *directed* discovery strategies are used in elementary school mathematics, the teacher assumes the role of facilitator. Kersh (7) has described two very different ways in which the child's progress can be facilitated. First, the teacher can give hints which help the child discover the generalization. The teacher is working with the student in step D above to facilitate formulation of better hypotheses. Second, the teacher can give hints which may help the child begin. The teacher is working with the child in step B to facilitate formulation of a workable strategy. These two guiding or facilitating processes have different objectives which deserve special consideration.

Facilitating Strategy Formulation.   When teachers engage in this behavior, they are helping children learn how to solve problems. When teachers pose questions which have several acceptable strategies, they help children learn that a problem can be attacked in more than one way. This procedure helps assure the teacher that the child is attacking the problem in a way which has meaning. There are many ways to solve problems, but some strategies are more sophisticated or elegant or efficient than others. When a teacher exposites, all the children learn by one strategy, the teacher's strategy. Helping children evolve their own strategies helps ensure that the procedures being used are meaningful to the learner, and the learner acquires experience and skill at the more general task of problem-solving. The discovery example in the chapter on addition and subtraction algorithms is a good example of this teacher facilitation.

Children are asked to solve a problem involving a new skill, addition of two two-digit numerals.

Facilitating Hypothesis Formulation. When teachers engage in this behavior, they are facilitating pupil discovery of the *particular generalization being examined.* Use of this approach helps children develop an understanding of the generalization by extracting it from a set of data. This approach can be used as one of the steps in the five-step problem-solving process as indicated in section two of the chapter on multiplication and division of rational numbers or it can be used by including only hypothesis formulation and testing.

When the five-step process is used, several simple story problems can be distributed to small groups. Each group works the problems and the teacher helps them set up the various number sentences and offers hints to foster recognition of the generalization.

When Awareness, Strategy Formulation and Data Collection (A, B and C) are omitted, the teacher can explore those steps with the class before working in groups. The teacher can establish a strategy, set up number sentences and ask the children to look for the generalization. The problem-solving strategies are presented expositorily and the children discover the generalization under study.

Another example of this approach is in the use of conjured mathematics examples to help children experience the enjoyment and pleasure of making discoveries. Activities of this sort are found in materials of the Madison Project and in most current textbook series. Robert Davis (5) has children look for numbers which can be used in placeholders of linear and quadratic equations or discover generalizations with geoboards. Example: Name some number pairs of the "truth set" for $\triangle + \square = 14$.

Characteristics. In guided discovery, children are involved. Challenging questions are raised to stimulate interest and curiosity, and appropriate materials are provided with which children can discover solutions. The teacher asks the questions, so guided discovery has structure. However, children are given freedom to answer the questions in ways which are consonant with their abilities and levels of understanding.

Children can seek out personalized solutions; most of the motivation is internalized. Since the teacher guides and directs children's efforts, success is not guaranteed but it is greatly enhanced. Nearly all children will experience success. The teacher can give relatively more guidance to those who are slow or who are having difficulty identifying an appropriate strategy or generalization.

Objectives Attained and Appropriate Uses. This mode is excellent when you wish to provide children with opportunities to develop problem-solving skills and meaningfully to learn new generalizations from analysis of patterns in data. It is a self-motivating strategy so it enhances interest and fosters good attitudes towards mathematics.

Guided or directed discovery can be used advantageously when new concepts are being introduced and when generalizations are to be learned. Many suggestions are included in later chapters for posing questions which challenge students to formulate problem-solving strategies, collect data, and verify or reject hypotheses. Small-group, laboratory-type settings are ideal for such activities because they offer rich opportunities for peer group interaction and manipulation of concrete materials in the discovery process.

Appraisal.   In relation to the four instructional criteria mentioned in the first section, the following statements can be made:

> A. One of the clearest strengths of discovery strategies is the strong motivational effect (8). The heightened interest of students who are involved in this mode seems to increase practice and learning. After the teacher utilizes an appropriate arousal strategy, the activities become more or less self-sustaining. The teacher aids students who have arrived at an impasse, and curiosity maintains interest.
> B. Since the teacher controls the presentation of concepts to be discovered, this mode can be used very effectively to present mathematics in a way which is structurally clear. Studies by several researchers have supported the hypothesis that discovery modes facilitate transfer of both generalizations and problem-solving strategies (heuristics) (13, 16, 17).
> C. Children can work with materials appropriate to their levels of understanding, so sequencing of learning activities can be controlled. The teacher can allow considerable latitude in pupil strategies; children can proceed from concrete to abstract as quickly or as slowly as they deem necessary and expedient.
> D. Success is determined externally in most cases but the child is given help through hints relative to strategies of data analysis which help assure success. The child is given whatever help he needs to make the discovery. The reinforcement and help will foster better attitudes.

Many guided discovery strategies are cited in succeeding chapters.

Expository Instruction

Teachers are notorious for their talkativeness. They probably have earned this distinction through the teaching style which typifies most instruction. Children and adults obviously learn when instructed in this style since most people have experienced such instruction in much of their formal education. Some of the characteristics, uses and advantages of expository instruction are explored in this section.

Characteristics.   Much expository instruction is *explaining*. Teachers tell and show students how to verify mathematical properties, how to use concepts and how to compute. Explaining often takes the form of a *deductive sequence,* i.e., the teacher presents a generalization or concept and gives several examples to demonstrate the uses or attributes. Following explanations or deductive sequences, students practice procedures or identify additional examples.

If the teacher expositorily presents the concept of commutativity of multiplication, $a \times b = b \times a$, the concept may be *demonstrated* on a number line, with sets, and with repeated addition. The students will then compute several commutative pairs with learning aids and then as number sentences. The generalization is given and explained; then the students practice for understanding and retention.

Expository instruction is a rather closed sequence. The teacher decides what will be studied (asks the questions), teaches it (answers the questions), and evaluates pupil practice on the concepts (determines success). There are few opportunities for student divergent thinking. The teacher who utilizes this mode must, because of its closed nature, assume most of the responsibility for sustaining motivation and interest through use of good materials and illustrations.

Expository instruction is also characterized by the narrow range of pupil skills allowed at any particular time and the lock-step pace which it requires. Students practice the skills or generalizations as they are presented and each student must move ahead as the presentation moves from one new topic to another. If the class is divided into two or three groups, this weakness is not as prominent but is still to be reckoned with.

Objectives Attained through Appropriate Uses. Expository instruction allows you to present a large amount of material in a relatively short period of time. It is particularly useful when you need to teach ideas which are not easily discovered or to review previous work.

Children cannot *discover* vocabulary or common symbols or notation. They must be told the names of concepts which have been learned and they need to be told how to write an equation or the standard way to set up a problem in vertical form or the symbols which represent addition, equal, place holder, etc.

After a concept or generalization has been discovered, expository instruction is appropriately used to review the concept, to point out its attributes and to explore its ramifications. If the students have discovered the essential ideas of regrouping in addition, you can help them write a computational procedure which describes symbolically those operations performed with concrete materials, and you can work some examples with them.

Appraisal. As you know, expository instruction can be and often is immensely boring. The skill, interest and enthusiasm of the teacher is a critical factor in its success or failure. As a method of instruction, the success of expository instruction hinges on the teacher. The strategy itself is not particularly motivating since the child is perceived as a receptacle to be filled. It is not very exciting and tends to arouse little natural curiosity. Since there is little challenge, arousal strategies are needed, and external incentives (rewards) must usually be employed. Broad objectives of internalized incentives and positive attitudes are difficult to attain in this mode.

Mathematical structure can be taught in this mode with the major drawback being that most children must progress at about the same rate. Some will move through the structure too slowly and others too quickly. Transfer can be built into such a manner of presentation since several studies have indicated that meaningful instruction (12, 15), instruction which emphasizes generalizations, (2) and instruction which emphasizes relationships between concepts and transfer-like situations (9) all enhance the amount of transfer likely to occur.

The teacher can control the sequence, too, but the same weakness of locked-step instruction will tend to decrease effectiveness. Children will not be ready to follow the sequence simultaneously.

Since the teacher asks the questions, success is determined externally. Some children will experience success nearly constantly, but some will experience success rarely since the structure and sequence of a locked-step curriculum is inappropriate for their needs.

Summary and Guidelines

In this section the three modes are collectively related to the criteria established. Other important variables are briefly discussed and summarized comments are presented.

Three Modes.   A summary of the three modes is presented in the following table relative to the four criteria used. As a general mode of instruction, expository is weakest on the basis of these four criteria and guided discovery is strongest.

	Motivation	Structure	Sequence	Reinforcement
Pure Discovery	Good	Weak	Weak	Good
Guided Discovery	Good	Good	Good	Good
Expository	Weak	Fair	Fair	Fair

Discovery strategies tend to be better motivators and reinforcers than expository strategies because the learner is involved in decision-making and evaluating his progress. He chooses his own questions or designs his own strategies and receives teacher guidance or decides his own success. Expository strategies tend to rely more upon external incentives and success criteria. The broader society desires education for its youth which instills love of learning. Discovery modes seem to contribute to this goal; they offer opportunities for development of problem-solving skills and divergent thinking. They make the child feel more positive about his abilities and, hence, himself.

Guided discovery does the most adequate job of presenting material in a sequence which is appropriate and which helps the learner grasp the structure of mathematics. It facilitates greater transfer. Guided discovery strategies, especially if used in small group work, offer opportunities for children to be working at all three levels of abstraction in the classroom at one time. The teacher as facilitator helps children move meaningfully from one level to another.

The major objective of this chapter has *not* been to convince you that you should use one mode exclusively. You should be aware of the strengths, weaknesses and appropriate uses of each mode. Your instruction should include special consideration of the mode or modes which will work best for you in helping you attain your objectives, to the extent that your objectives coincide with the four utilized in this chapter.

Other Important Variables.   The four criteria utilized are certainly important in building a solid curriculum. There are other variables which also influence day-to-day decisions. Some of these will now be considered. These may give you additional insights and help you make intelligent decisions.

Time. The time devoted to presentation in expository instruction is generally shorter. Discovery modes may require more time because of the amount of facilitation needed. You should remember, however, that transfer is greater in discovery modes so the extra time may be well spent.

Retention. Instruction in any mode can be meaningful instruction but the likelihood that it will be meaningful for the larger number of students favors a guided discovery mode since children are more inclined to be operating at an appropriate level of abstraction. Retention is greatest when 50 to 75 percent of instructional time is spent in developmentally meaningful activities and the remainder (less than half) of the time on practice or drill (14). Worthen found that while expository instruction yielded the greatest initial learning, discovery learning yielded greatest learning after five and eleven weeks (16).

Resources. Availability of appropriate aids might seem to be an important factor, but you will see in succeeding chapters that the resourceful teacher is surrounded with potential mathematics teaching devices. Rocks, tin cans and magazines are representative of items which are potentially useful in small groups or individual work.

Teacher Role. Your perception of your role in the classroom is a fundamentally important variable. If you are rigidly authoritarian, you will have difficulty with discovery modes. If you are bothered by student boredom or listlessness, you probably will seldom use expository instruction for concept presentation. The three modes run a gamut of structure and teacher control of pupil learning. Hopefully, you can use all three modes to accomplish the objectives for which each is best suited.

Summary.   The mode of instruction is an important variable in the teaching-learning process; so is the teacher. Success or failure of instruction is highly dependent upon the teacher's ability to carry it off. Ausubel (1) points out that expository instruction *can* be meaningful instruction. Much expository instruction is not meaningful, but that is the fault of the teacher and not the mode. He also points out that guided discovery strategies *can* be rote learning experiences. Teachers in the role of facilitator assume a responsibility which requires some skill. Most conscientious teachers can probably develop the skill.

Mathematics instruction is much more than skill development. Children need enjoyable experiences which foster positive attitudes and instill natural curiosity about learning in general and mathematics in particular. The best instructional decision is one which reflects a wise fit of modes to achieve short-range and long-range objectives.

Bibliography

1. Ausubel, David P. "Facilitating Meaningful Verbal Learning in the Classroom," *The Arithmetic Teacher* (February 1968), pp. 126–32.

2. Brownell, William A. and Harold E. Moser. "Meaningful vs. Mechanical Learning: A Study in Grade III Subtraction." *Duke University Studies in Education.* 8:1–207, 1949.

3. Bruner, Jerome S. *The Process of Education.* New York: Vintage Books, 1963.

4. Bruner, Jerome S. *Toward a Theory of Instruction.* New York: W. W. Norton and Company, Inc., 1968.

5. Davis, Robert B. "Discovery in the Teaching of Mathematics," from *Learning by Discovery: A Critical Appraisal.* Lee S. Shulman, Evan R. Keislar, eds. Chicago: Rand McNally, 1968, pp. 114–28.

6. DeVault, M. Vere and Thomas E. Kriewall. "Differentiation of Mathematics Instruction." *Mathematics Education: The Sixty-Ninth Yearbook of the National Society for the Study of Education.* Edward G. Begle, ed. Chicago: The University of Chicago Press, 1970.

7. Kersh, Bert Y. "Learning by Discovery: Instructional Strategies." *The Arithmetic Teacher* (1965), pp. 414–17.

8. Kersh, Bert Y. "The Motivating Effect of Learning by Directed Discovery." *Journal of Educational Psychology* (1962), pp. 65–71.

9. Kolb, John R. "Effects of Relating Mathematics to Science Instruction on the Acquisition of Quantitative Science Behaviors." *Journal of Research in Science Teaching* (June 1967), pp. 174–82.

10. McDonald, Frederick J. *Educational Psychology Second Edition.* Belmont, California: Wadsworth Publishing Company, Inc., 1965.

11. Overman, J. R. "An Experimental Study of the Effect of the Method of Instruction on Transfer of Training in Arithmetic." *Elementary School Journal* (November 1930), pp. 183–90.

12. Scandura, Joseph M. "An Analysis of Exposition and Discovery Modes of Problem Solving Instruction." *Journal of Experimental Education* (December 1964), pp. 148–59.

13. Shuster, Albert and Fred Pigge. "Retention Efficiency of Meaningful Teaching." *The Arithmetic Teacher* (January 1965), pp. 24–31.

14. Woody, Clifford. "Some Investigations Resulting from the Testing Program in Arithmetic: An Investigation to Determine the Transfer Effects of Three Different Methods of Teaching Three Different Types of Examples in Two-Place Addition (Second of 3 studies)." *Indiana University School of Education Bulletin* (April 1930), pp. 39–45.

15. Worthen, Blain R. "A Comparison of Discovery and Expository Sequencing in Elementary Mathematics Instruction." *Research in Mathematics Education.* Washington, D.C.: The National Council of Teachers of Mathematics, 1967, pp. 44–59.

16. Worthen, Blain R. "Discovery and Expository Task Presentation in Elementary Mathematics." *Journal of Educational Psychology* (February 1968), pp. 1–13.

Diagnosis of Mathematics Learning Difficulties

Good teaching begins where the child is. An immediate implication of this statment is that you need information concerning the existing level of mathematical competence and skill before beginning instruction.

When summer is ended and a new group of youngsters sit before you with their tanned, robust, gay and shiny faces, you have little knowledge of their present state of skill development and concept formation. You need information before you begin to plan the year's mathematics program.

As the year proceeds, you will introduce new topics in your instructional program. You will need to know if your strategies have been successful. Which children have attained mastery? Which ones need additional practice? Which ones need further developmental experiences?

In the following sections, these questions will be discussed and appropriate strategies and suggestions presented. Succeeding curriculum-content chapters of this book will build upon the ideas presented, offer specific suggestions and pose instructional problems for your reflection.

Three Types of Diagnosis

Two types of diagnosis were identified in the introduction: *general* or *survey diagnosis* and more *specific* or *ana-*

lytical diagnosis. In this section these two and a third, *clinical diagnosis,* will be defined.

Group Diagnosis of General Weaknesses

"Where shall I begin?" "What do these children know?" These two questions are commonly raised by teachers when confronted with a new group of youngsters in the fall. All too often, they remain unanswered in any direct sense. The rationale opted by many teachers, although rarely if ever stated, is as follows:

 I. The pupils were together last year, so they have had a common set of experiences.
 II. The book I am using is the next one in the series and the teacher last year got to page 270.
 III. I will give a review of the basic ideas of last year's work to accommodate the losses of retention over the summer.
 IV. Now I can proceed with new material.

Obviously, this rationale meets with some degree of success. However, there is a better way. Steps I, II, and III can be followed as indicated above. This would be similar to starting each day's lesson with a review of yesterday's work —help the children refresh rusty skills before making a formal assessment. Many rough spots may be taken care of with a day or two of review on each major concept or topic.

In his oft-quoted book, *Diagnostic and Remedial Teaching in Arithmetic,* Brueckner refers to such tests as *survey* or *inventory* tests:

> When survey tests can be given only once during the year, they probably should be given early in the school year instead of at its end, as it is often done, because then the data can be used as the basis of adjustment of instruction during the remainder of the year. About the end of the first month of school would seem to be the best time for these tests, since by then the "warming up process" or review work which is necessary to overcome the retrogression in ability in arithmetic which occurs during the summer vacation is completed and a more reliable picture of the conditions would be secured than by a test given immediately after the opening of school (2:63–64).

You should note that by the very nature of the breadth encompassed by such a test, broad areas of deficiency are revealed rather than specific weaknesses, e.g., addition or subtraction with regrouping but not particular instances such as problems involving zero in the minuend or regrouping hundreds.

An inventory or survey test in grade six might include all four operations with non-negative rational numbers and decimals. Such a test in grade two might include place value, addition and subtraction facts, inequalities and column addition.

The results of the general diagnostic test can be used to make a tentative plan of the year's instructional program. This test yields information which describes the general level of functioning of the class.

Group Diagnosis of Specific Weaknesses

The group diagnosis considered in this section will be aimed at short-term learning problems. As noted in the chapter on individualization of mathematics instruction, diagnosis is an integral component of the continuous instructional process. It provides the pupil with feedback relative to his performance on specified objectives and provides the teacher with feedback on the relative success of teaching strategies. The important components are summarized here.

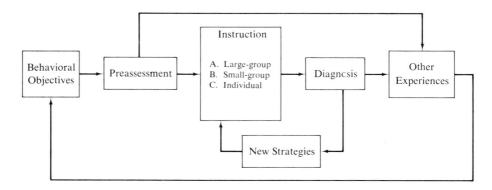

After instruction on a new major concept, a diagnostic test is administered to determine *specific weaknesses related to the concept(s) just presented*. Major concepts or skills of the unit are identified and broken down into subconcepts or subskills. This diagnostic test indicates which children are experiencing specific difficulties relative to unit subskills and subconcepts.

Diagnosis of Individual Learning Problems

After you have diagnosed through use of group survey and analytical tests, specific weaknesses begin to come into focus. The work of some children will reflect near-total mastery and the work of others will indicate only partial mastery of the subconcepts.

Some children, perhaps 5 to 15 percent of the class, will have attained only a minimal degree of understanding through the instruction which has occurred. For this group, further analysis on an individual basis is helpful. Such testing is often referred to as *clinical* diagnosis because it takes a deliberate, intensive and highly individual approach. Specific clinical techniques will be presented in this chapter and in the chapter on slow and fast learners.

A Diagnostic Model Based on Instructional Sequence

The major objective of this section is to relate two important aspects of instructional sequence to diagnosis: (1) structure, and (2) levels of learning. The outcome intended is an approach to diagnostic instruction which can be implemented by the average classroom teacher with limited time and resources.

Structure

A cursory examination of elementary school mathematics curricula quickly convinces you that for many topics a "typical" or "usual" sequence occurs. Addition usually precedes or is taught concurrently with subtraction; addition and subtraction usually occur before multiplication and division; operations on whole numbers precede operations on rational numbers and so on. This is part of the global structure of the K-6 curriculum. The more general or survey tests diagnose the performance of a group of students on portions of this broad continuum.

Within a given broad area such as addition of whole numbers there is also a typical sequence. Children encounter addition facts before they work with two-digit numerals in addition, and they learn to add two-digit numerals without regrouping ones to tens before they encounter situations requiring regrouping skills. These are sequences within the mathematics instructional sequence which are also important.

Levels of Learning

Concepts summarized in the psychology chapter also support the use of instructional sequencing of levels of learning. Pupil understanding of each new concept, subconcept, skill and subskill is enhanced through a concrete/semi-concrete/abstract sequence of instructional activities.

Sequence and Diagnosis

Instructional sequence can be likened to a three-beat musical score in which each measure is a mathematics subconcept or subskill; each *one, two, three* beat is the rhythm of concrete/semi-concrete/abstract, and each musical phrase is a major concept. Example:

> *Musical Phrase*—Addition of whole numbers
> *Measures*—Addition facts, sums of two-digit and one-digit numerals without regrouping, sums of two two-digit numerals without regrouping, sums of two- and one-digit numerals with regrouping, sums of two two-digit numerals with regrouping
> *Beats*—Concrete, semi-concrete, abstract

Tune: *Operations on Whole Numbers*

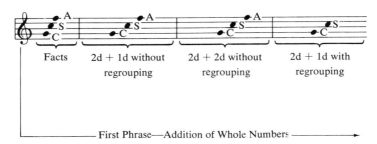

| Facts | 2d + 1d without regrouping | 2d + 2d without regrouping | 2d + 1d with regrouping |

First Phrase—Addition of Whole Numbers ⟶

Diagnosis evaluates the tune! If the child can play all the notes, he has achieved the objectives! The following translations of this analogy relate to the three forms of diagnostic tests:

> *Survey Tests*—only the *abstract* notes
> *Analytical Tests*—only the *semi-concrete* and *abstract* notes
> *Clinical Tests*—the whole tune with particular emphasis on beat one!
> (concrete)

Three Types of Diagnostic Information Obtained Through the Model: Implementation

This section will relate the three types of diagnostic tests (survey, analytical, and clinical) to the model based on instructional sequence.

Survey Tests

As indicated above, survey tests evaluate pupil understanding only at the abstract level. They are, therefore, especially useful in checking on skill development. You can construct a survey test by examining the chapter headings and subheadings of the previous year's text. You may wish to do it for the previous two or three years if your month's review experience in the fall indicates presence of some extended or cumulative deficiencies.

After you have selected the topics which you consider most important for success in the work of your tentative schedule, write two or three items on each topic and administer the test. The main criteria for the number of items will be reflected in the following:

> A. *The number of headings you have identified.* Will you look only at the four basic operations on whole numbers or will you include place value and other topics?
>
> B. *The total number of items you want.*

C. *The extent of follow-up of more specific diagnosis you anticipate.* Do you plan to administer analytical tests on topics of verified class deficiencies?

Selection of Commercial Tests. Many good survey tests are commercially available. You should be aware of the selection process through which you can go to find one which is appropriate. The following steps are suggested:

I. Decide what kind of test you need.
II. Locate three or four suitable tests in Buros' *Mental Measurements Yearbook* or talk with the school system's psychometrist if one is available.
III. Order samples.
IV. Make your final selection.

The steps are concerned with appropriate answers to the following questions relative to test selection:

What Kind of Test Do You Need? There are several factors which influence this decision. What grade level do you teach? What content do you wish to cover? Do you want to compare your students to other students in a normative population, e.g., national norms, children in urban areas, etc.? How much money do you have? How will the tests be scored? How will they be administered? How much time will you have for testing? How do you want the results reported? Jot down the answers to these questions first.

Is a Test Available Which Will Fulfill Your Needs? A chat with the school system's evaluation expert may give you just the lead you need. If such a person is not available, go to the local library and consult Buros' *Mental Measurements Yearbook*. The *Yearbook* is a compendium of testing information. Most tests which are commercially available are described, and most of the questions raised in the preceding paragraph are answered. New tests are evaluated by experts in the field. For example, new tests for elementary school mathematics will be listed and a brief evaluation of the test by a mathematics educator-evaluator will be included. Choose three or four which seem to accomplish your goals.

Which Test Best Meets Your Needs? After you have received the specimen sets, examine them carefully in light of your expectations, purposes and the limitations within which you work. Choose the one which is best or, if they are all unsatisfactory, develop your own diagnostic test. Here are the names of some common survey tests:

Arithmetic Essentials Test Grade Three, Steck-Vaughn Company
Basic Skills in Arithmetic, Science Research Associates
Los Angeles Diagnostic Tests: Fundamentals of Arithmetic, California Test Bureau
Stanford Diagnostic Arithmetic Tests Levels I and II, Harcourt Brace Jovanovich

Analytical Tests

Analytical tests look at the subconcepts and subskills in greater detail than do survey tests. After the subconcepts are identified, six questions on each subconcept should be included: three at the semi-concrete level (iconic) and three at the abstract level (symbolic). Three items are used to accommodate careless errors. If the child misses two or three of the three-group you would usually assume he has a problem with the item type.

When you construct your own test, first examine the major concept and attempt to identify the various subconcepts. In addition to the selective uses of exercise tests and specific problems provided in textbooks and teachers' manuals, *succeeding chapters of this book will include many specific suggestions for identifying appropriate hierarchies.* The following general guidelines can be used:

A. Break the unit into subunits, e.g., adding with and without regrouping.

B. Identify the specific types within each subunit in increasing order of complexity, e.g., adding ones, ones and tens, tens and tens.

Without Regrouping			*With Regrouping*		
2	15	26	8	16	26
+6	+ 3	+13	+9	+ 7	+39

C. Include at least *six* problems of each type: three semi-concrete and three abstract.

Analytical tests can be scored and results used easily by following this procedure: Construct the test in question groups of three, alternating semi-concrete and abstract with the simplest subconcept first and the most complex last. Grade student responses of the *entire class* in groups of three items. The name of each student who misses two or three of the group is placed on a summary sheet which has a box for each subconcept, semi-concrete and abstract. Example:

Subconcept	*Semi-concrete*	*Abstract*
Sums of two-digit and one-digit numerals with regrouping	John, Bill, Gary, Sue, Jane, Ellen	Harry, Monica, Gary, Ellen, Conrad, Joe, Susan, Mary

The children in the "abstract" group were not able successfully to complete the transition from semi-concrete so they should be provided additional experiences to facilitate the transition. The children in the "semi-concrete" group were not able successfully to complete the transition from concrete to semi-concrete so they should be provided additional experiences to facilitate this transition.

Clinical Diagnosis

Children who have continued difficulty making the transition from concrete to semi-concrete or who seem unable to master the concept at the concrete level pose a problem which may require additional diagnosis. An individual or clinical approach can be used. Several suggestions were given by Brueckner (2:66–70). In a given situation you can decide which are most suitable.

   A. Observe the child as he works.

   B. Analyze the child's written work.

   C. Analyze the child's verbal statements. Ask the child to explain his work; ask him to describe the relations between the manipulations and the symbolic notation.

   D. As a final approach, have an individual interview with the child to probe thought processes and uncover misconceptions.

Individual cases which cannot be accommodated through the model on individualized instruction are discussed in the chapter on slow and fast learners.

Summary

Three types of diagnostic tests were presented: survey, analytical and clinical. A model for diagnostic instruction was proposed, based on instructional sequence as related to the components of structure and levels of learning.

Survey tests were described as group tests which test pupil understanding of broad areas of mathematics at the abstract level; analytical tests were described as group tests which test pupil understanding of specific areas of mathematics at the semi-concrete and abstract levels, and clinical tests were described as individualized diagnosis with emphasis at the concrete level.

Problems and Projects

1. Examine Buros' *Mental Measurements Yearbook*.
2. Select a test from the yearbook which meets criteria you have established.
3. Make a survey test to be given at the beginning of the year for a grade level of your choice.
4. Choose a concept and write some items which evaluate pupil achievement at all three levels of abstraction.

Bibliography

1. Brueckner, Leo J. *Adapting Instruction in Arithmetic to Individual Differences.* Minneapolis: University of Minnesota Press, 1941.

2. Brueckner, Leo J. *Diagnostic and Remedial Teaching in Arithmetic.* Philadelphia: The John C. Winston Company, 1930.

3. Buros, Oscar K. *The Sixth Mental Measurements Yearbook.* Highland Park, New Jersey: Gryphon Press, 1965.

4. Buros, Oscar K. *The Fifth Mental Measurements Yearbook.* Highland Park, New Jersey: Gryphon Press, 1959.

5

Special Needs of Slow and Fast Learners

Slow and fast learners are rarely different in *kind;* they differ only in *degree*. They are at opposite ends of some descriptive continua. Recall some of the basic ideas of the first four chapters.

Learning Characteristics (Chapter 1)

The nature of intellectual growth and development appears to be characterized by an invariant chronological sequence. Hood (9) found a positive correlation between mental age (as measured by intelligence tests) and stage of cognitive development, and his results imply that slow learners pass through the stages more slowly than fast learners. This means that, in general, slow children need more work on concrete manipulations and will progress to more abstract logical operations at a later age. Fast children, on the other hand, pass through the stages more quickly. They will be able to perform abstract logical operations at an earlier age and will in general need to spend less time on concrete operations.

The learning environment must provide peer group interaction since such action facilitates transition from one developmental stage to another. Other benefits of peer group interaction include development of new insights and development of more realistic self-concepts.

Individualization (Chapter 2)

Special provisions for cognitive, social and emotional needs were outlined in the chapter on individualization. Fast students are filtered off during preassessment and after diagnosis. Fast learners are provided enrichment opportunities and the special needs of slow learners are met through use of a reteach group. Several combinations of individual, small and large groups were explored. Other specific suggestions are made in later sections of this chapter.

Learning Modes (Chapter 3)

Fast children tend to make discoveries more readily than do slow learners. However, the occasional use of pure discovery instructional experiences allows every child to experience the enjoyment of asking his own questions, seeking his own solution strategies and accepting or rejecting his hypotheses. Use of *guided* discovery strategies can further facilitate discoveries by slow students and give them experiences which tend to internalize motivation. Use of simple patterns, grouping students heterogeneously, use of hints and close supervision, and provision for demonstration of patterns without "giving away" the generalization will all help children achieve success.

Diagnosis (Chapter 4)

The individualization model assumed that most children will successfully complete work on new concepts through use of instructional and reteach phases. However, some children may fail to attain adequate mastery of concepts through this method. In such instances, special *clinical* diagnostic strategies are utilized. Procedures will be outlined for organization and implementation of clinical diagnosis for very slow learners.

Definitions

Fast learner refers to a child who is placed in the enrichment group of the individualization model. While this group will vary from one unit of instruction to another, certain youngsters will tend to remain in this group rather consistently. Their number will usually not exceed 15 percent of an average class. *Slow learner* refers to a child who is rather consistently in the reteach group, who, additionally, has continued difficulty with basic skills, remembering basic facts and who continues to function in the diagnostic reteach cycle at the concrete level. About 25 percent of an average class will be in the reteach group, but only 10 to 15 percent of the class will have such chronic problems.

Overview of the Chapter

Needs and characteristics of slow learners will be examined. Special attention will be given to diagnosis and specific remedial materials. Since *memory* problems (such as remembering addition facts or how to divide) greatly impede work with slow learners, the next section will discuss some relevant research and draw implications as to the instructional significance of research findings. The last section of the chapter presents characteristics, special needs and materials for mathematically gifted children.

Slow Learners in Mathematics

The use of the label *slow learner* is intended to communicate the assumption that *all* children can learn but some learn more quickly than others. Since some children learn more slowly than others, the obvious question is, "Why?" The two basic reasons are related to *ability* and *motivation*. Some children want to learn but seem to have difficulty developing concepts; they are assumed to have low ability. Other children do not demonstrate a desire or need to learn mathematics; they are assumed to have low motivation. Both types are *low-achievers;* however, the reasons why they are low-achievers are different. Children in the first group lack ability; children in the second group lack interest and motivation and these children are often referred to as *under-achievers*.

Children With Low Mathematics Ability

Some children master mathematics concepts more slowly than do the majority. They have difficulty conceptualizing mathematical ideas, understanding mathematical generalizations, and remembering computational procedures and basic facts when such ideas are presented in conventional ways. There are many reasons why children experience difficulties. An exhaustive treatise relative to the reasons is beyond the scope of this book; suffice it here to say that learning styles, socio-economic status, heredity and teacher-skill are but a few of the factors which are positively correlated with pupil success in mathematics.

Characteristics. Children with low mathematics ability are usually characterized by low-normal intelligence, poor reading achievement and poor memory. They are frequently from homes of lower-class culture and may have parents whose backgrounds reflect poor mathematics achievement and attitudes.

Instructional Guidelines. You can help low ability children by observing several important ideas:

A. Since intellectual development is correlated with mental age, expect slow children to perform at a less abstract level than bright and average children.

B. Since low-ability students progress more slowly, allow them more time at the concrete and semi-concrete levels of concept development.

C. Use a multi-sensory approach to accommodate various learning styles.

  D. Prevent practicing of errors through careful developmental work
and short sets of practice exercises.
  E. Introduce only one new idea at a time.
  F. Allow more time for development and more time for practice.

Transfer.   As noted in the previous chapter, transfer is more likely to occur
when the conditions are similar to the conditions in which the generalization is
applicable. Further, Thorndike (16) and other researchers found a positive
correlation between intelligence and ability to transfer, and Bruce (3) found that
overlearning—that is, learning which exceeds bare mastery—is necessary for
maximizing transfer. These three statements taken together seem to imply that
a teacher of children with low mathematics ability has an especially important
challenge to facilitate transfer by (1) providing frequent review and (2) utilizing
numerous social contexts.

Success.   As you would suspect, children with low mathematics ability often
develop a "failure syndrome." Failure creates lack of confidence and bad attitudes which result in diminished performance. This syndrome is more easily
avoided than overcome. *All* children need success. Previous suggestions indicate some of the ways of assuring success. Another way to hold down pupil
frustrations is to move at a slower pace. This can be accomplished by omitting
some difficult topics. Frequent diagnosis is essential, and repeated practice
for overlearning will help the child develop a sense of achievement.

Children with Low Mathematics Motivation

Many children do not function as well in mathematics instruction as their general
mental abilities and previous performance indicate possible. Such children are
often called *under-achievers* because they perform below the level of expectation
based on some valid and reliable criteria.

  Henry (8:7) studied families in poor urban ghettos and concluded that most
children in the urban ghettos are not oriented toward usual middle-class goals
of achievement and security. He feels that *hope* is the essential ingredient which
produces middle-class goal-striving. Hope implies a time-centered outlook on
life which views the future as "better" (hoped for) than the past or present;
there is a "striving for" which underlies the concept of hope. Without the time-
centeredness of hope, life loses much of its organization; it tends to become
random.

  Henry suggests that individuals in areas where hope is lacking lead very
random lives with respect to achievement and security. Without achievement
orientation, they become low-achievers because the will to succeed is not present. Achievement in the middle-class sense is not important.

  Henry (8) and Rosenbloom (15) draw some interesting implications from
characteristics of lower-class subcultures worthy of your consideration. Most
of the implications are familiar, but the underlying assumptions place
some interesting new perspectives and a somewhat different rationale behind
them:

A. The child is present-oriented and seeks immediate gratification. Typical children of the middle-class culture strive for academic achievement; they seek deferred gratification obtainable through good grades and advanced education; they seek far-off success; theirs is a delayed-reward system. Present-oriented children need positive reinforcement *today*. Daily success and daily feedback are highly desirable; the child needs frequent success data.

B. Success is maximized when subject matter increments are small. Success on each small step helps build a positive attitude through continuous *positive* feedback. Rosenbloom suggests that activities with immediate recreational value are good reinforcers; such is the case when children play games in which mathematical concepts are embedded.

C. Small increments also provide for frequent fresh starts. Each new task is of short duration so the child has frequent feelings of success; he can move on to new challenges with cumulative success experiences for support. This can be accomplished by breaking each major concept or skill into several smaller subconcepts or subskills.

D. Since, according to Henry, survival is the major thrust of the present-oriented subculture, relevance of mathematical experiences, especially in the intermediate grades, is gained through emphasis on social application of mathematics, especially in jobs and skills common to the community.

Problems of middle-class youngsters who lack motivation are somewhat more complex. These under-achievers tend to reject typical middle-class motivational patterns because of family circumstances and can frequently be helped by special guidance services. The teacher can work with these children by helping them see that mathematics meets a need through its recreational value, special-interest appeal or social utility. In many cases, the deferred gratification characteristic of the middle-class value system has been rejected and special needs can be met in much the same way as with the child who reflects a present-oriented existence.

Children with Low Motivation and Low Ability

Some children lack both motivation *and* ability. With children from middle-class homes, motivation is usually present during the primary grades but tends to be lost because of the failure syndrome. Children from lower-class or disadvantaged areas may lack *both* at the outset of formal schooling because of different cultural expectations and behavior patterns.

In the traditional instructional setting, the locked-step curriculum creates a cumulative learning deficit. As this graph illustrates, average and below-average ability children who begin at the same position at grade one (A) are separated in achievement more and more at each succeeding grade level. The low-ability child gets further and further behind. Similarly, the culturally disadvantaged child who is a low achiever begins with a deficit (B) and is cumulatively farther behind, too.

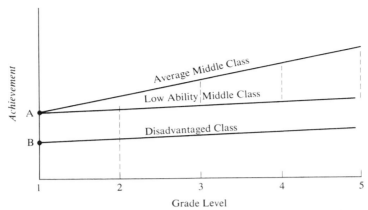

You can cope with the problem of low-achieving students. First, consider the motivational aspects of the problem. As outlined previously, discovery techniques are good motivators. Use these techniques when feasible. Allow children to discover computational procedures and solution strategies. Appeal to the child's learning style; use aids and strategies which require various sensory perceptions; these will also lend interest and variety.

Relevant material is also motivational. What is relevant material? For the young child in primary grades, *relevant* is nearly synonomous with *interesting*. Young children enjoy games and activities which are fun; if they are fun, they are interesting and relevant to the child's world. At the same time, you must remember that transfer is facilitated to everyday experiences when instruction emphasizes the relation between the mathematics concepts and their social utility. Therefore, social application of mathematics *within the realm of the young child's experiences* should be stressed. The behavior of the older child (intermediate grades) is characterized by *more imitative behavior*. Pre-adolescent behavior is characterized by increased interest and concern in adult activity; threfore, social situations in which mathematical concepts are utilized should be stressed even more. Care should be taken to identify adult activities which are most closely related to children's interests—budgeting an allowance, making purchases of clothing, building model planes, and so on. Less emphasis should be placed on life insurance, income taxes and similar topics which are in the conventional curriculum; they do not reflect the present orientation so typical of many low-achievers.

Diagnosis

The ability aspects of the problem of low-achievers are best countered through a carefully designed and executed program of diagnostic instruction.

For the slow learner with especially acute problems in mathematics, group tests will give you a good idea of the general level of functioning and the broad areas of difficulty but will not pinpoint the specific problems. A *clinical* approach is needed.

Example. Joe is in the fifth grade. After a month of review you administer a survey test and learn that Joe is functioning at third-grade equivalent in mathematics. As a follow-up in your diagnostic program, you give an analytical test over basic skills to determine pupil difficulties. This test includes addition, subtraction, multiplication and division facts and respective computational forms.

From the second test you find that Joe knows his addition facts but he has difficulty with some subtraction, multiplication and division facts. Further, he has weaknesses in all four computational procedures, especially multiplication and division.

Joe has problems! Further analysis on an *individual basis* is needed. As a starter, you work with the six children in the class who are having difficulty with subtraction facts. A small group diagnostic test is administered to determine *which* subtraction facts are not known. After the results are known, a page containing the 100 subtraction facts is provided for each child, and a felt pen is used to mark out the ones which are known. Joe knows all his one, two, three, four, five, six and eight facts. He is having trouble with zeros, sevens and nines.

As a result of the diagnosis, you provide Joe and each other child with worksheets. You ask them to work in pairs and explain the subtraction facts to each other with concrete materials. After this review of developmental procedures, game-like activities are provided which give the children practice on subtraction facts. They use their dittoed sheets of unknown facts as crutches and play games involving *all* the subtraction facts to create a feeling of success. Following a few activities of this sort, Joe and others with subtraction fact difficulties can work more advanced problems involving subtraction such as $29 - 14$ or $87 - 29$. They continue to use the "crutch sheets" for reinforcement.

For more complex problems, as in addition and subtraction, several strategies can be used. First, from the diagnostic test you can get some idea of the basic difficulty; you may notice that Joe has trouble with addition and subtraction computation only when zeros, sevens and nines are involved, or only when regrouping is needed or only when three digit numerals are used. If this information is not apparent, *ask Joe to work some subtraction and addition problems.* Study his incorrect responses to see if you can discover an error pattern. *Observe Joe* when he is working; ask him to *verbalize his thought processes* to ascertain faulty reasoning. Finally, you can *ask Joe to demonstrate* a sum or difference with concrete materials.

Each step will provide additional information about Joe's particular difficulties and make possible remedial work which is aimed at alleviating his unique problems.

When is it done? Here are a couple of ways to implement the sequence just presented. The grade level at which the sequence is used will be an important determining factor as to the most reasonable plan to implement.

One plan which is appropriate at all grade levels is to spend two periods each week on remedial work and enrichment. Identify two or three areas of difficulty. Divide the class into three or four groups relative to these areas and include one group which has no problem with any of the identified areas of weakness.

With such a plan it is important to provide all groups with materials of comparable interest and involvement so that negative attitudes do not develop.[1]

A second plan particularly applicable to intermediate grades is for the *school system* to establish priorities in the mathematics curriculum. Slow students can omit mathematics topics of low priority. Most classroom teachers are not fully qualified to make this decision independently and should use their *collective* judgment or seek the help of supervisors or consultants.

A third plan is a modification of the second. Children who need remedial work on essential skills will spend *less time* on low priority content rather than omit it entirely. This has the additional advantage of continuous or regular contact with the rest of the class.

A fourth plan is to have a period of remedial work for all subjects simultaneously. Some children can work on mathematics skills, others on reading skills and so on.

A fifth plan is to team with other teachers to group two or more classes on the basis of some identified common weakness.

Materials. Instructional materials for slow learners are commercially available. For example, the American Book Company and William H. Sadlier, Inc., publish books which require lower-than-average reading ability. The National Council of Teachers of Mathematics publishes *Experiences in Mathematical Ideas,* a set of duplicable pupil activity sheets and a teacher's guide with many suggestions for working with slow learners in intermediate and junior high school grades. Prepared by a special committee and field tested, it has received wide acclaim.

Charles E. Merrill Publishing Company and Imperial Productions, Incorporated, market *Mathematics Skilltapes* and the *Primary Math Skills Improvement Program,* respectively. They are typical of multi-sensory approaches to mathematics instruction and remedial work which are especially desirable for poor readers.

The School Mathematics Study Group (SMSG) publishes a special early-primary-grades mathematics program. It was designed for disadvantaged children.

Unipacs can be used for remedial work, too. Independent learning aids, which children can use individually or in small groups of two, three or four, can be incorporated.

Summary.   After general survey and analytical diagnosis, individual problems can be assessed by interview techniques, observing children's work habits, analyzing worksheets and listening to oral descriptions of thought processes. On the basis of information accumulated, remedial work can be planned. Several classroom organizational schema have been suggested in this chapter. If you desire additional detail, consult Brueckner's books which are listed in the bibliography of the chapter on diagnosis.

---

[1] Intermediate teachers will find *Experiences in Mathematical Ideas* an excellent resource.

Memory

Children must remember many facts and procedures to maintain a satisfactory level of mathematics achievement. There are 390 basic facts, several computational procedures, numerous definitions, and many properties and generalizations. Slow children usually retain information less well than fast children so it behooves every teacher to become aware of characteristics of memory processes and techniques and procedures for facilitating them.

In 1970, Harper & Row published a book by Michael J. A. Howe, *Introduction to Human Memory,* which is the primary source for this section. The major studies which seem to have implications for mathematics instruction are summarized and implications drawn. Since the studies are not in general related to mathematics instruction, the implications drawn in this section are somewhat tentative. However, since memory poses a great instructional dilemma for many teachers, especially with respect to slow learners, the implications will undoubtedly serve as guidelines from which successful teaching strategies may be derived.

In this section the importance of *meaning* and *attention* are discussed. Then some techniques for facilitating memory are presented.

Meaning Enhances Memory

According to the research in mathematics learning by Brownell and Moser (2) and Gray (6), memory or retention is greater for the learner when the material to be remembered has meaning to him. Meaning can be inherent in the concepts or facts to be remembered because of their interrelationships and their relationships to a broader or more expansive body of knowledge. Meaning can be discovered by the learner or meaning can be organized in advance.

Bruner (4) strongly supports structure to promote retention and feels that structure should be discovered by the learner so that meaning is maximal. The research of Worthen (18) supports this contention; he found that guided discovery yielded greater retention than did expository instruction.

Ausubel (1) feels that meaning is facilitated through use of *advance organizers*. The learner is provided with a structure skeleton upon which he can attach new knowledge in a meaningful way.

Whether the child discovers structure or is provided with a structural framework, structure lends meaning, and meaning facilitates retention.

Some Implications.   Meaning can be facilitated through either discovery or expository instruction. Use of discovery techniques enhances understanding because the child can discover structure. After children have made discoveries, you should help them place their discoveries into a broader context. Suppose children discover that the second digit from the right is groups of ten and the third is ten groups of ten. They can also see that a similar relation exists with groups of four, six or eight. Take time to help the children conceptualize the broader generalization from each of these separate discoveries by observing that the second position is groups and the third position is groups of groups.

The concept of structure can be utilized in expository instruction by establishing a frame of reference before beginning the details of the lesson. Try to help the children see where they are going. Map out the lesson before you begin. Tell the children that place value is a grouping system; grouping is helpful because it provides a short-hand method of describing objects in large quantities. Relate the approach you will take to candy bars, boxes of candy bars, and boxes of boxes of candy bars such as the candy truck delivers to the grocery store. Then begin with groups of three or four or five and work up to groups of ten.

Meaning is also facilitated through levels of learning. A *concrete* approach to mathematics instruction conveys the most meaning to a child. Semi-concrete and abstract approaches communicate less meaning to the child, respectively.

Attention Enhances Memory

People best remember material which has received their fullest attention. Teachers need to provide a learning atmosphere and learning strategies designed to increase the attention given by the child to the learning task. Certainly children will pay more attention to learning tasks which have *meaning* than to those which do not. Attention is greater when materials are meaningful, so retention is facilitated by attention and meaning.

Other factors which are related to attention and retention include child involvement, other stimuli in the learning environment, reflection and quantity of material.

Child Involvement.   Undoubtedly, one reason why discovery strategies are successful in facilitating retention is that the child can readily relate and respond to the meaning which he has created; another factor is his *involvement* in the learning experience. Involvement increases attention. Several research studies support the relation between involvement and retention. Gates (5) found that recitation to oneself or to another student facilitated retention more than simply reading silently to oneself. The retention was nearly linear, i.e., the more recitation, the more retention. Howe (10:30) distinguishes between short-term memory (less than one minute) and long-term memory (more than one minute). According to him, research supports the hypothesis that short-term memory is strongly receptive to auditory stimulation. Therefore, extensive auditory stimulation (recitation) keeps items in the short-term memory which in turn facilitates their storage in long-term memory.

Another factor related to pupil involvement is grouping of material. If some fourth-graders are having difficulty with addition facts, they should be encouraged to select a group of facts which *to them* are related. Some might choose a group with the same *first* addend ($9 + 5, 9 + 6, 9 + 7$, etc.); others might choose a group with the same *second* addend ($5 + 9, 6 + 9, 7 + 9$, etc.), and others might choose a group with the same *sum* ($4 + 8, 9 + 3, 6 + 6$, etc.).

Research by Winzenz and Bower (17) indicates that learner-imposed structure is more facilitative than experimenter-imposed structure. Howe (10:63–66) points out that *grouping is necessary*. Repetition without grouping aids retention much less than repetition with successive regrouping. Memory storage is seldom in little bits and pieces; it is nearly always in "chunks." The learner must arrange many bits into several chunks (usually three to seven). Retention seems to be better for student-imposed grouping than for teacher-imposed grouping.

Irrelevant Stimuli.   Non-essential noise and movement are distractions. Since slow children often have short attention spans and are easily distracted, unnecessary movement and noise should be kept to a minimum. Use of earphones in a language lab-type setting is one way to avoid distractions and enhance attention.

Reflection.   Howe (10:42) reports that retention seems to be related more to the total amount of time devoted to the presentation than to the number of times it was presented. There seems to be merit for built-in delays in the presentation to allow the learner "processing time." Hall's (7) research supported this same notion in relation to feedback. Children who received feedback (information relative to correctness of response) in ten seconds required more time to learn the task but retained it better than children who received feedback in zero-second or five-second intervals. Allow children some time to reflect on their responses.

Quantity.   Children can attend to only a limited number of facts at one time: four or five seem to be optimal. If they achieve success and retention, attention and motivation will increase.

Implications.   Attention facilitates retention and children are certainly more attentive to meaningful material. Attention is also greater when children are *involved*. When children manipulate objects, they are involved. Another form of involvement is recitation; if children are allowed to hear themselves when they work on memory items they will probably have greater attention and retention. Children might be encouraged to work together in pairs or small groups on number-fact activities with provision for recitation of number facts. They probably should say the whole fact, $3 + 4 = 7$, rather than just the answer. Research indicates that such auditory stimulation enhances memory. Another way in which children can be involved is through self-selection or self-organization of material to be remembered. Allow children to choose a set of facts to learn; encourage and allow them to establish a set of facts perceived by them as related in some way.

Attention is also enhanced when irrelevant stimuli are minimized. Try to keep miscellaneous noise and movement at a minimum. Memory is facilitated if you provide a quiet place for two or three children to recite number facts or work on some other material which must be remembered.

Delayed reinforcement or feedback is another device which will probably help children remember. When children respond to your questions or to questions in a small group setting, they probably should recite the entire question such as $8 - 2 = 6$ and then be allowed about ten seconds to work it out on their fingers or with some objects; this, too, seems to help.

Finally, the number of facts worked on should be kept at four, five or six. Children can attend to only about this many at a time.

Additional Retention Facilitators

In addition to *meaning* and *attention,* researchers have discovered other variables related to memory and retention. Amount of material, review, and rehearsal are important variables.

Amount of Material.　　The amount of information to be committed at one time should not exceed six pieces or items. Howe (10:22) reports that when more than five pieces are introduced, the middle ones tend to be lost quickly. A small number followed *immediately* by repetition is desirable. Allow the student a *choice* of items if there are many from which to choose; encourage him to choose four, five or six which he feels have something in common. Making his own small groups will promote his retention.

Review and Rehearsal.　　Lazar (12) found that immediate rehearsal or practice facilitates memory, and McDonald (13:235) reports that the greatest forgetting occurs immediately following instruction. Therefore, practice should *immediately* follow instruction. Frequency of successive reviews depends on the amount of repetition immediately following the initial learning and the extent to which material was encountered or applied after the original instruction.

An important related variable is the amount of *overlearning* which occurs. Overlearning is the degree of learning beyond bare mastery. Krueger (11) found that retention is nearly proportional to overlearning, i.e., the more overlearning, the better retention.

Immediate rehearsal increases the amount of overlearning and tends to increase retention by sustaining information in the short-term memory. This in turn seems to facilitate transfer to long-term memory.

Memory research tends to support extensive *immediate* rehearsal or practice within *minutes* after instruction since the greatest amount of forgetting of memory-type items occurs during the first few minutes.

Other Specific Techniques.　　Howe claims that on the basis of much research evidence, the short-term memory is highly responsive to auditory stimulation. When items are to be memorized, auditory stimuli should probably be used. This is supported by studies cited earlier which found recitation to be an effective means of increasing retention.

Finally, Roberts (14) found that recall of newer items before earlier items resulted in greater recall than chronological order when sets of items were memorized. When more than one chunk is being memorized in one day, review the most *recently* learned chunk first.

Fast Learners in Mathematics

The presence of fast learners in the classroom is challenging and oft-times perplexing. Three basic ways of handling the situation can be described as *acceleration, vertical enrichment* and *horizontal* or *lateral enrichment*. Acceleration is an administrative technique in which the child is placed in the next grade level; it is colloquially referred to as "skipping a grade." Acceleration can create special problems of social and emotional development and is being used less and less. Vertical and horizontal enrichment are the forms most commonly used.

Vertical Enrichment

One way to provide appropriate instruction for fast learners is to allow them to move through the regular curriculum at a quickened pace. The third-grader who grasps mathematics easily continues on in the third-grade book ahead of his peers. When he completes the third-grade text, he is commonly ushered into the fourth-grade text. Bruner (4:77) supports this form of enrichment for the mathematically gifted.

Several problems arise when vertical enrichment is utilized. Textbooks are written for the average range of ability so the fast or gifted child is moving more quickly through an "average" curriculum. The major criticism is that such an approach fails to provide the additional breadth and depth which such a child is capable of mastering.

Secondly, such an approach tends to be a very abstract, paper-and-pencil approach to mathematics. As such, it fails to take cognizance of the child's need to encounter concepts at increasing degrees of abstractness from concrete, action-oriented experiences to number manipulation. Children may fail to relate mathematics to everyday experiences and may memorize rather than search for meaning.

Thirdly, such an approach typically fails to accommodate children's needs for peer group and teacher interaction. "Good" students are shunted off to a corner where they work in isolation and are forgotten unless they initiate contact or create a disturbance.

Fourthly, vertical enrichment creates a problem for a child who moves on to a teacher who does not provide enrichment experiences. The child may be required to undergo the boring experience of repetition.

All these problems can be overcome, but they are the most common hazards. Special care must be taken to ensure that fast learners maintain good attitudes and motivation.

Lateral Enrichment

Lateral enrichment describes the strategy whereby all students are kept together part of the time. Additional experiences which provide depth and breadth of mathematics learnings are utilized to enhance growth of fast learners.

When children learn to add with regrouping in base ten, fast learners might explore non-decimal numeration systems. When some children need extensive review and practice of basic skills, fast learners can explore a topic not ordinarily included in the curriculum such as probability, statistics, modular arithmetic (clock arithmetic), historical developments, biographies of famous mathematicians and scientists, computational short-cuts and oddities, and so on.

Some of the problems associated with vertical enrichment are also present in lateral enrichment. It, too, can be an abstract, paper-and-pencil experience devoid of interaction.

For many teachers, accessibility of lateral enrichment materials is a problem. The following sources contain many ideas for enrichment. They suggest ideas, materials, games and activities for fast learners which will enrich their mathematics background, stimulate interest and curiosity, and help maintain a high level of motivation. Though utilization of the individualization model presented in an earlier chapter or some other form of non-graded or multi-age grouping, children's social and emotional needs can be more adequately met.

Sources of Enrichment Materials

A. *Activities for the Enrichment of Arithmetic,* by Herbert F. Spitzer (McGraw-Hill Book Company, 1964), is a book of teaching ideas for practice and development of elementary school mathematics concepts.

B. *Building Mathematics Concepts in Grades Kindergarten through Eight,* by L. Edwin Hirschi (International Textbook Company, 1970), lists such topics for enrichment in Chapter 10 as Goldbach's conjectures, Pythagorean numbers, historical algorisms, unusual ways to add, multiply and check results, non-decimal numerations, square root, absolute value and others; there are about twenty topics briefly described.

C. *Enriching the Teaching of Arithmetic,* by Herbert F. Spitzer (Houghton-Mifflin Company, 1954), is another book of ideas intended for all children and not simply fast learners.

D. *Enrichment Mathematics for the Grades* (1963) is the Twenty-Seventh Yearbook of the National Council of Teachers of Mathematics. Topics described include modular arithmetic, short-cuts, measurement, probability, geometry, topology and tricks. The Yearbook also includes several good bibliographies.

E. *Fun with Mathematics,* by Jerome S. Meyer (Harcourt, Brace & World, 1952), has many mathematical games, puzzles and tricks.

F. *Independent Learning Series* (Charles E. Merrill Publishing Company, 1968), includes booklets on probability and statistics, mental arithmetic, slide rule and other topics.

G. *Magic House of Numbers,* by Irving Adler (John Day Company, 1957), is a book of riddles, tricks and games which teach basic arithmetic concepts for intermediate grades.

H. *Mathematics in Everyday Things,* by William C. Vergara (Harper & Brothers, 1959), discusses the relation of mathematics principles to many scientific problems; it contains many diagrams.

I. *Numbers and Numerals,* by David Eugene Smith and Jekuthial Ginsburg (N. C. T. M. Monograph No. 1, 1937), relates the history of numbers and numerals.

J. *Numbers Old and New,* by Irving Adler and Ruth Adler (John Day Company, 1960), is a reference book for historical systems which can be read by older primary children.

K. *Paper Folding,* by Donovan Johnson (National Council of Teachers of Mathematics, 1957), contains many suggestions for demonstrating mathematics concepts with paper.

L. *Problems in the Teaching of Elementary School Mathematics,* edited by Klaas Kramer (Allyn & Bacon, 1970), includes in Part IV articles on geometry, algebra and probability and statistics for elementary school children by Irvin H. Brune, Robert B. Davis and Jack D. Wilkinson and Owen Nelson, respectively.

M. *Teaching Modern Mathematics in the Elementary School,* by Howard F. Fehr and Jo M. Phillips (Addison-Wesley Publishing Co., 1967), contains many enrichment topics in Chapter 10 which include Venn diagrams, clock arithmetic and integers.

Many other sources of lateral enrichment materials can be found in *bibliographies* in the following sources:

> *Arithmetic for Child Development,* by Lowry W. Harding (William C. Brown Company, Publishers, 1965), Part Three.
>
> *Enrichment Mathematics for the Grades,* Twenty-Seventh Yearbook of the National Council of Teachers of Mathematics, 1963, pp. 10–14.
>
> *Arithmetic Teacher,* "Bibliography of Books for Enrichment in Arithmetic," February 1959 and April 1960.

Summary. The model for individualization of instruction in a self-contained classroom proposed in Chapter 2 requires the use of lateral enrichment.

In addition to lateral enrichment activities which extend the fast learner's breadth and depth of understanding, various projects can also be utilized. Children can engage in library research on topics of interest and prepare oral or written reports, or they can build geometric models or set up experiments which demonstrate or utilize certain mathematical principles. They may enjoy preparing bulletin boards and exhibits from time to time or helping children experiencing difficulty in the class or at an earlier grade level.

Bibliography

1. Ausubel, David P. "Facilitating Meaningful Verbal Learnings in the Classroom." *The Arithmetic Teacher* (February 1968), 126–32.

2. Brownell, William A., and Harold E. Moser. "Meaningful vs. Mechanical Learning: A Study in Grade III Subtraction." *Duke University Studies in Education* (1949), 8:1–207.

3. Bruce, R. W. "Conditions of Transfer of Training." *Journal of Experimental Psychology* (1933), XVI, 343–61.

4. Bruner, Jerome S. *The Process of Education.* New York: Vintage Books, 1963.

5. Gates, A. I. "Recitation as a Factor in Memorizing." *Archives of Psychology* (1917), No. 40.

6. Gray, Roland F. "An Experiment in the Teaching of Introductory Multiplication." *The Arithmetic Teacher* (March 1965), 12:199–203.

7. Hall, John F. *The Psychology of Learning.* Philadelphia: J. B. Lippincott Co., 1966.

8. Henry, Jules. "Hope, Delusion, and Organization: Some Problems in the Motivation of Low Achievers." *The Low Achiever in Mathematics.* Washington, D.C.: U.S. Department of Health, Education and Welfare Bulletin No. 31, 1965.

9. Hood, H. Blair. "An Experimental Study of Piaget's Theory of the Development of Number in Children." *British Journal of Psychology,* (1962), 53: 273–86.

10. Howe, Michael J. A. *Introduction to Human Memory.* New York: Harper & Row, Publishers, 1970.

11. Krueger, W. C. F. "The Effect of Overlearning and Retention." *Journal of Experimental Psychology* (1929), 12:71–78.

12. Lazar, Gerald. "Retention as a Function of Successive Recall Trials Following Original Learning." *Psychological Reports* (1969), 25:567–74.

13. McDonald, Frederick J. *Educational Psychology,* 2nd Ed. Belmont, California: Wadsworth Publishing Company, Inc., 1965.

14. Roberts, William S. "The Priority of Recall of New Items in Transfer from Part List Learning to Whole List Learning." *Journal of Verbal Learning and Verbal Behavior* (1969), 8:645–52.

15. Rosenbloom, Paul C. "Implications of Psychological Research." *The Low Achiever in Mathematics.* Washington, D.C.: U.S. Department of Health, Education, and Welfare Bulletin No. 31, 1965.

16. Thorndike, E. L. "Mental Discipline in High School Studies." *Journal of Educational Psychology* (1924), 15:1–22, 83–98.

17. Winzenz, David, and Gordon Bower. "Subject-imposed Coding and Memory for Digit Series." *Journal of Experimental Psychology* (1970), 83:52–56.

18. Worthen, Blaine R. "A Study of Discovery and Expository Presentation: Implications for Teaching." *Journal of Teacher Education* (Summer 1968), 19:223–42.

6

Selection of
Teaching Materials

A good learning environment is much more than a comfortable room where children learn the world's accumulated wisdom. A good learning environment is one which allows children to learn because they *want* to learn. The quality of an environment can be measured by the enthusiasm, interest and curiosity which it generates. Children need to learn *how* to learn and to *want* to learn.

School learning need not be so very different from non-school learning. From your personal experiences and from the developmental theory summarized in the chapter on psychology, the need for socialization experiences and manipulation of materials must be quite evident. Children learn from each other, and through sensory experiences with the environment; they see, hear, touch and manipulate.

People tend to learn and to comprehend stimuli in varying strengths of their senses; some learn best from the sense of sight, others from touch, and so on.

> Even in the same person the results may differ at different times due to the internal conditions of that individual, which serves to determine how the stimuli attended to shall be organized into a perception. . . . Perception deals only with the salient, meaningful parts of the object being attended to. This sounds like a truism until one interprets it to mean that stimuli of equal strength need not be remembered or incorporated into a perception to the same degree. These perceptions which belong or fit into a pattern are those which are retained. . . . This whole subject of perception

may have more importance in the teaching of mathematics than in most subjects because there is less inherent meaning in a subject which must stress its abstractness (7:102).

Relative to Piaget's model, this statement by Syer reiterates that only meaningful stimuli are both assimilated *and* accommodated. Only a stimulus which can be meaningfully associated with other elements or beliefs can be integrated and retained as useful knowledge. Further, this statement supports learning at the concrete and semi-concrete levels in a *variety* of ways because there are many forms to which children can readily and meaningfully relate.

Accommodation of instruction to various meaningful learning patterns of children is the focus of this chapter. The research cited in various sections of this chapter constitute the case for variety. The thrust of the chapter will *not* be to convince you that a need exists but, rather, to help you *meet* the need.

Since the textbook is the most common learning aid, it will be briefly discussed first. The major portion of the chapter will be devoted to selection criteria and specific types of commercial and teacher-made learning aids. You will undoubtedly want to return to the last part of this chapter several times as you proceed through the remainder of this book.

The Super Aid

A good textbook is the teacher's best instructional aid. However, it should never be the teacher's *only* aid. Textbooks are usually written under joint authorship of mathematics educators and elementary school teachers. Texts are designed to bring you the best thinking of a highly qualified professional team in matters of elementary mathematics instruction.

Johnson and Rising (3) have stated that some of the strengths of a good textbook include: (1) content appropriate for the level, (2) appropriate structure and sequence, (3) provision for practice, (4) provision for independent study, and (5) provision for differentiated assignments. *A textbook by its very nature is abstract (computations) and semi-concrete (pictures and diagrams). Mathematics experiences should begin at the concrete level so the textbook should* **not** *be used during introductory work on new concepts.* Other important instructional aids are used in conjunction with the textbook to form a well-rounded program.

Making Wise Choices: A Balance of Many Factors

How does a teacher decide *what aids are needed?* How does a teacher decide *how to spend the money* in the instructional materials budget? How does a teacher decide *whether or not to make an aid?* These are questions you will undoubtedly encounter in your teaching career. This section is designed to make you aware of the variables impinging upon the decisions, and to consider the instructional aspects of the materials.

What Are the Factors?

Time vs. Expense.   If plenty of funds are available for instructional materials, you will probably purchase teaching aids. When funds are short, you will make some aids and purchase others. In the latter case, money and time must be wisely distributed to derive the maximum educational benefits for children. With this overriding factor, what educational variables should you consider?

Teacher-centered vs. Student-centered Aids.   Mathematics has traditionally been a teacher-centered subject. Instruction has been dominated by the expository mode. When new instructional aids are needed, the desirability and feasibility of pupil-manipulated materials should be weighed carefully. Children learn through experience; they learn by manipulating objects in the environment. Teacher aids for occasional demonstration are good to have, but they are even more effective when used in conjunction with individual or small-group activities on similar aids. Students will be more involved and probably more interested in the mathematics activity if they can *actively participate.*

When children learn place value concepts or addition of fractions, teachers typically work with flannel board materials, an abacus and other teacher-manipulated devices. Such materials can be used by children, too, but usually only one or two children can use the materials at any one time. Usually, children only handle the materials as participants in an expository lesson. Several devices such as bundles of tickets, bundles of popsicle sticks or graph paper, can be used by *all* the children, are very inexpensive, and commercial objects such as poppit beads or fraction kits or individual abacuses can be used. Objects for pupil manipulation can be used very advantageously in small groups for discovery of concepts. Children can *discover* that 23 popsicle sticks counted out individually can be grouped as one ten and thirteen ones or two tens and three ones; children can *discover* that $\frac{1}{5} + \frac{1}{5} = \frac{2}{5}, \frac{1}{3} + \frac{1}{3} = \frac{2}{3}$ and generalize to $\frac{1}{n} + \frac{1}{n} = \frac{2}{n}.$

Expository vs. Discovery Modes.   The teacher can demonstrate with a single, large aid but children can be afforded opportunities for discovery if they have aids for individual or small-group work. As noted previously, discovery modes usually generate stronger motivation. Children can ask their own questions and seek solutions. Such activities undoubtedly stimulate curiosity, enhance interest and make learning a richer, more enjoyable experience.

Development vs. Practice.   Activities can be categorized, although a bit artificially, into developmental activities and practice activities. The difference in teacher intent helps make the distinction: some activities, especially introductory, are for children to *understand a concept;* these are developmental activities. Other activities are for children to *remember a concept or skill;* these are practice activities.

Teaching aids should be available for development *and* practice. Most aids are for development. Such aids are greatly needed because research has supported the use of 50 to 75 percent of class time for developmental activities and 25 to 50 percent for practice (4, 5). However, practice is often a boring experience. Children are asked to work a page of problems. More game-like activities are needed which contain camouflaged practice!

Here are some activities and aids which exemplify the traits of pupil-centered/teacher-centered, development/practice, and expository/discovery:

A. *Pupil-centered—expository—development: concept of one-half.* Every child in the class needs a rectangular piece of paper. Fold the rectangle into two equal parts. *Ask:* Into how many parts is the paper separated by the crease? *Ask:* Does each part have the same size? Fold the paper again to verify that they do have the same size. Urge the pupils to suggest a name for one of the parts. If the response $\frac{1}{2}$ is not forthcoming, explain why one part is called $\frac{1}{2}$ of the piece of paper.

B. *Pupil-centered—practice: concept of congruence.* Have each child pair up with a member of the class. Ask them to find objects in their desks or somewhere in the room that are of the same size and shape.

C. *Teacher-centered—expository—development: concept of line segment.* Show the children that Tinkertoys can be used to represent line segments by joining short sticks and placing disks on the ends.

D. *Pupil involvement—practice: addition facts.* Prepare cards with addition facts. Cards are dealt so each child has the same number. The game is similar to rummy; the object is to get as many *books* as possible with a book consisting of two or more cards whose facts have the same sum. A player may add cards to a book after it has been placed on the table.

2	3	1	4		2	1	8	3
3	2	4	1		6	7	0	5

E. *Pupil involvement—practice: seriation.* The children would place in order of size or height, etc., from first to last or from smallest to tallest, etc., pictures or standups of themselves. The important thing is to have them arrange objects with which they are familiar.

F. *Pupil involvement—practice: cardinal number.* One person is fox and the rest of the children are chickens. Each has a line behind which he must stand. The fox calls out a time (3 o'clock) and the chickens take three big steps. When the fox calls "midnight" all the chickens run back to the starting line. If the fox catches one, that one then becomes another fox and the game is repeated.

Types of Reinforcement.   The four major sensory reinforcers in mathematics learning in children are visual (eye), auditory (ear), tactile (touch) and kinesthetic (muscular movement). The benefits of auditory stimulation emanating from the teacher have been greatly overvalued! Children do not have good attention spans, and they do not relate easily to near-meaningless mathematics jargon! Visual reinforcement has probably been overplayed, too. Many children fail to learn concepts after even two or three teacher demonstrations.

Child-centered mathematics instruction relies heavily upon tactile and kinesthetic reinforcement. If you hold three marbles in your hand, you *feel* (touch) three marbles; this is tactile reinforcement of "threeness." If you clap your hands three times (muscular movement), you *do something* three times; this is kinesthetic reinforcement. Hold a ring in your hand; this is tactile reinforcement of "circle." Trace a circle; this is kinesthetic reinforcement of "circle."

Your repertoire of instructional activities should include reinforcers of all four types. Combinations are common, too. For example, in the seriation example above children can see and touch the objects so they receive visual and tactile reinforcement. If they verbalize, they can also receive auditory reinforcement of the seriation. In the cardinal number example, the children can receive auditory, visual and kinesthetic reinforcement in the single activity; they can count (auditory), watch other children (visual) and take three steps (kinesthetic).

Classroom Organization. The extent to which you can use individually guided activities, small-group and large-group instruction may be influenced by the organization of your classroom. If the seats are attached to the floor, you may want to have a math-activity table where only one or two small groups can work while the remainder of the class carries out a different type of activity. Rooms which contain individual movable desks can be arranged front to front in groups of two, four or six, depending on the activity and availability of resources.

Selected Concepts. All mathematics concepts are not of equal importance nor of equal learning difficulty. Before purchasing or making aids, examine the class diagnostically, review the records of last year's class, talk to colleagues who teach the same grade level or talk with the teacher of the succeeding grade level to determine common deficiencies of children coming from the previous level.

You will want to place high priority on good instructional aids which help alleviate concept or developmental deficiencies. Further, you can go through the book to see if you have instructional materials for most of the major concepts.

Integration. The world is not dissected into mathematics, science, social studies, and so on. These barriers are erected to aid instruction. Activities should minimize these artificial barriers, so activities are needed which relate mathematics to other aspects of the total curriculum. Thus, science games with social settings such as playing store or the myriad of application-type situations help integrate the various components of the curriculum.[1] Studies have found that when skills are related to practical situations, attitudes (1) and attention (6) improve.

Storage. A consideration not to be overlooked is storage. Size and frequency of use may influence your decision to make or purchase an aid.

---

[1] The MINNEMAST Project seeks to integrate mathematics and science. The articles by Rosenbloom and Flournoy, and chapter seven of the book by Osborn *et al.* have many excellent ideas. See the bibliography in the next section of this chapter.

Versatility.   A small number of versatile aids will be less expensive, require less time to construct and present fewer storage problems. When you decide the concepts which need work, try to find a few aids which can be used or modified slightly for many purposes.

An example of a versatile object is the *clothespin*. Nearly *sixty* mathematics concepts are listed in the next section; each of them can be related instructionally to clothespins. A versatile commercial aid is the abacus. It can be used for place value, addition, subtraction, multiplication and division facts and algorithms, fractional number concepts, inequalities, cardinal numbers, decimal fractions and other concepts. Versatility can be within a grade level or across grade levels. Examine closely the aids of other teachers. The chances are very great that you can use many of them in your instructional program. Aids can also be versatile across subject matter lines. Globes, maps, and science and physical education equipment can be easily related to mathematics instruction.

What Is a Balance?

A balance is not a fifty-fifty split of teacher-student, expository-discovery, development-practice, and so on. A balance is a compromise between what is theoretically desirable and pragmatically possible; a balance reflects *you*. Management skills, tenor of the school administration, permissiveness-authoritarianism and many other factors enter into the determination of the appropriate balance. Most aids tend to be teacher-centered development aids. More student-centered development aids *and* practice aids are needed in most classrooms. The "right" balance is one which reflects the child's needs and the teaching style which best accommodates them.

Resources of the Immediate Environment

Resourcefulness is a characteristic of interested, dynamic teachers. They see the instructional potential of objects in their immediate surroundings. A few suggestions are made below to help the teacher generate new ideas.

Teacher-made Aids.   Teacher's manuals provide many valuable ideas on activities and aids to foster children's mathematics learnings. You can make such aids from accessible materials by using the pictures as guidelines or patterns. The pictures can be found in catalogs of companies listed in the next section, in teacher's manuals, textbooks and magazines. If you cannot buy an aid, try to make it yourself: enlist the help of students, parents, janitors, shop teachers and your spouse!

Common materials which can be used include:

Wire	Nails
Scrap wood	Various paper forms
Cardboard	Felt scraps
Washers	Magnetized rubber

Heard, Archer and Grossnickle give some practical ideas in the *Twenty-Second NCTM Yearbook,* and Johnson gives many clever ideas for using waxed and writing paper in his booklet on paper folding. Read Berger's comments in this *Yearbook* if you desire guidelines governing the use of teacher-made aids.

Many common objects have numerous uses in mathematics instruction. On several occasions I have asked a graduate student to bring a common object to class and the class would brainstorm the concepts which could be taught. Here are the results of one such session (we have had others dealing with such things as rocks, flannel boards, overhead projector and Tinkertoys):

Clothespins

I. Pre-Operational
   A. Sets
   B. Equivalent sets
   C. Non-equivalent sets
   D. Counting (1s, 2s, 5s)
   E. Cardinality
   F. Ordinality
   G. One-to-one correspondence
   H. One more than concept
   I. One less than concept
   J. One-to-many correspondence
   K. Place value (number men)

II. Addition
   A. Addition facts
   B. Horizontal addition
   C. Vertical addition
   D. Concrete addition
      (clothesline, table)
   E. Commutative property
   F. Associative property
   G. Identity element
   H. Regrouping
      (colored clothespins)

III. Subtraction
   A. Facts
   B. Vertical subtraction
   C. Concrete subtraction
   D. Identity element
   E. Regrouping
   F. Relationship of addition
      and subtraction

IV. Multiplication
   A. Commutative property
   B. Associative property
   C. Identity element
   D. Facts
   E. Concrete multiplication
   F. Relationship of addition
      and multiplication

V. Division
   A. Measurement
      division
   B. Relationship of
      multiplication
      and division
   C. Facts
   D. Identity element
   E. Concrete division

VI. Geometry
   A. Make shapes
   B. Compare shapes
   C. Line segments
   D. Angles

VII. Measurement
   A. Length
   B. Weight
   C. Area
   D. Volume

VIII. Fractions
   A. Fractional parts
      of a set
   B. Compare size of
      fractions
      ($\frac{1}{2}$ of set, $\frac{1}{4}$ of set)
   C. Equivalent fractions

Local businesses often have scrap materials which can be used in the classroom. A department store may have cloth remnants; a tool shop, metal strips of assorted shapes; an industry, cardboard or wood scraps, etc. You can look around the community and inquire of owners.

People as Resources.   Many parents and businessmen have responsibilities which are related to mathematics. If such individuals can come to your class and share ideas with children, applications of mathematics become clearer for the children, and relevance and interest are increased.

Places as Resources.   Businesses, central school offices and government offices use computers and various technology to perform their functions. Mathematics field trips can be arranged; children can become acquainted with some of the ways in which mathematics helps people.

Summary.   The immediate environment is rich in people, places and things which can be used to enrich the mathematics curriculum. Many common objects can be used for mathematics instruction, and teachers can make many others with the aid of diagrams from books and catalogs. Household items, hardware and lumberyard materials and throw-away items from local businesses and industries can be used by the resourceful teacher. Further pupil interest and motivation can be enhanced through local field trips and use of community resource people.

Commercial Resources

Many items can be *purchased* which will increase your effectiveness in mathematics instruction. Aids, children's books, games and machines are some of the most common ones.

Commercial Aids.   Many specific aids are mentioned throughout the remainder of this book. Here are some of the best known companies selling mathematics learning aids; most companies will send a catalog upon request.

Creative Playthings
Creative Publications
Cuisenaire Company of America, Inc.
EduKaid
Educational Teaching Aids
Ginn and Company
J. L. Hammett Company
Houghton Mifflin
Ideal School Supply Company
Instructo
Instructor
Judy Company
Math Media Division, h + m associates

Schoolhouse Visuals
Scott Foresman
SEE, selective educational equipment, inc.
WFF'N Proof

Children's Books. Often, mathematics concepts can be reinforced through children's literature. The National Council of Teachers of Mathematics has a booklet which lists many such books; *Mathematics Library, Elementary and Junior High School* by C. E. Hardgrove and H. F. Miller supplies an ample bibliography of appropriate books; and Harding lists many children's books in Part III of his teacher education text listed in the next section. Also, see the *Twenty-Seventh NCTM Yearbook.*

Games. Several interesting games have appeared on the market which develop and provide practice in mathematics concepts and skills. Here is a typical sampling:

Equations, WFF'N Proof (Primary, Intermediate)
On Sets, WFF'N Proof (Primary, Intermediate)
Say It, Garrard Press (Primary, Intermediate)
TUF, Creative Publications (Intermediate)
WFF, WFF'N Proof (Intermediate)
WFF'N PROOF: The Game of Modern Logic, WFF'N Proof
(Intermediate)

Many games can be found in the catalogs of Beckley-Cardy and J. S. Latta, Inc.

Machines. Many films and filmstrips are commercially available, and the 3M Company produces an extensive variety of overhead projector originals and duplication masters. In the *Twenty-Second Yearbook,* Woodby makes some good suggestions for making your own slides. Tape recorders can be used effectively for variety and for meeting special needs of poor readers. Finally, calculators and business machines can be used to develop special skills and increase interest.

Summary. Many commercial aids can be obtained from the companies listed. Aids should be selected according to the criteria outlined in the previous section. Motivation, positive attitudes and interest can be stimulated and maintained through development and practice of mathematics concepts, through children's literature, commercial games and use of machines.

A Selected Source Bibliography
of Mathematics Activities

Available to teachers are many commercial publications containing classroom activities for practice, skill development, and concept formation.

Journals

> *The Arithmetic Teacher*
> *The Instructor*
> *The Grade Teacher*

Books

> *Arithmetic for Child Development,* by Lowry W. Harding, 1965, Part III.
>
> *Early Childhood Curriculum—A Piaget Program, Teacher's Guide,* by Celia Stendler Lavatelli, 1970.
>
> *Emerging Practices in Mathematics Education,* the Twenty-Second Yearbook of the National Council of Teachers of Mathematics, 1954, Part II.
>
> *Enrichment Mathematics for the Grades,* the Twenty-Seventh Yearbook of the National Council of Teachers of Mathematics, 1963.
>
> *Extending Understandings of Mathematics,* by Roger Osborn, M. Vere DeVault, Claude C. Boyd and W. Robert Houston, 1969, Chapters 7, 8.
>
> *Math Activities for Child Involvement,* by Enoch Dumas, 1971.
>
> *Mathematics in Elementary Education,* edited by Nicholas J. Vigilante, 1969, pages 98 (Flournoy), 244 (Rosenbloom), 300 (Mariani), 424 (Williams).
>
> *Models for Mathematics in the Elementary School,* by Leonard M. Kennedy, 1967.
>
> *Paper Folding for the Mathematics Class,* by Donovan A. Johnson, 1967.
>
> *Piaget's Theory Applied to an Early Childhood Curriculum,* by Celia Stendler Lavatelli (1970), Chapters 4, 5, 6.
>
> *Plus, A Handbook for Teachers of Elementary Arithmetic,* by Mary E. Platts, 1964.
>
> *Problems in the Teaching of Elementary School Mathematics,* by Klaas Kramer (1970), Parts IV, VI.
>
> *The Teaching of Mathematics in the Elementary School,* by John W. Starr III (1969).

Bibliography

1. Dutton, Wilbur H. "Attitudes of Junior High School Pupils Toward Arithmetic." *School Review* (January 1956), 64:18–22.

2. *Emerging Practices in Mathematics Education.* Washington, D.C.: National Council of Teachers of Mathematics, 1954.

3. Johnson, Donovan A., and Gerald R. Rising. *Guidelines for Teaching Mathematics.* Belmont, California: Wadsworth Publishing Company, Inc., 1967.

4. Shipp, Donald E., and George H. Deer. "The Use of Class Time in Arithmetic." *The Arithmetic Teacher* (March 1960), 7:117–21.

5. Shuster, Albert, and Fred P. gge. "Retention Efficiency of Meaningful Teaching." *The Arithmetic Teacher* (January 1965), 12:24–31.

6. Stokes, C. Newton. "80,000 Children's Reactions to Meanings in Arithmetic." *The Arithmetic Teacher* (December 1958), 5:281–86.

7. *The Learning of Mathematics—Its Theory and Practice.* Washington, D.C.: National Council of Teachers of Mathematics, 1953.

PART II

Specific
Content
and
Methodology

A

Whole
Numbers

Pre-Operational Concepts of Mathematics

Children learn through manipulative experiences. Since young children are perception bound they naturally focus on characteristics of the environment which can be seen. Abstractions, such as *number*, which must be extracted from perceptions are less concrete, so they are formed later in the child's development.

The pre-operational mathematics curriculum, as outlined in this chapter, reflects the child's needs for manipulation and for movement from concrete to abstract. After a brief summary of mathematics knowledge of preschoolers, a fundamental mathematics concept, relation, is explored. It is examined first very concretely (qualitatively) and then more abstractly (quantitatively), e.g., sets are sorted by physical attributes such as color or size and then by number-related characteristics such as more than or less than. After pre-number relations are discussed, number relations are explored and instructional strategies for developing pre-operational concepts are elaborated.

Mathematics Concepts Possessed by Preschoolers

Children begin formal schooling at varying ages and with varying degrees of understanding of mathematical ideas, skills and concepts. Kindergarten and first-grade teachers provide appropriate learning experiences designed to build solid readiness foundations which aid in acquisition of number concepts. Several researchers have sought to summarize the mathematics skills and concepts of children who have reached school age. While all the studies naturally have limitations, the following summary will give you some feel for typicality.[1]

Almost all kindergarten children can count to ten and as many as half the kindergarten entrants can count to twenty or thirty. Some children can count only by rote (spiel off a sequence of sounds), but most can count rationally to ten (enumerate a set of objects; correctly answer the question, "How many are there?").

Nearly all kindergarten children can recognize a set of one, two, three or four objects immediately but must count to determine the number property of sets larger than four. Children can more easily determine that two sets have the same number property than find a subset of a given set which has the same number property as a given set, i.e., children can more easily determine that two sets have the same number of elements than to find a subset of a given set which matches a smaller set.

Most children can *write* the numerals 1, 2, 3, 4, 5 and some can *recognize* numerals through ten.

Most youngsters can solve simple addition and subtraction story problems. Some can answer addition questions but are unable to answer subtraction questions.

Also, many children are familiar with measuring instruments and terms, can tell time on the hour, can recognize pennies and nickels, circles and squares, and fractional parts half, third and fourth.

In most homes, the concepts just summarized are learned incidentally. Occasions arise in everyday circumstances in which counting, telling time, spending money, measuring, and other mathematics-related concepts and skills naturally arise. Children pick up vague notions which are frequently distorted and understood intuitively, i.e., they lack total comprehension of the skills and concepts. Acquired concepts are reinforced and clarified at school. Maturation and experience increase the degree of comprehension.

In recent years specialists in early childhood education and elementary school mathematics education have taken a critical look at early mathematics experiences provided in schools. Through careful study of Piaget's developmental theory and personal observations of young minds at work, they have concluded that the traditional mathematics sequence may be inappropriate; children may not be maturationally ready to study some mathematics concepts of the typical primary school mathematics curriculum.

For example, counting has traditionally been a skill practiced widely in early education. Counting can be rote or rational. Some children who count cannot answer the question, "How many buttons are there on your shirt?" Such a child

---

[1] Refer to the studies cited in the bibliography at the end of the chapter for further details.

is said to be counting by rote, i.e., the sequence of number names are given in proper order because they have been committed to memory, but the counting is non-functional in the sense of comparing the number of books on two shelves or stating the number of boys and girls in a class.

The ability to count rationally depends on mastery of other concepts. For example, many children who can count cannot establish one-to-one correspondences. Hence, counting should be preceded in the curriculum by work with other concepts. Further, the work of Piaget and many other researchers has indicated that not only are there prerequisite concepts to understand the concept of *number*, but many children do not master these concepts until $6\frac{1}{2}$ to 7 years of age!

I have taken my $4\frac{1}{2}$-year-old daughter to my university classes several times and engaged her in this discourse:

"Amy, will you place five of these little red blocks in my hand and count them as you do it, please?"

"One, two, three, four, five."

"Now, will you please place five in my other hand and count them as you do it?"

"One, two, three, four, five."

"Let's pretend these little red blocks are candy. Would you rather have this candy (one hand extended) or this candy (other hand extended) or wouldn't it make any difference?"

"It wouldn't make any difference."

"Okay. Now I will place these here in a little pile (hand emptied) and these here (other hand emptied; the piles are similarly spaced). Would you rather have this candy or this candy or wouldn't it make any difference?"

"It wouldn't make any difference."

(I then scatter one pile. There is now a compact group of five and five which are scattered.) "Now would you rather have this candy or this candy or wouldn't it make any difference?"

"I'd rather have this candy" (pointing to the scattered set).

Amy is in a stage through which all children pass. She is perception bound. What she *sees* takes precedence over what she counts. She *does not conserve number*. To her, the number property of a set depends on its position. For many children, the conviction or belief that number is independent of position does not occur until age seven years or after. Amy has not attained *reversibility*. She cannot undo the scattering in her mind and therefore conclude that this new scattered set has the same number property as the piled set. As Copeland says, "The idea of *reversibility* is inherent in conservation of number. Number does not change as objects are moved about because the objects can be placed back in their original position" (2:71).

Counting is a way to determine a characteristic of a given set; it helps determine a *quantitative* characteristic. With five red blocks, a child can more easily see that they all remain red when they are scattered than that they still have the property of "fiveness." "Redness" is a *qualitative* characteristic of the set.

Visual properties (qualities) can be identified by children more easily than number properties (quantities).

A given set of objects can be categorized by any characteristic, qualitative or quantitative: red-not red; hard-not hard; six-not six. Such classifications are derived from *relationships* existing among the objects or sets of objects. Relationships give rise to *relations* in mathematics.

Before moving into a detailed explanation of relations and other developmental concepts, you should note the following: the *precise* pedagogical significance of some of the ideas which follow in this chapter is uncertain. Whenever possible, suggestions and implications will be mentioned. Since there is still much to learn from research, some of the present knowledge can be used in three ways which, while they are far from creating a total picture, offer guidance to the perceptive teacher:

  I. Knowledge of mathematics sequences will help you provide a continuous strand of readiness experiences.
 II. Knowledge of child development will help you establish realistic expectations and provide you with insights into children's learning difficulties.
III. Knowledge of the content and the child reinforces your awareness that understanding is on a continuum; in between knowing and not-knowing is an expanse of partial-knowing which is related to maturation and appropriateness of learning experiences.

As Lovell states:

It is important to stress that our knowledge of the growth of thinking in children is not yet sufficient or exact enough to serve as a basis for a scientific pedagogy. An intensive understanding of children on the part of the teacher is still essential. But Piaget's work provides the best conceptional framework we yet have inside which we can discuss the growth of children's understanding of mathematics (8:x).

Relations and Conservation of Quantity

A relation is a way of pairing things. Examine some illustrations:

  A. *Relation: "weighs more than"*
Objects (elements): book (b), automobile (a), desk (d)
Statements: automobile *weighs more than* book, aRb
          automobile *weighs more than* desk, aRd
          desk *weighs more than* book, dRb
  B. *Relation: "is a cousin of"*
Objects (elements): Jane (j), Bill (b), Alice (a)
Statements: Jane *is a cousin of* Bill, jRb
          Bill *is a cousin of* Jane, bRj
          Jane *is a cousin of* Alice, jRa

Alice *is a cousin of* Jane, aRj
Bill *is a cousin of* Alice, bRa
Alice *is a cousin of* Bill, aRb

C. *Relation: "is less than"*

Objects (elements): 1, 2 + 3, 5

Statements: 1 *is less than* 2 + 3, 1R(2 + 3), 1 < 2 + 3
1 *is less than* 5, 1R5, 1 < 5

Each of the three relations makes possible the pairing of objects or elements. The first relation, "weighs more than," allows you to pair automobile and book, automobile and desk, and desk and book. Note that the order of the objects or elements in this relation is important. It is true that automobile weighs more than book, aRb, but it is *not true* that book weighs more than automobile, bRa. For this reason, order is important in a relation. Hence, for the relation "weighs more than" and objects automobile (a), book (b) and desk (d) the following hold:

True	*Not True*
aRb	bRa
aRd	dRa
dRb	bRd
	aRa
	bRb
	dRd

Write similar columns for B. "is a cousin of" and C, "is less than," for the elements given. Then check your lists with those on page 86.

Since order is important, *a relation is defined as a set of ordered pairs.* Thus aRb can be represented by (a, b) ∈ R.[2] The ordered pair (a, b) is an element of R.

R = {(a, b), (a, d), (d, b), . . .}. The three dots mean that all other object-pairs in which the first weighs more than the second are also in R. Since a train, (t), weighs more than an elephant, (e), tRe so (t, e) is in R. Translate each of the following to a verbal statement and indicate whether it is true or false. Check your responses on the next page.

x = Anna Freud	R_1 = is the daughter of
y = Sigmund Freud	R_2 = is the father of
z = Austria	R_3 = is located in
a = Europe	R_4 = has lived in

1. xR_1y	5. yR_2x
2. $(y, x) \in R_1$	6. xR_4z
3. aR_3z	7. $(y, a) \in R_4$
4. $(z, a) \in R_3$	8. aR_2z

---

[2] If you are unfamiliar with this notation, see the Appendix.

B. "is a cousin of"		C. "is less than"	
True	*Not True*	*True*	*Not True*
jRb	aRa	1R(2 + 3)	(2 + 3)R1
bRj	bRb	1R5	5R1
jRa	jRj		(2 + 3)R5
aRj			5R(2 + 3)
bRa			1R1
aRb			(2 + 3)R(2 + 3)
			5R5

Properties of Relations

Some relations exhibit special characteristics. Three very important characteristics are reflexivity, symmetry and transitivity.

Reflexivity. If for every element, g, in the relation it is true that gRg, then R
is said to be a reflexive relation. Since automobile *does not weigh more than*
automobile, Jane *is not a cousin of* Jane, and 2 + 3 *is not less than* 2 + 3,
none of the examples cited are reflexive. "Is as full as" is a reflexive relation
since for any meaningful g, gRg, e.g., the brown cup is as full as the brown cup,
and the barrel is as full as the barrel. Other reflexive relations include "lives at
the same house as," "is less than or equal to," "is congruent to," and "is as tall
as."

Symmetry. If for every aRb, bRa is also true, R is said to be a symmetric
relation. "Is a cousin of" is such a relation for surely if Jim is a cousin of
Bill, jRb, then Bill is a cousin of Jim, bRj. Other relations which are symmetric
include "belongs to the same bridge club as," "is a sibling of," and "is parallel
to." "Is heavier than" and "is less than" are *not* symmetric relations.

1. True: Anna Freud *is the daughter* of Sigmund Freud.
2. False: Sigmund Freud is *not* the daughter of Anna Freud.
3. False: Europe is *not* located in Austria.
4. True: Austria *is located in* Europe.
5. True: Sigmund Freud *is the father of* Anna Freud.
6. True: Anna Freud *has lived in* Austria.
7. True: Sigmund Freud *has lived in* Europe.
8. False: Europe is not the father of Austria.

Transitivity. If aRc when aRb and bRc, then R is a transitive relation.

　　A. *"weighs more than"*
When aRd, automobile weighs more than desk, and dRb, desk weighs
more than book, then aRb, automobile weighs more than book.

This is a transitive relation because aRd and dRb implies that aRb.
   B. *"is taller than"*
If aRb, Al is taller than Bill, and bRc, Bill is taller than Chuck, then aRc, Al is taller than Chuck.

Other relations which are transitive include "is a sibling of," "is shorter than" and "can carry more than."

RST—Reflexive, Symmetric, Transitive. Indicate by R, S, and T those properties possessed by each of the following relations. Check your answers wth those listed on page 88.

Relation	Set
A. "is the mother of"	people
B. "is heavier than"	animals
C. "is at least as old as"	people
D. "is the brother of"	males
E. "is older than"	cities
F. "is equal to"	counting numbers

Equivalence Relations

A relation which exhibits reflexivity, symmetry and transitivity is called an *equivalence relation*. Verify for yourself that each of the following is an equivalence relation: is symmetric to, is the same age as, is congruent to, is similar to, goes to the same school as, is the same length as, and equals.

Growth in Complexity

Some relations are reflexive or symmetric or transitive. Others exhibit two of these properties and others, equivalence relations, exhibit all three. If the child is fully to understand and be able to use equality, he must have an intuitive grasp of its properties. Equality is reflexive: $7 = 7$, number is conserved regardless of the position of objects. Equality is symmetric: if $3 + 4 = 7$ then $7 = 4 + 3$; one can be substituted for the other. Equality is transitive: if $3 + 4 = 7$ and $7 = 5 + 2$ then $3 + 4 = 5 + 2$; this is an important notion in the realization that numbers have many names.

You use many relations each day. Sometimes you use a single relation such as "tallness" or "weight" or "numerousness"; sometimes you use two or more such as tall and thin, number and height, width and breadth. Children in kindergarten, first and second grades (5 to 7 or 8 years) cannot work well with two relations at one time. As noted with Amy, she could work with number when spacing was roughly equivalent but when a new relation, dispersion, was introduced, she could no longer handle the ideas. This points out the problem with two relations. It also points out again the power of perception.

The young child's logical thought is closely tied to that which can be seen or imagined. For this reason, early experiences suggested in the next section

A. (none)	D. ST
B. T	E. T
C. RT	F. RST

will focus on *qualitative relations* since they are more readily perceived. Quantitative relations, especially those involving four or more objects, are more abstract and so will be delayed in the developmental sequence.

Pre-Number Relations: Number Readiness[3]

The transition from pre-operational thought to concrete operations occurs for most children between the ages of six and one-half and seven and one-half years. Of the factors which facilitate equilibration, experience and socialization are the ones upon which formal education must necessarily focus. The nature of the experiences provided must account for the growth in children's thinking skills.

Since children lack the ability to carry out abstract logical processes lacking concrete referents, experiences are provided which develop understanding of mathematics concepts at a pre-logical or intuitive level, i.e., experiences are correlated closely with concrete manifestations of the abstract mathematical concepts. When concrete materials are not used, concepts are related to object-imagery, i.e., instruction relates concepts to objects which can be conjured in the mind if not physically present. As Lovell states it, in intuitive thought,

> . . . thinking is greatly dependent on the total perception of the situation, and the child is largely unaware of the processes by which he arrives at his ideas. There is, as it were, a basic awareness, not yet formalized. Usually intuitive thinking depends upon considerable familiarity with the ideas involved, and almost always such thought is unable to detach itself completely from physical reality. For example, a pupil in the elementary school may have an intuitive grasp of negative numbers, but they will be embodied in concrete situations such as "temperature below freezing" or "number of feet below sea-level" (8:22).

Readiness.   Activities and learning which are intuitive in nature focus on associations of mathematics concepts with concrete experiences. They are readiness-related since they build bridges which facilitate abstract learnings on future pupil encounters with the same concepts on a higher, more mathematically sophisticated level. Research thus far has indicated that you cannot hurry abstract mastery of mathematics concepts. Rather, you should view your responsi-

---

[3] Before reading this section, you may want to review the developmental stages and implications of the Piaget summary in Chapter 1.

bility as one of providing appropriate experiences at intuitive levels which will aid in abstract mastery when the child has the intellectual maturation to grasp it.

Nearly all children who study place value can count out fourteen objects and place them in a group of ten and four (concrete); nearly all children can circle a group of ten and have four remaining when shown a picture of fourteen objects (semi-concrete), and nearly all children can fill the blanks: $14 = \underline{1}$ tens $\underline{4}$ ones (abstract). Yet, they still do not *totally understand* place value. Each of these three exercises is appropriate *but* each procedure can be done by *rote*. An important question to consider is, "What pupil behaviors are difficult to demonstrate from memory?" Specifically, what can you ask the child to do which rather definitely indicates he has near-total understanding that one ten is ten ones, that the position of a digit in a numeral is important? Here are some typical questions:

> *Concrete:* "Count out 25 blocks. Under the columns *Tens* and *Ones* write as many ways of naming 25 as you can. Remember, when the blocks are on the desk they are ones; when 10 blocks are placed in a tin can it is one ten. When you have completed this, do it again with groups of eight." (This assumes you have done this before in your instruction if this is a testing situation.)

Responses:	Tens	Ones		Eights	Ones
		25			25
	1	15		1	17
	2	5		2	9
				3	1

> *Semi-Concrete:* Repeat the concrete situation but with a dittoed sheet containing 25 fish or some other objects. The child works with one sheet for groups of ten and another sheet for groups of eight. If children place an acetate sheet over the dittoed paper and use a washable crayon, the dittoed sheets can be used many times.
>
> *Abstract:* Repeat the concrete and semi-concrete activities with only symbols. "Represent 25 as tens and ones as many ways as you can. Then repeat for groups of eight."

The abstract form is symbol manipulation and presupposes some sophistication in abstract number concepts which were hopefully gleaned from concrete experiences. The child who cannot do it has not made the transition from concrete-semi-concrete to abstract. Whether one argues lack of experiential or maturational readiness is a philosophical question which does not resolve the problem. The important lesson to be learned is that a child who is forced (yes, *forced*) to operate abstractly without having first attained meaningful associations at the concrete level is doomed to frustration. He has two alternatives, both of which are educationally unsound: (1) he can experience repeated failure at the abstract level with its attendant ills of psychological damage, or (2) he can learn to give the responses by rote which is also undesirable in a mathematics program stressing *meaning*.

Your level of expectations is crucially important. You must consider the level of development of the child who fails to grasp concepts at what might appear to be the "normal time" as determined by the curriculum or textbook. The child who has not intellectually matured to a point at which he can master the concept may be unduly frustrated. A child who is expected to function at a level which is beyond his comprehension may assimilate distorted concepts or develop negative attitudes towards mathematics. There is no pat formula at this time which will solve this problem for you, but your awareness of developmental processes and your classroom perceptivity will clearly enhance your effectiveness.

Qualitative Classification

Number is an abstract property of sets, so early number readiness experiences should provide children with many opportunities to create sets and systematically to study *qualitative* relations with respect to sets. Children can make sets from blocks, buttons, leaves and other common objects. Simple sorting exercises can then be made on the basis of one physical attribute such as color, shape, size, texture, or thickness. The single relation in such sorting exercises is "belongs to the set of." The sorted sets can be blue blocks, smooth leaves, round buttons and so on.

At first children can explore in a manner of pure discovery to see what attributes they can identify for sorting various sets of objects. Ideas can be shared. After working extensively with one attribute, two attributes can be used. Such sortings involve the relation twice. For example, children might sort blocks by color and shape. This would involve two applications of the "belongs to the set of" relation, e.g., belongs to the set of blue blocks and belongs to the set of cubes. Such sorting exercises would, in most cases, yield four subsets if the attributes exist in pairs.

Color \ Shape	Cube	Sphere
Blue	a	b
Red	c	d

Small children should carry out such double sortings with concrete materials since, as was mentioned previously, most kindergarten and many first-grade children cannot think about two attributes simultaneously. They *can* usually sort objects on the basis of two attributes; however, they may not be able to give a verbal description of their sortings.

If small objects are sorted on a desk, they can be placed into shoe boxes or other small containers. Larger objects can also be placed into large boxes. This works well for a single attribute. When two attributes are used the situation arises when objects belong to two sets simultaneously. You can begin with two pieces of yarn on a desk, or heavy yarn, rope or hula hoops on the floor. After the first

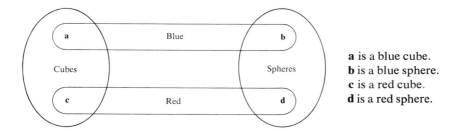

a is a blue cube.
b is a blue sphere.
c is a red cube.
d is a red sphere.

sorting is established, two more pieces of yarn or rope can be introduced to help identify the second application. Commercial aids such as *Materials for Attribute Games and Problems*, by Webster Division of McGraw-Hill Book Company, can be used, but the resourceful teacher is surrounded by many inexpensive materials.

Work with qualitative classifications lends itself to facilitation of pupil growth in logical thinking at the intuitive level. You can emphasize the following concepts.

Negation.   Objects can be sorted into two groups on the basis of a single attribute which is present or not present: blue-not blue; wheels-no wheels; round-not round; animal-not animal.

Inclusion.   Many children younger than nine years of age have difficulty dealing with inclusion relations abstractly. Inclusion relations are whole-part relations. An element is a member of a set which is itself a subset of a larger set. Such relations are hierarchical in nature. A dog is a mammal, and a mammal is an animal, so dogs are animals. Children have difficulty dealing with hierarchies. Concrete experiences can be provided where there are (A) many colored blocks, (B) red blocks and (C) red triangular-shaped blocks, and other such object groupings.

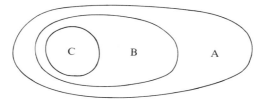

Conjunction.   Conjunction is like the "and" of set intersection. It is exemplified by the set which has two attributes. Consider red blocks and square blocks. Then the intersection contains those blocks which are both red and square.

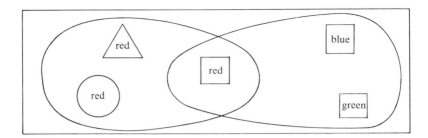

Diagramed questions can be raised such as:

$$A = \{\text{Boys with blue eyes}\}$$
$$B = \{\text{Boys with brown hair}\}$$

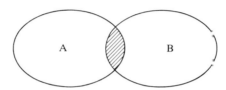

The shaded region is the conjunction; boys with blue eyes *and* brown hair. Similar questions can be raised and explored with objects or diagrams.

Dysjunction.   Dysjunction is related to set union, i.e., "or" relations. Hence, which children have (A) blue eyes *or* (B) brown hair *or* (A) blue eyes *and* (B) brown hair; which are red blocks *or* square blocks *or* red square blocks. *All* the shaded area in the diagram is in the union of A and B.

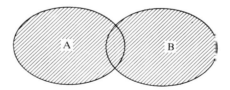

In addition to concrete manipulations involving one or two attributes, relations which are not physical attributes but which are intuitable can be explored *one at a time*. Such relations include the following; you can think of many more.

"is smaller than"	"is taller than"
"is as smooth as"	"is the aunt of"
"is the same color as"	"runs faster than"
"wears"	"lives on the same street as"
"holds less than"	"costs the same as'"

Such relations can be explored two-at-a-time provided they are preceded by extensive use of concrete materials with two relations.

Properties of Relations.   It is highly desirable for you to help children begin to intuit the nature of reflexivity, symmetry and transitivity as you explore relations with concrete materials and diagrams. Since an awareness of equivalence is a necessary prerequisite for working with one-to-one correspondence and conserving number, the RST properties are very important.

In discussing relations with children, refer to the properties; *not* to the names of the properties.

Example: "is taller than"   *Intuit*

   A. Is John taller than John? (no)   *Not* reflexive

   B. Is John taller than David? (yes)   *Not* symmetric
      Is David taller than John? (no)

   C. Is John taller than David? (yes)   *Is* transitive
      Is David taller than Philip? (yes)
      Is John taller than Phillip? (yes)

Example: "is the same shape as"   *Intuit*

   A. Is this box the same shape as itself? (yes)   *Is* reflexive

   B. Is this box the same shape as that box? (yes) *Is* symmetric
      Is that box the same shape as this box? (yes)

   C. Is this penny the same shape as this nickel? (yes)   *Is* transitive
      Is this nickel the same shape as this dime? (yes)
      Is this penny the same shape as this dime? (yes)

Look at three or four relations together. Examine them all for reflexivity, then all for symmetry, then for transitivity. From such experiences children should begin to intuit that some relations exhibit certain properties and others do not.

Seriation

Order is important in a system of numeration, and experiences can be provided which will help children learn to seriate at the concrete level. Objects of varying size by dimension can be provided and the child can order them shortest to tallest, narrowest to widest, smallest to largest. Such ordering can be done with Cuisenaire Rods or buttons, for example. You can begin with three objects and increase the number as the child is able to perform the task. Since most four-

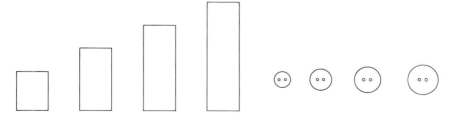

year-olds can seriate objects by size, nearly all kindergarten children should be able to handle such a task. Small children are seriating when they place plastic

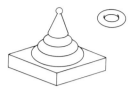

doughnut-shaped pieces on a cone. Children can also seriate by color in this exercise. A more complex task is to seriate on the basis of two attributes such as hue and size. Most small children cannot do this because it involves two relations. However, some may enjoy trying it.

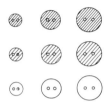

One-to-One Correspondence

The ability to pair objects is an important prerequisite to enumerating sets. Counting numbers are matched with objects to determine "how many." Children pass through stages of meaningfulness in their comprehension of correspondences. Small children (under 4 or 4½ years) usually cannot place objects in one-to-one correspondence; they tend to focus on length rather than matching. When asked if they can match blocks with pennies, they will display results such as these:

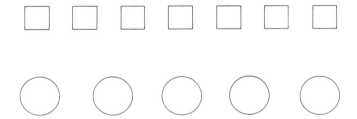

In the second stage, they can correctly match objects, but they do not believe there is an equal number of objects if one set is moved (think of Amy's comments). In the third and final stage, correspondences can be made and they are *conserved;* the child *believes* there are equal amounts regardless of position.

Teachers cannot hurry children from one stage to another. Growth seems to be tied to maturation. However, the teacher can provide opportunities for children to make one-to-one correspondences and take special care to maintain *visual* correspondences when they are instructionally needed. When discussing transitive relations, for example, *show* the transitivity. If the ducks can be placed into one-to-one correspondence with the birds, and the birds can be placed in one-to-one correspondence with the apples, then the ducks can be placed in one-to-one correspondence with the apples. If you disperse one set so that the correspondence is no longer visible, children in the second stage will not follow your explanation.

At the concrete level, children in stage two, especially, can benefit from one-to-one correspondence activities of various types. They can match buttons to button holes, items to be distributed to peers, flannel board materials and other activities which reinforce and relate to numerous activities in the home such as distributing snacks, setting the table, putting on articles of clothing and so on.

Pre-Number Quantitative Concepts

Some general notions related to quantity are *pre-number relationships.* These include "all," "some," "more than," "less than," and "the same as." Since young children are perception bound, earliest experiences with more and less can be arranged in such a way as to limit the influence of the visual model and to make certain that visual cues do not mislead the learner. Containers should be used which do not differ noticeably in size and proportion, and dispersions of objects on desks, tables or flannel boards should be similar at any one time.

In the following diagrams, the objects on the left lead the preconserver to think that $7 < 5$ whereas the one on the right leads him correctly to believe

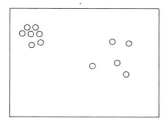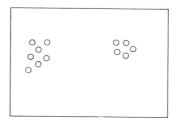

that $7 > 5$ because there are no misleading perceptual cues on the right. Similarly, the child may choose the "most" in the smaller container in the left

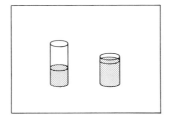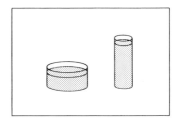

diagram because it looks "fuller," or he may choose the "most" in the tall container in the right diagram because it is higher. Try to maintain awareness and control of misleading perceptual cues.

When the child is in stage two or stage three of his understanding of one-to-one correspondence, sets of objects can be paired to determine which set has more, or less, or the same as a given set. Given one set of objects, the child can be asked to make another set which has fewer, the same, or more elements than the given set. Similar activities can, at a later time, be carried out with semi-concrete materials, e.g., pictures, dittoed sheets, or at the art easel.

Correct logical use of "all" and "some" does not come until nine or ten years of age. Concrete intuitive relations can be explored in a variety of circumstances to begin building understanding and readiness. Children have difficulty perceiving a group of objects as a set and a subset simultaneously. For example, the class is made up of boys and girls. "Boys" constitute a set, but "Boys" is also a subset of the class. "Boys" must be thought of as "all' and "some." This is difficult for young children to do.

Summary

Number is a property of sets. Exploration of physical (qualitative) attributes of sets helps the child become ready to explore number (quantitative) attributes. Early experiences focus on qualitative attributes which are examined concretely through sorting or classification exercises first with one attribute and then with two or more attributes. Study of relations includes intuitive explorations of reflexive, symmetric and transitive properties.

Relations explored through classifications, seriations and one-to-one correspondences build intuitive understandings. When the child has matured to appropriate levels, these readiness experiences facilitate mastery of concepts at more abstract levels.

Number Relations and Related Concepts

Children begin to conserve number at about the age of seven years. The experiences outlined in the previous section will build readiness for understanding of number concepts. What is not clear at this time is whether formal work with number ideas should be delayed until children conserve. More research is needed to answer this question, but for the present time the mathematics curriculum will continue to include number concepts in the kindergarten and first grades. Certainly children can learn number concepts in some form. Most first-graders and many preschoolers can count rationally, indicate "which is more," show one-to-one correspondences and demonstrate results of addition and subtraction facts. The major implication at the present time seems to be that teachers must remain aware that understanding of number concepts is *not complete* for most children. At the present time, the maturational factor seems to be very strong. You can help children achieve understanding *up to a point,* but then you must wait for equilibration. Probably the readiness activities facilitate equilibration.

Failure to conserve is consistent with the young child's inability to work with two relations simultaneously. When Amy worked only with the quantitative attributes of the two sets, she conserved number; she said they were the same. However, when an additional relation, area or space occupied, was introduced (varied), she immediately succumbed to the attribute which was most perceptible. When children are able to conserve number or quantity, they will no longer be "fooled" by perception.

Cardinal and Ordinal Number

Nearly all children can recognize, without counting, a set with one, two or three elements. Many sets can be constructed and compared through the establishment of one-to-one correspondences. Moving two or three objects about will help the child see that the number property remains constant. Three remains the property of a given set regardless of position. After sets of one, two, and three have been explored with objects of great variety, zero can be introduced as the cardinal number of the empty set. An empty cookie jar can be used. Children enjoy making up their own empty sets: people over ten feet tall, pink elephants and so on. Total mastery of the zero concept does not develop until eleven or twelve years of age, but an intuitive concept of zero can be developed in the first-grade mathematics program.

With cardinal numbers 0, 1, 2, and 3 established, children can acquire a sense of *order* in number concepts. By placing objects on the table, an association can be built of chronological sequencing of two after one and three after two. This ordering experience can be related to previous seriation activities by placing objects in stairstep fashion:

Hence, there is an ordering of numbers: one, two, three. With this order is associated the notion of position: first, second, third. The latter is referred to as *ordinal* usage of number. "Three" describes the cardinal number of a set; it tells "how many." "Third" describes the ordinal position of an object; it tells "which one." With these two related uses of number, children can learn to count rationally.

When the teacher says, "How many blocks are on the table?" one of several one-to-one correspondences can be made to answer the question. The teacher wants the *cardinal number* of the set. The question can be answered six different ways when there are three blocks. (See diagram at top of page 97.) If the teacher says "Which block is red, the first, the second or the third?" there is but *one* appropriate response. Ordinal usage of number implies an imposed ordering. If the teacher wants left-to-right, the only appropriate response is "first" if red is on the left. If the teacher wants right-to-left, the only appropriate response is "third" if red is on the left.

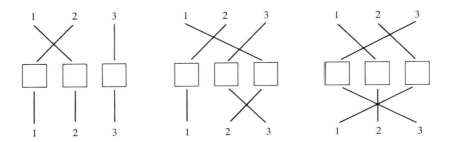

Counting and the One-More-Than Concept

Rote counting refers to the child's ability to say number names in sequence without the complementary ability to enumerate sets. When the child is able accurately to determine the cardinal number of a given set, he is said to have mastered *rational* counting. Rational counting can be introduced in the formal instructional program after one, two, and three have been learned. The development of one, two, and three can be paralleled with the development of first, second and third so that ordinal number is developed concurrently with cardinal number.

A set which has three elements can have *one more* element added and the word name for four introduced. A similar strategy of "one more" is generally used for five, six, seven, eight, and nine. Addition and subtraction facts are usually introduced as each new number is added to the set of number concepts.

Experiences which involve counting and set construction help develop an understanding of number seriation, and use of the one-more-than concept demonstrates the steady progression from each number to the next.

Numbers, Numerals and Sets

"Twoness" is a property of sets which have two elements. Related to twoness is a set, a standard numeral and a word name. The three components together constitute a *model set*.

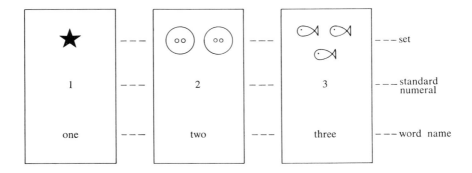

Model sets are available commercially, but teacher-made models are more desirable: they can be constructed with *real* objects whereas commercially made model sets are usually *pictures* of objects. By using picture-hanging hooks or adhesive putty, you can use buttons, coins, milk cartons, dolls, cowboys, straws, leaves or many other objects. A major advantage is that the objects can be changed perodically. Not only is this more interesting, but, more importantly, it helps the child learn that three is not related to doll nor two to leaf; that number is a characteristic of many different sets.

To help children learn the three related aspects of model sets, you can construct teaching aids such as this: make a two-dimensional birthday cake of cardboard with the corrugations running vertically. Make candles and place nails on the backs with adhesive tape. The nails will fit into the corrugations. Make "invitations" of sets, numerals, and word names. Pass out many invitations and children can come to the birthday party if they have one of the components of the appropriate model set. Invitations can also include simple addition or subtraction facts.

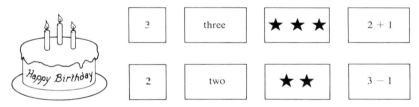

You can also use playing cards as model sets without word names and reinforce set-numeral relations with puzzle cards made of tagboard.

Numerals. A numeral is a name for a number. No one has ever seen "two" since twoness is an abstraction of sets. Two is quantitative in nature; you cannot see "two."

Betty Jones lives in Athens, Ohio. She is married and has three children. She is called by many names:

The milkman	calls her	Mrs. Jones
Her neighbor	calls her	Betty
Her husband	calls her	Honey
Her 2-year-old daughter	calls her	Mama
Her 8-year-old daughter	calls her	Mother
Her high school classmate	calls her	Betts

Each of Betty's names is appropriate under certain circumstances. She would be surprised if her daughter called her Mrs. Jones or the mailman called her Honey!

Just as people have many names, numbers also have many names. On a clock with roman numerals, you would not expect to see "3"; "III" is more appropriate. If you want to subtract twenty-one from fifty-two, 50 + 2 is an appropriate name for 52. However, if you wanted to subtract 25 from 52, 50 + 2 would *not* be the best name; 40 + 12 would be a much better name.

$$
\begin{array}{rr}
52 = 50 + 2 & \qquad 52 = 40 + 12 \\
-21 \quad 20 + 1 & -25 \quad 20 + \ 5
\end{array}
$$

If you wanted to multiply one-half by one-third, $\frac{1}{2}$ is a good name for one-half. However, $\frac{1}{2}$ is not a good name if you want to *add* one-half and one-third; $\frac{3}{6}$ would be a much better name.

Numerals are names for numbers. Children should be taught to examine problems with an eye for choosing best names for numbers. Classroom activities should be utilized which help children know (non-verbally) the difference between a number and a numeral. *Example:* How many *numbers* can you name by using one or more elements of this set $\{3, 3, +, \div\}$? Here are some: $\{3, 33, 1, 6, 8$ (reverse one three and "put them together"!)$\}$ How many *names* for three can you write using one or more elements of this set: $\{0, 1, 2, 3, 4, 5, +, -\}$? Here are some: $\{0 + 3, 1 + 2, 2 + 1, 3 - 0, 5 - 2, 3\}$.

You need to be aware of the difference between a number and its name (numeral) since pupil difficulties can arise from inability to distinguish between the two. Your knowledge and awareness helps you look for this as a source of difficulty. Children may say 3 + 3 = 33, or half of 8 is zero, or 3 + 3 = 8. These responses reflect inappropriate applications of mathematical operations on *numerals* rather than *numbers*. You should say *numeral* whenever you are referring to the name. "John, write the numerals on the number line." "Mary, what is the sum of these numbers?" Try to make the distinction when you can, but it is probably best not to insist that children make the distinction. A general rule-of-thumb is, "When in doubt, say number." Number has been traditionally used in everyday language to refer to both numbers and numerals. The two main points are that the teacher should know the difference, and the *teacher* should reinforce the difference with appropriate terminology when possible.

The numeral in the model set is called the standard numeral because it is the standard name or the one which comes to mind when the number is recited: "three" calls to mind "3."

In this book, the word *numeral* is used whenever the *name* is clearly called for, e.g., "26 is a two-digit numeral" and "numerals are placed on number lines." The word *number* is used whenever the abstract concept is the referent, e.g., "the number of elements in the set is two" or "what numbers can be added which have a sum of 5?" When number and numeral are both referents, one or the other may be used for clarity since sentences may be awkward and wordy otherwise.

Precise: Add these numbers named by two-digit numerals.

Acceptable: Add these two-digit numbers. Add these two-digit numerals.
Problems: Numbers do not have digits, and one cannot add numerals.
One adds numbers, and numerals have digits.

Children can learn to make numerals by tracing sandpaper cutouts. If there is
a sandbox in the room, you can make the numerals in the sand and the children
can trace them. Other techniques include numerals cut from cardboard (the
"hole" can be used as well as the numeral removed from the piece of cardboard),
plaster of paris models, tracing over dittoed numeral sheets and plywood models.

Seriation and Inequalities.   Inequalities of *less than* and *greater than* were
explored in conjunction with one-to-one correspondences. Children will also
learn that *less than* and *more than* can be determined by relative position in the
counting sequence, i.e., the first number in the sequence is smallest. Children
also learn to place numerals in serial order. In an activity, children can be given
an opportunity to seriate number and numeral by using a strip of cardboard cut
into ten pieces with pictures of sets and an appropriate numeral on each. They
"fit" only one way because of the cuts in the strip (like a puzzle). The "walk-on"
number line is also an excellent aid for these concepts. A strip of oilcloth can be

used nicely or you can simply place strips of masking tape on the floor. Numeral
cards can be made with tagboard. You can make them collapsible for easy storage; place a paper clip on the overlapping sections on the bottom.

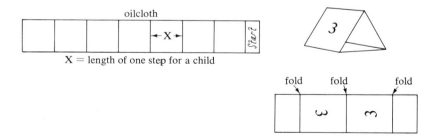

oilcloth

X = length of one step for a child

Objectives of the Pre-Operational Mathematics Program

Emphasis should be placed on manipulative experiences. Piagetian theory indicates that children learn through actions on objects. Hence, the major thrust of
the pre-operational program should be on an introduction to mathematics con-

cepts at the concrete level. As a child's understanding of a given concept grows, semi-concrete learning experiences can be utilized.

Behavioral objectives can be written on the concepts which cover concrete and semi-concrete levels of concept development. In this chapter, attention will not be given to the individualization model since kindergarten programs are generally unstructured. Following is a sample listing of major pre-operational mathematics concepts.

I. Pre-number
  A. Common qualitative relations—classification
  B. Common quantitative relations
  C. Seriation
  D. Properties of relations—reflexivity, symmetry, transitivity
  E. Equivalence relations
  F. Conjunction, dysjunction, negation, inclusion exercises
  G. One-to-one correspondence
II. Number
  A. Cardinal number
  B. Ordinal number
  C. Counting—rational
  D. Numeral

Obviously, the pre-number concepts should precede the number concepts. The order within the pre-number category can vary considerably since these are readiness experiences and are for the most part not sequential in nature. The number items *do* form a sequence which should not be greatly altered. Cardinal and ordinal number can be learned concurrently. The number category repeats itself as each new number is introduced, e.g., two; second; one, two; 2 and then three; third; one, two, three; 3.

Sample Objectives:
  I. A. (Concrete) The child will be able to divide a set of blocks on the basis of color. (One attribute)
  I. A. (Concrete) The child will be able to partition a set of blocks by shape and color. (Two attributes)
  I. D. (Concrete) The child will be able to determine whether a given relation such as "is longer than" is reflexive, symmetric, and/or transitive by manipulating appropriate materials. (The RST terminology would *not* be used. You might say, "Billy, pick up one of your blocks. Is it longer than itself?" This is reflexivity. "Billy, pick up two of your blocks of different size. Is this one longer than that one? Is that one longer than this one?" This is symmetry. Transitivity can be done similarly.)
  I. F. (Concrete) The child will be able to divide a set of blocks into *red* and *not red*. (Negation)
  II. B. (Concrete) The child will be able to go to the second seat in the row. (Ordinal number)

II. A. (Semi-concrete) The child will be able to place Xs on a given number of objects in a page.

One last comment: Since children vary developmentally, they will vary in the extent to which they attain your objectives.

Discussion and Projects

1. What household objects can be used for qualitative and quantitative pre-number classification? What attributes do they exhibit?
2. Name some qualitative attributes, other than length, color, hue, and diameter, which can be seriated.
3. List some additional relations. Which ones are reflexive? symmetric? transitive? equivalence relations (RST)?
4. What are some occasions, naturally arising at home, which are one-to-one correspondences? one-to-two correspondences? one-to-many?
5. Write some other behavioral objectives on pre-operational concepts.
6. Make up an activity which is designed to aid children in learning the three components of model sets.

Additional Resources for College Students

Filmstrips

    Numbers in Color, Cuisenaire
    Modern Mathematics Sets: 1–5, Society for Visual Education
    Modern Mathematics Sets: 5–9, Society for Visual Education

Films

    Beginning Number Concepts, National Council of Teachers of Mathematics
    Sets, Numerals and Numbers, Science Research Associates

Bibliography

1. Bjornerud, C. E. "Arithmetic Concepts Possessed by Pre-School Children." *The Arithmetic Teacher* (November 1960), 7:347–50.
2. Copeland, Richard W. *How Children Learn Mathematics.* London: The Macmillan Company, 1970.
3. Dutton, W. H. "Growth in Number Readiness in Kindergarten Children." *The Arithmetic Teacher* (May 1963), 10:251–55.

4. Flavell, John H. *The Developmental Psychology of Jean Piaget.* New York: Van Nostrand Reinhold & Company, 1963.

5. Grossnickle, Foster E., Leo J. Brueckner, and John Reckzeh. *Discovering Meanings in Elementary School Mathematics,* 5th ed. New York: Holt, Rinehart and Winston, Inc., 1968.

6. Lavatelli, Celia Stendler. *Early Childhood Curriculum—A Piaget Program Teacher's Guide.* Boston: American Science and Engineering, Inc., 1970.

7. Lavatelli, Celia Stendler. *Piaget's Theory Applied to an Early Childhood Curriculum.* Boston: American Science and Engineering, Inc., 1970.

8. Lovell, Kenneth. *The Growth of Understanding in Mathematics.* New York: Holt, Rinehart and Winston, Inc., 1971.

9. Piaget, Jean. *The Child's Conception of Number.* New York: W. W. Norton & Company, Inc., 1965.

10. Priore, Angela. "Achievement by Children Entering the First Grade." *The Arithmetic Teacher* (March 1957), 4:55–60.

8

Teaching Basic Concepts of Addition and Subtraction

Two small sets of objects can be enumerated by counting, but when you wish to find the number of elements in two large sets, counting is inefficient. To increase your efficiency you need computational procedures for finding sums.

An *operation* is a rule which assigns a new element to given elements of a set. A *binary* operation is one which assigns an element to *two* given elements. Addition is an example of a *binary operation*. Consider the set of *counting numbers,* $\{1, 2, 3, 4, 5, \ldots\}$. When you begin with two counting numbers and find a sum, a third counting number is obtained. Thus, in addition of counting numbers you begin with two counting numbers and use the rule to find a new element: $2 + 3 \rightarrow 5$. When you begin with the counting numbers 2 and 3, you perform the binary operation addition to obtain a third element, 5, which is also a counting number.

An *inverse operation* is a second operation which "undoes" a given operation. Subtraction is the inverse operation of addition. Thus, $2 + 3 = 5$ is the addition sentence which has two related inverse subtraction sentences, $5 - 2 = 3$ and $5 - 3 = 2$. An operation can have but one result, e.g., $2 + 3 = 5$, and there is no number which is the sum of 2 and 3 which is not 5.

A computational procedure is called an *algorithm*. The word *algorism* is also used. The computational procedure which you use to find $36 + 47$ is called the *standard algorithm* of addition, and the computational procedure which you use to find the difference

62 − 15 is the *standard algorithm* for subtraction. You did not use standard algorithms efficiently until you learned the addition and subtraction facts. In the system of numeration which you have learned and worked with all your life there are 10 *digits:* 0, 1, 2, 3, 4, 5, 6, 7, 8, and 9. An *addition fact* is a combination which is the sum of two digits. The subtraction facts are those which are the inverse statements of the addition facts.

This chapter contains a summary of important addition and subtraction readiness concepts. Specific techniques for developing pupil understanding will be explored, and the properties of addition and subtraction will be examined and uses presented. Following a discussion of subtraction types and practice suggestions some important concepts of addition and subtraction will be related to specific objectives of instruction and discovery techniques. The extension of these concepts to algorithms will be presented in the next chapter.

Addition and Subtraction Readiness

Readiness for work with addition and subtraction depends on experiential and maturational factors. These will be considered separately.

Experiences

Nearly all the activities described in the chapter on pre-operational concepts were readiness activities for addition and subtraction. Children learn to make numerals, seriate, count, make one-to-one correspondences, and so on. Counting is a very important part of the readiness program for addition and subtraction since the addition sentence 2 + 3 = 5 can be related to a set of two and a set of three which when joined (union) yield a set which has cardinality five. Similarly, removing two objects from a set which has cardinality five is related to subtracting two, and removing three objects from a set which has five objects is related to the mathematical sentence 5 − 3 = 2. Children can work such problems by counting.

Other activities related to addition and subtraction are those which involve grouping and separating objects. Children can be given five objects and a sheet of paper with a line down the middle. They can be challenged to determine how many different ways they can place five objects on the sheet of paper using the line as a separation between two sets. Here are some of the possible ways.

 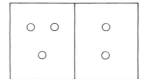 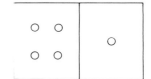

Subtraction readiness can be built similarly by placing five objects on a sheet of paper and removing two or four or one and so on, as indicated below.

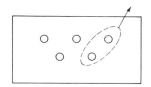 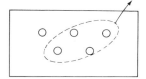

Maturation

Children cannot totally understand addition and subtraction until they conserve quantity. Many children do not conserve until they are about seven years of age. In a research study by Van Engen and Steffe (11), five pieces of candy were presented to 100 first-graders. The candy was separated into sets of two and three. About half the first-graders thought 2 + 3 pieces of candy was more than five pieces of candy. You will recall that Amy's responses were similar to these results. When children do not conserve, they cannot totally understand equality.

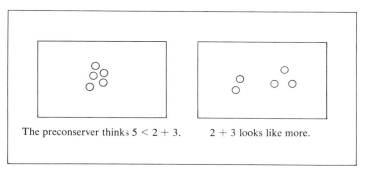

The preconserver thinks 5 < 2 + 3.   2 + 3 looks like more.

The number sentence 2 + 3 = 5 and the number sentence 2 + 3 = 4 + 1 indicate that the number which is named in each instance is the same number. In mathematics the equal sign means *names the same number as.* Children who cannot conserve quantity cannot fully understand this renaming process. Since children do not conserve until about the age of seven there are many children for whom 2 + 3 = 5 will have limited meaning. They will be able to take a set of two and a set of three and determine by counting that there are five elements; however, they may not really *believe,* in the sense of conservation, that 2 + 3 and 5 name the same quantity.

Equality is an equivalence relation. It is reflexive (5 = 5); it is symmetric (2 + 3 = 5 and 5 = 2 + 3); it is transitive (when 2 + 3 = 5 and 5 = 4 + 1 then 2 + 3 = 4 + 1). Knowledge of the transitive property is also related to conservation of quantity. Transitivity is very important in the renaming process. Children can work with objects to see at the intuitive level that equality is reflexive, symmetric, and transitive. However, they will not attain full mastery of this equivalence relation until they have achieved conservation of quantity.

Understanding of inverse operations is dependent upon reversibility of thought, and reversibility is also related to conservation. Since subtraction is the inverse of addition, children who have not attained conservation of quantity cannot fully comprehend the nature of an inverse relation. Thus, children may have difficulty with equations of the form $2 + \square = 5$ even though they can determine $2 + 3 = \square$. Prior to conservation children can work with such equations by using concrete objects; however, the logical abstraction will not be mastered until children conserve quantity.

In summary, you should be aware that conservation of quantity is essential for total mastery of addition, subtraction and the inverse nature of their relationship. Pre-conservers can work with these concepts at the intuitive level by manipulating concrete objects. You must also be aware that children who do not conserve have a limited understanding of addition and subtraction sentences at the abstract level. Work performed by first-graders indicates they can indeed work with addition and subtraction concepts. It is the relationship between those abstract manipulations and the physical reality which is very unstable in the pre-conserver. Pre-conservers are often asked to work with addition and subtraction facts on a sheet of paper without concrete objects. When this occurs, teachers must take care to provide recurring experiences with concrete objects. Then when a given child does begin to conserve, the relation between the abstract manipulations and concrete materials will become firmly embedded in his conception of reality.

Pedagogical Importance of Addition and Subtraction Properties

There are many addition and subtraction facts to be learned and computational procedures to be mastered. Certain important properties of addition and subtraction help the child learn basic facts and computational procedures. The following chart indicates the properties of addition and subtraction which will be discussed in this section.

	Addition	Subtraction
Commutativity	yes	no
Associativity	yes	no
Identity	yes	no (right)
Closure	yes	no

Commutativity

Addition is commutative, e.g., $2 + 3 = 3 + 2$. Subtraction is *not* commutative: $3 - 2 \neq 2 - 3$.

One very important reason that commutativity of addition is helpful to children is that it reduces the memory work by enabling the child to relate pairs of facts having the same addends and the same sum. If the child learns $2 + 3 = 5$

and understands that addition is commutative, then he also knows $3 + 2 = 5$. So for each fact he learns, he actually knows *two* facts since $6 + 7 = 7 + 6$. The commutative property is also valuable in conjunction with the associative property. This relation is explored in the next section.

In helping children understand the commutative property, physical spacing or dispersion is important. You already noted that some children have not acquired conservation and for them the perception of objects usually overrides the results of counting. Two sets of objects can be placed on a table. When the child stands on one side of the table he sees a set of three on the left and a set of four on the right and can write the appropriate number sentence: $3 + 4 = 7$. If he walks around to the other side of the table, he can now see a set of four on the left and a set of three on the right and can write the appropriate number sentence: $4 + 3 = 7$. If he then writes both the number sentences on a piece of paper, he has $3 + 4 = 7$ and $4 + 3 = 7$. Several such experiences will help him begin to intuit that addition is commutative.

Children can also place dominoes on their desks and write $1 + 5 = 6$, turn the domino 180° and write $5 - 1 = 6$. Similar types of activities can be carried out by taking a paper plate, marking it through the center and placing objects on each section of the paper plate. A sheet of paper and some pebbles can be used, too.

Associativity

Addition is associative on the set of whole numbers, i.e., $(2 + 3) + 4 = 2 + (3 + 4)$ since $5 + 4 = 2 + 7$. Subtraction is *not* associative: $(6 - 3) - 2 \neq 6 - (3 - 2)$ since $3 - 2 \neq 6 - 1$.

The associative property is particularly useful in helping children learn addition facts with sums greater than ten. To determine $7 + 5$, the 5 can be renamed as $3 + 2$. Now the statement is $7 + (3 + 2)$. Since addition is associative, the parentheses can be changed to $(7 + 3) + 2$. $7 + 3$ is 10 and $10 + 2$ is another name for 12.

$7 + 5$	Question
$7 + (3 + 2)$	Rename
$(7 + 3) + 2$	Associativity
$10 + 2$	Add or rename
12	Add or rename

Associativity also plays a very important role in addition of numbers which have two digits. By using renaming and associativity, you can find sums of numbers using an algorithm. Examine the following sequences which are possible because of the place value characteristics of the number system.

$32 + 4$	Given	
$(30 + 2) + 4$	Rename	32
$30 + (2 + 4)$	Associativity	$+\ 4$
$30 + 6$	Add or rename	$\overline{36}$
36	Add or rename	

Commutativity and associativity together play a vital role in procedures for computing sums and differences. If you wish to find the sum of several single digit numbers you can use the associative and commutative properties to regroup various combinations in groups of ten. Study the following example:

$(6 + 8) + 4$	Given
$6 + (8 + 4)$	Associativity
$6 + (4 + 8)$	Commutatvity
$(6 + 4) + 8$	Associativity
$10 + 8$	Add or rename
18	Add or rename

$$10 \begin{cases} 6 \\ 8 \\ 4 \end{cases}$$
$$\overline{18}$$

Commutativity and associativity are also used together in the standard algorithm for addition. Study this example to see how they play a very important role.

Standard Algorithm

$26 + 13$	Given
$(20 + 6) + 13$	Rename
$20 + (6 + 13)$	Associativity
$20 + (13 + 6)$	Commutativity
$20 + [(10 + 3) + 6]$	Rename
$20 + [10 + (3 + 6)]$	Associativity
$20 + (10 + 9)$	Add or rename
$(20 + 10) + 9$	Associativity
$30 + 9$	Add or rename
39	Add or rename

$$\begin{array}{r} 26 \\ +13 \\ \hline 39 \end{array}$$

The number system is remarkable in the ease with which you are able to compute sums. The three properties of associativity, commutativity, and renaming allow you to find the sum $26 + 13$ in the very short manner shown on the right above. The relationships between these properties and the development of standard algorithms will be discussed extensively in the next chapter.

The basic idea of associativity is that when you have three numbers the third can be added to the sum of the first two, or the sum of the last two can be added to the first, $(a + b) + c = a + (b + c)$. To help children understand this property, three sets of objects can be placed on the desk. A piece of string or yarn can be placed around the two sets on the left. Children can add the third set to the sum of the first two sets. Then the piece of string can be moved to encompass the two sets on the right. The sum of the two enclosed sets can be found and added to the objects on the outside. Such experiences will help children see that $(2 + 3) + 4 = 2 + (3 + 4)$. In addition to many concrete manipulative experiences, you may wish also to place magnetic pieces on the chalk board and draw a chalk mark around two sets at a time and ask children to write the appropriate equation. You could do the same type of exercise with the flannel board. If you wish to make large sets on the floor, you can use rope, string, yarn or hula hoops.

To help children relate to commutativity and associativity simultaneously you can ask them to engage in activities similar to the following: Give the children three different sets, each set having a different cardinal number. Ask them to find as many different number sentences as they can to show the sum. If they have two airplanes, three marbles, and four pennies, they could find the total number of objects with any one of the following number sentences.

$$2 + 3 + 4 = 9 \qquad 4 + 2 + 3 = 9$$
$$3 + 2 + 4 = 9 \qquad 2 + 4 + 3 = 9$$
$$4 + 3 + 2 = 9 \qquad 3 + 4 + 2 = 9$$

Such activities will help children learn that numbers can be added in any order without effecting the sum.

Identity

Addition has an identity element, zero, since $3 + 0 = 0 + 3 = 3$. Subtraction has no identity element. There is no element such that $3 - e = e - 3 = 3$. Identity elements must commute. When an identity element is not commutative, it is described as a right-hand or left-hand identity element. Subtraction has a right-hand identity element, zero, since $3 - 0 = 3$. The additive identity element plays a special role as a place holder in the number system. Zero is a troublesome concept for youngsters throughout primary grades. It is a source of difficulty in place value, addition and subtraction. The concept of zero was one of the last characteristics of the number system developed, and this late historical development may be one small clue to its sophisticated nature. Most children do not fully understand the concept of zero until the stage of logical or formal operations (about eleven or twelve years of age).

Closure

Addition is closed over the set of whole numbers, 0, 1, 2, 3, 4, ... When you add two whole numbers, the sum is a whole number. When you subtract two whole numbers, *sometimes* the difference is a whole number. Many subtraction questions have no answers in the set of whole numbers: $2 - 5 = \square$. If the answer is *always* in the set, an operation is said to be closed over the set. Addition is closed on the set of whole numbers; subtraction is not.

Lack of subtraction closure on the set of whole numbers can be a source of difficulty for children. Since they cannot understand closure at the abstract level, the lack of closure can be developed intuitively by use of concrete materials. If you have two marbles you cannot take away five marbles. You should avoid saying to children, "You cannot subtract 5 from 2." This is not true. The answer is -3. What you mean is that the child does not know how to work with negative numbers or that you cannot remove five objects from a set of objects which contains only two objects. When presenting subtraction to children, try to use terminology which is consistent with what must be learned later. If you say "You cannot subtract 5 from 2," they will have to unlearn this at a later time when integers are encountered. Either say to them, "We do not have the numbers necessary to do this problem," or relate the discussion to concrete materials. When children raise questions relative to subtraction, relate their questions to the inverse nature of subtraction and addition. $5 - 7 = \square$ has the related addition question $\square + 7 = 5$. Since the child has no number for the latter, he has no number for the former. This question could also be answered concretely by relating the child's question to a thermometer.

A word of caution with respect to situations similar to the one described in the preceding paragraph: the teacher who observes due caution in relating the "whys" and "why nots" to children can greatly reduce the emotional and intellectual discomfort wrought by teacher-imposed *unlearning*. In every possible way, present instruction should be continuous and in agreement with later mathematics concepts. Observe caution in answering pupil questions. As you continue, you will see that questions can nearly always be answered in a way which is understandable to the child and mathematically correct.

Summary

The properties of addition are very important in learning number facts and understanding computational procedures. Total mastery of these concepts is dependent upon the child's ability to conserve quantity. Baumann (1) found that commutativity and closure were difficult concepts for second-grade pupils. You should work extensively with these properties at the concrete or intuitive levels. Children who are conservers will begin to atttain mastery at the abstract level. Children who cannot conserve will have these valuable readiness experiences upon which to build when they have matured to the point where they also can conserve.

Addition and Subtraction Facts

There are 100 addition facts and 100 subtraction facts. They can be represented compactly in tabular form as indicated in the diagram on page 113.

The table is read as follows: If you wish to find the sum $2 + 3$, locate the "2" in the left-hand column and the "3" across the top. Then follow across from the "2" and down from the "3" until the two lines intersect; they intersect at the answer, "5." This tells you that $2 + 3 = 5$. If you wish to know $3 + 2$, locate "3" on the left, "2" at the top and you find the intersection "5" indicating that $3 + 2 = 5$, also.

The table can also be used for subtraction facts. If you wish to know $15 - 7$, find the "7" across the top and go down the column until you come to "15." Go to the left-hand column to find "8." This tells you that $15 - 7 = 8$.

If you think of a diagonal running from the upper-left corner to the lower-right corner of the table, you will notice that the two halves of the table are symmetric. In other words, each numeral on the upper-right side of the diagonal has a corresponding numeral on the lower-left side of the diagonal on which it

+	0	1	2	3	4	5	6	7	8	9
0	0	1	2	3	4	5	6	7	8	9
1	1	2	3	4	5	6	7	8	9	10
2	2	3	4	5	6	7	8	9	10	11
3	3	4	5	6	7	8	9	10	11	12
4	4	5	6	7	8	9	10	11	12	13
5	5	6	7	8	9	10	11	12	13	14
6	6	7	8	9	10	11	12	13	14	15
7	7	8	9	10	11	12	13	14	15	16
8	8	9	10	11	12	13	14	15	16	17
9	9	10	11	12	13	14	15	16	17	18

would coincide or superimpose if the table were folded on the diagonal. This is an easy way to see all the commutative addition pairs. When you fold the table on the diagonal the two 5s of $3 + 2 = 5$ and $2 + 3 = 5$ will coincide. Of the 100 addition facts there are 45 such duplications. The number facts on the diagonal have no commutative pairs. Notice this very interesting fact: There are 45 addition fact pairs with identical addends and sums. These are the 45 which are not shaded.

The left-hand answer column represents the number facts which have the additive identity, 0, as the second addend: $2 + 0 = 2, 7 + 0 = 7$, and so on. There are 10 such facts. With the aid of commutativity and the identity element the number of addition facts with different addends is 45.

The easiest facts for children to learn are those which have "1" as the second addend. These facts make up the second column in the table: $2 + 1 = 3$, $3 + 1 = 4, 4 + 1 = 5$, and so on. You will notice that within the 55 shaded facts there are nine such facts. Thus, with the aid of commutativity, the identity element, and the one-more-than concept the number of addition facts with different addends is reduced to 36: 45 addition facts have identical addends because they are commutative pairs, and of the remaining 55, 10 are identity element facts and 9 have "1" as an addend. If children fully understand these properties of addition, the number of addition fact number pairs to be remembered is only 36!

If addition facts were taught after children learned to conserve, at which time they would be able to understand the properties of addition, it would be reasonable to work upon the 36 facts just described. However, nearly every textbook series on the market begins work on addition in grade one. Many first-grade children do not conserve. At this time the experiences must be largely intuitive rather than abstract. Children learn to remember addition and subtraction facts before they fully comprehend the meaning of addition and subtraction.

Most mathematics programs today expect that nearly all children will know the 200 addition and subtraction facts by the end of grade two. The usual approach is to begin with addition and subtraction facts which use numbers less than ten; then place value is taught, and the number facts are steadily increased until eighteen is included. Most programs attempt to make the child's task easier by building families of related facts and working with addition and subtraction concurrently. As each new number is introduced, the addition and subtraction facts which constitute the related facts for that number are introduced. When the number 7 is introduced the following facts are studied.

Set of Related Facts for 7   *Fact Family*

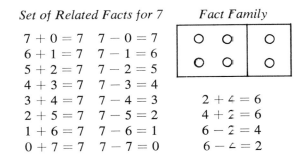

$$7 + 0 = 7 \quad 7 - 0 = 7$$
$$6 + 1 = 7 \quad 7 - 1 = 6$$
$$5 + 2 = 7 \quad 7 - 2 = 5$$
$$4 + 3 = 7 \quad 7 - 3 = 4$$
$$3 + 4 = 7 \quad 7 - 4 = 3 \qquad 2 + 4 = 6$$
$$2 + 5 = 7 \quad 7 - 5 = 2 \qquad 4 + 2 = 6$$
$$1 + 6 = 7 \quad 7 - 6 = 1 \qquad 6 - 2 = 4$$
$$0 + 7 = 7 \quad 7 - 7 = 0 \qquad 6 - 4 = 2$$

A *fact family* is a set of three related numbers which have four addition and subtraction facts related to them. Consider the domino which has two dots on one end and four dots on the other end. There are six dots all together. For two, four, and six there are four addition and subtraction facts as noted above. Sets of related facts and fact families can be used to help children relate various combinations.

Research. Several research studies have been done relative to addition and subtraction facts. Some are old studies but are still quite valid. MacLatchy (9) found that children who count well tend to learn addition facts easily. Buckingham (3) found that teaching addition and subtraction facts together as was suggested here with the sets of related facts tends to increase achievement, too. And, as you would have expected from Chapter 1, research has supported the use of manipulative materials for increasing understanding of addition facts. Ekman (5) found that understanding of addition is higher when using manipulative materials than when using only pictures. And, finally, Breed and Ralston (2) found that achievement was higher and addition and subtraction facts were learned more quickly when practice of facts was built into examples rather than simply rote practice on work sheets. Children can solve word problems or practice facts within more difficult problems such as $36 + 29$ or $84 - 19$.

Operational Definitions of Addition and Subtraction

When addition is taught to young children it is defined intuitively as an operation associated with combining sets (union). Two sets of objects are identified and then the combined total of objects in the two sets is subsequently determined. Addition is the number operation associated with the union of disjoint sets. As indicated in the following picture, you begin with two sets; one set has cardinality two, and the other, three. The union of the two sets is indicated by the dotted line. Two and three are, respectively, the cardinal numbers of the

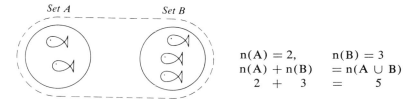

$$n(A) = 2, \qquad n(B) = 3$$
$$n(A) + n(B) \quad = n(A \cup B)$$
$$2 \;+\; 3 \quad = \quad 5$$

two sets. When the two sets are operated on by the operation union, addition is the corresponding operation on the cardinal numbers. In other words, $2 + 3 = 5$ is the number sentence related to the union of sets A and B. Or, if $n(A)$ represents the cardinal number of A and $n(B)$ represents the cardinal number of B then $n(A) + n(B) = n(A \cup B)$.

The corresponding addition sentence is true only if two sets are disjoint. Let A = {Alice, Bill, John} and B = {Alice, Mary, Keith}. Suppose these two groups of people are going swimming. You would usually assume that if two groups of people were going swimming you could add the number of people in each group to determine the total number of swimmers. However, Alice is in both groups so the sentence $3 + 3 = 6$ does not describe the situation. The addition sentence is true only if the two sets are disjoint, that is to say if there is no person who is in both sets. Suppose the Bridge Club has 18 people and the Garden Club has 14 people. The two organizations plan a bus trip. When the officers hire the bus, they tell the bus company there will be 32 people because $18 + 14 = 32$. However, 6 people who are in the Garden Club are also members of the Bridge Club. Only 26 people are paying fares! This is another example of sets which are *not* disjoint. When sets are not disjoint, the usual addition sentence is not true.

Since addition is taught as the union of disjoint sets, an instructional procedure which emphasizes the inverse relation between subtraction and addition should emphasize subtraction as the removal of a subset. Introductory work in addition is related to the union of disjoint sets, and introductory work in subtraction is related to the removal of a subset. You should be aware, however, that there are other kinds of subtraction situations. Once children have grasped the basic idea of subtraction in this take-away sense, they should be provided opportunities to examine subtraction as it occurs in other situations.

Consider this question: "Bill had eight marbles and gave five of them to Jerry. How many marbles did Bill have left?" This is a *take-away* subtraction question.

You can easily imagine a set of eight marbles from which five are taken away. Now consider this question, "Bill has eight marbles and Jerry has five marbles. How many more marbles has Bill than Jerry?" In this situation no marbles were taken away. This is a *comparison* subtraction question. Imagine one row of marbles which has eight and another row of marbles placed into one-to-one correspondence which has five. In comparing the two sets you determine that one set has three more than the other. Consider this question, "Jerry has four marbles, but he needs ten. How many more marbles does he need?" In this situation there is but one row of four marbles. You want to determine the number of marbles needed to make a row of ten. This is called the *additive* concept of subtraction.

Take-Away	Comparison	Additive
5 − 2 = ☐	4 + ☐ = 7 7 − 4 = ☐	4 + ☐ = 9 9 − 4 = ☐

Teachers should be able to distinguish between the various types of subtraction. The take-away concept is the one which should probably be used in introductory subtraction experiences because it is so closely related to the inverse operation, addition. Children tend to have more difficulty with the comparative and additive subtraction situations so teachers should take special care to help them see the types of diagrams that demonstrate or represent these situations. Children need exposure to all three types, but they also need to be aware that subtraction occurs in more than one type of situation. The main point is do not teach only take-away and then expect children to work all three types. Work with all three types in your instruction. Begin with take-away and then teach the other two types through word problems and diagrams.

Practice

Mastery of addition and subtraction concepts is only half the battle. Many experiences must be provided to help children *remember* as well as understand. Eventually children must be able to state results of addition and subtraction facts spontaneously and without hesitation so that they can efficiently use standard addition and subtraction algorithms. Activities and techniques for practice and drill which are fun and interesting are most desirable. When children spend a great deal of time in rote memorization of addition and subtraction facts, bad side effects may result. Poor mathematics attitudes may be developed through such exercises in boredom.

Class activities in which all the children work on their facts can be used if not overdone. When you ask addition and subtraction facts, you need to know which children are making right responses and the approximate number of children making incorrect responses. Following are some techniques which can be used.

A. Give each child a set of numeral cards, one each of every digit except one. There should be two numeral cards for one. This allows the child to pick up either one card or two cards since the answers of all addition and subtraction facts are 0 through 18. When you say "6 + 7," each child picks up the 1 and the 3 and holds it above his head. Children should respond together. You can say "6 + 7" and then give a "one, two, three," so that all the children will respond simultaneously. This way you will get a better idea which children know the answers and which ones do not. Plastic numerals can be used to carry out this type of activity.

B. Children can use their fingers for addition and subtraction facts with answers through ten. They can place their hands under their desks and play a game called *Nobody Early, Nobody Late*. When you say "4 + 3," the children, hands under the desks, get seven fingers ready to show you. You say, "One, two, three, up!" and each child places the correct number of fingers above his head to show you the correct answer. This can also be used for addition and subtraction facts through fifteen by using one hand for ones and one hand for tens.

C. Give each child a piece of acetate, a napkin or paper towel, and a wax crayon. When you say "9 − 3," the child writes the numeral "6" on the acetate sheet. At the appropriate time, each child holds up his acetate sheet, and you take a quick look around to see who and how many missed the question. Magic slates can be used in the activity described in this paragraph.

One strategy for improving basic facts skills is to allow children to use an addition and subtraction chart like the one described earlier in this chapter. By using the chart, they can continue to more advanced work in addition and subtraction while continuing to practice the basic facts. By using the addition and subtraction chart children begin to remember some of the answers and, over an extended period of time, will rely less and less upon the chart as they increase in confidence and achievement.

A similar method is to give a timed diagnostic test on addition and subtraction facts three times as indicated in the chapter on diagnostic instruction. Run off some dittoed sheets which have the 100 addition and 100 subtraction facts. Take a felt-tip marker and mark off those facts which the child consistently gets correct. Allow the child to use the sheet as a crutch as he continues in the mathematics program. After an interval of one month or six weeks, administer a diagnostic test again. Mark off additional facts which each child has learned. This method is good because it allows each child to see his progress. Children will use crutches consistently at the beginning, but most children will begin to guess the answers before they look. After repeated positive reinforcement, they will rely upon the crutch less and less.

A third method is to use game-like activities which camouflage practice. For example, you can make up a Bingo-type game which has on the Bingo cards answers to addition and subtraction facts. *Competitive* games can be detrimental to proper attitude formation if slow children are asked to compete with fast children. There are ways to use competitive games and avoid this problem. One technique is to divide the children into groups for competitive games on the basis of comparable mathematics achievement. A second alternative is to make success or failure in the game independent of success or failure in answering mathematics questions. An example might be for a child to draw a card which asks a question such as $3 + 4$. Use a game board on which objects are moved in conjunction with the set of cards. On the problem card, $3 + 4$, is indicated the number of moves or other specific directions related to the game. The child then carries out the activity on the game board *irrespective of right or wrong responses* for the addition fact, $3 + 4$. Many activities of the types described here are suggested in the books listed in the bibliography of the materials of instruction chapter. Try to help each child feel that he is succeeding and continuing to learn.

Column Addition

After children have worked with basic facts they can begin to work with groups of three or more numbers. When adding $8 + 7 + 6$, the child encounters a new difficulty. Since addition is a binary operation, the child must find the sum of the first two numbers, 8 and 7, remember that sum, 15, and then add 6 to 15. This is more difficult for children than it might appear. One of the addends, 15, is not seen. It must be remembered from the previous sum. An appropriate readiness experience for column addition is to find sums of three or more numbers horizontally. Hence, $8 + 7 + 6$ could be placed horizontally and then underneath it $15 + 6$, and then 21.

Other Specific Materials and Discovery Strategies

Around the home and school are many common objects which can be used to develop addition and subtraction concepts. Here is a sampling:

pebbles	straws	coffee stirrers
bottle caps	Tinker toys	tin cans
washers	dolls	pencils
nuts and bolts	coins	paper clips
paper cups	tongue depressors	crayons

Because of the difficulty young children experience with the inclusion relation, addition and subtraction problems related to inclusion should not be used in the first and second grades. When Piaget (10) gave children some brown wooden beads and some white wooden beads, the children could easily distinguish whether there were more brown beads or white beads. When asked whether there were more brown beads or wooden beads, the children who did not understand inclusion said there were more brown beads. Situations of this type should be avoided. In introductory work in addition and subtraction, you would do well to focus on a single attribute. The inclusion relation generally requires the child to focus on more than one attribute. If you begin with objects of the same type—all pencils or all pebbles or all marbles—there are no extraneous attributes to confuse the child. Children should definitely work with more than one type of object, but it would be best at the beginning to work with one type of object at any one given time and avoid whole-part relations which focus on more than one attribute.

In addition to the many objects found around the home and school, there are many commercial aids which can be used to develop addition and subtraction concepts. In the remainder of this section several commercial aids will be mentioned and then some discovery suggestions will be made.

Many schools today are using Cuisenaire Rods. The rods have a cross section of one square centimeter and vary in length from one centimeter to ten centimeters. In working with whole numbers the ten rod lengths correspond to 1, 2, 3, 4, 5, 6, 7, 8, 9, and 10. The rods do not have marks to indicate length. Each rod is a different color. To find $3 + 4 = \square$, the child takes a 3-rod and a 4-rod, places them end to end and then finds a rod which has the length of the combined 3- and 4-rods. To show subtraction such as $7 - 4 = \square$, the child takes a 7-rod and places next to it a 4-rod and then finds a rod that will complete the length from the 4-rod to the other end of the 7-rod as illustrated. Cuisenaire Rods can

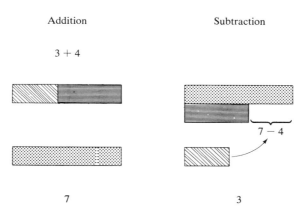

Addition   Subtraction

$3 + 4$

$7 - 4$

7   3

also be used to show commutativity and associativity. The 3-rod and the 4-rod together have the same length as the 4-rod and the 3-rod. When placed end to end, this reinforces the commutative concept as illustrated at the top of page 120. You will recall that associativity involves three numbers. The child can take the 2-rod and the 3-rod and place with it a 4-rod; then he can take a 3-rod

Commutativity

3 + 4

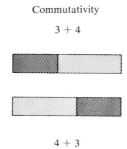

4 + 3

and a 4-rod and place to its left the 2-rod. This will reinforce the associative property. Cuisenaire Rods can also be used to demonstrate the place value concept in finding sums of numbers greater than ten. To find 8 + 7 the child

Associativity

(2 + 3) + 4

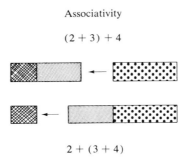

2 + (3 + 4)

can place the 8-rod and the 7-rod end to end and place below it one group of ten which is the 10-rod. He then determines the rod which must be placed next to the 10-rod to complete the length to the end of the 7-rod as illustrated. When the child has placed the 10-rod and the 5-rod, he can see that $8 + 7 = 10 + 5$ which is 15.

Sums Greater than Ten

8 + 7

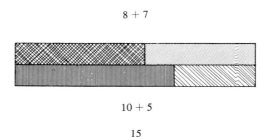

10 + 5

15

Sterns Blocks are similar to Cuisenaire Rods except they have different dimensions and they *do* have markings on them to allow children to count. The 3-rod has two markings on it as illustrated to show that there are three sections. To show 4 + 5, the child can find one rod with four sections, another rod with

Sterns Blocks

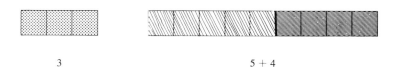

3   5 + 4

five sections and count nine sections altogether. The uses of Sterns Blocks are similar to those mentioned relative to Cuisenaire Rods.

Teaching aids similar to Cuisenaire Rods and Sterns Blocks can be easily made by using large, one-inch-square graph paper and writing appropriate numerals on the strips as shown in the following diagram:

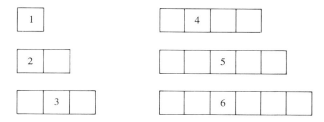

Counting rods such as the one illustrated can be purchased commercially. They can be made with a piece of wire and wooden beads. Such beads can be

purchased at lumber yards and hardware stores. Children can use these for counting and demonstrating addition and subtraction facts. By placing five beads to the right and putting his hand over the ones on the left, the child can easily determine the set of related addition facts of five by moving the beads one-at-a-time to the right or left to get $5 + 0 = 5$; $4 + 1 = 5$; $3 + 2 = 5$; $2 + 3 = 5$; $1 + 4 = 5$; $0 + 5 = 5$.

The materials just described allow children to manipulate objects to find addition and subtraction facts. Two rulers can be used to find addition and subtraction facts in a more semi-concrete manner. By placing two rulers together as illustrated, the child can determine that $4 + 5 = 9$ using ordinary rulers

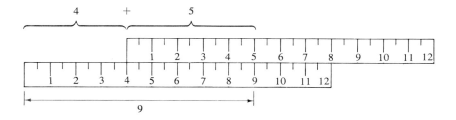

which are marked off in inches or centimeters. On a one-foot rule children can calculate addition and subtraction facts using numbers 12 and less.

The number line is another very useful semi-concrete aid. A number line can be dittoed on a sheet of paper and placed under an acetate sheet. Children can then use the same number line many times by using erasable crayon and a paper napkin. A teacher with a little ingenuity can think of many variations of number lines which can be used to help develop addition and subtraction concepts. As with concrete materials, the best use of number lines is made when *each child* has his own number line to use. One interesting variation is the walk-on number line described in the chapter on pre-operational concepts. Children can determine sums and differences by walking on the number line. If you are in a room with floor tile, pieces of masking tape can be placed to mark the intervals between paces.

Children can bring twenty objects of some kind from home. They can trade these every few days and this way they gain work with addition and subtraction concepts from a variety of manipulative aids. The variety is very essential because children must learn that mathematics concepts are independent of materials even though they may be demonstrated by or related to many different kinds of materials. Teachers who use a single aid run the risk of creating in the mind of the child the idea that number concepts are related to particular kinds of materials rather than representing a model of many kinds of materials.

Many materials for student manipulation have been mentioned in this chapter. According to Piaget's developmental theory, children learn through actions on concrete materials. It is very important that the textbook *not* be the starting place because textbooks by their very nature cannot provide the concrete manipulative experiences needed for children to comprehend mathematical concepts. After much exploratory work with concrete materials, semi-concrete materials such as pictures, number lines and drawings can be used. Finally, at the abstract level, manipulation of numerals can be mastered by children. Textbooks naturally provide semi-concrete and abstract experiences. Teachers must be aware that concrete materials are needed and must be creative in finding interesting materials for children to manipulate.

Discovery Strategies

Children in primary grades can be given many interesting opportunities to discover mathematical relationships. A few suggestions will now be made and the reader can devise many of his own.

Sets of Related Facts for Six.   Have the children count out six objects. Then ask them to find out how many addition sentences they can write which have the number six as the answer. A variation would be to have the children work in groups of two, three, or four. Maybe one could be a secretary and the other two could manipulate objects. A similar type of exercise can be done to find the set of subtraction facts. Another variation of this would be to give children the sentence $\square + \triangle = 6$ and ask them to find all the number pairs for box and triangle that will make this a true statement.

Odd and Even. Give children some small objects or a peg board and pegs. Ask them to make rectangles or two rows of pegs for each of the numbers 1 through 10. Through a guided discovery approach, help them see that 2, 4, 6, 8, and 10 have all pairs but 1, 3, 5, 7, and 9 have one left over. By having them see all of these in front of them at one time you can help them begin to intuit a distinction between even and odd numbers.

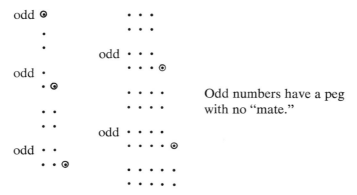

Odd numbers have a peg with no "mate."

Commutativity. Ask children to place a certain number of objects on a sheet of paper with a line down the middle, for instance, three on one side, two on the other side. Ask them to write the number sentence $3 + 2 = 5$ and then ask them to turn the sheet of paper around and write the number sentence $2 + 3 = 5$. Ask the children to do this for several number combinations. Some of them will begin to see that the second number sentence is the same as the first except the addends are reversed. Another activity is to give children a sheet with several problems, the answers of which are to be determined with concrete materials. The first question can be something like $3 + 2$ and the second one $2 + 3$. After four or five commutative pairs they will begin to see a pattern emerge in the answers. You do not want them to get the correct answers because of an answer pattern: 3, 3; 4, 4; 9, 9; etc. To prevent this pattern, place some questions in the list which do not follow the pattern. Then children will begin to look for commutative pairs as they work.

Commutativity and Associativity. Give the children three-addend problems such as the following: Bill has four pennies, Mary has five pennies and Jerry has three pennies. How many have they altogether? Ask the children working alone or in small groups to write as many number sentences as possible by which the total can be determined. A variation of this exercise would be to give a problem such as $\square + \triangle + \bigcirc = 12$ and ask the children to find as many triplets of numbers as possible to put in the three shapes which make a true statement. They can, of course, use counters, Cuisenaire Rods or other materials if they wish.

Accommodation of Individual Differences

The discussion in this section will relate primarily to the model presented in the chapter on individualization of instruction. Objectives, preassessment, instruction, diagnosis, and grouping will be examined.

Objectives

Children should first be provided an opportunity to explore mathematics concepts with concrete materials without relating them to the numerals and operational symbols. After some readiness work they should begin to use symbols with the manipulations of materials. When children seem to be developing an understanding of the mathematical concepts in relation to materials, semi-concrete materials such as pictures, diagrams, and number lines can be used. Finally, children will learn to use symbols without aids. Following are some of the major concepts explored in the chapter.

A. Sets of related addition and subtraction facts
B. Fact families
C. Commutativity
D. Associativity
E. Identity element

Since each concept is to be explored at each of the four levels identified, instructional objectives covering the various levels should be written. The following are samples. First examine A.

Concrete without symbols. Given two sets the child will be able to state the cardinal number of each set and the cardinal number of the union of the two sets.

Concrete with symbols. Given two sets of elements, the child will be able to write an addition sentence corresponding to the two sets.

Semi-concrete with symbols. Given a picture depicting two sets, the child will be able to write the addition or subtraction sentence associated with the picture.

Symbols or abstract. Given a set of addition and subtraction sentences the child will be able to fill in the place holders without the use of aids.

Here is one for the commutative property at the abstract level: Given a set of flash cards with intermittently placed commutative pairs the child will be able to answer the second question of the commutative pair without hesitation.

Preassessment

When the class is ready to work on a new concept, you can preassess either formally or informally to determine whether or not there are some children who have already attained the objectives of the next unit of instruction. You can do this informally by observing the children during the previous units of instruction. This will give you insights as to whether or not there may be one or more students who will not need to participate in this unit of instruction. A formal diagnostic procedure is to administer a brief quiz on the objectives of the next unit to see if there are some children who have already attained the objectives. Some children may have attained the objectives at the concrete level which means they are ready to work at the semi-concrete level. If there are some children who have attained the objectives at both the concrete and semi-concrete levels, they can work on the concept at the abstract level. If there are some who have attained the objectives at all three levels, they can go into some of the enrichment activities described later.

Instructional Phase

If guided discovery strategies are used, children can work in small groups and use objects to answer questions. If you choose to use a large-group instructional approach, keep it child-centered. If you feel it is important to use aids for demonstration, attempt whenever possible to use them in conjunction with individualized concrete manipulative materials. One-to-one contact with materials and peer-group socialization experiences are very important for development of mathematics concepts. When you feel that several children have attained the objectives of the unit, it is time to administer a diagnostic test.

Diagnosis

You will recall that a diagnostic test is one which determines the extent to which children have attained objectives. The objectives which you identified define the questions that you ask. If children are to see objects and write equations, then you will provide the objects and the children will write the equations. If the children are to show problems on a number line, you will provide the problems and the number line and the children will draw the diagram. If children are to answer questions at the symbolic level, i.e., without the use of instructional aids, you will administer some type of timed test so that children will not have the opportunity to count anything, including their fingers! On the basis of the results of the diagnostic test, children should be regrouped. Some will go into a practice group, some will go into a reteach group, and others who have attained the objectives of instruction will go into the enrichment group.

Grouping

Children who have not attained the concept can be placed into a reteach group where they can be provided additional experiences for developing and understanding concepts with concrete materials. These children should be allowed to work together and they may need more teacher help than the other two groups. In working with number facts children may be expected only to attain objectives at the concrete and semi-concrete levels during introductory work since children usually do not learn all the basic combinations until the end of grade two. Therefore, your objectives will probably focus on concrete and semi-concrete levels. Children who have attained the concept at the concrete level may be placed in a practice group where they have additional experiences at the semi-concrete level. These children can work with the number line, pictures, and diagrams. They can also make up their own problems and solve them by drawing pictures.

Children who have attained these concepts at the concrete and semi-concrete levels can be placed in an enrichment group. Enrichment activities may include the use of concepts just mastered. These children might play mathematical games such as *Equations* or *On Sets* (available commercially). The children might also work on developmental exercises related to addition and subtraction concepts in other number bases, especially activities related to place value. By using Unipacs, programmed materials or work sheets, the children can be provided opportunities to explore areas of interest. They can add in groups of five or learn to subtract in base six by looking at basic facts in other bases. They might construct addition and subtraction tables similar to the ones described in this chapter. Whatever the enrichment activities provided, children should be given the opportunity to choose whenever possible. This will help foster positive attitudes toward mathematics.

Additional Resources for Teacher Training

Filmstrips

> *Addition and Subtraction Are Related,* Popular Science (3H–2)
> *Mathematical Sentences,* Popular Science (5H–2)

Films

> *Open Sentences and the Number Line,* Madison Project
> *Addition and Its Properties,* National Council of Teachers of Mathematics
> *Subtraction,* National Council of Teachers of Mathematics

Elementary School Textbooks

> The Macmillan Co. (1970), Grade 1, *Developing Mathematics One,* by J. Phillips, W. Sanders, T. Thoburn, J. F. Fitzgerald.
> > Student Text: pp. 65–77, 84–103, 118–25, 168–73, 216–26.
> Harper & Row (1970), Grade 1, *New Dimensions in Mathematics,* by C. D'Augustine, F. Brown, J. Heddens, C. Howard.
> > Student Text: pp. 63–108, 135–68.
> > Teacher Edition: pp. 88–136, 166–202.

Bibliography

1. Baumann, Reemt R. "Children's Understanding of Selected Mathematical Concepts in Grades Two and Four." University of Wisconsin, 1965. *Dissertation Abstracts* (March 1966), 26:5219–220.

2. Breed, Frederick S., and Alice L. Ralston. "The Direct and Indirect Methods of Teaching the Addition Combination." *Elementary School Journal* (December 1936), 37:283–94.

3. Buckingham, B. R. "Teaching Addition and Subtraction Facts Together or Separately." *Educational Research Bulletin* (May 25, 1927), 6:228–29, 240–42.

4. Copeland, Richard W. *How Children Learn Mathematics.* London: The Macmillan Company, 1970.

5. Ekman, L. G. *A Comparison of the Effectiveness of Different Approaches to the Teaching of Addition and Subtraction Algorithms in the Third Grade* (Volumes I and II). Minnesota: University of Minnesota (unpublished), 1966.

6. Flavell, John H. *The Developmental Psychology of Jean Piaget.* New York: Van Nostrand Reinhold & Company, 1963.

7. Grossnickle, Foster E., Leo J. Brueckner, and John Reckzeh. *Discovering Meanings in Elementary School Mathematics,* 5th ed. New York: Holt, Rinehart and Winston, Inc., 1968.

8. Lovell, Kenneth. *The Growth of Understanding in Mathematics.* New York: Holt, Rinehart and Winston, Inc., 1971.

9. MacLatchy, Josephine H. "Counting and Addition." *Educational Research Bulletin* (February 17, 1932), 9:96–100).

10. Piaget, Jean. *The Child's Conception of Number.* New York: W. W. Norton & Company, Inc., 1965.

11. Van Engen, H. and L. P. Steffe. "First Grade Children's Concept of Addition of Natural Numbers." Research and Development Center for Learning and Re-Education. Madison, Wisconsin: University of Wisconsin, 1966.

9

Systems of Numeration

Place value is a rogue! Many children in grades one, two, three and
four do not understand place value concepts even after repeated
exposure. Many teachers do not fully understand place value either.
Even though you are capable of sophisticated number manipulations
which require use of place value concepts, you may be doing so by
rote! If you cannot answer these questions, you do not fully
understand place value:

A. If "one two" is "twelve" then "thirteen" is "one three";
"one three" follows "one two" in groups of ten. What follows
"one two" in groups of eight?

B. What precedes "one four" in groups of five?

C. What precedes "one zero zero" (one hundred) in groups
of ten? What precedes "one zero zero" in groups of eight?
groups of seventeen?

D. What is 27 + 38 in groups of ten? groups of nine?
groups of twelve?

If you can answer these questions easily without converting to
groups of ten (base ten), the grouping system you always use, you
are well on your way towards mastery of place value concepts.

Th difficulties encountered by most elementary school students
led me to a concentrated study of place value and the problems
related to it. As a result of this study, I accumulated evidence that
understanding is possible through relating place value in base ten

to grouping systems in general. In other words, I concluded that if children (and adults) could see many grouping systems, they would view base ten as simply another instance of grouping systems in general.

As I observed children and adults working with non-decimal numeration systems I noticed that they exhibited a strong tendency to convert other systems to base ten, compute results, and convert back. They were already so firmly indoctrinated in a given system that they experienced great difficulty in "breaking out" of a preconceived base ten mental set.

Obviously, people who have no engrained system do not have the difficulty described in the preceding paragraph. Who are they?—first-graders who have not yet encountered place value.

Although little has been done with non-decimal (not base ten) systems of numeration below grade three, I have evidence to support my belief that first-graders can explore operations in other bases with understanding. Over a three-month period I worked with a bright first-grade boy to determine the extent to which he could work with other systems.

There were three youngsters at first. They were in grade one and had not yet encountered the place value concept. We began by working with pencils. We gathered around my desk, and I talked to Erik on the toy phone:

"Hello, Erik. Do you have any pencils over at the storeroom?"

"Yes."

"How many?"

"Four."

After asking several such questions using only pencils, a *box of pencils* was placed in front of Erik. I asked him how many pencils there were now. He thought for a moment and then guessed that there were six pencils in the box. I pulled them out one at a time and showed him there were more than six. Mary guessed eight, and Bill guessed ten. They were similarly shown to be wrong. The three youngsters decided with a little help to call it a "box of pencils." We resumed the phone conversation:

"Erik, how many pencils are on the shelf?"

"One box of pencils."

"How many now?"

"Three boxes of pencils."

"How many pencils are on your desk?"

"Four."

"How many are on the shelf and on your desk altogether?"

"Three boxes and four." (Pause) *"That's seven!"*

This failure to distinguish between pencils and boxes of pencils as "different" entities is a place value problem. There is a difference between *one* when it describes a single pencil and *one* when it describes a box of pencils just as the important distinction must be made between *one one* and *one ten*.

After a few days the concept was handled adequately at the verbal level, and all three youngsters were able to add and subtract verbally with the use of pencils or other objects. I would place two boxes and three pencils and one box and four pencils. They could tell me these were three boxes and seven all together. They were simply carrying out the operations in the *enactive* mode. After a couple weeks, two children ceased instruction. Much time was being lost entertaining two while I worked with and probed the third.

The most difficult problem encountered was one of appropriate symbolism. A pencil *looks* different from a box of pencils. However, *ten ones, 10,* does not look different from *one ten, 10.* The numeral 10 is sometimes used to refer to one ten and sometimes to ten ones, just as 10 cents may refer to one dime or ten pennies. After much thought I was able to create a visual distinction with symbols. One ten was denoted by ⓵ and ten ones was denoted by 10. Special notations were created which readily permitted visual discrimination of groups of three, four, five, and six.

After three months, the one child with whom I continued to work had successfully learned to add and subtract at the enactive, iconic and symbolic levels *with regrouping*. Then two other upper-average children went through a revised sequence in six weeks and, finally, two others who were at the bottom of the class (I. Q.s in lower-normal range) also went through the sequence in about six weeks.

There is no doubt in my mind that the child who has mastered the concept of place value as a grouping process has a solid base upon which to build understanding of algorithms for all four whole-number operations. Further, the teacher who has a solid grasp of place value concepts is in a position to provide good instruction in whole number operations.

The materials which follow are based upon the work with first-graders. They have been modified for college instruction through a programmed format. They are of little use if you do not work with the materials and follow instructions carefully. Unless you can add and subtract in other bases *without* using the addition and subtraction facts of the base ten system, your mastery of numeration systems is incomplete. These materials are designed to enhance it.

The next section consists of auto-tutorial materials. As concepts are developed, you are asked to answer questions to stimulate reflection and increase your comprehension. Behavioral objectives are listed below and a self-test is included at the end of the programmed materials to allow you to determine whether or not you have attained the objectives.

Systems of Numeration

Objectives

After completing this unit you will be able to:

(1) List the characteristics of the decimal numeration system.
(2) Indicate which of the three systems discussed possesses a given characteristic and give an illustration supporting your statement.

(3) Indicate whether or not given counting sequences in non-decimal systems of numeration are correct.
(4) Work illustrations which demonstrate the use of the associative property of addition in regrouping.
(5) Add and subtract in bases 3, 4, 5, 6, and 10 with the two following algorithmic forms using either the special notation developed or standard notation:

     A. Vertical expanded notation

     B. Vertical standard or traditional algorithm

(6) Demonstrate with concrete teaching aids the steps in each of the above algorithms.

Materials needed

Since the basic idea emphasized in this unit is place value as a grouping process, you need objects which you can group. Paper clips, pennies, poker chips, pencils or straws will do quite well. Since another basic idea is *groups* and *single entities* (called *ones* in our numerations system), you need a visual reference for a group. If you use paper clips, you can use a quarter-sheet of paper:

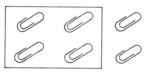 1 group of four and 2

You can place four paper clips on a piece of paper when you wish to think of a *group of four* or simply place four paper clips on your desk when you wish to think of them as *four separate entities* rather than a group. You can do something similar to this with pennies. If you use poker chips, you can use the paper groupings again or you can place a chip of a different color on top when you wish to think of it as a group, e.g., three blue chips with a red one on top is a *group of four* but a stack of four blue chips is *four separate entities* (ones). If you use pencils or straws, they are separate entities unless you place a rubber band around them; then they are a group.

It is *extremely* important for you to do the counting and manipulating called for in this unit. **Do not** skip them just because you think you understand the point being made.

Whenever questions are asked, decide what the answer should be, write down all steps, and then look at the correct response on the second page following. **All answer frames are indicated parenthetically. A question on frame N–9 is answered on frame (N–9).**

N–1

Historical Background

The Egyptian System

The symbols used to represent numbers are called *numerals,* i.e., "2" is a numeral which represents the number two; "14" is a numeral which represents the number fourteen. Early Egyptians used groups of tallies as numerals for numbers less than 10. The symbols were called *hieroglyphics*

Decimal System: 1   2   3   4   5   6   7   8   9

Egyptian System: /   //   ///   ////   //   //⁝   ///   ////   ///

CONTINUE TO N–2.

N–2

When a group of ten was counted, a new symbol, ∩, was used. Hence, 64 was represented by ∩∩∩ //// and 76 was represented by ∩∩∩∩ ///.

For 100, still another symbol, ℮ , was used. Thus, 435 was represented by ℮℮℮℮∩∩// .

    (a) How would you write 238 in hieroglyphics?

    (b) Express in the decimal system: (1)   ℮℮℮℮∩∩∩ ///

                                         (2)   ℮℮℮∩∩ ///

COMPARE YOUR ANSWERS WITH THOSE
ON (N–2) TWO PAGES FOLLOWING.

N–3

Notice these characteristics of hieroglyphics:

I. The symbols represent powers of 10:

Decimal	*Egyptian*
$1 = 10^0$	/
$10 = 10^1$	∩
$100 = 10^2$	℮

II. Each symbol is used nine times, and then the entire group is replaced by another symbol:

///
/// add one / and you   get ∩
///
9 +   1   =   10

∩∩∩
∩∩∩   add one ∩ and you   get ℮
∩∩∩
90   +   10   =   100

CONTINUE TO N–4.

III. The values of the symbols are added:

꠸ꪈ ∩∩∩
ꪈꪈ ∩∩//   is $(100 + 100) + (10 + 10 + 10 + 10 + 10) + (1 + 1)$

IV. The order of the symbols would not change the number represented:

ꪈꪈ∩∩∩//// is the same as   ∩ ꪈ∩∩/// ꪈ/

Order is dictated more or less by custom.

CONTINUE TO N–5.

In other words, the Egyptian system:

  I. has different symbols representing each power of ten

 II. is repetitive in a given power

III. is additive

IV. is non-positional

CONTINUE TO N–6.

Question:

What is meant by the following statement?

    "The Egyptian system has a different symbol to represent each power of ten."

SEE ANSWER FRAME (N–6).

N–7

Question:

What is meant by the following statement?

"The Egyptian system is repetitive in a given power."

SEE ANSWER FRAME (N–7).

(N–2)

(a) ℓℓ∩∩∩ ////⁄////

(b) 433
     323

CONTINUE TO N–3.

N–8

Question:

What is meant by the following statement?

"The Egyptian system is additive."

SEE ANSWER FRAME (N–8).

Question:

What is meant by the following statement?

    "The Egyptian system is non-positional."

SEE ANSWER FRAME (N–9).

The Roman System

The Romans used numerals which are familiar to most people today.

Decimal System	Roman System
1	I
5	V
10	X
50	L
100	C
500	D
1000	M

Which of the following are characteristics of the Roman system?

    (a) It is repetitive.

    (b) It is additive.

    (c) It has a subtractive principle. What do you think is the meaning of this statement?

    (d) It is positional.

    (e) All the symbols represent powers of 10.

SEE ANSWER FRAME (N–10).

Instead of using the same symbols 0–9 as you use in the decimal system, the Egyptians used different symbols to represent ones, tens, hundreds, and so on. In the Egyptian system, ∩ represents 10 and ℓ represents 100. As the powers of ten increase, new symbols are introduced, i.e.,

$$10^0 = \quad 1 \leftrightarrow /$$
$$10^1 = \quad 10 \leftrightarrow ∩$$
$$10^2 = 100 \leftrightarrow ℓ$$

Notice that in your system such is *not* the case.

CONTINUE TO N–7.

(N–7)

There is but one symbol to represent each power of ten, i.e., in the ones there is only a tally, in the tens there is only ∩ , and in the hundreds there is only ℓ . Contrast this to your system: 6 means six ones but in hieroglyphic notation, six had to be represented by a *repetition* of the symbol which stood for one: $\frac{///}{///}$.

In the decimal system you can say 42 is four groups of ten and two ones. However, the Egyptian system was repetitive because it had no way to show several ones or groups except to repeat the symbol used for one and ten. Hence 42 was ∩∩∩∩ //.

CONTINUE TO N–8.

N–11

The Hindu-Arabic System

The exact origins of the present decimal system of numeration are not known. However, a likely conjecture is that the digits 1, 2, 3, 4, 5, 6, 7, 8, and 9 were invented by the Hindus. Perhaps they became familiar with the symbol 0 used by Greek astronomers. They probably also knew of the Babylonian positional usage in the sexagesimal system (base 60).

The characteristics of the Hindu-Arabic system are as follows:

   I. It uses 10 symbols (digits): 0, 1, 2, 3, 4, 5, 6, 7, 8, 9.

  II. Numbers are expressed in powers of ten:
$$462 = (4 \times 10^2) + (6 \times 10^1) + (2 \times 10^0).$$

 III. The system is additive: $462 = 400 + 60 + 2$.

 IV. It has place value: $64 \neq 46$ (positional).

CONTINUE TO N–12.

(N–8)

The number represented by a collection of symbols was found by *adding* the values of each symbol shown. Example:

$$ℓ∩∩/// \text{ is } ℓ + ∩ + ∩ + / + / + / \quad or$$
$$100 + 10 + 10 + 1 + 1 + 1 = 123$$

Your system, the decimal system, is also additive since
$$123 = 1 \text{ hundred} + 2 \text{ tens} + 3 \text{ ones} \quad or$$
$$100 \quad + \quad 20 \quad + \quad 3$$

CONTINUE TO N–9.

In the decimal system, which is positional, the "2" in 123 is "2 tens." If you write 213, the "2" is no longer "2 tens." However, in the Egyptian system "∩" is "1 ten" whether you write ℮∩/ or ∩℮/ or ℮/∩ .

The decimal system is said to have *place value* since there is a ones place (position), a tens place (position) and so on. The Egyptian system, on the other hand, has no place value; the symbols for one, ten and hundred can be placed at will. Hence, the Egyptian system is *non-positional*.

CONTINUE TO N–10.

(a) Yes—XXIII is 23, two groups of ten and three ones: there is repetition.

(b) No—While it frequently is, as in CCLV = 100 + 100 + 50 + 5, there are exceptions as in CXL = 100 − 10 + 50 or 100 + 50 − 10.

(c) When two symbols are in inverse order by value, the first is subtracted from the second as in (b).

(d) No—There is no "ones place," "tens place," etc.

(e) No—Some, such as I, X, C, M, do. Others, such as V, L, D, do not.

CONTINUE TO N–11.

Before elaborating upon these characteristics take a look at systems of numeration more closely.

Suppose you are asked, "How many groups of four are there in this picture?"

> • • • • •
>
> • • • • •

You could simply draw rings around sets of four and get 2 groups of four and 3 left over.

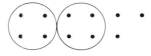

Use some small objects to count out 2 groups of four and 3. *Describe the total as each new one is placed* by using the terminology of the next frame.

CONTINUE TO N–13.

N–13

Here is the counting sequence. Try it. Read through it and then duplicate it *verbally* while using your counting objects. This is important so don't hurry!

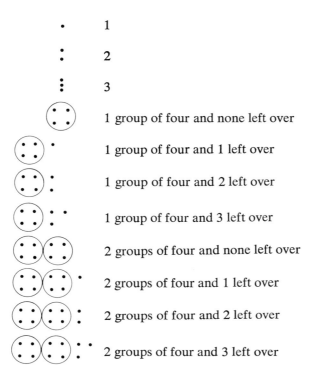

•	1
:	2
⁝	3
	1 group of four and none left over
	1 group of four and 1 left over
	1 group of four and 2 left over
	1 group of four and 3 left over
	2 groups of four and none left over
	2 groups of four and 1 left over
	2 groups of four and 2 left over
	2 groups of four and 3 left over

CONTINUE TO N–14.

N–14

When you count, you say:

1	one	3	three	5	five	7	seven	9	nine
2	two	4	four	6	six	8	eight	10	ten

Although there is no "signal" in a verbal change from nine to ten, you can *see* a signal when you observe the *numerals*. Ten is the first numeral with two digits. It signifies *one group of ten and no ones*.

CONTINUE TO N–15.

N–15

Collect your materials (objects). Make 2 groups of five and 3 left over. Now pick them up. Place them in front of you one-at-a-time and use the counting sequence similar to the one at the top of the page. Remember, you want groups of *five* this time. Check yourself on the second page following.

SEE ANSWER FRAME (N–15).

Make groups which match this picture.

(a) How many are in each of the tallest stacks?

(b) How many tall stacks?

(c) How many in the short stack?

(d) What would you call the total? _____ groups of four and _____ left over

(e) Now *count out* another set which matches the set which you already have before you.

SEE ANSWER FRAME (N–16).

Count your fingers. Instead of thinking of them as ten fingers, consider that they are in groups of five. Write the sequence on a piece of paper and check your sequence with the one listed on the second page following.

SEE ANSWER FRAME (N–17).

The transition from "left over" to groups is the most essential idea of this pattern. For example, if you have "3 groups of five and 4 left over" as indicated, then by placing one more,

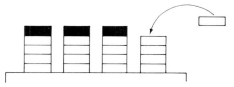

you would get "4 groups of five and none left over." Then the counting sequence repeats itself:

Groups	Left Over	Verbalize
4	1	four one
4	2	four two
4	3	four three
4	4	four four

CONTINUE TO N–19.

N–19

Now use your objects to count in groups of seven from one through four groups of seven. As you *place each object,* say to yourself,

"1, 2, . . . , 1 group of seven and none left over, 1 group of seven and 1 left over, ..."

Then go back and repeat the sequence as on the previous frame. Verbalize:

		Groups	*Left Over*
"One three" for	"1 group of seven and 3 left over"	1	3
"One four" for	"1 group of seven and 4 left over"	1	4
"One five" for	"1 group of seven and 5 left over"	1	5

SEE ANSWER FRAME (N–19).

N–20

The following pictures represent colored blocks and paper plates. You can relate them to your materials. When three blocks are placed on a paper plate, you will say "1 group of three" or "one zero." Hence:

   "1 group of three" or "one zero"

   "1 group of five" or "one zero"

When additional blocks are placed on the *table* but *not on a plate,* you will say that they are "left over." Hence:

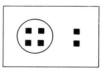   "1 group of four and 2 left over" or "one two"

CONTINUE TO N–21.

(N–15)

1
2
3
4

1 group of five and none left over
1 group of five and 1 left over
1 group of five and 2 left over
1 group of five and 3 left over
1 group of five and 4 left over

2 groups of five and none left over
2 groups of five and 1 left over
2 groups of five and 2 left over
2 groups of five and 3 left over

⟶ Be sure to repeat this part each time.

CONTINUE TO N–16.

(a) 4   (b) 2   (c) 3   (d) 2 groups of four and 3 left over

(e)   1
             2
             3

1 group of four and none left over   2 groups of four and none left over
1 group of four and 1 left over   2 groups of four and 1 left over
1 group of four and 2 left over   2 groups of four and 2 left over
1 group of four and 3 left over   2 groups of four and 3 left over

CONTINUE TO N–17.

             1
             2
             3
             4

1 group of five and none left over   1 group of five and 3 left over
1 group of five and 1 left over   1 group of five and 4 left over
1 group of five and 2 left over   2 groups of five and none left over

IF YOUR SEQUENCE IS IN *ERROR*, GO TO FRAME N–18.
IF YOUR SEQUENCE IS CORRECT, GO TO FRAME N–20.

What would you call this?

(a) 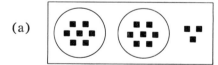 (b)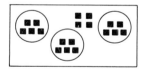

Show these with paper plates and blocks or some other objects:

(c) "2 groups of eight and 1 left over"

(d) "5 groups of six and 3 left over"

(e) *Count out twelve objects.* Count them in groups of six using this
sequence:

one	five	one three
two	one zero	one four
three	one one	one five
four	one two	two zero

Repeat for groups of five and groups of four.

SEE ANSWER FRAME (N–21).

(N–19)

Groups	Left over	Verbally	Groups	Left over	Verbally
	1	one	1	2	one two
	2	two	1	3	one three
	3	three	1	4	one four
	4	four	1	5	one five
	5	five	1	6	one six
	6	six	2	0	two zero
1	0	one zero	2	1	two one
1	1	one one	etc.	etc.	etc.

CONTINUE TO N–20.

N–22

Study this new symbolism:

"1 group of three"   —   (three sides)

"1 group of four"   —   (four sides)

"1 group of five"   —   (five sides)

"1 group of six"   —   (six segments)

"1 group of ten"   —   (like 10)

"2 groups of three"   —

"3 groups of five"   —

CONTINUE TO N–23.

N–23

Complete the following. The first one is done for you.

(a) "3 groups of four"   —

(b) "4 groups of six"   —

(c) "2 groups of three"   —   2

(d) "7 groups of ten"   —   ?

(e) "_____ groups of four"   —

(f) "5 groups of _____"   —

(g) "_____ groups of _____"   —

(h) "3 groups of _____"   —

SEE ANSWER FRAME (N–23).

The number of line segments in the placeholder tells how many are in each group or how many are on *each* paper plate. Hence:

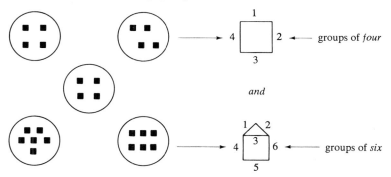

and

CONTINUE TO N–25.

N–25

The *numeral in the placeholder* tells *how many groups* or paper plates there are.

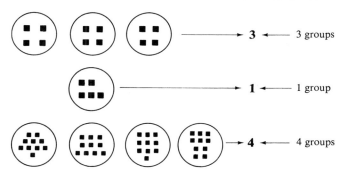

CONTINUE TO N–26.

(N–21)

(a) "2 groups of seven and 3 left over" or "two three"

(b) "3 groups of five and 4 left over" or "three four"

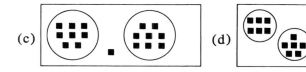

(e)

Groups of five	*Groups of five*	*Groups of four*	*Groups of four*
one	one two	one	one three
two	one three	two	two zero
three	one four	three	two one
four	two zero	one zero	two two
one zero	two one	one one	two three
one one	two two	one two	three zero

CONTINUE TO N–22.

N–26

Thus:

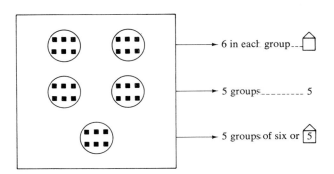

CONTINUE TO N–27.

N–27

Now try these:

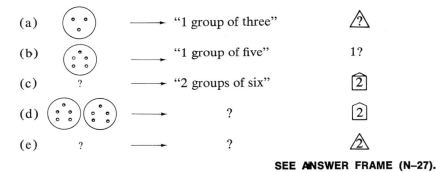

SEE ANSWER FRAME (N–27).

(N–23)

(b) 4

(c) △

(d) ⑦

(e) 2

(f) six

(g) 2, six

(h) five, 3

IF YOU GOT ALL CORRECT OR MISSED ONLY ONE, GO
TO N–28. IF YOU MISSED MORE THAN ONE, GO TO N–24.

Next you need a way of accounting for the "left overs." You will simply say,

"<u>1</u> group of three and <u>2</u> left over"

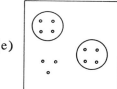 + <u>2</u>

"<u>2</u> groups of four and <u>3</u> left over"

2 + <u>3</u>

CONTINUE TO N-29.

N-29

Draw pictures or use concrete materials for these:

(a) 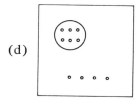 + <u>1</u>   (b) ① + <u>4</u>   (c) 3 + <u>2</u>

Write expressions for these:

(d)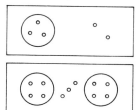

(e)

(f)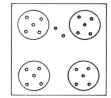

SEE ANSWER FRAME (N-29).

N-30

Use the objects to answer the following questions. *Be sure to use the devices.* They will help develop intuitive understanding. After you place the objects, *count* them.

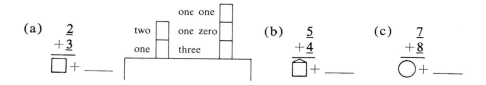

(a) $\begin{array}{r} 2 \\ +\underline{3} \\ \hline \end{array}$ □+ ____

(b) $\begin{array}{r} 5 \\ +\underline{4} \\ \hline \end{array}$ + ____

(c) $\begin{array}{r} 7 \\ +\underline{8} \\ \hline \end{array}$ ○+ ____

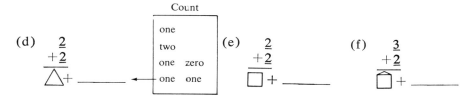

(d) $\begin{array}{r} 2 \\ +\underline{2} \\ \hline \end{array}$ △+ ____

(e) $\begin{array}{r} 2 \\ +\underline{2} \\ \hline \end{array}$ □+ ____

(f) $\begin{array}{r} 3 \\ +\underline{2} \\ \hline \end{array}$ + ____

SEE ANSWER FRAME (N-30).

N–31

Use your objects to find these sums (be sure to *use* the aids):

(a) $\boxed{1}$ + $\underline{1}$
    + $\boxed{1}$ + $\underline{2}$
    ————————
    $\boxed{2}$ + $\underline{3}$

(b) $\textcircled{2}$ + $\underline{3}$
    + $\textcircled{1}$ + $\underline{6}$
    ————————

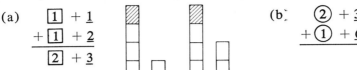

(c) $\widehat{2}$ + $\underline{1}$
    + $\boxed{2}$ + $\underline{2}$
    ————————
    $\bigcap$ + ————

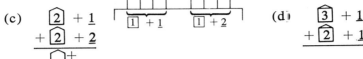

$\boxed{1}$ + 1 $\boxed{1}$ + 2

(d) $\boxed{3}$ + $\underline{1}$
    + $\widehat{2}$ + $\underline{1}$
    ————————

SEE ANSWER FRAME (N–31).

(N–27)

(a) 1

(b) $\bigcap$

(c)

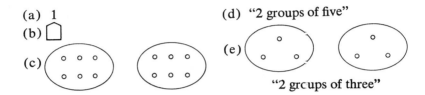

(d) "2 groups of five"

(e)

"2 groups of three"

CONTINUE TO N–28.

N–32

Now you can move to something new and challenging. Place $\boxed{2}$ + $\underline{3}$ objects in front of you. Separate these *visually* from the next grouping. Now, place $\boxed{1}$ + $\underline{4}$ objects in front of you. Now you have $\boxed{2}$ + $\underline{3}$
$\boxed{1}$ + $\underline{4}$

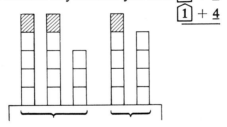

Since the custom is to start on the right, place the 3 and 4 together and *count* to get:

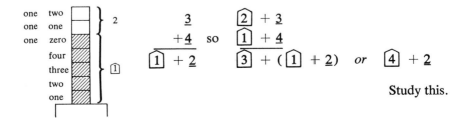

one   two
one   one   } 2
one   zero
       four
       three   } $\boxed{1}$
       two
       one

$\boxed{1}$ + $\underline{2}$

$\begin{array}{r} 3 \\ +\underline{4} \\ \end{array}$ so

$\boxed{2}$ + $\underline{3}$
$\boxed{1}$ + $\underline{4}$
————————
$\boxed{3}$ + ($\boxed{1}$ + $\underline{2}$)   *or* $\boxed{4}$ + $\underline{2}$

Study this.

CONTINUE TO N–33.

Use your objects to verify this:

$\boxed{1} + \underline{3}$ *One, Two, Three,*   *Four, Five, One zero, One one, One two*

3   +   5 $= \widehat{1} + \underline{2}$

$\boxed{2} + \underline{5}$

$\boxed{3} + (\boxed{1} + \underline{2})$ *or* $\boxed{4} + \underline{2}$

Notice the use of the associative property of addition:

$\boxed{3} + (\boxed{1} + \underline{2}) = (\widehat{3} + \widehat{1}) + \underline{2} = \boxed{4} + \underline{2}$

CONTINUE TO N–34.

(a)   (b)   (c)

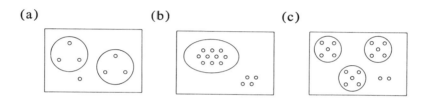

(d) $\widehat{1} + \underline{4}$ (e) $\boxed{2} + \underline{3}$ (f) $\boxed{4} + \underline{2}$

CONTINUE TO N–30.

(a) $\boxed{1} + \underline{1}$ *Be sure you count!*
(b) $\widehat{1} + \underline{3}$
(c) $\bigcirc{1} + \underline{5}$ $3 + 4 = \bigcap + \underline{\quad}$?
(d) $\triangle + \underline{1}$
(e) $\boxed{1} + \underline{0}$
(f) $\widehat{0} + \underline{5}$

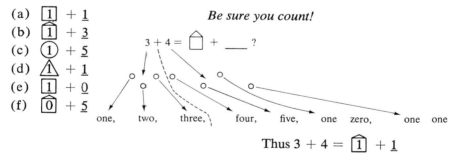

one,   two,   three,   four,   five,   one zero,   one one

Thus $3 + 4 = \widehat{1} + \underline{1}$

This will help you understand how a first-grader "figures out" the sum of six and seven.

If you say $3 + 4 = 7$
$\qquad 7 - 6 = 1$ *Foul Ball!*
so $3 + 4 = \boxed{1} + \underline{1}$, you are missing the point! The child has no such reference system. *He must count.*

CONTINUE TO N–31.

(N–31)

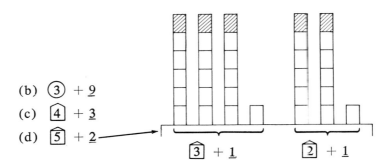

(b) ③ + 9

(c) ④ + 3

(d) ⑤ + 2 ——→

③ + 1   ② + 1

CONTINUE TO N–32.

N–34

Use your objects to find these sums.

Be sure to *count* to get the sums, and then use the associative property.

(a)   ☐1 + 2   (b)   ⑵ + 4
     + ☐1 + 3   + ⑴ + 4

(c)   ⌢1 + 5   (d)   ① + 9
     + ⑵ + 5   + ② + 7

SEE ANSWER FRAME (N–34).

N–35

Now you are in need of a method which will enable you to find such sums *without* the help of manipulative devices.

Before continuing, see if you can find the following sums *without* using the counting aids.

        ☐1 + 3   ⑵ + 4
      + ☐1 + 3   + ⑴ + 4

Hint: Count on your fingers!

NOW EXAMINE THE POSSIBILITIES ON N–36.

$$\boxed{1} + \underline{3}$$
$$+\ \boxed{1} + \underline{3}$$

$$\boxed{2} + \underline{4}$$
$$+\ \boxed{1} + \underline{4}$$

You want to know how many groups of four are in $\underline{3} + \underline{3}$. Hold up three fingers on your left hand and three on your right hand. When you group them visually you see $\boxed{1} + \underline{2}$.

Another way: Hold up three fingers on each hand and count them—

       one two three, one zero, one one, one two

    1,   2,   3, $\boxed{1} + \underline{0}$, $\boxed{1} + \underline{1}$, $\boxed{1} + \underline{2}$

Another way: Counting in groups of four, you can start at $\underline{3}$ and then go $\underline{3}$ more using the fingers on only *one* hand, i.e., $\underline{3}$, $\boxed{1} + \underline{0}$, $\boxed{1} + \underline{1}$, $\boxed{1} + \underline{2}$.

Try the second problem before continuing.

CONTINUE TO N–37.

$$\boxed{2} + \underline{4}$$
$$+\ \boxed{1} + \underline{4}$$

1. Count: $(\boxed{1} + \underline{3})$

      Left Hand   *Right Hand*

   $(\underline{1},$ $2,$ $\underline{3},$ $\underline{4}),$ $(\boxed{1} + \underline{0},$ $\boxed{1} + \underline{1},$ $\boxed{1} + \underline{2},$ $\boxed{1} + \underline{3}$ $)$
one, two, three, four, one zero, one one, one two, one three
(or use your fingers and regroup them visually)

2. Place the sum

3. Add the groups

4. Use the associative property and find the "grand sum," $\boxed{4} + \underline{3}$

CONTINUE TO N–38.

Now look at one in the decimal system:

$$\left.\begin{array}{l} 36 = \circled{3} + \underline{6} \\ +\ 28 \quad \circled{2} + \underline{8} \end{array}\right\} Step\ 1 \qquad \text{Count}$$

$$\underbrace{\circled{5}}_{Step\ 3} + \underbrace{(\circled{1} + \underline{4})}_{Step\ 2} = (\circled{5} + \circled{1}) + \underline{4} \atop = \circled{6} + \underline{4} = 64 \Big\} Step\ 4$$

1. Count: Hold up 8 fingers and start with the six you already have:

      seven, eight, nine, $\circled{1} + \underline{0},$ $\circled{1} + \underline{1},$ $\circled{1} + \underline{2},$
(6), 7,   8,   9,   one zero, one one, one two,
                  $\circled{1} + \underline{3},$ $\circled{1} + \underline{4}.$
                one three, one four

2. Place the sum

3. Add the groups

4. Use the associative property and find the "grand sum"

CONTINUE TO N–39.

N–39

Your turn!

Try this:

$$\boxed{1} + \underline{2}$$
$$+ \boxed{1} + \underline{4}$$

COUNT!

COUNT!   COUNT!

(Be sure *not* to divide or subtract; pretend you don't know how!)

COUNT!

SEE ANSWER FRAME (N–39).

(N–34)

(a) $\boxed{2} + (\boxed{1} + 1) = (\boxed{2} + \boxed{1}) + 1 = \boxed{3} + \underline{1}$

(b) $\boxed{3} + (\boxed{1} + \underline{3}) = (\boxed{3} + \boxed{1}) + 3 = \boxed{4} + \underline{3}$

(c) $\boxed{3} + (\boxed{1} + \underline{4}) = (\boxed{3} + \boxed{1}) + 4 = \boxed{4} + \underline{4}$

(d) $\enclose{circle}{3} + (\enclose{circle}{1} + \underline{6}) = (\enclose{circle}{3} + \enclose{circle}{1}) + 6 = \enclose{circle}{4} + \underline{6}$

How's your counting?

CONTINUE TO N–35.

N–40

Use your objects to count in groups of four up to three three. Count as you place each object.

Groups	Left over		Groups	Left over
	one			1
	two			2
	three			3
one	zero		1	0
one	one		1	1
one	two		1	2
one	three		1	3
two	zero		2	0
	etc.			etc.

List the next four numbers in each of the following sequences:

(a) After one four in groups of six

(b) After two six in groups of eight

(c) After one in groups of three

SEE ANSWER FRAME (N–40).

Count in groups of eight from zero to 4 groups of eight. Your objects will help you if you are unsure. Now write down the sequence as indicated and compare your sequence with the one listed on the second page following.

Groups of eight	*Left over*
•	•
•	•
•	•
1	2
1	3
1	4
•	•
•	•
•	•

SEE ANSWER FRAME (N–41).

Just one more.

Write the sequence from 0 to 4 groups of six.

$$\begin{array}{cc}
 & 1 \\
 & 2 \\
 & 3 \\
 & • \\
 & • \\
 & • \\
1 & 2 \\
1 & 3 \\
 & \text{etc.}
\end{array}$$

Compare your response with the sequence listed on the answer frame.

SEE ANSWER FRAME (N–42).

Remember to *count* when you add. Pretend you don't know about sums in base ten.

$$\boxed{1} + \underline{3}$$
$$\boxed{1} + \underline{4}$$
$$(\boxed{1} + 2)$$

Step 1
Hold up three fingers and four fingers. Count 1, 2, 3, 4, 1 0, 1 1, 1 2.

Step 2
Add the groups.

Step 3
Use the associative property to find the "grand sum."

CONTINUE TO N–44.

(N–39)

$$\boxed{1} + \underline{2}$$
$$+ \boxed{1} + \underline{4}$$
$$\overline{\boxed{2} + (\boxed{1} + \underline{1})}$$
$$(\boxed{2} + \boxed{1}) + \underline{1}$$
$$\boxed{3} + \underline{1}$$

$\underline{1}$ one
$\underline{2}$ two
$\underline{3}$ three   COUNT!
$\underline{4}$ four
$\boxed{1} + \underline{0}$ one zero
$\boxed{1} + \underline{1}$ one one

IF YOU HAD TROUBLE WITH THIS ONE, REVIEW N–12
THROUGH N–19. IF YOU BREEZED THROUGH THIS
ONE, GO TO THE NEXT FRAME, N–40.

N–44

Try this one!

$$\boxed{1} + \underline{3}$$
$$+ \boxed{2} + \underline{5}$$

COUNT!

SEE ANSWER FRAME (N–44).

(N–40)

(a) one five	(b) two seven	(c) two
two zero	three zero	one zero
two one	three one	one one
two two	three two	one two

IF THIS IS PERFECTLY CLEAR, GO TO N–43;
OTHERWISE CARRY ON TO N–41!

Groups of eight	*Left over*

```
                                   1
                                   2
                                   3
                                   4
                                   5
                                   6
                                   7
1------------------------0              Okay?
1                        1         Notice the repetition
1                        2         on the right.
1                        3
1                        4
1                        5
1                        6
1                        7
2------------------------0
```

(cont.)

CONTINUE TO N–42.

```
            0                 2    2
            1                 2    3
            2                 2    4
            3                 2    5
            4                 3    0
            5                 3    1
        1   0                 3    2
        1   1                 3    3
        1   2                 3    4
        1   3                 3    5
        1   4                 4    0
        1   5
        2   0         If you are a little uncertain,
        2   1         do this with your objects.
```

CONTINUE TO N–43.

... and this one:

$$③ + \underline{6}$$
$$+ ① + \underline{7}$$

Notice that you don't have to count 0 through 6. Just hold up seven fingers and count (6), 7, 8, 9, 1 0, 1 1, 1 2, 1 3. (Pretend you don't know that $6 + 7 = 13$.)

SEE ANSWER FRAME (N–45).

N–46

If you can do these, and the ones in the next frame, you graduate with honors on this section. If you are having trouble, better go back to N–29 and review those aspects which are giving you trouble.

(a)   [1] + 1
   + [2] + 2

(b)   (2) + 2
   + [1] + 4

(c)   ⌂1 + 4
   + ⌂1 + 2

COUNT!

SEE ANSWER FRAME (N–46).

(N–44)

⌂1 + 3
[2] + 5
⌂3 + (⌂1 + 2)
(⌂3 + ⌂1) + 2
[4] + 2

IF YOU *COUNT*, AND THESE ARE NOW EASY FOR YOU, GO TO N–48. SOME ADDITIONAL EXPLANATION AND PRACTICE IS GIVEN IN THE NEXT SEQUENCE OF FRAMES. GO TO N–45.

N–47

(a)   △1 + 2
   +   1

(b)   (3) + 4
   + (3) + 9

(c)   ⌂4 + 4
   + ⌂1 + 1

(d)   ⌂1 + 2
   ⌂1 + 5
   + ⌂1 + 5

(e)   ⌂1 + 4
   ⌂1 + 3
   +   4

(f)   ⌂1 + 3
   + [2] + 4

(BE SURE TO COUNT!)

SEE ANSWER FRAME (N–47).

N–48

Now that you have mastered addition, how about trying your hand at subtraction? Try these easy ones first:

(a) $\begin{array}{r} \boxed{3} \\ -\ \boxed{1} \\ \hline \end{array}$ (b) $\begin{array}{r} \underline{6} \\ -\ \underline{2} \\ \hline \end{array}$ (c) $\begin{array}{r} \widehat{\boxed{4}} \\ -\ \widehat{\boxed{3}} \\ \hline \end{array}$ (d) $\begin{array}{r} \textcircled{9} \\ -\ \textcircled{5} \\ \hline \end{array}$

SEE ANSWER FRAME (N–48).

N–49

These are easy, too:

(a) $\textcircled{1} - \underline{4} =$ (e) $\triangle\!\!\!\!1 - \underline{1} =$

(b) $\widehat{\boxed{1}} - \underline{3} =$ (f) $\boxed{1} - \underline{2} =$

(c) $\widehat{\boxed{1}} - \underline{1} =$ (g) $\widehat{\boxed{1}} - \underline{1} =$

(d) $\triangle\!\!\!\!1 - \underline{2} =$

Convince yourself with the objects if you fail to see it readily.

SEE ANSWER FRAME (N–49).

(N–45)

$$\begin{array}{r} \textcircled{3} + \underline{6} \\ + \textcircled{1} + \underline{7} \\ \hline \textcircled{4} + (\textcircled{1} + \underline{3}) \\ (\textcircled{4} + \textcircled{1}) + \underline{3} \\ \textcircled{5} + \underline{3} \end{array} \qquad \begin{array}{r} 36 \\ +17 \\ \hline 53 \end{array}$$

CONTINUE TO N–46.

(N–46)

(a) □3 + 3　　　(b) □3 + (□1 + 1)　　　(c) ⬠2 + (⬠1 + 0)

　　　　　　　　　　　(□3 + □1) + 1　　　　　　　(⬠2 + ⬠1) + 0

　　　　　　　　　　　　　□4 + 1　　　　　　　　　　⬠3 + 0

CONTINUE TO N–47.

N–50

Use your materials to do this one:

$$⬠1 + 5$$
$$-\quad 3$$

Be sure to use the aids; you need the visual and manual reinforcement.

SEE ANSWER FRAME (N–50).

(N–47)

(a) △1 + (△1 + 0)　　(b) ◯6 + (◯1 + 3)　　(c) □5 + 5

　　　(△1 + △1) + 0　　　　　(◯6 + ◯1) + 3

　　　　　△2 + 0　　　　　　　　◯7 + 3

(d) ⬠3 + (⬠2 + 0)　　(e) □2 + (□2 + 1)　　(f) ⬠3 + (⬠1 + 1)

　　　(⬠3 + ⬠2) + 0　　　　(□2 + □2) + 1　　　　(⬠3 + ⬠1) + 1

　　　　　⬠5 + 0　　　　　　　　□4 + 1　　　　　　　⬠4 + 1

CONTINUE TO N–48.

(a) $\boxed{2}$

If you start with 3 groups of four and take away 1 group of four you will have 2 groups of four remaining. Try it with your objects if you are not convinced.

(b) 4

If you had 6 left over and removed two of them, you would have only 4 left over.

(c) ⌂1

(d) ④

$90 - 50 = 40$

CONTINUE TO N–49.

(a) 6   (e) 2
(b) 2   (f) 2
(c) 4   (g) 5
(d) 1

CONTINUE TO N–50.

Now you can do these easily:

(a) $\boxed{4} + 2$
$-(\boxed{1} + 1)$

(b) $③ + 8$
$-(① + 5)$

(c) $\boxed{3} + 2$
$-(\boxed{1} + 1)$

Verify at least one of these with your materials.

> The use of the parenthesis is important because
> $-(\boxed{1} + 1) \neq -\boxed{1} + 1$ since
> $-(6 + 1) \neq -6 + 1$
> $-7 \neq -5$

SEE ANSWER FRAME (N–51).

N–52

Subtract this and do an addition check:

$$\boxed{4} + \underline{3}$$
$$- (\boxed{1} + \underline{2})$$

SEE ANSWER FRAME (N–52).

(N–50)

$$\boxed{1} + \underline{5}$$
$$- \quad \underline{3}$$
$$\boxed{1} + \underline{2}$$

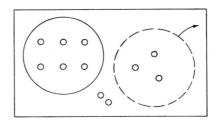

CONTINUE TO N–51.

N–53

Find this difference by

COUNTING:

$$\boxed{1} + \underline{2}$$
$$- \quad \underline{4}$$

Check your results by addition.

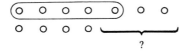

Think of:

$$8$$
$$- 3$$

Start with 3 and put up a finger for each number until you get to 8

4,   5,   6,   7,   8
1 + 1 + 1 + 1 + 1 = 5

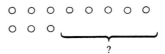

SEE ANSWER FRAME (N–53).

Remember that addition and subtraction are inverse operations, i.e., $9 - 3 = 6$ means that $6 + 3 = 9$.   Hence:

$$\boxed{1} + 2 \qquad \qquad means \quad ? + \underline{4} = \boxed{1} + \underline{2}.$$
$$\underline{ - \qquad 4}$$
$$?$$

An easy way to answer this is to place 4 *red* poker chips before you. Begin placing *blue* poker chips and counting in groups of five. The number of *blue* poker chips necessary to arrive at $\boxed{1} + \underline{2}$ is the result.

CONTINUE TO N–55.

Like this:

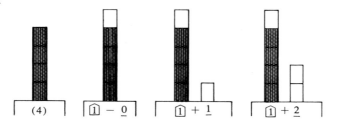

Three additional chips were needed to increase the total from $\underline{4}$ to $\boxed{1} + \underline{2}$.

Thus:
$$\boxed{1} + \underline{2} \qquad and \qquad 3$$
$$\underline{ - \qquad 4} \qquad \qquad \underline{+4}$$
$$3 \qquad \qquad \qquad \widehat{1} + \underline{2}$$

CONTINUE TO N–56.

(a) $\widehat{3} + \underline{1}$
(b) $\textcircled{2} + \underline{3}$
(c) $\boxed{2} + \underline{1}$

Verify at least one of these with objects.

CONTINUE TO N–52.

(N–52)

CONTINUE TO N–53.

N–56

Another example: [1] + 2
                    —   5

Think: I have 5;   then there is [1] + 0 or one zero 1 ⎤
                                       [1] + 1 or one one   1 ⎬ 3
                                       [1] + 2 or one two   1 ⎦

You put up a finger each time and find the difference is 3

CONTINUE TO N–57.

(N–53)

(four), one zero, one one, one two
          1 + 1 + 1 = 3

Check:

              3
            +4   COUNT!
           [1] + 2

IF YOU UNDERSTAND THIS, GO TO N–57;
OTHERWISE, GO TO FRAME N–54.

Try this:

    (a)   1̄ + 1   COUNT!
          −   2   COUNT!

    (b) Check it by addition.   COUNT!

SEE ANSWER FRAME (N–57).

N–58

(a) ① + 2 − 5	(b) 1̂ + 1 − 3	(c) 1̂ + 2 − 5
(d) △̇ + 1 − 2	(e) ① + 1 − 6	(f) 1 + 2 − 3

Check a couple of them.

    COUNT!   COUNT!   COUNT!

SEE ANSWER FRAME (N–58).

N–59

Make this with your objects: 2̄ + 1.

Now take away 4.

You should now have 1̄ + 2.

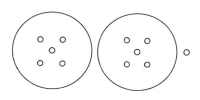

CONTINUE TO N–60.

N–60

When you did the previous problem, you probably followed one of two procedures:

(1) 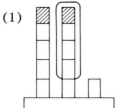   (2)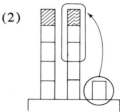

You took the 4   *or*   you took the 1 which was left-over
from one of the   and then took the other three from
groups of five and   a group of five to get a total of 4.
then added the
left-overs,

Use method (1) to find these differences with your objects:

$$\boxed{3} + 2 \\ \underline{-\qquad 4}$$ $$\boxed{3} + 1 \\ \underline{-\qquad 3}$$

SEE ANSWER FRAME (N–60).

N–61

The mathematical steps involved are as follows: $$\boxed{4} + 2 \\ \underline{-\qquad 4}$$

(1) In terms of concrete objects,   (2) 4 from 1 group of five
    you could say, "I can't take   is 1, and 2 more is 3.
    4 from the left-overs because
    there are only 2. Therefore,   (3) There are 3 groups of
    I will take the 4 from one of   five remaining.
    the groups."

$$\boxed{3} + (\boxed{1} + 2) \\ \underline{-\qquad\qquad 4} \\ 1 + 2$$

CONTINUE TO N–62.

N–62

This procedure is based on the associative property which says (a + b) + c = a + (b + c) like this:

Step 1	*Step 2*	*Step 3*
$\boxed{3} + 1$	$(\boxed{2} + \boxed{1}) + 1$	$\boxed{2} + (\boxed{1} + 1)$
$-\qquad 2$	$-\qquad\qquad 2$	$-\qquad\qquad 2$
		$\boxed{2} + (2 + 1)$ *or*
		$\boxed{2} + 3$

CONTINUE TO N–63.

(a) <u>4</u> ◄——— three   If you missed this, do it again but
                 four   use the manipulative materials this
                 one zero   time.
                 one one

(b)   4   If this hasn't cleared up the diffi-
     +2   culty, look at frames N–53 through
   ─────   N–56 again.
   $\boxed{1} + \underline{1}$

CONTINUE TO N–58.

(a) <u>7</u>   If you still have a problem, think about this question
(b) <u>4</u>   for a while: "How could I find 13 − 8 if I couldn't
(c) <u>3</u>   remember my addition and subtraction facts?"

(d) <u>2</u>   Remember how you used to count on your fingers?
(e) <u>5</u>
                    nine   1
(f) <u>3</u>   ten   2
                    eleven   3
                    twelve   4
                    thirteen   5

CONTINUE TO N–59.

Similarly:

$$\boxed{4} + \underline{1} \quad = \quad (\boxed{3} + \boxed{1}) + \underline{1} \quad = \quad \boxed{3} + (\boxed{1} + 1)$$
$$-\quad\underline{4} \qquad\qquad -\qquad\qquad \underline{4} \qquad\qquad -\qquad\qquad\qquad \underline{4}$$
$$\boxed{3} + (2 + \underline{1})$$
$$\boxed{3} + \underline{3}$$

Show these steps with your objects.

CONTINUE TO N–64.

(N–60)

(1) $\widehat{2}$ + 4   (2) $\boxed{2}$ + 2

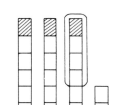   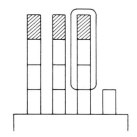

CONTINUE TO N–61.

N–64

Examine the steps in this problem:

$\boxed{4}$ + 1   ($\widehat{3}$ + $\boxed{1}$) + 1 $\boxed{3}$ + ($\boxed{1}$ + 1)
—   4   —   4   —   4

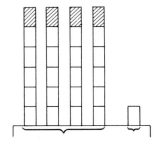   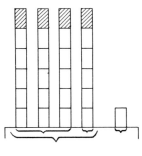   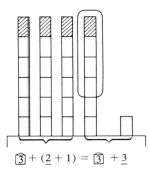

$\boxed{3}$ + (2 + 1) = $\boxed{3}$ + 3

CONTINUE TO N–65.

N–65

Use objects and method (1) as just discussed to work (a). Try to set up the steps for (b) and then check by addition.

(a) $\boxed{3}$ + 2   (b) $\widehat{4}$ + 4
—   4   —   5

SEE ANSWER FRAME (N–65).

Now practice.

Remember to use the associative property and subtract from *one group*.

(a) ② + 3
  −   8

(b) ④ + 1
  −   3

SEE ANSWER FRAME (N–66).

Now the pinnacle!

Example: (Do this with your materials.)

⑤ + 1 = ④ + (① + 1)
−(① + 3)   −(① + 3)
              ③ + (3 + 1)
              ③ + 4

You try this one:

      ④ + 1
  −(① + 3)

Check it!

Now do it with your concrete materials.

SEE ANSWER FRAME (N–67).

Now practice:

(a)   ③ + 1
   −(① + 2)

(b)   ④ + 0
   −(① + 2)

(c)   ⑤ + 4
   −(① + 9)

(d)   ⑤ + 4
   −(③ + 5)

(e)   ④ + 8
   −(① + 6)

(f)   ② + 0
   −(① + 2)

SEE ANSWER FRAME (N–68).

N–69

A real challenge—the mix:

(a)   [1] + 2
    +[1] + 4

(b)   ⟨1⟩ + 1
    +[2] + 4

(c)   (5) + 6
    −((1) + 2)

(d)   [2]
    +[1] + 2

(e)   ⟨1⟩ + 1
    [1] + 4
    +[1] + 5

(f)   ⟨3⟩ + 2
    −([1] + 5)

When in doubt, count or use your materials.

SEE ANSWER FRAME (N–69).

N–70

(a)   (3) + 7
    +(4) + 9

(b)   [2] + 2
    +[1] + 2

(c)   [4] + 2
    −([1] + 4)

(d)   (8) + 3
    −((2) + 0)

(e)   ⟨4⟩ + 2
    −([1] + 3)

SEE ANSWER FRAME (N–70).

(N–65)

(a)   [2] + 3

(b)   [4] + 4   =   ([3] + [1]) + 4   =   [3] + ([1] + 4)
      −   5   −   5   −   5
                                        ⟨3⟩ + (1 + 4)
                                        [3] + 5

Check:
    ⟨3⟩ + 5
  +   5
    ⟨3⟩ + ([1] + 4)
    [4] + 4

CONTINUE TO N–66.

(a) $\bigcirc\!\!\!2 + \dfrac{3}{8}$ $= \dfrac{(\bigcirc\!\!\!1 + \bigcirc\!\!\!1) + 3}{8}$ $= \dfrac{\bigcirc\!\!\!1 + (\bigcirc\!\!\!1 + 3)}{8}$

$\bigcirc\!\!\!1 + (2 + \underline{3}) = \bigcirc\!\!\!1 + \underline{5}$

(b) $\dfrac{\boxed{4} + \underline{1}}{+ \underline{3}}$ $= \dfrac{(\boxed{3} + \boxed{1}) + \underline{1}}{3}$ $= \dfrac{\boxed{3} + (\boxed{1} + \underline{1})}{3}$

$\boxed{3} + (2 + \underline{1}) = \boxed{3} + \underline{3}$

If you are having difficulty, review N–59 through N–66 at this time.

CONTINUE TO N–67.

$$\dfrac{\boxed{4} + \underline{1}}{-(\boxed{1} + \underline{3})} \qquad \dfrac{\boxed{3} + (\boxed{1} + \underline{1})}{-(\boxed{1} + \qquad \underline{3})} \qquad \textit{Check:} \quad \dfrac{\boxed{2} + \underline{3}}{+ \boxed{1} + \underline{3}}$$

$$\boxed{2} + (2 + \underline{1}) \qquad\qquad \boxed{3} + (\boxed{1} + \underline{1})$$
$$\boxed{2} + \underline{3} \qquad\qquad\qquad \boxed{4} + \underline{1}$$

CONTINUE TO N–68.

(a) $\boxed{1} + \underline{3}$ (a) $\dfrac{\boxed{3} + \underline{1}}{-(\boxed{1} + \underline{2})}$ $= \dfrac{\boxed{2} + (\boxed{1} + \underline{1})}{-(\boxed{1} + \underline{2})}$

(b) $\boxed{2} + \underline{3}$

(c) $\bigcirc\!\!\!3 + \underline{5}$ $\boxed{1} + (2 + \underline{1})$

(d) $\widehat{1} + \underline{5}$ $\boxed{1} + \underline{3}$

(e) $\bigcirc\!\!\!3 + \underline{2}$

(f) $\underline{1}$

CONTINUE TO N–69.

(N–69)

(a) $\boxed{3}$ + 1   (d) $\boxed{3}$ + 2

(b) $\widehat{\boxed{3}}$ + 5   (e) $\widehat{\boxed{4}}$ + 4

(c) $\boxed{4}$ + 4   (f) $\widehat{\boxed{1}}$ + 3

IF YOU WANT MORE PRACTICE, GO TO FRAME N–70.
IF YOU FEEL CONFIDENT, GO TO FRAME N–71.

(N–70)

(a) ⑧ + 6   (d) ⑥ + 3

(b) $\boxed{3}$ + 4   (e) $\widehat{\boxed{2}}$ + 5

(c) $\widehat{\boxed{2}}$ + 3

CONTINUE TO N–71.

N–71

You have been utilizing the very important concept of *place value*. Now look at the decimal system to gain additional insights. Notice these parallels:

$$26 = ② + 6 \qquad\qquad 26 = 20 + 6$$
$$+\ 48 = ④ + 8 \qquad\qquad +\ 48 = 40 + 8$$
$$\overline{} \qquad\qquad\qquad \overline{}$$
$$⑥ + (① + 4) \qquad\qquad 60 + 14$$
$$(⑥ + ①) + 4 \qquad\qquad 60 + (10 + 4)$$
$$⑦ + 4 \qquad\qquad (60 + 10) + 4$$
$$74 \qquad\qquad\qquad 70 + 4$$
$$\qquad\qquad\qquad\qquad 74$$

Notice that ① = 10. The special notation helps identify ten as *one group of ten,* ①, rather than ten ones, 10.

CONTINUE TO N–72.

Similarly, in subtraction:

$$82 = ⑧ + 2 = (⑦ + ①) + 2 = ⑦ + (① + 2)$$
$$-45 = -(④ + 5) = -(④ + 5) = -(④ + 5)$$
$$③ + 7 = 37$$

$$82 = 80 + 2 = (70 + 10) + 2 = 70 + (10 + 2) =$$
$$-45 = -(40 + 5) = -(40 + 5) = -(40 + 5) =$$

$$70 + 12$$
$$-(40 + 5)$$
$$\overline{30 + 7}$$
$$37$$

Notice: $① + \underline{0} = ① = 10$

CONTINUE TO N–73.

N–73

Study these counting sequences:

Groups of 10			*Groups of 6*		
1	one	1	1	one	1
2	two	2	2	two	2
3	three	3	3	three	3
4	four	4	4	four	4
5	five	5	5	five	5
6	six	6	$\widehat{1} + \underline{0} =$	one zero	10
7	seven	7	$\widehat{1} + \underline{1}$	one one	11
8	eight	8	$\widehat{1} + \underline{2}$	one two	12
9	nine	9	$\widehat{1} + \underline{3}$	one three	13
$① + \underline{0} =$	one zero	10			
$① + \underline{1}$	one one	11			
$① + \underline{2}$	one two	12			
$① + \underline{3}$	one three	13			

CONTINUE TO N–74.

N–74

Study the previous frame carefully.

1 group of ten is 1 group of ten and none left over

$$① = ① + \underline{0}$$

1 group of six is 1 group of six and none left over

$$\widehat{1} = \widehat{1} + \underline{0}$$

13 in groups of ten is $① + \underline{3}$

13 in groups of six is $\widehat{1} + \underline{3}$

CONTINUE TO N–75.

N–75

Think about this:

How could you do these similarly?

$$
\begin{array}{r}
④ + \underline{5} = ④\,5 \\
+ ② + \underline{8} = ②\,8 \\
\hline
⑦\,3
\end{array}
$$

$$
\begin{array}{r}
☖1 + \underline{4} \\
+ \widehat{3} + \underline{4} \\
\hline
\end{array}
\qquad
\begin{array}{r}
☖1 + \underline{3} \\
+ ☖2 + \underline{4} \\
\hline
\end{array}
$$

COUNT!

SEE ANSWER FRAME (N–75).

N–76

Now,

How would you do this?

$$
\begin{array}{r}
☖1 + \underline{4} = \overset{1}{☖1}\,4 \\
+ \widehat{3} + \underline{3} = \widehat{3}\,3 \\
\hline
\widehat{5}\,1
\end{array}
$$

$$
\begin{array}{r}
☖2 + \underline{3} \\
+ ☖1 + \underline{4} \\
\hline
\end{array}
$$

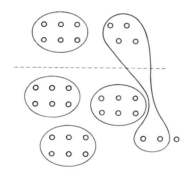

SEE ANSWER FRAME (N–76).

N–77

Try these:

(a)
$$
\begin{array}{r}
☖1\,2 \\
+ \widehat{2}\,3 \\
\hline
\end{array}
$$

(b)
$$
\begin{array}{r}
☖1\,3 \\
+ ☖2\,1 \\
\hline
\end{array}
$$

(c)
$$
\begin{array}{r}
②\,5 \\
+ ④\,6 \\
\hline
\end{array}
$$

(d)
$$
\begin{array}{r}
⑥\,1 \\
+ ②\,3 \\
\hline
\end{array}
$$

(e)
$$
\begin{array}{r}
☐1\,2 \\
+ \quad 3 \\
\hline
\end{array}
$$

(f)
$$
\begin{array}{r}
☖1\,3 \\
4 \\
+ ☖1\,4 \\
\hline
\end{array}
$$

COUNT!

SEE ANSWER FRAME (N–77).

Now another look at subtraction is in order.   Look at groups of 10.

$$
\begin{array}{rcccl}
72 & = & ⑦ + 2 & = & ⑥ + (① + 2) \\
- 25 & = & - (② + 5) & = & - (② + \quad 5) \\
\hline
& & & & ④ \quad + \quad 7 = 47
\end{array}
$$

$$
\begin{array}{rcccl}
72 & = & ⑦\,2 & = & ₆⑦¹2 \\
- 25 & = & - ②\,5 & = & - ②\,5 \\
\hline
& & & & ④\,7 = 47
\end{array}
$$

These are just handy short-cuts. Study them carefully.

CONTINUE TO N–79.

N–79

Now compare groups of 10 with groups of 6.

Look at these groups of 10:

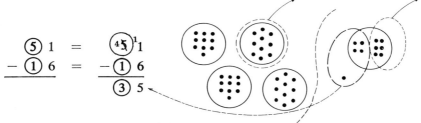

$$
\begin{array}{rcl}
⑤\,1 & = & ₄⑤¹1 \\
- ①\,6 & = & - ①\,6 \\
\hline
& & ③\,5
\end{array}
$$

Can you do this one in groups of 6?

$$
\begin{array}{r}
⑤\,1 = \\
- ②\,4 = \\
\hline
\end{array}
$$

SEE ANSWER FRAME (N–79).

N–80

Look at this one the long and short ways. Then try the second problem both ways. *Example:*

Expanded or
Long Form:

$$
\begin{array}{rcccl}
④\,1 & = & ④ + 1 & = & ③ + (① + 1) \\
- ①\,3 & = & - (① + 3) & = & - (① + \quad 3) \\
\hline
& & & & ② + 3 \;=\; ②\,3
\end{array}
$$

Traditional or
Short Form:

$$
\begin{array}{rcl}
④\,1 & = & ⍣\,1 \\
- ①\,3 & = & - ①\,3 \\
\hline
& & ②\,3
\end{array}
$$

Try this:

$$
\begin{array}{r}
③\,1 \\
- ①\,2 \\
\hline
\end{array}
$$

SEE ANSWER FRAME (N–80).

(N–75)

$$\begin{array}{r} \boxed{1}\,{}^{1}4 \\ \boxed{3}\;4 \\ \hline \boxed{5}\;2 \end{array} \qquad \begin{array}{r} \boxed{1}\,{}^{1}3 \\ \boxed{2}\;4 \\ \hline \boxed{4}\;2 \end{array}$$

CONTINUE TO N–76.

(N–76)

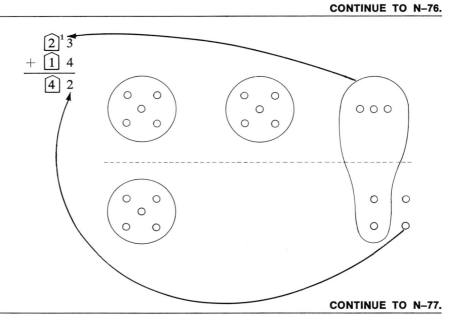

$$\begin{array}{r} \boxed{2}\,{}^{1}3 \\ +\;\boxed{1}\;4 \\ \hline \boxed{4}\;2 \end{array}$$

CONTINUE TO N–77.

(N–77)

(a) $\boxed{3}$ 5

(b) $\boxed{3}$ 4

(c) $\boxed{7}$ 1

(d) $\boxed{8}$ 4

(e) $\boxed{2}$ 1

(f) $\boxed{4}$ 1

IF YOU ARE HAVING DIFFICULTY,
REVIEW N–71 THROUGH N–76.
CONTINUE TO N–78.

By now you should have a pretty good grasp of this shorter algorithm. If you have trouble with these three, review N–78 through N–80.

(a) ⑤ 2
  − ③̂ 5

(b) △̂ 1
  − △̂ 2

(c) ⑧ 2
  − ④ 9

SEE ANSWER FRAME (N–81).

⑤ 1 = ④̂³ 1¹
− ②̂ 4 = − ②̂ 4
_____
       ②̂ 3

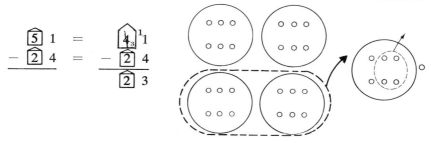

Just as:

⑤ + 1   =   ④ + (① + 1)
− (②̂ + 4) = − (②̂ +   4)
_____
            ②̂ +   3

CONTINUE TO N–80.

Long   3 1 =   3 + 1 = 2 + (1 + 1)
      − 1 2 = − (1 + 2) = − (1 +   2)
_____
                          1 + 3
                          1 3

Short   3 1 =   3̷₂¹ 1
       − 1 2 = − 1 2
_____
                1 3

CONTINUE TO N–81.

N–82

Scramble the addition and subtraction; find these sums and differences:

(a) ② 5
    + ③ 7

(b) ④ 1
    − ① 2

(c) ④ 3
    − ① 1

(d) ① 2
    + ① 1

(e) ⑧ 2
    − ④ 5

(f) ④ 1
    − ① 3

SEE ANSWER FRAME (N–82).

N–83

Now return to the characteristics of the Hindu-Arabic system.

(a) It uses ten symbols (digits):

0, 1, 2, 3, 4, 5, 6, 7, 8, 9

(b) Numbers are expressed in powers of ten:

Ones $= 10^0 =$ left-overs
Tens $= 10^1 =$ groups of ten
Hundreds $= 10^2 =$ ten groups of ten

(c) The system is additive:

$462 = 400 + 60 + 2$
$= $ (4 groups of ten groups of ten) $+$ (6 groups of 10) $+$ 2 left over

(d) It has place value:

46 means 4 groups of ten and 6 left over but 64 means 6 groups of ten and 4 left over. Also, 6 means six left over but 60 means 6 groups of ten.

CONTINUE TO N–84.

N–84

Look at N–83 and see if you can make some corresponding statements about groups of six.

SEE ANSWER FRAME (N–84).

(a) ⬠1⬠ 3   (b) 2   (c) ③ 3

CONTINUE TO N–82.

Let's return to counting:

		Groups of three	*Verbally*
	1	•	one
	2	• •	two
△1	0	(• • •)	one zero
△1	1	(• • •) •	one one
△1	2	(• • •) • •	one two
△2	0	(• • •)(• • •)	two zero
△2	1	(• • •)(• • •) •	two one
△2	2	(• • •)(• • •) • •	two two
△1 △0	0	(• • •)(• • •)(• • •)	one zero zero

(Groups   (Groups)
 of groups)

CONTINUE TO N–86.

		Groups of four
	1	x
	2	x x
	3	x x x
☐1	0	(x x x x)
☐1	1	(x x x x) x
☐1	2	(x x x x) x x
☐1	3	(x x x x) x x x
☐2	0	(x x x x)(x x x x)
☐2	1	(x x x x)(x x x x) x
☐2	2	(x x x x)(x x x x) x x
☐2	3	(x x x x)(x x x x) x x x
☐3	0	(x x x x)(x x x x)(x x x x)
☐3	1	(x x x x)(x x x x)(x x x x) x
☐3	2	(x x x x)(x x x x)(x x x x) x x
☐3	3	(x x x x)(x x x x)(x x x x) x x x
☐1 ☐0	0	(x x x x)(x x x x)(x x x x)(x x x x)

(Groups   (Groups)
 of groups)

CONTINUE TO N–87.

(N–82)

(a) ⑥2   (d) [2] 3

(b) [2̂] 5   (e) ③7

(c) [3] 2   (f) [2̂] 3

CONTINUE TO N–83.

N–87

Study the following. Supply information where needed.

Group Size	Counting Sequence	Place Value		
		Groups of Groups	Groups	Left-overs
10	1, 2, 3, 4, 5, 6, 7, 8, 9, 1 0, 1 1, . . .	100s 10^2	10s 10^1	1s 10^0
6	1, 2, 3, 4, 5, 1 0, 1 1, 1 2, . . .	36s 6^2	(b) 6^1	1s 6^0
4	(a)	(d) (e)	(c) 4^1	1s 4^0
3	1, 2, 1 0, 1 1, 1 2, 2 0, . . .	(j) (k)	(h) (i)	(f) (g)

SEE ANSWER FRAME (N–87).

(N–84)

(a) It uses six symbols (digits):

  0, 1, 2, 3, 4, 5

(b) Numbers are expressed in powers of six:

  Ones $= 6^0 =$ left-overs
  Sixes $= 6^1 =$ groups of six
  Thirty-sixes $= 6^2 =$ six groups of six

(c) The system is additive

(d) It has place value

CONTINUE TO N–85.

In the Hindu-Arabic system, the numeral 467 means:

4 groups of (ten groups of ten)	$4 \times 100 = 4 \times (10 \times 10)$
6 groups of ten	$6 \times 10 = 6 \times 10^1$
7 left over	$7 \times 1 = 7 \times 10^0$

In an 8 grouping system, the numeral 467 means:

4 groups of (eight groups of eight)
6 groups of eight
7 left over

Each system has:

ones (left over)
groups
groups of groups

CONTINUE TO N–89.

New notation:

$\textcircled{1} = 10_{10}$

$\boxed{1}\,\widehat{} = 10_6$

$\boxed{1} = 10_5$

$\boxed{1} = 10_4$

$\triangle = 10_3$

Examples:

$\widehat{1}\ 4 = 14_6 = 10_6 + 4_6$

$\boxed{2}\ 3 = 23_5 = 20_5 + 3_5$

$\boxed{3}\ 1 = 31_4 = 30_4 + 1_4$

$\triangle\!\!1\ 2 = 12_3 = 10_3 + 2_3$

$\textcircled{4}\ 7 = 47_{10} = 40_{10} + 7_{10}$

CONTINUE TO N–90.

When you want to add:

$$\begin{array}{r} \boxed{2}\ 4 \quad = \quad {}^12\ 4_5 \\ + \boxed{1}\ 3 \quad = \quad 1\ 3_5 \\ \hline 4\ 2_5 \end{array}$$

Or subtract:

$$\begin{array}{r} \widehat{4}\ 1 \quad = \quad {}^3\!\!\not{4}\,{}^11_6 \\ - \widehat{1}\ 3 \quad = \quad -1\ 3_6 \\ \hline 2\ 4_6 \end{array}$$

COUNT! *Add this one with both notational forms*

$$\begin{array}{r} \widehat{3}\ 4 \qquad 3\ 4_6 \\ + \widehat{1}\ 4 \qquad +1\ 4_6 \\ \hline \end{array}$$

Subtract this one with both notational forms

$$\begin{array}{r} \boxed{4}\ 1 \qquad 4\ 1_5 \\ - \boxed{1}\ 3 \qquad -1\ 3_5 \\ \hline \end{array}$$

Use expanded notation and the associative property.

SEE ANSWER FRAME (N–90).

N–91

Solve these with expanded notation. You may omit the associative steps.

(a) 27_{10}
      $+16_{10}$

(b) 13_6
      $+24_6$

(c) 21_5
      $+13_5$

(d) 84_{10}
      -39_{10}

(e) 52_6
      -31_6

(f) 42_5
      -14_5

Check your results with concrete materials. For convenience, you may omit the subscripts in intermediate steps.

SEE ANSWER FRAME (N–91).

(N–87)

(a) 1, 2, 3, 10

(b) 6s

(c) 4s

(d) 16s

(e) 4^2

(f) 1s

(g) 3^0

(h) 3s

(i) 3^1

(j) 9s

(k) 3^2

CONTINUE TO N–88.

N–92

Solve these in standard algorithmic form.

Example   *Example*

$\overset{1}{3}7$
$+45$
$\overline{82}$

$\overset{1}{1}4_6$
$+24_6$
$\overline{42_6}$

12_3
$+\ 2_3$

13_4
$+13_4$

34_5
$+\ 3_5$

15_6
$+23_6$

42_6
-14_6

31_4
-13_4

SEE ANSWER FRAME (N–92).

(a) $\quad$ 27 = 20 + 7
$\underline{+16 = 10 + 6}$
 30 + 13
optional $\left\{ \begin{array}{l} 30 + (10 + 3) \\ (30 + 10) + 3 \end{array} \right.$
 40 $\;+\;$ 3
 43

(b) 13_6 = 10 + 3
$\underline{24_6 = 20 + 4}$
 30 + 11
 40 + 1
 41_6

(c) $\quad 21_5$ = 20 + 1
$\underline{+13_5 = 10 + 3}$
 30 + 4
 34_5

(d) $\quad 84_{10}$ = 80 + 4 = 70 + (10 + 4) = (70 + 10) + 4 = 70 + 14
$\underline{-39_{10}}$ 30 + 9 optional 30 + 9
$\phantom{-39_{10} = 80 + 4 = 70 + (10 + 4) = (70 + 10) + 4 =}$ 40 + 5
$\phantom{-39_{10} = 80 + 4 = 70 + (10 + 4) = (70 + 10) + 4 =}$ 45

(e) $\quad 52_6$ = 50 + 2
$\underline{-31_6 = 30 + 1}$
 20 + 1
 21_6

(f) $\quad 42_5$ = 40 + 2 = 30 + 12
$\underline{-14_5 = 10 + 4 = 10 + 4}$
 20 + 3
 23_5

CONTINUE TO N–92.

12_3	13_4	34_5	15_6	42_6	31_4
$+ \; 2_3$	$+13_4$	$+ \; 3_5$	$+23_6$	-14_6	-13_4
21_3	32_4	42_5	42_6	24_6	12_4

THE END.

$\boxed{3}\,4 = \boxed{3} + 4$
$\underline{+\boxed{1}\,4 = \boxed{1} + 4}$
$\phantom{+\boxed{1}\,4 =}$ $\boxed{4} + (\boxed{1} + 2)$
$\phantom{+\boxed{1}\,4 =}$ $(\boxed{4} + \boxed{1}) + 2$
$\phantom{+\boxed{1}\,4 =}$ $\boxed{5} + 2$
$\phantom{+\boxed{1}\,4 =}$ $\boxed{5}\,2$

$34_6 = 30_6 + 4_6$
$\underline{+14_6 = 10_6 + 4_6}$
 $40_6 + 12_6$
 $40_6 + (10_6 + 2_6)$
 $(40_6 + 10_6) + 2_6$
 $50_6 \;+\; 2_6$
 52_6

$\boxed{4}\,1 = \boxed{4} + 1 = (\boxed{3} + \boxed{1}) + 1 = \boxed{3} + (\boxed{1} + 1)$
$\underline{-\boxed{1}\,3}$ $\boxed{1} + 3$ $\boxed{1}$ $\phantom{+ \boxed{1}) +}$ + 3 $\boxed{1} \;+\; 3$
$\phantom{\boxed{4}\,1 = \boxed{4} + 1 = (\boxed{3} + \boxed{1}) + 1 = }$ $\boxed{2} \;+\; 3$
$\phantom{\boxed{4}\,1 = \boxed{4} + 1 = (\boxed{3} + \boxed{1}) + 1 = }$ $\boxed{2}\,3$

$41_5 = 40_5 + 1_5 = (30_5 + 10_5) + 1_5 = 30_5 + (10_5 + 1_5) = 30_5 + 11_5$
$\underline{-13_5}$ $10_5 + 3_5$ 10_5 $+ 3_5$ $10_5 +$ 3_5 $10_5 + 3_5$
 $20_5 + 3_5$
 23_5

CONTINUE TO N–91.

Numerations Self-Test

1. List three characteristics of the decimal numerations system.

2. Which of the three systems, Egyptian, Roman and Decimal, are always additive?

3. Which of the following sequences are correct?

    A. 4, 5, 6, 7, 10, 11 in groups of 7
    B. 1, 2, 3, 10, 11, 12 in groups of 3
    C. 12, 13, 14, 15, 16 in groups of 12
    D. 1, 2, 3, 10, 11, 12 in groups of 4

4. Use the renaming and the associative property to find this sum: $36 + 2$.

5. Find the sums and differences in traditional notation and in the special notation presented in this chapter.

$$13_6$$
$$+24_6$$

$$82_{10}$$
$$-37_{10}$$

Answers to Numerations Self-Test

1. It is additive.
   It has ten digits (symbols).
   It has place value.

2. Egyptian, Decimal

3. C and D

4. $36 + 2 = (30 + 6) + 2 = 30 + (6 + 2) = 30 + 8 = 38$

5.

$$
\begin{array}{r}
13_6 \\
+24_6 \\
\hline
\end{array}
\quad = \quad
\begin{array}{r}
10_6 + 3_6 \\
20_6 + 4_6 \\
\hline
30_6 + 11_6 \\
41_6
\end{array}
$$

$$
\begin{array}{r}
\boxed{1}\,3 \\
+\,\boxed{2}\,4 \\
\hline
\end{array}
\quad = \quad
\begin{array}{r}
\boxed{1} + 3 \\
\boxed{2} + 4 \\
\hline
\boxed{3} + \boxed{1}\,1 \\
\boxed{4}\,1
\end{array}
$$

$$
\begin{array}{r}
82 \\
-37 \\
\hline
\end{array}
\quad = \quad
\begin{array}{r}
80 + 2 \\
30 + 7 \\
\hline
\end{array}
\quad = \quad
\begin{array}{r}
70 + 12 \\
30 + 7 \\
\hline
40 + 5 \\
45
\end{array}
$$

$$
\begin{array}{r}
\textcircled{8}\,2 \\
-\textcircled{3}\,7 \\
\hline
\end{array}
\quad = \quad
\begin{array}{r}
\textcircled{8} + 2 \\
\textcircled{3} + 7 \\
\hline
\end{array}
\quad = \quad
\begin{array}{r}
\textcircled{7} + \textcircled{1}\,2 \\
\textcircled{3} + 7 \\
\hline
\textcircled{4} + 5 \\
\textcircled{4}\,5
\end{array}
$$

Summary

Number bases are elegant grouping systems. Our system, the decimal numeration system, uses groups of ten. Computers use groups of two, and other systems can be seen in the environment; for example, adding feet and yards is similar to base three, and adding quarts and gallons is similar to base four.

Helping children work with concrete objects and pictures in groups of three, four, five and six *before* working with groups of ten will probably facilitate mastery of place value concepts. They will perceive groups of ten as another example of "ways in which things can be grouped." In this way, they can extract a structural generalization about grouping systems rather than operating in base ten by rote.

A numeral describes groups:

> 13 in groups of ten is 1 ten and 3 ones
> 13 in groups of four is 1 four and 3 ones
> 13 in groups of seventy-five is 1 seventy-five and 3 ones
> The first place on the right is always ones (left-overs).
> The second place always tells how many groups.
> The third place always tells how many groups-of-groups.

Groups of ten	*Groups of four*
ten ones $=$ 10	four ones $=$ 10
ten groups of ten $=$ 100	four groups of four $=$ 100
ten groups of	four groups of
(ten groups of ten) $=$ 1000	(four groups of four) $=$ 1000

10

Teaching Addition and Subtraction Algorithms

After children understand developmental concepts of addition and subtraction, computational procedures are developed which allow them to calculate sums and differences of numbers, the size of which make counting an inefficient and impractical way to determine results. Computational procedures are called *algorithms*. In this chapter you will learn how to teach children to use addition and subtraction algorithms *with meaning*.

This chapter is divided into three sections:

Content and Specific Methodology
General Methods and Specific Materials of Instruction
Accommodation of Individual Differences

In section one you will be presented with behavioral objectives and auto-tutorial materials for attaining them. Section one concludes with a self-test to help you determine the extent to which you have attained the desired behaviors.

Section two relates addition and subtraction algorithms more specifically to the general treatments in this text on discovery learning and materials of instruction.

Section three explores more specifically the relations between various algorithms and the individualization model. Ideas related to objectives, readiness, diagnosis, slow and fast learners, evaluation, and psychology are discussed.

Content and Specific Methodology

After you have read the following list of behavioral objectives, you may wish to take Part I of the self-test at the end of this section. If you perform satisfactorily you may wish to skim the addition section quickly or to omit it. Then proceed to Part II on subtraction algorithms and follow a similar pattern.

Algorithms for Addition

Objectives

When you have completed this unit, you will be able to
> (1) Describe and illustrate the development of the standard algorithm for addition of whole numbers by the following sequence:
>> A. Horizontal—expanded notation
>> B. Vertical—expanded notation
>> C. Vertical—partial sums
>> D. Standard algorithm
> (2) Demonstrate the steps in each of the *four algorithms* with concrete materials.
> (3) Find sums by writing *all steps* (standard form) in all *four algorithms* with
>> A. A two-digit and a one-digit numeral* with and without regrouping
>> B. Two two-digit numerals* with and without regrouping

Instructional Aids

Get a piece of paper. Cut it into strips about $\frac{3}{4}$-inch in width. Cut three of the strips into ten small squares. Graph paper works especially well. Mark off each strip into ten sections of equal size.

1 ten   1 one

Assumptions

> A. Children know all addition facts through $9 + 9 = 18$.

---

* You cannot add *numerals,* but *numbers* do not have digits, either. You add numbers whose numerals have two and one digits. To avoid wordiness, only *numeral* is used in these statements. You could say "numbers between 0 and 10 or between 9 and 100."

B. Place value has been taught through sets as it was developed in other numerations.

C. Children think of 18 as one set of ten and eight.

D. Children can use renaming and the associative property as follows:

$$9 + 9 = 9 + (1 + 8)$$
$$= (9 + 1) + 8$$
$$= 10 + 8$$
$$= 18$$

E. Children can think flexibly of number names.

F. Children can add tens.

The approach utilized in the development of the standard algorithm for addition of whole numbers will follow this sequence:

A. Sums of two-digit numerals and one-digit numerals *without* regrouping ones to tens, e.g., $14 + 3 = 17$

B. Sums of two-digit numerals and one-digit numerals *with* regrouping of ones to tens, e.g., $17 + 6 = 23$

C. Sums of two two-digit numerals *without* regrouping ones to tens, e.g., $23 + 44 = 67$

D. Sums of two two-digit numerals *with* regrouping of ones to tens, e.g., $27 + 39 = 66$

The four algorithms or slight variations of them are used in most current text series. Familiarity with them will enhance your grasp of the continuity of the sequence in developing pupil understanding. If you use a discovery mode in your instruction, these four algorithms or variations of them will commonly be discovered by children. Knowledge of these four should increase your ability to identify correct pupil-created algorithms which may differ only slightly from these.

Answer all questions in the following section on a piece of paper and compare them with responses listed on the second page following. Pages are divided into three sections. If the question is in the middle section, the answer is two pages later in the middle section.

A. *Sums of two-digit numerals and one-digit numerals without regrouping of tens.*

The *associative property of addition* and *expanded notation* will be needed.

1. *Associative Property:* $2 + (3 + 4) = (2 + 3) + 4$

$$2 + \quad 7 \quad = \quad 5 \quad + 4$$
$$9 \quad = \quad 9$$

The associative property allows one to regroup.

2. *Expanded Notation:* Sets of ten and ones

$$27 = 20 + 7 = \textcircled{2} + 7$$

Example:		
	$23 + 6$	Problem
	$(20 + 3) + 6$	Expanded Notation
	$20 + (3 + 6)$	Associative Property
	$20 + 9$	Add or Rename
	29	Add or Rename

This problem was written *horizontally* and *expanded notation* was used.

CONTINUE TO FRAME A–2.

Another example in horizontal-expanded notation:

$42 + 5$	Problem
$(40 + 2) + 5$	Expanded Notation
$40 + (2 + 5)$	Associative Property
$40 + 7$	Add or Rename
47	Add or Rename

> Notice that only
> *one change* is made
> in each step.

You try these: (a) $14 + 3$ (b) $81 + 6$

COMPARE YOUR RESPONSES WITH THOSE LISTED IN ANSWER FRAME (A–2).

Problem: $42 + 5$

From your unit on numerations, you know you could easily say (42), 43, 44, 45, 46, 47, and get the answer by counting. However, you are now trying to build skills helpful in attacking problems in which number magnitude or size make counting unreasonable. Examine what happens when you add $42 + 5$.

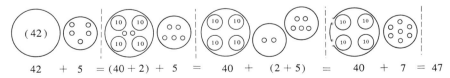

$$42 \quad + \ 5 \quad = (40 + 2) + \ 5 \quad = \quad 40 \ + \quad (2 + 5) \quad = \quad 40 \ + \ 7 = 47$$

Show with the paper strips what happens when you add $32 + 6$. Compare your analysis with the diagrams on the second page following. Use a *strip for one ten* and a *small square for each one.*

SEE ANSWER FRAME (A–3).

A–4

B. *Sums of two digit numerals and one digit numerals* with *regrouping of tens.* Notice that the first four steps are the same.

34 + 9	Problem
(30 + 4) + 9	Expanded Notation
30 + (4 + 9)	Associative Property
30 + 13	Add or Rename

―――――――――――――――――A child doesn't know that 30 + 13 = 43

30 + (10 + 3)	Expanded Notation	Notice the transition from 10 ones to 1 ten.
(30 + 10) + 3	Associative Property	
40 + 3	Add or Rename	Notice that expanded nota-
43	Add or Rename	tion and the associative prop-erty were used *twice*.

You try this one: 86 + 7. Write the steps and use your strips to show each step.

SEE ANSWER FRAME (A–4).

A–5

Try a couple more: (a) 14 + 7   (b) 26 + 4

Use the paper strips to show what happens in each step. Be sure to include *all* steps. Remember, there must be *one* reason which explains why each step is "legal." Compare your results with the steps on the answer page. They should agree.

SEE ANSWER FRAME (A–5).

A–6

C. *Sums of two digit numerals and two digit numerals* without *regrouping tens.*

This time you must utilize the commutative property of addition, e.g., 3 + 4 = 4 + 3. It allows you to reverse the order of sums. Study this carefully:

23 + 31	Problem	
(20 + 3) + 31	Expanded Notation	
20 + (3 + 31)	Associative Property	
*20 + (31 + 3)	*Commutative Property	An additional set
(20 + 31) + 3	Associative Property	of brackets is in-

[20 + (30 + 1)] + 3	Expanded Notation	troduced here for
[(20 + 30) + 1] + 3	Associative Property	clarity.
(50 + 1) + 3	Add or Rename	
50 + (1 + 3)	Associative Property	
50 + 4	Add or Rename	
54	Add or Rename	

> You might note that such problems have *many* possible routes. The main criterion is that only *one* change can be made in each step.

CONTINUE TO FRAME A–7.

A–7

That was long! However, the steps were precise and well-defined. Elementary school students will not do that. For *you,* especially, this process is important to master. In such a "simple" problem as 23 + 31, you can gain some insights into the *degree of sophistication* required to work such problems with *understanding.* Certainly, answers can be found without understanding process because you do it frequently. However, such process is esthetically pleasing and is important in helping children understand the structure of mathematics. Return to A–6 and try this: 46 + 23.

SEE ANSWER FRAME (A–7).

(A–2)

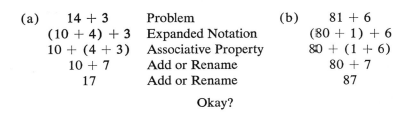

(a)	14 + 3	Problem	(b)	81 + 6
	(10 + 4) + 3	Expanded Notation		(80 + 1) + 6
	10 + (4 + 3)	Associative Property		80 + (1 + 6)
	10 + 7	Add or Rename		80 + 7
	17	Add or Rename		87

Okay?

CONTINUE TO FRAME A–3.

(A–3)

32 + 6 = (30 + 2) + 6 = 30 + (2 + 6) = 30 + 8 = 38

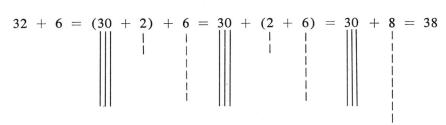

(Each long line represents a 10-strip and each short line represents a one-square.)

CONTINUE TO FRAME A–4.

This is another semi-concrete form for working with tens and ones.

10 = 1 ten-strip
o = 1 one square

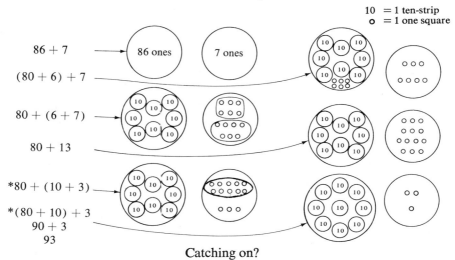

86 + 7

(80 + 6) + 7

80 + (6 + 7)

80 + 13

*80 + (10 + 3)

*(80 + 10) + 3
90 + 3
93

Catching on?

* Transition. Trade 10 squares for 1 strip.

CONTINUE TO A–5.

(a)			(b)	
	14 + 7	Problem		26 + 4
	(10 + 4) + 7	Expanded Notation		(20 + 6) + 4
	10 + (4 + 7)	Associative Property		20 + (6 + 4)
	10 + 11	Add or Rename		20 + 10
	*10 + (10 + 1)	Expanded Notation		30
	*(10 + 10) + 1	Associative Property		
	20 + 1	Add or Rename		
	21	Add or Rename		

* Transition. Trade 10 squares for 1 strip. This embodies the critical transition from 10 as ten ones to 10 as one ten.

CONTINUE TO A–6.

The structure of mathematics in general and the Hindu-Arabic numeration system in particular makes such solutions possible.

    The four main ideas utilized were:

1. Place value
2. Additive property (expanded notation)
3. Associativity: $(30 + 4) + 8 = 30 + (4 + 8)$
4. Commutativity: $30 + (4 + 20) = 30 + (20 + 4)$
          or $4 + 20 \ = 20 + 4$

Can you do this one without looking at the steps? 74 + 13. Show each step with the paper strips. Keep the 74 and the 13 separated visually so that *movement* occurs when parentheses are used.

SEE ANSWER FRAME (A–8).

(A–7)

	Another way	*Another way*
46 + 23	46 + 23	46 + 23
(40 + 6) + 23	(40 + 6) + 23	46 + (20 + 3)
40 + (6 + 23)	40 + (6 + 23)	(46 + 20) + 3
40 + (23 + 6)	40 + (23 + 6)	[(40 + 6) + 20] + 3
(40 + 23) + 6	40 + [(20 + 3) + 6]	[(6 + 40) + 20] + 3
[40 + (20 + 3)] + 6	40 + [20 + (3 + 6)]	[6 + (40 + 20)] + 3
[(40 + 20) + 3] + 6	40 + (20 + 9)	(6 + 60) + 3
(60 + 3) + 6	(40 + 20) + 9	(60 + 6) + 3
60 + (3 + 6)	60 + 9	60 + (6 + 3)
60 + 9	69	60 + 9
69		69

Okay?

CONTINUE TO A–8.

A–9

Maybe the parentheses and brackets are confusing you. Just remember that they are used to *help* you.

Hence: 3 + [4 + 5] = 3 + (4 + 5)

In proceeding from (70 + 13) + 4 to [70 + (10 + 3)] + 4, you do so to help remember that 70 + 13 was still being grouped together but with a different name, 10 + 3. It would have been more confusing to put (70 + 13) + 4 = (70 + (10 + 3)) + 4.

Try one more: 23 + 64

SEE ANSWER FRAME (A–9).

A–10

D. Sums of two two-digit numerals with regrouping of tens.
This is like the previous sequence in the first ten steps.

1.	25 + 38	8.	(50 + 8) + 5
2.	(20 + 5) + 38	9.	50 + (8 + 5)
3.	20 + (5 + 38)	10.	50 + 13
4.	20 + (38 + 5)		- - - - - - - - - - - - - Here it changes
5.	(20 + 38) + 5	11.	50 + (10 + 3)
6.	[20 + (30 + 8)] + 5	12.	(50 + 10) + 3
7.	[(20 + 30) + 8] + 5	13.	60 + 3
		14.	63

Use the paper strips to see if you can tell what happened in each step.

CONTINUE TO A–11.

Try this one: $42 + 39$

Refer to frame A–10 for help.

SEE ANSWER FRAME (A–11).

Here is one done a different way:

$$46 + 27$$
$$46 + (20 + 7)$$
$$(46 + 20) + 7$$
$$[(40 + 6) + 20] + 7$$
$$[(6 + 40) + 20] + 7$$
$$[6 + (40 + 20)] + 7$$
$$(6 + 60) + 7$$
$$(60 + 6) + 7$$
$$60 + (6 + 7)$$
$$60 + 13$$
$$60 + (10 + 3)$$
$$(60 + 10) + 3$$
$$70 + 3$$
$$73$$

The number of steps is not important. The important point is that only *one* property or operation is done in each step. There are many ways to get the answer and the number of steps will vary considerably depending on the route taken in the solution.

CONTINUE TO A–13.

IF YOU GOT MIXED UP, CONTINUE TO A–9. OTHERWISE, GO ON TO A–10.

A–13

How can you help children understand without overwhelming them? The horizontal-expanded notation has been presented for each of the four cases. Other algorithms can also be used. Vertical forms are helpful.

A. Sums of two-digit numerals and one-digit numerals without regrouping of tens.

Horizontal	Vertical-Expanded Notation		Vertical
			Partial Sums
$16 + 3$	$16 \quad = \quad 10 + 6$		
$(10 + 6) + 3$	$\underline{+ \quad 3 \quad = \qquad 3}$		16
$10 + (6 + 3)$	$10 + 9$		$\underline{+ \quad 3}$
$10 + 9$	19	9 ones and $\Big\{$	9
19		1 ten which $\Big\{$	$\underline{10}$
		is 19 $\longrightarrow$	19

CONTINUE TO A–14.

(A–9)

There are several ways to work this problem. This is one such way:

$23 + 64$	Problem
$(20 + 3) + 64$	Expanded Notation
$20 + (3 + 64)$	Associative Property
$20 + (64 + 3)$	Commutative Property
$(20 + 64) + 3$	Associative Property
$[20 + (60 + 4)] + 3$	Expanded Notation
$[(20 + 60) + 4] + 3$	Associative Property
$(80 + 4) + 3$	Add or Rename
$80 + (4 + 3)$	Associative Property
$80 + 7$	Add or Rename
87	Add or Rename

Notice again that only *one* change occurred in each step.

CONTINUE TO A–10.

A–14

Try these in expanded notation horizontally and vertically and in partial sums (vertical).

     (a) $34 + 5$

     (b) $91 + 7$

SEE ANSWER FRAME (A–14).

$42 + 39$	Problem	$(70 + 9) + 2$	Add or Rename
$(40 + 2) + 39$	Exp. Notation	$70 + (9 + 2)$	Assoc. Prop.
$40 + (2 + 39)$	Assoc. Prop.	$70 + 11$	Add or Rename
$40 + (39 + 2)$	Comm. Prop.	$70 + (10 + 1)$	Exp. Notation
$(40 + 39) + 2$	Assoc. Prop.	$(70 + 10) + 1$	Assoc. Prop.
$[40 + (30 + 9)] + 2$	Exp. Notation	$80 + 1$	Add or Rename
$[(40 + 30) + 9] + 2$	Assoc. Prop.	81	Add or Rename

CONTINUE TO A–12.

A–15

B. *Sums of two-digit numerals and one-digit numerals with regrouping of tens.*

Horizontal-Expanded Notation

Standard Form		Shortened Form	
$36 + 7$	-----------	$36 + 7$	
$(30 + 6) + 7$	-----------	$(30 + 6) + 7$	
$30 + (6 + 7)$	-----------	$30 + (6 + 7)$	Important here
$30 + 13$	-----------	$30 + 13$	to emphasize
$30 + (10 + 3)$	-----------	$30 + 10 + 3$	this property.
$(30 + 10) + 3$	-----------		
$40 + 3$	-----------	$40 + 3$	
43	-----------	43	

Don't bother to memorize which step is omitted. It varies from text series to text series. The *shortened form* is included here to show you that children do not usually do all the steps of the standard *form;* some are done mentally.

CONTINUE TO A–16.

A–16

Vertical forms of B, two-digit and one-digit **with** *regrouping.*

	Expanded	*Partial Sums*	One should say:
$36 =$	$30 + 6$	36	"$6 + 7 = 13$"
$+\ 7$	7	$+\ 7$	"3 tens + 0 tens = 3 tens"
	$\overline{30 + 13}$	$\overline{13}$	"$3 + 0 = 3$"
	$30 + (10 + 3)$	30	"1 ten + 3 tens = 4 tens"
	$(30 + 10) + 3$	$\overline{43}$	
	$40 + 3$		
	43		

These statements reinforce *basic facts.* Children are not required to remember $10 + 30 = 40$ translated as "Ten plus thirty equals forty." Try this all three ways: Horizontal and two Vertical— $47 + 8$

SEE ANSWER FRAME (A–16).

A–17

C. *Sums of two two-digit numerals* without *regrouping tens.*

Standard Form	*Shortened Form*
23 + 41	23 + 41
(20 + 3) + 41	(20 + 3) + (40 + 1)
20 + (3 + 41)	(20 + 40) + (3 + 1)
20 + (41 + 3)	60 + 4
(20 + 41) + 3	64
[20 + (40 + 1)] + 3	
[(20 + 40) + 1] + 3	A bit easier?! This was *horizontal-ex-*
(60 + 1) + 3	*panded notation.* Don't bother to re-
60 + (1 + 3)	member which steps were combined
60 + 4	and/or omitted. It varies from one text
64	series to another.

Children will use some shortened form.

CONTINUE TO A–18.

A–18

Now look at vertical forms of C.

	Expanded	*Partial Sums*
23 =	20 + 3	23
+41	40 + 1	+41
	60 + 4	4
	64	60
		64

Try all three forms (horizontal short form, expanded and partial sums) on this one: 61 + 32.

SEE ANSWER FRAME (A–18).

(A–14)

	Horizontal-Expanded Notation	*Vertical-Expanded Notation*	*Vertical-Partial Sums*
(a)	34 + 5	34 = 30 + 4	34
	(30 + 4) + 5	+ 5 5	+ 5
	30 + (4 + 5)	30 + 9	9 ⎫ 3 tens and
	30 + 9	39	30 ⎭ 9 ones
	39		39
(b)	91 + 7	91 = 90 + 1	91
	(90 + 1) + 7	+ 7 7	+ 7
	90 + (1 + 7)	90 + 8	8 ⎫ 9 tens and
	90 + 8	98	90 ⎭ 8 ones
	98		98
	91 + 7	91 = ⑨ + 1	
	(⑨ + 1) + 7	+ 7 7	
	⑨ + (1 + 7)	⑨ + 8	
	⑨ + 8	98	
	98		

CONTINUE TO A–15.

Try these, using the short form for horizontal notation and both vertical forms.

(a) 33 + 24   (b) 62 + 14

SEE ANSWER FRAME (A–19).

D. *Sums of two two-digit numerals* with *regrouping of tens.*

Standard Form	*Short Form*
34 + 29	34 + 29
(30 + 4) + 29	(30 + 4) + (20 + 9)
30 + (4 + 29)	(30 + 20) + (4 + 9)
30 + (29 + 4)	50 + 13
(30 + 29) + 4	50 + 10 + 3
[30 + (20 + 9)] + 4	60 + 3
[(30 + 20) + 9] + 4	63
(50 + 9) + 4	
50 + (9 + 4)	Try this one using the *short form:*
50 + 13	67 + 25. Show the steps with
50 + (10 + 3)	your paper strips.
(50 + 10) + 3	
60 + 3	
63	

SEE ANSWER FRAME (A–20).

Horizontal   *Vertical*

47 + 8
(40 + 7) + 8
40 + (7 + 8)
40 + 15
40 + (10 + 5)
(40 + 10) + 5
50 + 5
55

Expanded

47 = 40 + 7
+ 8 = 8
40 + 15
40 + (10 + 5)
(40 + 10) + 5
50 + 5
55

Partial Sums

47
+ 8
15
40
55

- - - - - - - - - -

47 + 8
((4) + 7) + 8
(4) + (7 + 8)
(4) + 15
(4) + ((1) + 5)
((4) + (1)) + 5)
(5) + 5
55

47 = (4) + 7
+ 8 = 8
(4) + 15
(4) + ((1) + 5)
((4) + (1)) + 5
(5) + 5
55

(4)7
8
(1)5
(4)
(5)5
55

CONTINUE TO A–17.

A–21

Vertical forms of D, two two-digit numerals **with** *regrouping.*

		Expanded	*Partial Sums*
34	=	30 + 4	34
+29	=	20 + 9	+29
		50 + 13	13
		50 + (10 + 3)	50
		(50 + 10) + 3	63
		60 + 3	
		63	

Try all three forms on this one (horizontal-short form and both vertical forms): 17 + 15

SEE ANSWER FRAME (A–21).

(A–18)

Horizontal	*Vertical*

			Expanded		*Partial Sums*
61 + 32		61	=	60 + 1	61
(60 + 1) + (30 + 2)		+32		30 + 2	+32
(60 + 30) + (1 + 2)				90 − 3	3
90 + 3				93	90
93					93

Notice this, too:

61 + 32

(⑥ + 1) + (③ + 2)

(⑥ + ③) + (1 + 2)

⑨ + 3 = 93

61	=	⑥ + 1
32	=	③ + 2
		⑨ + 3
		93

IF YOU ARE CONFIDENT, SKIP
A–19 AND GO TO A–20.

A–22

Try a couple more (all three ways):

     (a)   34 + 49

     (b)   27 + 64

SEE ANSWER FRAME (A–22).

	Horizontal-Short Form	*Vertical*	

(a) 33 + 24   *Expanded*   *Partial Sums*

$$
\begin{array}{lll}
(30 + 3) + (20 + 4) & 33 = 30 + 3 & 33 \\
(30 + 20) + (3 + 4) & +24 = 20 + 4 & +24 \\
50 + 7 & \overline{}50 + 7 & \overline{}7 \\
57 & 57 & \underline{50} \\
& & 57
\end{array}
$$

(b) 62 + 14

$$
\begin{array}{lll}
(60 + 2) + (10 + 4) & 62 = 60 + 2 & 62 \\
(60 + 10) + (2 + 4) & +14 = 10 + 4 & +14 \\
70 + 6 & \overline{}70 + 6 & \overline{}6 \\
76 & 76 & \underline{70} \\
& & 76
\end{array}
$$

CONTINUE TO A–20.

67 + 25

(60 + 7) + (20 + 5)

(60 + 20) + (7 + 5)

80 + 12

80 + 10 + 2

90 + 2

92

CONTINUE TO A–21.

From partial sums, the *standard algorithm* can easily be developed.

Partial Sums	*Standard Algorithm*

$$
\begin{array}{ll}
31 & 31 \\
+42 & 42 \\
\overline{3} & \overline{73} \\
70 & \\
\overline{73} & \\
\end{array}
$$

Think: 1 one plus 2 ones is 3 ones. *3 tens* plus *4 tens* is *7 tens.* *Not* thirty plus forty is seventy. Reinforce those basic facts!

Find these sums in all three vertical forms:

$$
\begin{array}{ll}
26 & 125 \\
+41 & +213 \\
\hline
\end{array}
$$

SEE ANSWER FRAME (A–23).

(A–21)

Horizontal		Vertical	
	Expanded		*Partial Sums*
$17 + 15$			
$(10 + 7) + (10 + 5)$	$17 \ = \ 10 + 7$		17
$(10 + 10) + (7 + 5)$	$+15 \qquad 10 + 5$		$+15$
$20 + 12$	$\overline{20 + 12}$		$\overline{12}$
$20 + 10 + 2$	$20 + (10 + 2)$		$\underline{20}$
$30 + 2$	$(20 + 10) + 2$		32
32	$30 + 2$		
	32		

**IF YOU HAVE THIS DOWN, SKIP
A–22 AND GO TO A–23.**

A–24

Partial Sums　　　　　　　　　　*Standard Algorithm*

　　　　38　　　　　　　　　　　　　　38
　　$+45$　　　　　　　　　　　　　　45
　　$\overline{13}$　　　　　　　　　　　　　　$\overline{83}$
　　　　70
　　$\overline{83}$

Think:　8 ones plus 5 ones is 13 which
is 1 ten and 3 ones. Write down the 3

Try these in all three
vertical forms:

ones.

1 ten and 3 tens is 4 tens.
4 tens and 4 tens is 8 tens.
Write down the 8 tens.

(a)　　77　(b)　　139
　　$+56$　　　　$+183$

SEE ANSWER FRAME (A–24).

(A–22)

	Horizontal		Vertical	
(a)	$34 + 49$	$34 \ = \ 30 + 4$		34
	$(30 + 4) + (40 + 9)$	$+49 \qquad 40 + 9$		$+49$
	$(30 + 40) + (4 + 9)$	$\overline{70 + 13}$		$\overline{13}$
	$70 + 13$	$70 + (10 + 3)$		70
	$70 + 10 + 3$	$(70 + 10) + 3$		$\overline{83}$
	$80 + 3$	$80 + 3$		
	83	83		
(b)	$27 + 64$	$27 \ = \ 20 + 7$		27
	$(20 + 7) + (60 + 4)$	$+64 \qquad 60 + 4$		$+64$
	$(20 + 60) + (7 + 4)$	$\overline{80 + 11}$		$\overline{11}$
	$80 + 11$	$80 + (10 + 1)$		80
	$80 + 10 + 1$	$(80 + 10) + 1$		$\overline{91}$
	$90 + 1$	$90 + 1$		
	91	91		

CONTINUE TO A–23.

In regrouping tens to hundreds, you can begin by using tens only. You should eventually regroup as hundreds, however. Examine these:

$$89 \;=\; 80 + 9$$
$$+42 \;=\; \underline{40 + 2}$$
$$120 + 11$$
$$120 + (10 + 1)$$
$$12 \text{ tens} + 1 \text{ ten}$$

$$89 \;=\; 80 + 9$$
$$+42 \;=\; \underline{40 + 2}$$
$$120 + 11$$
$$100 + 20 + 10 + 1$$
$$100 + 30 + 1$$

THE END.

(a)
$$77 = 70 + 7$$
$$+\ 56 = \underline{50 + 6}$$
$$120 + 13$$
$$120 + (10 + 3)$$
$$(120 + 10) + 3$$
$$130 \quad + 3$$
$$133$$

$$77$$
$$\underline{+\ 56}$$
$$13$$
$$120$$
$$133$$

$$77$$
$$\underline{56}$$
$$133$$

12 tens + 1 ten is 13 tens

(b)
$$139 = 100 + \ 30 + \ 9$$
$$+\ 183 = \underline{100 + \ 80 + \ 3}$$
$$200 + 110 + 12$$
$$200 + 110 + (10 + 2)$$
$$200 + 120 + 2$$
$$200 + (100 + 20) + 2$$
$$300 + \ 20 + \ \ 2$$
$$322$$

$$139$$
$$\underline{+\ 183}$$
$$12$$
$$110$$
$$\underline{200}$$
$$322$$

$$139$$
$$\underline{+\ 183}$$
$$322$$

CONTINUE TO A–25.

$$26 = 20 + 6$$
$$+\ 41 = \underline{40 + 1}$$
$$60 + 7$$
$$67$$

$$26$$
$$\underline{+\ 41}$$
$$7$$
$$\underline{60}$$
$$67$$

$$26$$
$$\underline{+\ 41}$$
$$67$$

$$125 = 100 + 20 + 5$$
$$+\ 213 = \underline{200 + 10 + 3}$$
$$300 + 30 + 8$$
$$338$$

$$125$$
$$\underline{+\ 213}$$
$$8$$
$$30$$
$$\underline{300}$$
$$338$$

$$125$$
$$\underline{+\ 213}$$
$$338$$

CONTINUE TO A–24.

Algorithms for Subtraction

Objectives

When you have completed this unit, you will be able to:

    (1) Use a two-step algorithm to solve subtraction problems which do not involve regrouping and demonstrate the steps with concrete materials.

    (2) Use a three-step algorithm to solve subtraction problems involving regrouping and demonstrate the steps with concrete materials.

    (3) Use a five-step algorithm to solve subtraction problems involving regrouping and demonstrate the steps with concrete materials.

Materials Needed

Paper strips, some of which are cut into ten equal lengths as noted in the *Addition Algorithms*. Recommended, too, are some objects such as pencils or playing cards which can be bundled in groups of ten with a rubber band. It is highly desirable from the child's point of view if the strips are marked off into ten equal segments. Graph paper works especially well.

Assumptions

    A. Children know all subtraction facts through $18 - 9 = 9$.

    B. Children have had considerable work with "many names for a number." For example, six has many names: 6, VI, $///$, $5 + 1$, $7 - 1$, $10 - 4$, 12_4, $\boxed{1}\,1$, and so on.

    C. Children can give a number many names based on sets of ten: 52, $50 + 2$, $40 + 12$, $30 + 22$, $20 + 32$, and so on.

As with addition, subtraction will be discussed in four steps:

    (1) Two-digit numerals minus one-digit numerals *without* regrouping of tens, e.g., $26 - 2 = 24$.

    (2) Two-digit numerals minus two-digit numerals *without* regrouping of tens, e.g., $46 - 13 = 33$.

    (3) Two-digit numerals minus one-digit numerals *with* regrouping of tens, e.g., $34 - 7 = 27$.

    (4) Two-digit numerals minus two-digit numerals *with* regrouping of tens, e.g., $51 - 14 = 37$.

Horizontal notation will *not* be utilized with B, C, and D. There is a tendency inappropriately to transfer the use of the associative property. An illustration will be helpful:

Correct	*Incorrect*
25	$25 - 13$
$-\ 13$	$25 - (10 + 3)$
12	$(25 - 10) + 3$
	$15 + 3$
	18

Horizontal forms can be and are used in subtraction forms but only with type A in *introductory* work in subtraction of whole numbers.

Another use of symbolism which you should watch for is the appropriate use of the equal sign. This is more troublesome in subtraction than in addition.

Addition: Correct

$$23 \ = \ 20 + 3$$
$$+\ 42 \qquad 40 + 2$$
$$\overline{\qquad} \qquad \overline{60 + 5}$$
$$65$$

Subtraction: Incorrect

$$58 \ = \ 50 + 8$$
$$-\ 25 \qquad -\ 20 + 5$$
$$\overline{\qquad} \qquad \overline{30 + 13}$$
$$43$$

One of several patterns can be used:

Step 1   *Step 2*

$$58 \qquad 50 + 8$$
$$-\ 25 \qquad 20 + 5$$
$$\overline{\qquad} \qquad \overline{30 + 3}$$
$$33$$

$$58 \ = \ 50 + 8$$
$$-\ 25 \qquad -\ (20 + 5)$$
$$\overline{\qquad} \qquad \overline{30 + 3}$$
$$33$$

Note that if equal signs had been used here, they would not be true in the bottom or subtrahend.

$-\ 25 \neq 20 + 5$ because $-\ 25 \neq 25$

Note the use of parentheses. They are essential because

$$-\ 20 + 5 \neq -\ (20 + 5) \ since$$
$$-\ 15 \neq -\ 25$$

Simply ask yourself, "Have I written a true statement?"
"$-25 = -20 - 5$" is another possibility.

All subtraction diagrams in this chapter utilize the **take-away** *concept of subtraction.*

S–1

A. Two-digit numerals minus one-digit numerals without regrouping tens.

	Step 1	*Step 2*	

$$
\begin{array}{r} 26 \\ -\ 4 \\ \hline \end{array}
\qquad
\begin{array}{r} 20 + 6 \\ 4 \\ \hline 20 + 2 \\ 22 \end{array}
\qquad
\text{Use the paper strips and squares to show what has happened.}
$$

To facilitate pupil understanding, provide each child with manipulative materials which can be manually and visually grouped. Put rubber bands around straws or popsicle sticks or transfer 10 objects to paper plates or cups.

SEE ANSWER FRAME (S–1).

S–2

B. Two-digit numerals minus two-digit numerals without regrouping tens.

Step 1   *Step 2*   Another notational form:

$$
\begin{array}{r} 67 \\ -\ 42 \\ \hline \end{array}
\qquad
\begin{array}{r} 60 + 7 \\ 40 + 2 \\ \hline 20 + 5 \end{array}
\qquad
\begin{array}{r} 67 \\ -\ 42 \\ \hline \end{array}
\qquad
\begin{array}{r} 60 + 7 \\ -\ (40 + 2) \\ \hline 20 + 5 \\ 25 \end{array}
$$

Use the paper strips to show what has happened. The teacher should say "6 tens minus 4 tens," *not* "sixty minus forty." Children do not learn sixty facts or forty facts, but they *do* learn 6 facts and 4 facts. Teachers should try to relate this new experience to the basic subtraction facts.

SEE ANSWER FRAME (S–2).

S–3

C. Two-digit numerals minus one-digit numerals with regrouping of tens.

To find the difference between 41 and 5, the child must be able to convert 1 ten to 10 ones. He needs many manipulative experiences to develop a "feel" for this relationship since the system of notation makes no distinction.

$$41 = \quad 40 + 1 \quad = \quad (30 + 10) + \quad 1 \quad = \quad 30 + \quad (10 + 1) \quad = \quad 30 + 11.$$
$$41 = 4 \text{ tens } 1 \text{ one} = (3 \text{ tens } 1 \text{ ten}) 1 \text{ one} = 3 \text{ tens } (10 \text{ ones } 1 \text{ one}) = 3 \text{ tens } 11 \text{ ones}.$$

Step 1	*Step 2*	*Step 3*	Note these steps in the

$$
\begin{array}{r} 41 \\ -\ 5 \\ \hline \end{array}
\qquad
\begin{array}{r} 40 + 1 \\ -\ 5 \\ \hline \end{array}
\qquad
\begin{array}{r} 30 + 11 \\ -\quad 5 \\ \hline 30 + \ 6 = 36 \end{array}
$$

$$
\begin{array}{r} 41 \text{ ones} \\ -\ 5 \text{ ones} \\ \hline \end{array}
\qquad
\begin{array}{r} 4 \text{ tens } 1 \text{ one} \\ -\quad 5 \text{ ones} \\ \hline \end{array}
\qquad
\begin{array}{r} 3 \text{ tens } 11 \text{ ones} \\ -\quad 5 \text{ ones} \\ \hline 3 \text{ tens } \ 6 \text{ ones} \\ 36 \end{array}
$$

Note these steps in the special notation used in the numeration chapter:

Step 1   *Step 2*   *Step 3*

$$
\begin{array}{r} ④\ 1 \\ -\quad 5 \\ \hline \end{array}
\qquad
\begin{array}{r} ④ + 1 \\ -\ 5 \\ \hline \end{array}
\qquad
\begin{array}{r} ③ + 11 \\ -\quad 5 \\ \hline ③ + \ 6 \\ 36 \end{array}
$$

CONTINUE TO S–4.

One of the major problems faced by children is the determination of when to think of 10 as "1 ten" and when to think of it as "10 ones." This problem is squarely encountered in the present problem $41 - 5$. Notice:

Step 1   Step 2   Step 3

$$\begin{array}{r} 41 \\ -\ \ 5 \\ \hline \end{array} \qquad \begin{array}{r} ④+1 \\ -\ \ 5 \\ \hline \end{array} \qquad \begin{array}{r} ③+11 \\ -\ \ 5 \\ \hline ③+\ 6 = 36 \end{array}$$

Use paper strips to show these steps.

In going from Step 2 to Step 3, the child must be thoroughly aware of the procedure in going from *4 tens and 1 one* to *3 tens and 11 ones:* 1 ten was "changed into" 10 ones to enable the ones subtraction to be carried out easily.

SEE ANSWER FRAME (S–4).

Now, even though *you* may understand this algorithm, you need to bear in mind the great importance of developing pupil understanding through *many* and varied concrete experiences. Notice here the role of the associative property. The physical model associated with the regrouping (changing parentheses) is the change from 1 ten to 10 ones.

Step 1   Step 2   Step 3   Step 4   Step 5

$$\begin{array}{r} 53 \\ -\ 5 \\ \hline \end{array} \quad \begin{array}{r} 50+3 \\ -\ 5 \\ \hline \end{array} \quad \begin{array}{r} (40+10)+3 \\ -\ 5 \\ \hline \end{array} \quad \begin{array}{r} 40+(10+3) \\ -\qquad 5 \\ \hline \end{array} \quad \begin{array}{r} 40+13 \\ -\ \ 5 \\ \hline 40+\ 8 \\ 48 \end{array}$$

Use the paper strips to see if you can tell what happened at each step.

Write the five steps for this problem: $93 - 8$.

SEE ANSWER FRAME (S–5).

D. Two-digit numerals minus two-digit numerals with regrouping of tens.

The basic pattern is much the same as for two-digit minus one-digit.

Step 1   Step 2   Step 3   Step 4   Step 5

$$\begin{array}{r} 82 \\ -37 \\ \hline \end{array} \quad \begin{array}{r} 80+2 \\ -(30+7) \\ \hline \end{array} \quad \begin{array}{r} (70+10)+2 \\ -(30+\ \ 7) \\ \hline \end{array} \quad \begin{array}{r} 70+(10+2) \\ -(30+\ \ 7) \\ \hline \end{array} \quad \begin{array}{r} 70+12 \\ -(30+\ \ 7) \\ \hline \end{array}$$

Note the use of the associative property. What would this problem look like with the special notation, i.e., use ① = 1 ten and 10 = 10 ones.

SEE ANSWER FRAME (S–6).

(S–1)

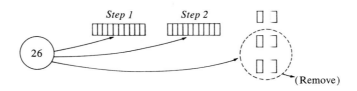

Good verbal reinforcement of the concrete materials:

"Twenty-six is 2 tens and 6 ones. '

It is visually helpful to keep the ten-strips to the left of the one-squares since this reinforces tens left of ones in a numeral.

CONTINUE TO S–2.

(S–2)

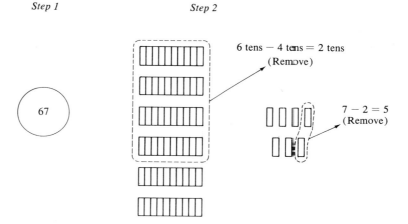

Keep the tens left of ones.

CONTINUE TO S–3.

S–7

A way to increase efficiency is to write the subtrahend in expanded notation *first* to help decide *which name* for the minuend will be best.

Step 1	Step 2	and	Step 3
82			70 + 12
−37	30 + 7		

The three steps here are actually combined into two:

$$\begin{array}{rl} 82 & = \quad 70 + 12 \\ -37 & \quad\ \ 30 + 7 \\ \hline \end{array}$$

Step 1	Step 2	and	Step 3
89			80 + 9
−37	30 + 7		

The size of the subtrahend *ones* determines the best name for 82 or 89.

CONTINUE TO S–8.

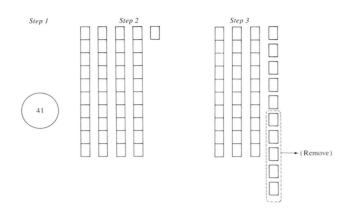

CONTINUE TO S–5.

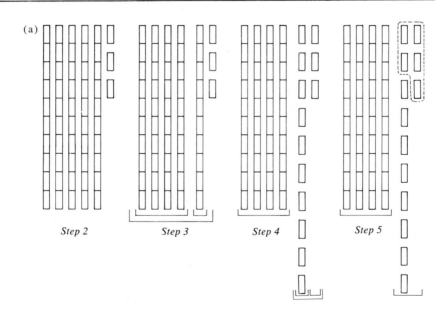

(b)   93   90 + 3   (80 + 10) + 3   80 + (10 + 3)   80 + 13
     − 8 −   8 −   8 −   8 −   8

GO ON TO S–6.

82   ⑧+ 2   (⑦ + ①) + 2   ⑦ + (10 + 2)   ⑦ + 12
−37   −(③ + 7)   −(③ + 7)   −(③ + 7)   −(③ + 7)
                                                       ④ + 5
                                                        45

CONTINUE TO S–7.

Try these:

Use the Five-step Method on (a)	*Use the Three-step Method on (c) and*
and (b): (a) 31 (b) 27	*(d):* (c) 47 (d) 85

$$\begin{array}{rr} \text{(a)} \quad 31 & \text{(b)} \quad 27 \\ -\ 9 & -18 \end{array} \qquad \begin{array}{rr} \text{(c)} \quad 47 & \text{(d)} \quad 85 \\ -28 & -39 \end{array}$$

Combine Steps 2 and 3 of the Three-step Method on (e) and (f)

$$\begin{array}{rr} \text{(e)} \quad 46 & \text{(f)} \quad 72 \\ -17 & -\ 6 \end{array}$$

Convince yourself with the paper strips that you know what is happening in each step.

SEE ANSWER FRAME (S–8).

The Five-step Method utilizes the associative property of addition and expanded notation to regroup ones and tens. Observe that the sequence of steps in subtraction regrouping is identical to the sequence of steps in addition regrouping *in reverse order*.

Addition
Regrouping

$$34$$
$$30 + 4$$
$$(20 + 10) + 4$$
$$20 + (10 + 4)$$
$$20 + 14$$

$$\begin{array}{r} 34 \\ -18 \end{array} = \begin{array}{l} 30 + 4 \\ 10 + 8 \end{array} = \begin{array}{l} (20 + 10) + 4 \\ \underline{10 \qquad + 8} \end{array} =$$

$$\begin{array}{l} 20 + (10 + 4) \\ \underline{10 \quad + \quad 8} \end{array} = \begin{array}{l} 20 + 14 \\ 10 + 8 \end{array}$$

Subtraction
Regrouping

$$\begin{array}{r} 16 \\ +18 \end{array} = \begin{array}{l} 10 + 6 \\ 10 + 8 \end{array}$$

$$\overline{20 + 14} = 20 + (10 + 4) =$$

$$(20 + 10) + 4 = 30 + 4 = 34$$

Write the steps to regroup (1) 3 tens 1 one as 2 tens 11 ones, (2) 2 tens 11 ones as 3 tens 1 one, (3) show the steps with your paper strips and squares.

SEE ANSWER FRAME (S–9).

"Choosing the correct name" is a game which can be played with children to practice regrouping. In problems involving 62 in the minuend children can decide whether to use $60 + 2$ or $50 + 12$ to subtract. In three-digit numerals there are four possibilities:

    A. No regrouping as in $634 - 213$, i.e., $600 + 30 + 4$

    B. Regrouping ones only as in $634 - 217$, i.e., $600 + 20 + 14$

    C. Regrouping tens only as in $634 - 253$, i.e., $500 + 130 + 4$

    D. Regrouping tens and ones as in $634 - 257$, i.e , $500 + 120 + 14$

CONTINUE TO S–11.

(S–8)

(a) $\quad$ 31 $\quad$ 30 + 1 $\quad$ (20 + 10) + 1 $\quad$ 20 + (10 + 1) $\quad$ 20 + 11
$\quad\quad$ − 9 $\quad\quad$ − 9 $\quad\quad\quad\quad\quad\quad$ − 9 $\quad\quad$ − $\quad$ 9 $\quad\quad\quad$ − $\quad$ 9
$\quad\quad\quad\quad\quad\quad\quad\quad\quad\quad\quad\quad\quad\quad\quad\quad\quad\quad\quad\quad\quad$ 20 + $\quad$ 2
$\quad\quad\quad\quad\quad\quad\quad\quad\quad\quad\quad\quad\quad\quad\quad\quad\quad\quad\quad\quad\quad\quad$ 22

(c) $\quad$ 47 $\quad$ 40 + 7 $\quad$ 30 + 17 $\quad\quad\quad$ (e) $\quad$ 46 $\quad\quad$ 30 + 16
$\quad\quad$ −28 $\quad$ 20 + 8 $\quad$ 20 + $\quad$ 8 $\quad\quad\quad\quad\quad$ −17 $\quad$ −(10 + $\quad$ 7)
$\quad\quad\quad\quad\quad\quad\quad\quad\quad$ 10 + $\quad$ 9 $\quad\quad\quad\quad\quad\quad\quad\quad\quad$ 20 + $\quad$ 9
$\quad\quad\quad\quad\quad\quad\quad\quad\quad\quad$ 19 $\quad\quad\quad\quad\quad\quad\quad\quad\quad\quad\quad$ 29

CONTINUE TO S–9.

(S–9)

(1) $\quad\quad$ 31 $\quad\quad\quad$ (2) $\quad\quad$ 20 + 11
$\quad\quad\quad\quad$ 30 + 1 $\quad\quad\quad\quad\quad\quad$ 20 + (10 + 1)
$\quad\quad\quad$ (20 + 10) + 1 $\quad\quad\quad\quad$ (20 + 10) + 1
$\quad\quad\quad$ 20 + (10 + 1) $\quad\quad\quad\quad\quad$ 30 + 1
$\quad\quad\quad\quad$ 20 + 11 $\quad\quad\quad\quad\quad\quad\quad$ 31

(3) *Step 1* $\quad\quad\quad\quad$ *Step 2* $\quad\quad\quad\quad$ *Step 3* $\quad\quad$ *Step 4*

② + 11 = ② + (10 + 1) = (② + ①) + 1 = ③ + 1 = 31

CONTINUE TO S–10.

S–11

Regrouping which involves addition *and* subtraction is not clearly yes or no as is the case for addition and subtraction separately.

$\quad\quad\quad\quad$ *Addition—Yes* $\quad\quad\quad\quad\quad\quad\quad$ *Subtraction—No*

$\quad$ 8 + (4 + 1) = (8 + 4) + 1 $\quad\quad$ 8 − (4 − 1) ≠ (8 − 4) − 1
$\quad\quad\quad$ 8 + 5 $\quad$ = $\quad\quad$ 12 + 1 $\quad\quad\quad\quad$ 8 − 3 $\quad$ ≠ $\quad$ 4 − 1
$\quad\quad\quad\quad$ 13 $\quad$ = $\quad\quad\quad$ 13 $\quad\quad\quad\quad\quad\quad$ 5 $\quad\quad$ ≠ $\quad\quad$ 3

$\quad\quad\quad\quad$ *Addition and Subtraction—Sometimes*

$\quad$ 8 + (4 − 1) = (8 + 4) − 1 $\quad\quad$ 8 − (4 + 1) ≠ (8 − 4) + 1
$\quad\quad\quad$ 8 + 3 $\quad$ = $\quad\quad$ 12 − 1 $\quad\quad\quad\quad$ 8 − 5 $\quad$ ≠ $\quad$ 4 + 1
$\quad\quad\quad\quad$ 11 $\quad$ = $\quad\quad\quad$ 11 $\quad\quad\quad\quad\quad\quad$ 3 $\quad\quad$ ≠ $\quad\quad$ 5

Less confusion arises when work with subtraction is developed intuitively, i.e., subtraction of ones from ones and tens from tens can be done because it agrees with manipulations carried out with concrete materials. Most textbooks do, however, include the use of horizontal-expanded notation and parentheses on case A, two-digit minus one-digit without regrouping. This is not associativity since associativity is a property of a *single operation*. This helps build an intuitive belief in the symbolic pattern of working with ones and tens separately.

THE END.

Addition-Subtraction Self-Test

Part 1. Addition Algorithms

In exercises 1–4, solve each problem with the four algorithms explained: horizontal-expanded notation, vertical-expanded notation, partial sums, and traditional. Include all steps.

1. 43 + 2

2. 13 + 24

3. 35 + 8

4. 26 + 47

5. Demonstrate each of the steps in item 3 above as you would for a child. Use paper strips and squares.

Part II. Subtraction Algorithms

Use expanded notation with the number of steps indicated.

Two steps	*Three steps*	*Five steps*
6. 96	7. 46	8. 81
−41	− 19	−37

9. Demonstrate with concrete materials each of the steps in items 6 and 8 above.

Answers to Addition-Subtraction Self-Test

1.
$$
\begin{array}{lllll}
43 + 2 & 43 & = & 40 + 3 & 43 & 43 \\
(40 + 3) + 2 & + \ 2 & & + \quad 2 & + \ 2 & + \ 2 \\
40 + (3 + 2) & & & 40 + 5 & 5 & 45 \\
40 + 5 & & & 45 & 40 & \\
45 & & & & 45 &
\end{array}
$$

2.
$$
\begin{array}{lllll}
13 + 24 & 13 & = & 10 + 3 & 13 & 13 \\
13 + (20 + 4) & +24 & & 20 + 4 & +24 & +24 \\
(13 + 20) + 4 & & & 30 + 7 & 7 & 37 \\
[(10 + 3) + 20] + 4 & & & 37 & 30 & \\
[(3 + 10) + 20] + 4 & & & & 37 & \\
[3 + (10 + 20)] + 4 & & & & & \\
(3 + 30) + 4 & & & & & \\
(30 + 3) + 4 & & & & & \\
30 + (3 + 4) & & & & & \\
30 + 7 & & & & & \\
37 & & & & &
\end{array}
$$

3. $\quad$ 35 + 8 $\qquad$ 35 $\quad$ = $\quad$ 30 + 5 $\qquad\qquad$ 35 $\qquad$ 35
$\quad$ (30 + 5) + 8 $\qquad$ + 8 $\qquad\qquad$ + $\quad$ 8 $\qquad$ + 8 $\qquad$ + 8
$\quad$ 30 + (5 + 8) $\qquad\qquad\qquad$ 30 + 13 $\qquad\qquad$ 13 $\qquad$ 43
$\qquad$ 30 + 13 $\qquad\qquad\qquad$ 30 + (10 + 3) $\qquad\quad$ 30
$\quad$ 30 + (10 + 3) $\qquad\qquad$ (30 + 10) + 3 $\qquad\quad$ 43
$\quad$ (30 + 10) + 3 $\qquad\qquad$ 40 + 3
$\qquad$ 40 + 3 $\qquad\qquad\qquad\qquad$ 43
$\qquad\quad$ 43

4. $\qquad$ 26 + 47 $\qquad$ 26 $\quad$ = $\quad$ 20 + 6 $\qquad\qquad$ 26 $\qquad$ 26
$\quad$ 26 + (40 + 7) $\qquad$ +47 $\qquad\qquad$ 40 + 7 $\qquad\qquad$ +47 $\qquad$ +47
$\quad$ (26 + 40) + 7 $\qquad\qquad\qquad$ 60 + 13 $\qquad\qquad$ 13 $\qquad$ 73
$\quad$ [(20 + 6) + 40] + 7 $\qquad\qquad$ 60 + (10 + 3) $\qquad$ 60
$\quad$ [(6 + 20) + 40] + 7 $\qquad\qquad$ (60 + 10) + 3 $\qquad$ 73
$\quad$ [6 + (20 + 40)] + 7 $\qquad\qquad$ 70 + 3
$\qquad$ (6 + 60) + 7 $\qquad\qquad\qquad$ 73
$\qquad$ (60 + 6) + 7
$\qquad$ 60 + (6 + 7)
$\qquad\quad$ 60 + 13
$\qquad$ 60 + (10 + 3)
$\qquad$ (60 + 10) + 3
$\qquad\quad$ 70 + 3
$\qquad\qquad$ 73

5. See frame (A–4), page 189.

6. $\quad$ 96 $\quad$ = $\quad$ 90 + 6
$\quad$ −41 $\qquad\quad$ 40 + 1
$\qquad\qquad\quad$ 50 + 5
$\qquad\qquad\qquad$ 55

7. $\quad$ 46 $\quad$ = $\quad$ 40 + 6 $\quad$ = $\quad$ 30 + 16
$\quad$ −19 $\qquad\quad$ 10 + 9 $\qquad\quad$ 10 + $\quad$ 9
$\qquad\qquad\qquad\qquad\qquad$ 20 + $\quad$ 7
$\qquad\qquad\qquad\qquad\qquad\quad$ 27

8. $\quad$ 81 = 80 + 1 = (70 + 10) + 1 = 70 + (10 + 1) = 70 + 11
$\quad$ −37 $\quad$ 30 + 7 $\qquad$ 30 $\qquad$ + 7 $\qquad$ 30 + $\qquad$ 7 $\qquad\qquad$ 30 + $\quad$ 7
$\qquad\qquad\qquad\qquad\qquad\qquad\qquad\qquad\qquad\qquad\qquad\qquad$ 40 + $\quad$ 4
$\qquad\qquad\qquad\qquad\qquad\qquad\qquad\qquad\qquad\qquad\qquad\qquad\qquad$ 44

9. Item 6—see frames S–2 and (S–2), pages 202 and 204.
$\quad$ Item 8—see frame (S–5), page 205.

General Methods and Specific Materials of Instruction

The Bead Frame produced by Science Research Associates is a commercial aid which lends itself well to development of pupil understanding of addition and subtraction algorithms. It is an open-ended abacus with stackable red and yellow beads. Here is a sequence of steps through which pupil understanding of addition can be maximized:

A. Use beads of one color for 26 + 17. Group them in tens and separate the addends. Re-arrange the stacks of tens and ones to get 4 tens and 3 ones.

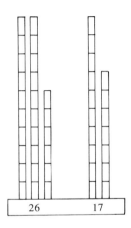

B. Place a different colored bead as the *tenth* on each stack.

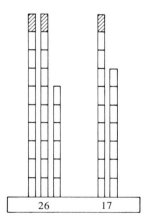

C. Use the different color *only*
   as a group of ten.

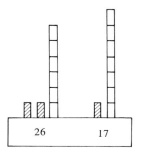

D. Use the different color *only*
   as a group of ten and *stack*
   them.

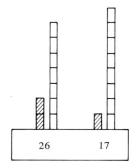

This sequence will provide excellent visual imagery for the child to distinguish between tens and ones. The procedure will help the child *intuitively*
believe in the procedures. A to B to C to D is an instructional sequence which
would rarely occur in one or two days, except as a review. More likely, it
would occur in four or five days with review of previous stages as each new one
is introduced.

The SRA Bead Frame is large and can be used for teacher demonstrations.
Children can get *individual experiences* with small colored stackable pegs
available commercially from the Judy Company.

A twenty-bead abacus like the one illustrated here is also effective. Beads
not in use are hidden by the partition. The major advantage of a twenty-bead

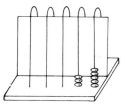

abacus is that it allows one to show problems with regrouping such as 7 +
6 = 13 visually on one position before converting the 13 to 1 ten and 3 ones.
Such an abacus can be made with wire and washers.

Cuisenaire Rods, Dienes Blocks and Sterns Blocks are also effective in facilitating meaningful work in addition. For 26 + 17, Cuisenaire Rods can be placed as shown.

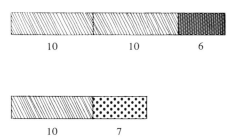

The tens and ones can be regrouped and then a substitution made by comparing lengths.

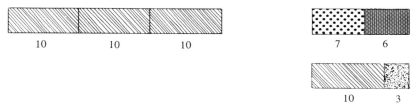

Other items commonly used are straws, tongue depressors and popsicle sticks with rubber bands to bundle groups of ten. Pennies and dimes can also be used effectively.

The most crucial step is always regrouping. A visual and tactile model in the hands of the child can greatly enhance his accommodation of 13 = ① + 3, i.e., 13 is 1 ten and 3 ones. His intuitive *belief* is essential if this sequence of steps is to be meaningful.

In selecting materials, choose those which can be used by the teacher *and* the student or which can be closely coordinated. Remember that, as a matter of transfer, the child will be able to replicate or apply new knowledge in relation to the similarity between the original and the new experience. If the child follows your explanation with the Bead Frame, you cannot be certain that he will be able to transfer his understanding immediately to popsicle sticks! Attempt to use teacher and student aids which are similar in design, color and use. Finally be certain to *use more than one aid*. This accomplishes at least three things: (1) it helps prevent children from associating regrouping in addition with a specific aid; use of two or more helps the child realize that the operations are independent of *specific* objects but *characteristic* or *descriptive* of many objects; (2) it facilitates transfer to a wider range of experiences in which the concept is applicable; the concept will transfer to situations "like" Bead Frames and "like" popsicle sticks and "like" straws so generalizability is broader; and (3) children who fail to conceptualize regrouping in addition and subtraction with one aid will have an opportunity to accommodate the concept with a different aid which is more akin to or in harmony with previous experience.

As always, the teacher does not begin with the textbook since it is not concrete. The following four steps are suggested.

> A. Use concrete materials and verbalization *without symbols.* Example: Ask children to make 46 with 4 bundles of ten and 6 ones and 37 with 3 bundles of ten and 7 ones. Then ask them to decide how many there are altogether. Talk through a couple of problems.
>
> B. Use concrete materials in conjunction with symbols. Write the steps of an appropriate algorithm which correspond to the concrete manipulations.
>
> C. Use pictures and symbols. "Write the number sentence represented by this picture."
>
> D. Use symbols, solely. "What is the sum of 37 and 29?"

After experiences with *concrete aids,* children can begin to work with pictorial representations (semi-concrete) which are found in textbooks and workbooks. The child may also wish to draw his own pictures and sets to help conceptualize addition and subtraction algorithms. Eventually the child will work solely with abstract symbols (numerals) in computation. He should not be hurried! Encourage children to use objects or draw pictures as they need them; failure to encourage them may create pressures to *memorize* algorithms. It is much more desirable for the child to *understand* an algorithm.

Helping children develop computational accuracy is a challenge to every teacher. Clark and Vincent (1) found that checking answers facilitates accuracy; it is probably better to give a smaller number of problems which will be checked than to give a larger number with no checking.

Discovery

How can a primary teacher help children discover an acceptable algorithm for addition? In the programmed section of this chapter you were introduced to several algorithms. Four were given, and there are certainly others. Since an algorithm is, loosely speaking, a short-cut computational procedure, there are as many algorithms as short-cuts! The teacher must be able to recognize which short-cuts are mathematically acceptable and which are not.

It is assumed that your mathematics background, combined with the experiences with the material of this chapter, makes you such a person. Your teaching task, as represented in the opening question, is to help children find a short-cut.

A good technique is to start with a problem situation requiring the desired skill. Such a problem can be created through a story about boxes of popsicles for your class and the class next door. Since in guided discovery the teacher provides subtle, leading information toward the desired end, the problem can easily involve boxes which contain ten popsicles each. Further, popsicle sticks can be provided. The children can bundle ten sticks together to represent enough for 31 children and 28 children, i.e., three bundles and one for one class and two bundles and eight for the other class.

Before continuing, stop and think. What are three or four possible ways the total number of popsicles might be determined by a second- or third-grader? After you have reflected on the question, turn to page 215 and look at the partial listing of short-cuts.

Now examine response A. This child is exhibiting the most unsophisticated strategy but he is getting the answer. His response has meaning for him. Your challenge is to increase his efficiency while at the same time maintaining a balance in understanding. What alternatives do you have?

There are several. Three will be examined. First, help the child realize (intuitively believe) that tens can be added together and that the resultant sum will agree with ones. This can be done by using bundled and unbundled sticks and writing it notationally like this:

20	2 tens		40	4 tens
+ 30	+ 3 tens		+ 30	+ 3 tens
50	5 tens		70	7 tens

Second, lead a class discussion based on the various solutions without placing evaluative judgments as to their relative merit. Then work another problem. Many times children will understand a different way and see that it is more efficient; they just did not happen to think of it. Third, have the child work with two-digit plus one-digit addition such as 14 + 3 to see that he can count 14, *15, 16, 17.*

Through teacher guidance children can increase their efficiency in finding totals *with concrete materials.* Further, all but the grossly retarded will get the answer eventually. This gives every child the feeling of success and self-respect.

After the preceding activities have been carried out in the classroom for a day or two, the teacher can move to a concrete-manipulation-with-symbolization stage. In other words, concrete materials will be utilized in conjunction with an algorithm. A problem may be posed and the teacher can place on the chalkboard algorithms which describe the verbal descriptions given by pupils. Examples:

3 tens	1 one		30 + 1
2 tens	8 ones		20 + 8
5 tens	9 ones		50 + 9
	59		59

Of course, there will be more variation when the concept of regrouping is introduced. When many of the children have attained the concept, a diagnostic test can be administered.

A. Unbundle all the sticks and count: 1, 2, 3, . . . , 59

B. Count by tens and then by ones: 10, 20, 30, 40, 50, 51, . . . , 59

C. Count by tens and count by ones to determine place values:
$$\left.\begin{array}{l} \text{(1)} \quad 10, 20, 30, 40, 50 \\ \text{(2)} \quad 1, 2, 3, 4, 5, 6, 7, 8, 9 \end{array}\right\} 50 + 9 = 59$$

D. Start with 31; then count by tens and ones:
31, 41, 51, 52, 53, . . . , 59

E. Add the tens, add the ones:
$$\left.\begin{array}{l} 30 + 20 = 50 \\ 1 + 8 = 9 \end{array}\right\} 59$$

F. Unbundle one set of sticks and count by ones:
31, 32, 33, . . . , 59

Accommodation of Individual Differences

The steps of the individualization model are:

A. Objectives on concept A
B. Preassessment
C. Instruction
D. Diagnosis
E. Grouping

Examine these in more detail.

Objectives. You want to formulate behavioral objectives which encompass the material to be learned. Objectives should account for the ranges of concrete-abstractness and the levels of difficulty of the major concept. In this case, you should include these areas:

Concept	*Levels*
A. Two-digit numerals plus or minus one-digit numerals without regrouping, e.g., $16 + 3 = 19$ or $19 - 3 = 16$.	I. Concrete II. Semi-concrete III. Abstract

A. Two-digit numerals plus or minus one-digit numerals without regrouping, e.g., $16 + 3 = 19$ or $19 - 3 = 16$.

                                  I. Concrete
                                  II. Semi-concrete
                                  III. Abstract

B. Two-digit numerals plus or minus two-digit numerals without regrouping, e.g., $23 + 45 = 68$ or $68 - 23 = 45$.

C. One-digit numerals plus one-digit numerals with regrouping, e.g., $6 + 8 = 14$.

D. Two-digit numerals plus or minus one-digit numerals with regrouping, e.g., $26 + 8 = 34$ or $34 - 8 = 26$.

E. Two-digit numerals plus or minus two-digit numerals with regrouping, e.g., $16 + 47 = 63$ or $63 - 47 = 16$.

You could write 30 or more specific objectives but usually the wording can be made more general to include several of the components at one time.

Specific

Concept A—Level I: The child will be able to determine the sums of two-digit and one-digit numerals without regrouping by using popsicle sticks and rubber bands.

Concept D—Level III: The child will be able to compute differences of two-digit and one-digit numerals with regrouping without the use of manipulative aids.

General

The child will be able to find sums of one- and two-digit numerals involving regrouping with the use of teaching aids utilized in class.

Note that this last objective covers addition in concept-levels C-I, D-I, and E-I for a variety of concrete experiences.

Preassessment. If the discovery strategy is used, an informal preassessment can be made simply by observing those children who can successfully carry out the task in the most efficient manner. If these pupils demonstrate a satisfactory level of achievement, they can be given enrichment activities. Specific suggestions are discussed below.

Instruction. After informal discovery experiences, the class may work as a unit or can work on individualized materials such as Unipacs or IPI materials discussed in the chapter on individualization.

Diagnosis. When the teacher feels that *many* children have mastered the concept, or when *individuals* are ready if experiences are totally individualized, a diagnostic test is administered. The test, you will recall from the discussion of diagnostic tools, samples the behaviors outlined in your objectives. On the basis of performance, the children will be given additional work. The analytical diagnostic test should sample semi-concrete and abstract behaviors. Individual diagnosis can be used as a follow-up at the concrete level for problem cases.

There are three very common errors in subtraction which deserve mention. First, many children do not know their facts; second, they have many problems with regrouping; third, zero is especially troublesome in the top numeral. To accommodate the first problem, you can introduce subtraction algorithms with easy combinations or provide children with crutches such as 5 × 7 note cards with troublesome facts. Most children with regrouping problems should be referred to concrete materials or pictorial representations for verification. Build a solid relation between the physical reality and the arithmetical model. Beware of the situation like the little girl who said $23 - 16 = 13$ with numerals and $23 - 16 = 7$ with toothpicks! Finally, avoid zeros in introductory exercises. Since children do have difficulty with problems like $60 - 26$, avoid such problems initially until the children have experienced considerable success with other combinations.

Grouping. Children who have not developed the concept will be given *new* developmental experiences. They will be encouraged to use concrete materials. They may need to be sub-grouped on the basis of common strengths and weaknesses.

Children who have mastered the concept but need additional practice can work on story problems, play games which involve addition of two-digit numerals or work a page in a workbook now and then.

Children who have mastered this concept can be given lateral enrichment activities. Some which are appropriate for this unit are (1) addition in other bases including historical systems, (2) modular arithmetic, (3) exploring the relations between regrouping in addition and measurements, (4) helping other students, or (5) writing story problems involving the concept. Each of these can become boring. Give variety and choice whenever possible.

Psychology. Note how readiness is given meaning in relation to ideas of Bruner, Gagné and Piaget discussed previously. Bruner's claim that the child is always ready implies that the teacher determines appropriate strategies and aids through which addition algorithms can be taught. Readiness is in the hands of the teacher. According to Gagné, the teacher should preassess in relation to important subskills for addition with regrouping. Then children lacking important subskills will be given learning experiences to develop them. In this view, too, readiness is the responsibility of the teacher. Piaget's developmental stages are accommodated through use of appropriate levels of abstraction; the teacher allows children to learn through concrete materials without unduly hurrying their progress so as to increase meaningful contact with mathematics. Readiness is the responsibility of the teacher.

The major point of emphasis is *ready for what?* If the teacher has one concept to present one way and gives one assignment, readiness is an empty word. But when a concept is encompassed in its totality with varying degrees of difficulty, appropriate levels of abstraction, and attention to prerequisite subskills, readiness is a very meaningful concept which will orient teachers' contacts with children.

Teachers who have taught the subskills have provided readiness for addition with regrouping, and the teachers who teach this concept provide readiness experiences for all concepts later to be learned to which this skill is related: partial sums provide readiness for partial products; regrouping in addition provides readiness for regrouping in subtraction and multiplication; use of the associative and commutative properties in addition with regrouping provides readiness for associativity and commutativity in multiplication, etc. Each teacher builds upon the readiness experiences provided by the child's previous teachers and provides readiness experiences to meet future needs. Readiness is a continuing, building process; this is the essence of the spiraling curriculum.

Finally, once concepts are mastered they must not be dropped. Fragile memories that we have, we must *overlearn* to facilitate retention. This does not mean spaced *drill* on addition and subtraction with regrouping; it means spaced *exposure*. Teachers working on new topics can, especially through word problems, provide disguised practice on mastered skills.

Discussion and Projects

1. What other materials, commercial or homemade, can be used to teach addition and subtraction with regrouping?
2. Demonstrate addition and subtraction with regrouping on aids mentioned in this chapter or others available to you.
3. Outline a discovery lesson on subtraction with regrouping. What are some other problem situations which can be used to introduce the work on addition and subtraction algorithms? What different pupil strategies can you anticipate for the alternatives?
4. What might the teacher do for each of the other children in the lesson cited in this chapter?
5. Write specific and general objectives for this unit of work.
6. Locate specific references which can be used as source materials for enrichment.
7. Write six items to evaluate pupil understanding of addition and subtraction with regrouping. Write two for each level of abstractness.
8. Discuss ways the teacher can evaluate pupil understanding at the concrete level (a) individually and (b) in a large-group setting.
9. How can a tape recorder be utilized in teaching this unit to second- and third-graders?
10. List some concepts which are prerequisite (serve as readiness) for understanding addition and subtraction with regrouping.
11. If the teacher decided to spend time with the practice group, what are some activities which could involve the members of the development group by themselves or working with the enrichment group?

Additional Resources

Filmstrips

>   *Names for Numbers,* Filmstrip-of-the-Month (1201)
>   *Place Value and Subtraction,* Filmstrip-of-the-Month (1211)

Films

>   *Addition Algorithms,* National Council of Teachers of Mathematics.
>   *Subtraction,* National Council of Teachers of Mathematics.
>   *Helping Children Discover Arithmetic,* Wayne State University.

Elementary School Textbooks

Harper & Row (1970), Grade 2, *New Dimensions in Mathematics,* by C. D'Augustine, F. Brown, J. Heddens, C. Howard.
　　Student Text: pp. 83–94, 129–52.
　　Teacher Edition: pp. 108–19, 158–83.

Harper & Row (1970), Grade 3, *New Dimensions in Mathematics,* by C. D'Augustine, F. Brown, J. Heddens, C. Howard.
　　Student Text: pp. 78–97.
　　Teacher Edition: pp. 102–21.

Houghton-Mifflin Company (1970), Grade 2, *Modern School Mathematics,* by E. Duncan, L. Capps, M. Dolciani, W. Quast, M. Zweng.
　　Student Text: pp. 158–83, 249–59.
　　Teacher Edition: pp. 186–220, 294–304.

Houghton-Mifflin Company (1970), Grade 3, *Modern School Mathematics,* by E. Duncan, L. Capps, M. Dolciani, W. Quast, M. Zweng.
　　Student Text: pp. 94–125.
　　Teacher Edition: pp. 118–51.

Bibliography

1. Clark, J.R. and E.L. Vincent. "A Study of the Effect of Checking Upon Accuracy in Addition." *The Mathematics Teacher* (February 1926), Vol. 19, pp. 65–71.

2. *Mathematics for Elementary School Teachers.* Washington, D.C.: National Council of Teachers of Mathematics, 1966.

11

Teaching Multiplication and Division Concepts

As noted in the chapter on addition and subtraction concepts, a binary operation is a rule which assigns to two elements of a set a third element of the set. Thus, addition assigns to the whole numbers 2 and 3 a third whole number, 5; this relationship is sometimes expressed like this: $(2,3) \xrightarrow{+} 5$. Write similar notation for 6 and 2 under the operations of subtraction, multiplication and division. Check your answers with those listed on the next page.

In this chapter the operations of multiplication and division are explored in detail. After readiness considerations, instructional techniques for teaching multiplication and division and properties of addition, subtraction, multiplication and division are presented. Then the relationships among the four operations are explored. Following a detailed scrutiny of basic facts, the broad topics of instructional materials, discovery strategies, and individualized instruction are examined.

Multiplication and Division Readiness

Readiness is both maturational and experiential in nature. According to Piaget's theory of cognitive development, children can master new dimensions of thought at successive stages of the developmental sequence because of such factors as conservation, liberation from egocentrism and so on. Many activities can be carried out which develop intuitive understanding of concepts. Through such experiences children become ready to learn the concepts at more abstract levels.

Maturational Factor of Readiness

Before children can totally understand multiplication and division concepts they must be able to conserve quantity and, related to this, construct and conserve one-to-one correspondences. They must also have reversibility of thought if they are to understand the inverse relationship between these two operations.

Subtraction: $(6, 2) \Rightarrow 4$
Multiplication: $(6, 2) \overset{\times}{\Rightarrow} 12$
Division: $(6, 2) \overset{\div}{\Rightarrow} 3$
Note that order is important since $(2, 6) \overset{\div}{\Rightarrow} \frac{1}{3}$

The thought processes involved in multiplication and division are basically the same as for addition and subtraction. Since most children attain these cognitive skills around the age of seven, extensive work on developmental concepts of multiplication and division in grade three is appropriate for nearly all children since most third-graders are at least eight years old.

Children of this age are in the stage of concrete operations. Mathematics concepts should be related extensively to manipulations of objects, pictures and diagrams (Bruner's enactive and iconic modes). Those few children who are still functioning pre-operationally should have continued work with concrete materials. This will develop intuitive understanding of concepts which will in turn facilitate complete mastery when youngsters are *maturationally* ready.

Experiential Factor of Readiness

Children who are functioning pre-operationally can have a variety of learning experiences designed to develop an intuitive grasp of concepts and familiarize them with the various approaches and aids utilized. Children who are functioning at the concrete level of operations also benefit from the experiences described since, according to Piaget and Bruner, abstract mastery (symbolic) is a process of successive internalization of manipulations with concrete materials (enactive) and diagrams or other schematic forms (iconic).

Children can be familiarized with materials and with the mathematical approaches. Number lines, arrays and sets are the most commonly used approaches for multiplication and division instruction. Since number lines are used with addition and subtraction concepts, familiarity with this aid will facilitate smooth transition to these new operations, especially repeated sums and differences such as $3 + 3 + 3 = \square$ and $12 - 3 - 3 - 3 - 3 = \square$, respectively.

An array is a rectangular pattern of rows and columns. Teachers can use them to add as a readiness experience for multiplication or to subtract as a readiness experience for division. Thus, corresponding to an array with three rows and four columns are the following four operations.

```
· · · ·     4
· · · ·     4
· · · ·   +4
3 × 4 =   12
```

$$
\begin{array}{rc}
12 & \\
- 4 & 1 \\
\hline
8 & \\
- 4 & 1 \\
\hline
4 & \\
- 4 & + 1 \\
\hline
0 & \\
\end{array}
$$

$$12 \div 4 = 3$$

Objects of many different designs, colors and shapes can be placed in rectangular arrays or merely arranged into equivalent disjoint sets. Addition of cardinal numbers of equivalent disjoint sets is a readiness experience for multiplication, and removal of equivalent disjoint subsets is a readiness experience for division.

Skip counting backwards and forwards also builds readiness for multiplication and division. When a child says, "3, 6, 9, 12," he is having an experience related to $3 + 3 + 3 + 3 = \square$ and $4 \times 3 = \square$ or "12, 9, 6, 3, 0" is related to $12 - 3 - 3 - 3 - 3 = \square$ and $12 \div 3 = \square$.

Developing the Concept of Multiplication and Its Inverse

There are five ways in which multiplication is commonly introduced. Each way can also be used to show that multiplication is a commutative operation and that division "undoes" multiplication, i.e., is its inverse operation.

Sets. The operations of multiplication and division can be related to sets. Multiplication is the operation associated with the union of equivalent disjoint sets. The sets must be equivalent because they must have the same number of elements in each set. 3×2 is interpreted "three sets of two";

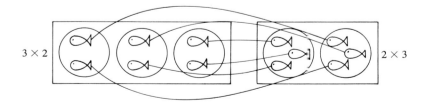

there must be two in each set. The sets must be disjoint because of the same rationale used in establishing this relation between sets for the operation of addition. Children can make many sets of identical cardinality. They can rearrange two sets of three into three sets of two. Many experiences at interchanging the number and size of sets will help children understand that multiplication is commutative, e.g., $2 \times 3 = 3 \times 2$—two sets of three elements have the same total as three sets of two.

The inverse of multiplication, division, can be related to sets also by *removing* equivalent disjoint subsets.

Multiplication

$3 \times 2 = 6$

How many is three sets of two?

Division

$6 \div 2 = 3$

How many sets of two in six?

The product 3×2 is *arbitrarily* interpreted as 3 sets of 2. It could just as easily be interpreted as 2 sets of 3. The distinction is pedagogical. It is a convenient *instructional interpretation* which allows the learner to grasp the meaning of multiplication. The distinction also provides an instructional "handle" for teaching commutativity since the learner can see that 3 sets of 2 is the same number of objects as 2 sets of 3. These comments also apply to other distinctions such as the number line and array interpretations of multiplication which follow.

Addition.   Multiplication can be taught in conjunction with objects by utilizing addition skills. "2×3" is "two threes" or "three used as an addend two times." Thus, $2 \times 3 = 3 + 3 = 6$ and $3 \times 2 = 2 + 2 + 2 = 6$. This approach will also help children see that multiplication is commutative, e.g., $2 \times 3 = 3 \times 2$.

Just as multiplication can be related to repeated addition, so, too, can division be related to repeated subtraction. "$6 \div 2$" means "how many twos in six?"

$$6 - 2 = 4; \quad 4 - 2 = 2; \quad 2 - 2 = 0$$
$$1 \quad + \quad 1 \quad + \quad 1 = 3$$
$$6 \div 2 = 3$$

Since multiplication is related to addition, and subtraction "undoes" addition, the relations among these four operations can be used to help children understand that division "undoes" multiplication.

Number Line.   Multiplying "3×2" can be interpreted as "three jumps of two" on a number line. Start at zero and jump to the right. "2×3" means "two jumps of three." By making this distinction between *number of jumps* and *size of jump,* commutativity becomes more apparent, e.g., $3 \times 2 = 2 \times 3$.

$3 \times 2 = 6$

$2 \times 3 = 6$

Inverse operations addition and subtraction move in opposite directions on the number line, as do multiplication and division. $6 \div 2 = \square$ may be interpreted, "How many jumps of two are needed to get to zero from six?" There are two ways this is commonly shown.

$6 \div 2 = 3$

$6 \div 2 = 3$

Arrays. A multiplication sentence represented by an array is read *rows times columns.* The *rows are horizontal* and the *columns are vertical.* Look at this array and then turn your book 90 degrees. Arrays can also be used to demonstrate the commutative property of multiplication.

$3 \times 5 = 15$ $5 \times 3 = 15$

A "Tiger Bite" can be used to show division. Make a story about a tiger getting loose from the zoo and chewing up your arrays. The total number of dots in the array was fortunately up in the corner. Children can help you decide how many rows there were so you can make new ones.[1]

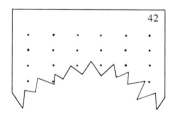

42

Cross-products. A cross-product or Cartesian Product is a set of ordered pairs. If Mary has two skirts and three blouses, her outfits can be represented as follows:

---

[1] My thanks to my colleague, Dr. Charles W. Smith, for this clever idea.

Blouses	Skirts	Outfits: (Blouse, Skirt)	
Red = R	Tan = T	(R, T)	(G, B)
Green = G	Black = B	(R, B)	(W, T)
White = W		(G, T)	(W, B)

When there are three skirts and two blouses, there are six outfits (ordered pairs). They could also have been represented as follows:

Blouses	Tan	Black
Red	✕	✕
Green	✕	✕
White	✕	✕

or

Blouses   Skirts

Red — Tan
Green — Black
White

or

```
        T   B
   R ---+---+---
   G ---+---+---
   W ---+---+---
```

Hervey (2) found that children did not conceptualize multiplication as readily with cross-products as with other methods which she tried. Cross-products are important in mathematics so some examples should be used in the classroom.

Division Types

You should learn to discern between two different types of division questions. One type is referred to as the *measurement* concept of division, and the other is referred to as the *partition* or *partitive* concept of division.

Measurement. Some division questions can be answered by removing subsets in a repeated subtraction sequence. Example: "How many tables will be needed if I place twenty-four people four at each table?" or "If Bill wants to play marbles with his eighteen marbles and each player receives six marbles, how many players will there be?" In each of these problems you can imagine objects being placed into equivalent sets and then counting the total number of sets.

Partition. Other division questions begin with the number of sets known; they require that the *size* of each set be determined. Example: "How many people will be seated at each table if there are six tables for twenty-four people?" or "If Bill wants to play marbles with his two friends, how many marbles will each of the three boys get if eighteen marbles are distributed equally?" In each of these situations you can imagine the objects divided into a given number of sets and then counting to determine how many are in each set.

Contrast. The relation between the measurement and partitive concepts of division can be represented as follows:

	Partitive	Measurement
Number of sets:	Known	Unknown
Size of Sets:	Unknown	Known

Measurement can be likened to dealing a deck of cards four-at-a-time to see how many piles of four are contained in a deck. Partition can be likened to dealing cards to four people one-at-a-time to see how many cards will be dealt to each person.

A mnemonic device to use is the following: When the number items in a problem agree in units, the question is a measurement question.

Measurement: There are *twenty-four marbles* to be distributed *four marbles* for each boy. How many boys will receive marbles?

Measurement: Each child will receive *three cookies;* if there are *thirty-six cookies,* how many children can receive a share?

Not measurement: There are *twenty-four marbles* for *six boys;* how many marbles will each boy receive?

Not measurement: If *thirty-six cookies* are given to *six children,* how many cookies will each child receive?

In measurement questions the units of numbers agree:

24 *marbles;* 4 *marbles*
3 *cookies;* 36 *cookies*

When the units of numbers do *not* agree, the problem is *not* a measurement question:

24 *marbles;* 6 *boys*
36 *cookies;* 6 *children*

In general, the measurement concept should be used in introductory work with division in grades two and three. Zweng (3) found that children can understand the measurement concept more readily. Further, the measurement concept as associated with removal of subsets is related to the repeated subtraction concept in division; this approach is the one most commonly used.

Commutativity

Several ways have been indicated by which children can learn that multiplication is a commutative operation, i.e., a $\times$ b = b $\times$ a. Of what practical significance is this property?

There are 100 multiplication facts. If a child knows 6 $\times$ 7 = 42 and truly understands the commutative relation, he also knows that 7 $\times$ 6 = 42. With the aid of commutativity, there are only 55 multiplication facts which have different factors. (There are ten facts having no commutative statements which reduce memory required since there is only *one* in 4 $\times$ 4 = 4 $\times$ 4, etc.)

Associativity

Multiplication is associative since a $\times$ (b $\times$ c) = (a $\times$ b) $\times$ c.

$$2 \times (3 \times 4) = (2 \times 3) \times 4$$
$$2 \times 12 = 6 \times 4$$
$$24 = 24$$

Of what practical significance is this property?

Products of three or more numbers can be checked by using associativity as in the illustration above.

When children are introduced to products of ones and tens, the associative property can be used as follows:

$$3 \times 60$$
$$\left.\begin{array}{l} 3 \times (6 \times 10) \\ (3 \times 6) \times 10 \end{array}\right\} \quad \text{associativity}$$
$$18 \times 10$$
$$180$$

Associativity can be taught through illustrations of the following type. "How many thread holes are on these buttons?"

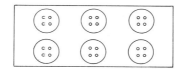

rows × (columns × holes/button = (rows × columns) × holes/button
$$2 \times (3 \times 4) = (2 \times 3) \times 4$$
2 rows × 12 holes each = 6 buttons × 4 holes each

Apples and seeds can be used, too, or two muffin pans with three rows and four columns each, or four houses with six window frames with eight panes each. These and many other instances which occur in everyday life indicate to the student that this property is useful when multiplication situations involving three factors are encountered.

Distributivity

Multiplication is distributive over addition on the set of whole numbers.

$$2 \times (3 + 4) = (2 \times 3) + (2 \times 4)$$
$$2 \times 7 = 6 + 8$$
$$14 = 14$$

A 2-by-7-array can be broken into a 2-by-3-array and a 2-by-4-array: $2 \times 7 = 2 \times (3 + 4) = (2 \times 3) + (2 \times 4)$.

$$7$$
$$3 + 4$$

$$2 \quad \begin{array}{l} \cdots\ \vdots\ \cdots \\ \cdots\ \vdots\ \cdots \end{array}$$

$$(2 \times 3) + (2 \times 4)$$

The distributive property plays a crucial role in nearly all multiplication algorithms.

$$3 \times 21$$
$$3 \times (20 + 1)$$
$$(3 \times 20) + (3 \times 1)$$
$$60 + 3$$
$$63$$

It is the distributive property which allows you to multiply ones and tens separately.

The distributive property can most easily be taught to children with arrays. The children can find many names for a given number to determine that the product is always the same.

$$3 \times 4$$
$$3 \times (3 + 1) = (3 \times 3) + (3 \times 1) = 9 + 3 = 12$$
$$3 \times (2 + 2) = (3 \times 2) + (3 \times 2) = 6 + 6 = 12$$
$$3 \times (1 + 3) = (3 \times 1) + (3 \times 3) = 3 + 9 = 12$$

The commutative, associative and distributive properties are used together extensively in the development of algorithms as presented in the next chapter.

Whole Number Operations: Properties and Interrelationships

A brief summary of the properties of and relationships among addition, subtraction, multiplication and division will now be presented to enable you to review and study their interrelatedness. Doing so will help you grasp more completely the unifying role of sets and the continuous nature of the K–4 mathematics curriculum.

Properties of Whole Number Operations

Make a chart with the four operations—addition, subtraction, multiplication, and division—across the top. Write the properties down the left as they are mentioned and write "yes" or "no" under each operation.

Commutativity. Addition is commutative, e.g., $3 + 4 = 4 + 3$. Any operation, *, is said to be commutative when for any two elements of the defined set $a * b = b * a$. Use 3 and 4 as the elements to decide if the other three operations are probably commutative. Check your answer with the ones listed at the top of the following page.

Associativity. Addition is associative, e.g., $12 + (6 + 2) = (12 + 6) + 2$ or $12 + 8 = 18 + 2$. Any operation, *, is said to be associative when for any three elements of the set it is true that $a * (b * c) = (a * b) * c$. Use 12, 6, and 2 to decide if the other three operations are probably associative. Check your answers with those on the middle of the following page.

> *Commutativity:*
>
> Subtraction: $3 - 4 \neq 4 - 3$ no
> Multiplication: $3 \times 4 = 4 \times 3$ yes
> Division: $3 \div 4 \neq 4 \div 3$ no

Identity Element. Addition has an identity element, e.g., $3 + 0 = 0 + 3 = 3$. An operation, $*$ is said to have an identity element, e, if for any element of the set it is true that $b * e = e * b = b$. When $* = +$, $e = 0$. Can you find elements for $* = -$, $* = \times$, and $* = \div$? Check your answers with the ones listed on the top of the following page.

> *Associativity:*
>
> Subtraction: $12 - (6 - 2) \neq (12 - 6) - 2$
>   since $12 - 4 \neq 6 - 2$ no
> Multiplication: $12 \times (6 \times 2) = (12 \times 6) \times 2$
>   since $12 \times 12 = 72 \times 2$ yes
> Division: $12 \div (6 \div 2) \neq (12 \div 6) \div 2$
>   since $12 \div 3 \neq 2 \div 2$ no

Closure. Addition is closed over the set of whole numbers. An operation, $*$ is said to be closed if every pair of elements operated upon yields another element of the set, i.e., if a and b are elements of the set, then $a * b$ is also an element of the set. Three and four are whole numbers, and $3 + 4$ is a whole number. Use 3 and 4 to decide if the other operations are closed on the set of whole numbers. Check your responses with those on page 230.

Summary. Your table should now look like this:

	Addition	Subtraction	Multiplication	Division
Commutative	yes	no	yes	no
Associative	yes	no	yes	no
Identity Element	yes	no (right)	yes	no (right)
Closure	yes	no	yes	no

Addition and multiplication are referred to as *primary operations*. As you can see, they exhibit properties not possessed by their inverse operations, subtraction and division. In a sense, subtraction and division derive their meaning from addition and multiplication; subtraction is the operation which "undoes" addition, and division is the operation which "undoes" multiplication.

Identity elements:

Subtraction:	$3 - e = e - 3 = 3$	There is no e
Multiplication:	$3 \times e = e \times 3 = 3$	$e = 1$
Division:	$3 \div e = e \div 3 = 3$	There is no e

Subtraction and division are true for $3 - e = 3$ (zero) and $3 \div e = 3$ (one). Since they are only true when *e* is on the right, subtraction and division are said to have *right-hand identity* elements.

Distributivity.   A property sometimes exhibited by two different operations is the distributive property. *Multiplication is distributive over addition* over the set of whole numbers. Example: $2 \times (3 + 4) = (2 \times 3) + (2 \times 4)$ and $(3 + 4) \times 2 = (3 \times 2) + (4 \times 2)$; multiplication is distributive on the left and the right, respectively. Distributivity communicates *left and right. Right-hand* or *left-hand* is indicated if only one is true. One operation, *, is said to be distributive over another operation, #, if for any three elements of the set it is true that *a * (b # c) = (a * b) # (a * c)* and *(b # c) * a = (b * a) # (c * a)*. If only one case is true, * is said to be distributive over # on the left or right, respectively.

   Use $a = 12$, $b = 6$, and $c = 2$ to determine whether either or both cases of distributivity probably occur for division over addition; multiplication over subtraction, division over subtraction. Check your responses on page 231.

Closure:

Subtraction:	$3 - 4$ is not a whole number
Multiplication:	3×4 is a whole number
Division:	$3 \div 4$ is not a whole number

Sets and Operations

You have seen how each of the four basic operations can be related to sets. Addition is the operation associated with the union of disjoint sets; subtraction is that associated with the removal of a subset; multiplication is the opera-

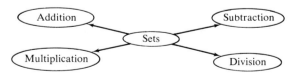

tion associated with the union of equivalent disjoint sets and division is that associated with the removal of equivalent disjoint subsets. In this manner sets can be emphasized as a basic idea throughout the K–4 curriculum.

Distributivity

Division over Addition:

Left*: $12 \div (6 + 2) \neq (12 \div 6) + (12 \div 2)$ because
          $12 \div \quad 8 \quad \neq \quad 2 \quad + \quad 6$ no

Right: $(6 + 2) \div 12 = (6 \div 12) + (2 \div 12)$ because
          $\frac{8}{12} \quad = \quad \frac{6}{12} \quad + \quad \frac{2}{12}$ yes

Multiplication over Subtraction:

Left*: $12 \times (6 - 2) = (12 \times 6) - (12 \times 2)$ because
          $12 \times \quad 4 \quad = \quad 72 \quad - \quad 24$ yes

Right: $(6 - 2) \times 12 = (6 \times 12) - (2 \times 12)$ because
          $4 \quad \times 12 = \quad 72 \quad - \quad 24$ yes

Division over Subtraction:

Left*: $12 \div (6 - 2) \neq (12 \div 6) - (12 \div 2)$ because
          $\frac{12}{4} \quad \neq \quad \frac{12}{6} \quad - \quad \frac{12}{2}$ no

Right: $(6 - 2) \div 12 = (6 \div 12) - (2 \div 12)$ because
          $\frac{4}{12} \quad = \quad \frac{6}{12} \quad - \quad \frac{2}{12}$ yes

 * Left—the operation being distributed is on the left side of the parenthetical expression.

Each new operation can be related to sets and, through sets, to other operations. Subtraction is the inverse of addition, and division is the inverse of multi-

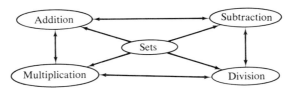

plication. Multiplication can be related to repeated addition, and division can be related to repeated subtraction. Thus, with sets as a curriculum nucleus, operations can be seen to form an interrelated core of mathematics concepts.

Teaching Multiplication and Division Facts

As with addition and subtraction, a multiplication or division fact is the relationship between three numbers at least two of which can be represented by a single digit. A multiplication fact is the product of two single-digit numerals such as $5 \times 9 = 45$, and a division fact is the division of a single- or two-digit numeral and a single-digit numeral in which the quotient is a single-digit numeral, e.g., $8 \div 2 = 4$ or $45 \div 9 = 5$. There are 100 multiplication facts. There are only 90 division facts since there can be no zero divisors.

Earliest experiences with multiplication usually begin with the two-facts since they can be related to addition facts, e.g., $2 \times 6 = 6 + 6 = 12$. Children can work with sets, array, number lines, cross-products and repeated addition to attach meaning to this operation. Division can be introduced concurrently to emphasize the "undoing" of the inverse operation.

Along with the two-facts, the corresponding commutative facts can be explored such as 6×2, 5×2, and 8×2. Skip counting can be used for these facts. To multiply 5×2, the child can hold up five fingers and count "2, 4, 6, 8, 10" as he points to, looks at or wiggles each finger.

Children can engage in renaming activities to begin to develop an understanding of the distributive property. When working with the twos, you can ask them to rename the second factor. Have the youngsters make sets of arrays

$$2 \quad \times \quad 6 \quad = \quad 12$$

first factor   second factor   product

to show that the product can be represented in a new way. This property is very useful in extending knowledge of multiplication facts.

$$2 \times 6 = 12 \qquad (2 \times 4) + (2 \times 2)$$

$$2 \times 4 = 8 \rightarrow 3 \times 4 = (2 + 1) \times 4$$
$$(2 \times 4) + (1 \times 4)$$
$$8 \quad + \quad 4$$
$$12$$

Exploration of the distributive property in relation to the twos, threes and fours builds an understanding of the concept. While extensive work with concrete materials is both desirable and necessary for early number facts, the increase in sheer number size dictates that concrete materials will be used relatively less as larger products are encountered. After 4×9 or 5×9, so many objects (greater than 45) are needed that number lines, arrays and abstract number patterns through the distributive property are used in increasing frequency. Specific strategies for using the distributive property are presented in the next section.

As children work with new facts, they can begin to build a multiplication chart similar to the addition table for reference and study. The table can be used by children to discover patterns and to work more sophisticated problems even though they have not committed the facts to memory. The particular problems associated with the identity, and zero in multiplication, and division by zero are examined in the next section.

The use of the chart is similar to the one for addition and subtraction: to locate the product of 6 and 7 find 6 in the left column and 7 across the top; the answer 42 is located at the intersection.

As with addition facts, 45 of the 100 multiplication facts are commutative pairs. Of the remaining 55, 10 are zero facts and 9 are identity element facts. With the aid of commutativity, zero facts and the identity element, the number of facts with different factors is only 36.

X	0	1	2	3	4	5	6	7	8	9
0	0	0	0	0	0	0	0	0	0	0
1	0	1	2	3	4	5	6	7	8	9
2	0	2	4	6	8	10	12	14	16	18
3	0	3	6	9	12	15	18	21	24	27
4	0	4	8	12	16	20	24	28	32	36
5	0	5	10	15	20	25	30	35	40	45
6	0	6	12	18	24	30	36	42	48	54
7	0	7	14	21	28	35	42	49	56	63
8	0	8	16	24	32	40	48	56	64	72
9	0	9	18	27	36	45	54	63	72	81

$2 \times 4 = 8$

located in left column

located across the top

intersection of "2" row and "4" column

Many activities for learning new facts are needed in the teaching repertoire of the third-grade teacher. Here are some ideas:

A. *Sets of related facts for twelve.* Ask the children to use pegboards to demonstrate these equations.

$$1 \times 12 = 12 \qquad 6 \times 2 = 12 \qquad 12 \div 3 = 4$$
$$2 \times 6 = 12 \qquad 12 \times 1 = 12 \qquad 12 \div 4 = 3$$
$$3 \times 4 = 12 \qquad 12 \div 1 = 12 \qquad 12 \div 6 = 2$$
$$4 \times 3 = 12 \qquad 12 \div 2 = 6 \qquad 12 \div 12 = 1$$

B. *Fact family for {3, 4, 12}.* Ask children to write fact family cards for number triplets.

$$3 \times 4 = 12 \qquad 12 \div 3 = 4$$
$$4 \times 3 = 12 \qquad 12 \div 4 = 3$$

C. *Patterns—Skip counting; multiples.* Ask children to count or mark off multiples on a number line.

$$2, 4, 6, 8, 10, 12, \ldots$$
$$3, 6, 9, 12, 15, 18, \ldots$$
$$4, 8, 12, 16, 20, 24, \ldots$$

D. *Distributive Property*. Ask children to rename one factor in as many ways as possible.

$$4 \times 7 = 4 \times (4 + 3) = 16 + 12 = 28$$

Refer to the addition and subtraction chapter for a review of activities and factors to consider in providing *practice* of facts.

Gray (1) found that instruction which emphasized the distributive property had several good effects. Pupil achievement was higher than from other methods, and children were able to proceed to new combinations independently. Teaching for structure seems to pay dividends. He also found that children did not develop an understanding of the distributive property unless it was specifically taught.

Other Materials and Discovery Strategies

In addition to the materials already described, Cuisenaire Rods, Sterns Blocks and other length-associated aids can be used. For detailed descriptions of these commercial materials consult manuals printed by appropriate companies.

Objects can be used in more than one way to show multiplication and division. Rod-type materials can be placed as illustrated to show $3 \times 8 = \square$.

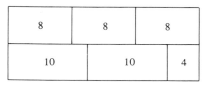

$$3 \times 8 = 20 + 4 = 24$$

To show $24 \div 6 = \square$ or $21 \div 6 = \square$ the rods can be placed as in the following figures.

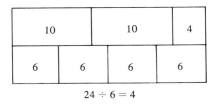

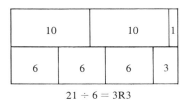

$$24 \div 6 = 4 \qquad\qquad 21 \div 6 = 3R3$$

Pegboards and pieces of graph paper are excellent manipulative aids for illustrating arrays.

Discovery

Children can be led to discover most of the multiplication and division properties, facts and relationships. Here are some examples; you can think of others.

A. *Commutativity*. Give children worksheets with intermittently spaced commutative pairs of problems to be solved with sets, arrays or number lines. Make the pairs increasingly frequent in the list to ensure success of discovery.

B. *Associativity and Commutativity*. Use some problem situations involving three factors. Challenge small groups to explain several ways to compute the result. Example: Bill and Joe have six dimes each. How many suckers can they buy if suckers are three-for-a-dime?

$$\text{Boys} \times \text{dimes} \times \text{suckers/dime}; 2 \times 6 \times 3$$
$$\text{Boys} \times \text{suckers/dime} \times \text{dimes}; 2 \times 3 \times 6$$
$$\text{Suckers/dime} \times \text{dimes} \times \text{boys}; 3 \times 6 \times 2$$

Others: Muffins—2 rows, 3 columns, 4 pans
Windows—3 houses, 6 windows, 4 panes
Horses—4 teams, 3 rows, 2 columns

C. *Distributivity*. Give a set of problems involving a sum and a product. Instruct the small groups to see how many ways they can answer the question. Example: "There are three boys and four girls. How many cookies will be needed if each person receives two?"

$$\text{cookies} \times (\text{boys} + \text{girls}) = 2 \times (3 + 4)$$
$$(\text{cookies} \times \text{boys}) + (\text{cookies} \times \text{girls}) = (2 \times 3) + (2 \times 4)$$

A more abstract experience is to play with arrays. Have each group work with an array of a different size. Ask them to write down the product, fold the array between two rows or two columns, rename the folded side and represent the three products. A dittoed sheet would be helpful.

Array: 4 × 7		
Name	Single Product	Sum of Products
$7 = 6 + 1$	$4 \times (6 + 1)$	$(4 \times 6) + (4 \times 1)$
$4 = 1 + 3$	$(1 + 3) \times 7$	$(1 \times 7) + (3 \times 7)$

D. *Facts*. After children have worked with the distributive property, they can use it to discover new facts. Challenge them to use renaming and the distributive property to find 6×7 after they have worked with the fives. They may write $6 \times (5 + 2) = (6 \times 5) + (6 \times 2) = 30 + 12 = 42$ or any one of several other ways.

E. *Operational Relationships*. Have children guess a rule for associating numbers. Example: Choose a rule such as $3 \times \square + 1 = \triangle$ and set up columns for the relation. Children give you values for $\square$, and you indicate the corresponding value for $\triangle$. Instead of telling the rule the child is challenged to give a value of $\square$ *and* $\triangle$ to test his hypothesis. Films of the Madison Project have activities similar to this.

F. *Division by Zero is Undefined.* Give youngsters a set of simple division facts to solve by the repeated subtraction method. Include a zero divisor. Example: $8 \div 2 = \square$, $6 \div 3 = \square$, $12 \div 4 = \square$, $6 \div 0 = \square$, $9 \div 3 = \square$. Children will discover that removal of empty sets will never exhaust the set of 6! You can also include some division by zero examples in a set to be verified by using inverse statements, e.g., $12 \div 3 = \square$ relates to $\square \times 3 = 12$, so $\square = 4$. When the child comes to $6 \div 0 = \square$ he relates it to $\square \times 0 = 6$. There is no such number! For $0 \div 0 = \square$, the inverse statement $\square \times 0 = 0$ has many answers so this, too, is undefined since operations can have only *one* answer.

G. *Patterns.* Children can use sequences to discover multiplication and multiplication-addition patterns. They can use a hundreds chart to do this, too.

1. 2, 4, 6, 8, ____, ____, ____, ____ $(2 \times n)$
2. 4, 8, 12, ____, ____, ____, ____ $(4 \times n)$
3. 3, 7, 11, ____, ____, ____, ____ $(4 \times n - 1)$

Cross out all multiples of two or three or six on the chart. Children can discover visual patterns and number patterns. For example, all multiples of 6 are also multiples of two and multiples of three. A hundred chart has ten rows of ten counting numbers like this:

1	2	3	4	5	6	7	8	9	10
11	12	13	14	15	16	17	18	19	20

(and so on to 100)

Accommodation of Individual Differences

Introductory work on multiplication and division will necessarily focus upon the child's *mastery* of the concepts; *memory* will be emphasized after mastery. Therefore, objectives which focus upon concrete and semi-concrete behaviors relative to *facts* are most appropriate.

Here is a partial list of the concepts:

A. Multiplication	F. Identity
B. Division	G. Distributivity
C. Inverse Relation	H. Set of Related Facts
D. Commutativity	I. Fact Family
E. Associativity	J. Number Sentences

And here are some sample objectives:

A & B. (Concrete) Given a multiplication or division fact, the child will be able to determine the product or quotient with the use of objects provided.

A & B. (Semi-Concrete) Given a multiplication or division fact, the child will be able to determine the product or quotient with a number line.

A & B. (Abstract) Given a multiplication or division fact, the child will be able to determine the product or quotient with repeated addition or repeated subtraction.

Children can also be *given* sets, number line pictures and repeated addition or subtraction equations and asked to write the appropriate multiplication or division sentences.

G. (Concrete) the child will be able to demonstrate a given distributive statement on a pegboard.

G. (Semi-Concrete) Given an array with a vertical line through the middle the child will be able to write an appropriate distributive sentence.

G. (Abstract) Given two factors, the child will be able to rename one of the factors and write the corresponding distributive sentence.

As a result of preassessment, the children who have acquired the concept(s) of the unit can work on activities which will help them remember the basic combinations (facts). The rest of the class can work with concrete materials such as popsicle sticks, pebbles and buttons, or number lines or arrays, depending on their respective levels of development. They can work individually, or, more preferably, in small groups.

When several children have attained adequate mastery of the concept, you can diagnose. You can usually rely upon your observations of pupil work to decide which ones are still functioning at the concrete level *if you jot down some observation notes*. Then you can base your diagnostic test primarily on the semi-concrete and abstract behaviors since these lend themselves a bit more readily to large-group evaluation.

Children who perform well at both the semi-concrete and abstract levels can be placed in the enrichment group which will focus on activities designed to help children *remember* basic facts. Children who perform satisfactorily on semi-concrete activities but encounter difficulty on abstract relationships can work in a practice group in which the focus is semi-concrete and abstract developmental exercises. And those whose performance is weak at the semi-concrete level should be encouraged to join the reteach group in which activities are focused on mastery at the concrete and semi-concrete levels.

When all the children in the reteach group have developed the concepts, bring the class back together and move to the next unit of instruction. If everyone has not reached this level, you may need to go on anyway because of time considerations or class restlessness. In such a case, use the techniques described in the chapter on slow and fast learners to accommodate the specific needs of those who are unusually slow in attaining mastery.

Consult the development of addition and subtraction chapter and the content and bibliography of the chapter on materials of instruction for activities and suggestions in addition to those described in this chapter.

Project and Discussion Topics

1. Make up some division questions or locate some in a third- or fourth-grade textbook. Decide if each one is a measurement or a partition question.

2. Suggest other ways to demonstrate the multiplicative commutative and associative properties and distributivity of multiplication over addition.

3. Suggest other activities for *developing* multiplication and division facts.

4. Suggest other activities for *practicing* multiplication and division facts.

5. Suggest other activities for *discovering* patterns, commutativity, associativity, fact families and distributivity.

6. Write other behavioral objectives on the major concepts of this chapter at the concrete, semi-concrete and abstract levels.

7. Write evaluation items which measure pupil achievement on the objectives listed in this chapter and/or the objectives which you wrote in the previous question.

8. Suggest some appropriate activities for the practice group following diagnosis.

Additional Resources

Filmstrips

> *Two Properties of Multiplication: Commutative and Associative,* Popular Science (4H–3)
> *Multiplication Forms and the Distributive Property,* Popular Science (4H–4)
> *Solution Sets,* Popular Science (7H–2)
> *Modern Mathematics: Number Line—Whole Numbers,* Society for Visual Education (A532–6)

Films

> *Creative Learning Experiences,* Madison Project
> *An Excerpt from Operations of Arithmetic,* Madison Project
> *Multiplication and Its Properties,* National Council of Teachers of Mathematics

Division, National Council of Teachers of Mathematics

Elementary School Textbooks

Silver Burdett (1970), Grade 2, *Modern Mathematics Through Discovery,* by R. Morton, M. Ross, H. S. More, M. Gray, E. Sage, W. Collins.

Student Text: pp. 177–78, 181–86, 205–08, 235–36, 251–56.

Silver Burdett (1970), Grade 3, *Modern Mathematics Through Discovery,* by R. Morton, M. Ross, H. S. More, M. Gray, E. Sage, W. Collins.

Student Text: pp. 152–68, 230–51.

Houghton-Mifflin Company, (1970), Grade 2, *Modern School Mathematics,* by E. Duncan, L. Capps, M. Dolciani, W. Quast, M. Zweng.

Student Text: pp. 281–318.

Houghton-Mifflin Company (1970), Grade 3, *Modern School Mathematics,* by E. Duncan, L. Capps, M. Dolciani, W. Quast, M. Zweng.

Student Text: pp. 126–59, 190–209.

Bibliography

1. Gray, Roland F. "An Experiment in the Teaching of Introductory Multiplication." *The Arithmetic Teacher* (March 1966), 13:187–91.

2. Hervey, Margaret A. "Children's Responses to Two Types of Multiplication Problems." *The Arithmetic Teacher* (April 1966), 13:288–92.

3. Zweng, Marilyn J. "Division Problems and the Concept of Rate." *The Arithmetic Teacher* (December 1964), 11:547–56.

12

Teaching Multiplication and Division Algorithms

As with the previous chapter on algorithms, this chapter is also divided into three sections: Content and Specific Methodology; General Methods and Specific Materials of Instruction; and Accommodation of Individual Differences.

Section one has behaviorally stated objectives which you will attain by going through the auto-tutorial materials presented in a programmed format. At the end of the section, you will find a self-test and answers on which you may evaluate your performance.

Section two relates multiplication and division algorithms more specifically to the general treatments in this text on guided discovery learning and materials of instruction. Relevant research is cited and translated.

Section three explores more specifically the relations between the algorithms of section one and others created by students. The individualization model with specific suggestions on objectives, readiness, diagnosis, slow and fast learners, evaluation and psychology is also expanded.

Content and Specific Methodology

After you have read the following list of behavioral objectives, you may wish to take Part I of the self-test at the end of this section. If you perform satisfactorily, you may wish to skim the multiplication section quickly or to omit it. After Part I, proceed to Part II on division algorithms and follow a similar pattern.

Multiplication Algorithms

Objectives

When you have completed this unit, you will be able to describe and illustrate the development of the standard algorithm for multiplication of whole numbers. You will be able to:

(1) Multiply two-digit by one-digit numerals with and without regrouping and two two-digit numerals without regrouping using a horizontal-expanded notation algorithm.

(2) Multiply two two-digit numerals with regrouping by using a shortened horizontal form.

(3) Multiply one- and two-digit numerals in all three vertical forms:
A. Expanded Notation
B. Partial Products
C. Standard or Traditional Algorithm.

(4) Use arrays and paper strips to demonstrate the steps in an algorithm.

Materials Needed

Arrays will be used to develop pupil understanding of multiplication computational procedures. An easy way to make arrays is to mark off sheets of paper in squares and make dots on the intersections. Another simple way is to get some graph paper and shade in every other or every third section. The following arrays are needed: 3 × 13, 4 × 12, 4 × 13, 12 × 23.

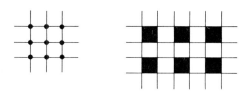

The paper strips from addition and subtraction will also be used.

⊞⊞⊞⊞⊞⊞⊞⊞⊞⊞ —1 strip of paper is *one ten.*

☐ —ten small pieces are *10 ones.*

Assumptions:

A. Children know all multiplication facts through $9 \times 9 = 81$.

B. Children have worked extensively with expanded notation and names for numbers.

C. Children are familiar with the commutative and associative properties of multiplication.

D. The teacher has developed pupil understanding of the distributive property of multiplication over addition on the set of whole numbers.

These are arrays:

(a) · · · ·   (b) · · · · ·   (c) · ·   (d) · · ·
· · · ·   · · · · ·   · ·   · · ·
                     · · · · ·   · ·   · · ·
                                                            · · ·

An array is always described in terms of its rows and columns *in that order.* For example (a) above is a 2 × 4 (two by four) array. What are each of the others? The order is important.

This array is a 3 × 4 array: · · · ·
                                 · · · ·
                                 · · · ·

(e) Turn your book 90°. Now what is the array?
(f) Make a 5 × 4 array.

LOOK AT ANSWER FRAME (M–1).

The simple manipulation of rotation represents a visual model which shows that a 3 × 4 array is the same (has the same number of dots) as a 4 × 3 array: 3 × 4 = 4 × 3. This helps show that multiplication is commutative.

You used groups of ten in addition and subtraction:

$$
\begin{array}{rcl}
36 &=& 30 + 6 \\
+\,47 &=& 40 + 7 \\
\hline
&& 70 + 13 \\
&& 83
\end{array}
\qquad
\begin{array}{rcl}
42 &=& 30 + 12 \\
-\,13 &=& -(10 + 3) \\
\hline
&& 20 + 9 \\
&& 29
\end{array}
$$

You will also use groups of ten in developing multiplication algorithms.

CONTINUE TO FRAME M–3.

Arrays are of special significance in multiplication because they help you develop understanding of distributivity. A 4 × 5 array can be separated or partitioned into a 4 × 2 array and a 4 × 3 array.

· · · · ·   · · | · · ·
· · · · ·   · · | · · ·
· · · · ·   ↔   · · | · · ·
· · · · ·   · · | · · ·

A 4 × 5 array is made up of a 4 × 2 array and a 4 × 3 array. Renaming the five: 4(2 + 3) = (4 × 2) + (4 × 3)

This important property of multiplication and addition is particularly useful when grouping in 10s. Study the next frame carefully to see how the distributive property can be illustrated with an array and paper strips.

CONTINUE TO M–4.

M–4

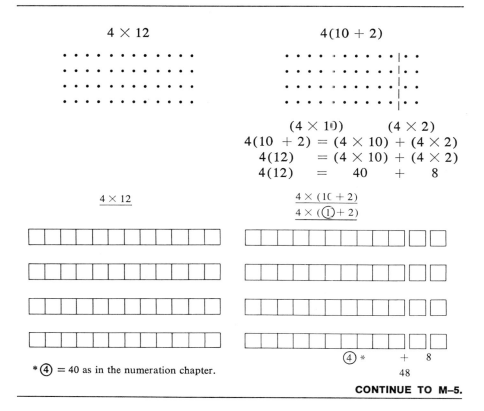

$$4 \times 12 \qquad\qquad\qquad 4(10 + 2)$$

$$(4 \times 10) \qquad (4 \times 2)$$
$$4(10 + 2) = (4 \times 10) + (4 \times 2)$$
$$4(12) \quad = (4 \times 10) + (4 \times 2)$$
$$4(12) \quad = \quad 40 \quad + \quad 8$$

4 × 12

$$4 \times (10 + 2)$$
$$4 \times (\textcircled{1} + 2)$$

$$\textcircled{4} * \qquad + \quad 8$$
$$48$$

* $\textcircled{4}$ = 40 as in the numeration chapter.

CONTINUE TO M–5.

M–5

Make a 3 × 13 array and fold it to show this product:

$$3 \times 13$$
$$3 \times (10 + 3)$$
$$(3 \times 10) + (3 \times 3) \qquad\qquad \text{Then show it with paper strips.}$$
$$30 + 9$$
$$39$$

SEE ANSWER FRAME (M–5).

M–6

As with addition and subtraction, the standard or traditional algorithm will be developed through a sequence of four levels of difficulty:

   A. Two-digit numeral times one-digit numeral *without* regrouping of ones and tens. Example: $4 \times 12 = 48$
   B. Two-digit numeral times one-digit numeral *with* regrouping of ones and tens. Example: $4 \times 13 = 52$
   C. Two-digit numeral times two-digit numeral *without* regrouping of ones and tens. Example: $13 \times 12 = 156$
   D. Two-digit numeral times two-digit numeral *with* regrouping of ones and tens. Example: $14 \times 16 = 224$

CONTINUE TO M–7.

(b) 3 by 5   (f) $\cdot$ $\cdot$ $\cdot$ $\cdot$
(c) 3 $\times$ 2 $\cdot$ $\cdot$ $\cdot$ $\cdot$
(d) four by three $\cdot$ $\cdot$ $\cdot$ $\cdot$
(e) 4 $\times$ 3 (four by three) $\cdot$ $\cdot$ $\cdot$ $\cdot$
                                               $\cdot$ $\cdot$ $\cdot$ $\cdot$

CONTINUE TO M–2.

M–7

A. *Two-digit numeral times one-digit numeral* without *regrouping of ones and tens*.

Make a 4 $\times$ 12 array and use the paper strips.

Show that $4 \times 12 =$ $4 \times (10 + 2)$ Expanded Notation
                     $= (4 \times 10) + (4 \times 2)$ Distributivity
                     $=$ $40 + 8$ Multiplication
                     $=$ 48 Addition or Renaming

SEE ANSWER FRAME (M–7).

M–8

B. *Two-digit numeral times one-digit numeral* with *regrouping of ones and tens*.

Make a 4 $\times$ 13 array and use the paper strips.

Show the following:
          (a) 4×13 Problem
          (b) $4 \times (10 + 3)$ Expanded Notation
          (c) $(4 \times 10) + (4 \times 3)$ Distributive Property
          (d) $40 + 12$ Multiplication
          (e) $40 + (10 + 2)$ Expanded Notation
          (f) $(40 + 10) + 2$ Associative Property
                       $50 + 2$ Add or Rename
                         52 Add or Rename

The sequence from step (e) to step (f) is a change from 10 ones to 1 ten and can be made clear with "bundling" or replacing ten-unit paper pieces with one ten-strip:

          $\text{④} + (10 + 2)$ 4 tens + (10 ones + 2 ones)
          $(\text{④} + \text{①}) + 2$ (4 tens + 1 ten) + 2 ones

SEE ANSWER FRAME (M–8).

M–9

You supply the reasons:

(a)	5(17)	5(17)
(b)	5(10 + 7)	5(①) + 7)
(c)	(5 × 10) + (5 × 7)	(5 × ①)) + (5 × 7)
(d)	50 + 35	⑤) + 35
(e)	50 + (30 + 5)	⑤) + (30 + 5)
(f)	(50 + 30) + 5	(⑤) + ③)) + 5
(g)	80 + 5	⑧) + 5
(h)	85	85

Notice as with addition that only one change occurs in each step.

SEE ANSWER FRAME (M–9).

(M–5)

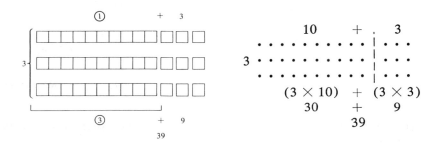

$$(3 \times 10) + (3 \times 3)$$
$$30 + 9$$
$$39$$

CONTINUE TO M–6.

M–10

As you probably have guessed, children wouldn't be expected to duplicate all these steps. Consider this:

All Steps	Shortened Form
6 × 17	6 × 17
6 × (10 + 7)	6 × (10 + 7)
(6 × 10) + (6 × 7)	(6 × 10) + (6 × 7) — optional*
60 + 42	60 + 42 ⟶ 42 60
60 + (40 + 2)	+ 60 or +42
(60 + 40) + 2	102 ⟵ 102 102
100 + 2	
102	

Children know that addition is commutative.

* The inclusion of this step should depend on how well the pupils understand the concept. If they are weak, they should include it.

CONTINUE TO M–11.

Do these both ways. Include the optional step.   3 × 18   3 × 13

SEE ANSWER FRAME (M–11).

4 × 12

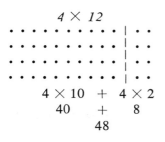

4 × 10 + 4 × 2
  40   +   8
      48

No regrouping was necessary.

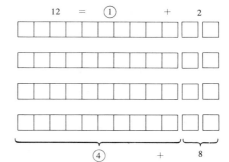

CONTINUE TO M–8.

(a)   *4 × 13*
                10   +   3
(b)

4

(c)   4 × 10   4 × 3
(d)   40   +   12

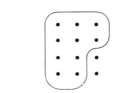

(e)   40   + (10 + 2)
(f)   (40   + 10) + 2

Replace ten ☐ with
one

④ + ① + 2
⑤ + 2
52

CONTINUE TO M–9.

(M–9)

    (a) Problem

    (b) Expanded Notation

    (c) Distributivity

    (d) Multiplication

    (e) Expanded Notation

    (f) Associativity

    (g) Add or Rename

    (h) Add or Rename

CONTINUE TO M–10.

M–12

On these two, work formal proofs with reasons (all steps) and the short form without option.

$$6 \times 12 \qquad\qquad 7 \times 13$$

Verify your work with arrays.

SEE ANSWER FRAME (M–12).

M–13

C. Two-digit numeral times two-digit numeral without regrouping.

This time you will use the distributive property three times, as indicated by the underlined sections below.

$$12 \times 23$$

$$
\begin{aligned}
&12 \times 23 \\
&12(20 + 3) \\
&(12 \times 20) + (12 \times 3) \\
&[(10 + 2)20] + [(10 + 2)3] \\
&*[(10 \times 20) + (2 \times 20)] + \\
&\quad [(10 \times 3) + (2 \times 3)] \\
&*(200 + 40) + (30 + 6) \\
&[(200 + 40) + 30] + 6 \\
&[200 + (40 + 30)] + 6 \\
&200 + 70 + 6 \\
&276
\end{aligned}
$$

* Can you identify each of these products on the diagram?

Relate the steps of the problem to your array.

How would you say 10×20, 2×20, 10×3 and 2×3 to build upon and to reinforce basic facts?

SEE ANSWER FRAME (M–13).

All Steps	Short Form With Option	Short Form Without Option
3×18	3×18	3×18
$3 \times (10 + 8)$	$3 \times (10 + 8)$	$3 \times (10 + 8)$
$(3 \times 10) + (3 \times 8)$	$(3 \times 10) + (3 \times 8)$	
$30 + 24$	$30 + 24 \longrightarrow 24$	$30 + 24 \longrightarrow 24$
$30 + (20 + 4)$	$+30$	$+30$
$(30 + 20) + 4$	$54 \longleftarrow 54$	$54 \longleftarrow 54$
$50 + 4$		
54		

3×13	3×13	3×13
$3(10 + 3)$	$3 \times (10 + 3)$	$3 \times (10 + 3)$
$(3 \times 10) + (3 \times 3)$	$(3 \times 10) + (3 \times 3)$	
$30 \quad + \quad 9$	$30 \quad + \quad 9$	$30 + 9$
39	39	39

**IF YOU GOT THESE ALL RIGHT, SKIP FRAME
M–12, AND GO ON TO FRAME M–13.**

M–14

The child could do it like this:

$$12 \times 23$$
$$12(20 + 3)$$
$$(12 \times 20) + (12 \times 3)$$
$$(10 + 2)20 + (10 + 2)3$$
$$200 + 40 + 30 + 2 \longrightarrow 2$$
$$30$$
$$40$$
$$200$$
$$272 \longleftarrow 272$$

Draw a diagram and work this one both ways:

$$21 \times 42$$

Because the distributive property is used three times, this algorithm is usually not included in elementary school textbooks.

SEE ANSWER FRAME (M–14).

M–15

Try this using the short form:

(a) 14×21

Try this one using all steps: (b) 7×26

SEE ANSWER FRAME (M–15).

D. *Two two-digit numerals* **with** *regrouping.*

$$24 \times 37$$
$$24(30 + 7)$$
$$(24 \times 30) + (24 \times 7)$$
$$[(20 + 4)30] + [(20 + 4)7]$$
$$[(20 \times 30) + (4 \times 30)] + [(20 \times 7) + (4 \times 7)]$$
$$(600 + 120) + (140 + 28)$$

$[600 + (100 + 20)] + (140 + 28)$	$700 + [(100 + 60) + 28]$
$[(600 + 100) + 20] + (140 + 28)$	$700 + [100 + (60 + 28)]$
$(700 + 20) + (140 + 28)$	$(700 + 100) + (60 + 28)$
$700 + [20 + (140 + 28)]$	$800 + (60 + 28)$
$700 + [(20 + 140) + 28]$	$800 + [60 + (20 + 8)]$
$700 + [(140 + 20) + 28]$	$800 + [(60 + 20) + 8]$
$700 + \{[(100 + 40) + 20] + 28\}$	$800 + 80 + 8$
$700 + \{[100 + (40 + 20)] + 28\}$	888

Supply reasons for each step.

SEE ANSWER FRAME (M–16).

(M–12)

6×12	Problem	7×13
$6 \times (10 + 2)$	Expanded Notation	$7 \times (10 + 3)$
$(6 \times 10) + (6 \times 2)$	Distributive Property	$(7 \times 10) + (7 \times 3)$
$60 + 12$	Multiplication	$70 + 21$
$60 + (10 + 2)$	Expanded Notation	$70 + (20 + 1)$
$(60 + 10) + 2$	Associativity	$(70 + 20) + 1$
$70 + 2$	Add or Rename	$90 + 1$
72	Add or Rename	91

$$6 \times 12$$
$$6 \times (10 + 2)$$
$$60 + 12 \longrightarrow 12$$
$$\underline{+ 60}$$
$$72 \longleftarrow 72$$

$$7 \times 13$$
$$7 \times (10 + 3)$$
$$70 + 21 \longrightarrow 21$$
$$\underline{+ 70}$$
$$91 \longleftarrow 91$$

CONTINUE TO M–13.

(M–13)

	20	+ 3
	10 × 20 array	10 × 3
10 + 2	(200)	(30)
	2 × 20 array (40)	2 × 3

"1 ten times 2 tens is 2 hundreds"
"2 times 2 tens is 4 tens"
"1 ten times 3 is 3 tens"
"2 times 3 is 6"

Reinforce and build upon those basic multiplication facts!

CONTINUE TO M–14.

M–17

The preceding frame was a rather detailed analysis of the steps involved. The short form is like this:

$$24 \times 37$$
$$24(30 + 7)$$
$$(24 \times 30) + (24 \times 7)$$
$$(20 + 4)30 + (20 + 4)7$$
$$600 + 120 + 140 + 28$$

$$\begin{array}{r} 28 \\ 140 \\ 120 \\ 600 \\ \hline 888 \end{array}$$

$$888 \longleftarrow 888$$

Try this one: 17×39 (short form). You need not learn the long form steps.

SEE ANSWER FRAME (M–17).

(M–14)

All Steps

$$21 \times 42$$
$$21(40 + 2)$$
$$(21 \times 40) + (21 \times 2)$$
$$[(20 + 1)40] + [(20 + 1)2]$$
$$[(20 \times 40) + (1 \times 40)] + [(20 \times 2) + (1 \times 2)]$$
$$(800 + 40) + (40 + 2)$$
$$[(800 + 40) + 40] + 2$$
$$[800 + (40 + 40)] + 2$$
$$800 + \quad 80 \quad + 2$$
$$882$$

Short Form

$$21 \times 42$$
$$21(40 + 2)$$
$$(21 \times 40) + (21 \times 2)$$
$$(20 + 1)40 + (20 + 1)2$$
$$800 + 40 + 40 + 2 \longrightarrow 2$$

$$\begin{array}{r} 40 \\ 40 \\ 800 \\ \hline 882 \end{array}$$

$$882 \longleftarrow 882$$

	40	+ 2
20	800	40
+		
1	40	2

IF YOU HAVE MASTERED THIS, SKIP THE NEXT FRAME, M–15.

(M–15)

(a)

$$14 \times 21$$
$$14(20 + 1)$$
$$(14 \times 20) + (14 \times 1)$$
$$(10 + 4)20 + (10 + 4)1$$
$$200 + 80 + 10 + 4$$
$$294$$

(b)

$$7 \times 26$$
$$7(20 + 6)$$
$$(7 \times 20) + (7 \times 6)$$
$$140 + 42$$
$$(100 + 40) + (40 + 2)$$
$$[(100 + 40) + 40] + 2$$
$$[100 + (40 + 40)] + 2$$
$$100 + 80 + 2$$
$$182$$

CONTINUE TO M–16.

(M–16)

Problem	Commutativity
Expanded Notation	Expanded Notation
Distributive Property	Associative Property
Expanded Notation	Add
Distributive Property	Associative Property
Renaming or Multiplication	Associative Property
Expanded Notation	Add
Associative Property	Expanded Notation
Add	Associative Property
Associative Property	Add
Associative Property	Add

CONTINUE TO M–17.

M–18

Before proceeding to vertical algorithmic forms, try these to see if you have mastered all four horizontal types.

Show all steps

(a) $14 \times 2 = 2 \times 14$
(b) $26 \times 3 = 3 \times 26$ $\Big\}$ Distribute these on the right side this time.
(c) 21×14

Use the Short Form

(d) 26×47 Expand the 26 first this time.

SEE ANSWER FRAME (M–18).

M–19

You have examined horizontal forms for each type. Now take a look at *vertical forms* for each type:

A. *Two-digit times one-digit* without *regrouping*.

Horizontal	*Vertical*	
	Expanded Notation	*Partial Products*

$$4 \times 21$$
$$4 \times (20 + 1)$$
$$(4 \times 20) + (4 \times 1)$$
$$80 + 4$$
$$84$$

	Expanded Notation	Partial Products
	21 = 20 + 1	21
	× 4 × 4	× 4
	80 + 4	4
	84	80
		84

Note that 4×20 would be "four times two tens which is 8 tens."

Try this one all three ways: 4(32)

SEE ANSWER FRAME (M–19).

$$17 \times 39$$
$$17(30 + 9)$$
$$(17 \times 30) + (17 \times 9)$$
$$(10 + 7)30 + (10 + 7)9$$
$$300 + 210 + 90 + 63$$
$$663$$

63
90
210
300
663

CONTINUE TO M–18.

B. *Two-digit times one-digit* with *regrouping.*

Horizontal	*Vertical*	
	Expanded Notation	*Partial Products*

$$4 \times 16$$
$$4 \times (10 + 6)$$
$$(4 \times 10) + (4 \times 6)$$
$$40 + 24$$
$$40 + (20 + 4)$$
$$(40 + 20) + 4$$
$$60 + 4$$
$$64$$

Expanded Notation:

$$16 = 10 + 6$$
$$\times\ 4$$
$$\overline{40 + 24}$$
$$64$$

Partial Products:

$$16$$
$$\times\ 4$$
$$\overline{24}$$
$$40$$
$$\overline{64}$$

Try this one all three ways: 6×16

SEE ANSWER FRAME (M–20).

C. *Two two-digit numerals* without *regrouping.*

Horizontal

$$21 \times 22$$
$$21 \times (20 + 2)$$
$$(21 \times 20) + (21 \times 2)$$
$$(20 + 1)20 + (20 + 1)2$$
$$[(20 \times 20) + (1 \times 20)] + [(20 \times 2) + (1 \times 2)]$$
$$(400 + 20) + (40 + 2)$$
$$400 + [20 + (40 + 2)]$$
$$400 + [(20 + 40) + 2]$$
$$400 +\qquad 60 \qquad + 2$$
$$462$$

Vertical
Expanded Notation

$$21 = 20 + 1$$
$$\times 22 \qquad 20 + 2$$
$$\overline{400 + 20 + 40 + 2}$$
$$462$$

Partial Products

$$21$$
$$\times 22$$
$$\overline{2}$$
$$40$$
$$20$$
$$400$$
$$\overline{462}$$

Try this one all three ways: 12×13

SEE ANSWER FRAME (M–21).

D. *Two-digit times two-digit* with *regrouping.*

Horizontal (Short Form)

$$37 \times 42$$
$$(30 + 7) \times 42$$
$$(30 \times 42) + (7 \times 42)$$
$$30(40 + 2) + 7(40 + 2)$$
$$1200 + 60 + 280 + 14$$
$$1554$$

Vertical

Expanded Notation   *Partial Products*

$$
\begin{array}{rl}
37 & = \quad 30 + 7 \\
\times 42 & \qquad 40 + 2 \\
\hline
& 1200 + 280 + 60 + 14 \\
& \qquad 1554
\end{array}
$$

$$
\begin{array}{r}
37 \\
\times 42 \\
\hline
14 \\
60 \\
280 \\
1200 \\
\hline
1554
\end{array}
$$

Try this one horizontally and with partial products: 62×47. Draw a diagram to show the partial products.

SEE ANSWER FRAME (M–22).

(a) 14×2
$$(10 + 4) \times 2$$
$$(10 \times 2) + (4 \times 2)$$
$$20 + 8$$
$$28$$

(c) 21×14
$$21 \times (10 + 4)$$
$$(21 \times 10) + (21 \times 4)$$
$$(20 + 1)10 + (20 + 1)4$$
$$[(20 \times 10) + (1 \times 10)] + [(20 \times 4) + (1 \times 4)]$$
$$(200 + 10) + (80 + 4)$$
$$200 + [10 + (80 + 4)]$$
$$200 + [(10 + 80) + 4]$$
$$200 + \qquad 90 \qquad + 4$$
$$294$$

(b) 26×3
$$(20 + 6) \times 3$$
$$(20 \times 3) + (6 \times 3)$$
$$60 + 18$$
$$60 + (10 + 8)$$
$$(60 + 10) + 8$$
$$70 + 8$$
$$78$$

(d) 26×47
$$(20 + 6) \times 47$$
$$(20 \times 47) + (6 \times 47)$$
$$20(40 + 7) + 6(40 + 7)$$
$$800 + 140 + 240 + 42$$
$$1222 \longleftarrow$$

$$
\begin{array}{r}
42 \\
240 \\
140 \\
800 \\
\hline
1222
\end{array}
$$

CONTINUE TO M–19.

Horizontal

$$4 \times 32$$
$$4 \times (30 + 2)$$
$$(4 \times 30) + (4 \times 2)$$
$$120 + 8$$
$$128$$

Vertical

Expanded Notation   *Partial Products*

$$
\begin{array}{rl}
32 & = \quad 30 + 2 \\
\times 4 & \qquad \times 4 \\
\hline
& 120 + 8 \\
& \qquad 128
\end{array}
$$

$$
\begin{array}{r}
32 \\
\times 4 \\
\hline
8 \\
120 \\
\hline
128
\end{array}
$$

CONTINUE TO M–20.

M–23

Now you have seen the development leading to the *standard algorithm* through utilization of the very important *distributive property*. You have seen how horizontal and vertical notation help develop pupil understanding of the operation *multiplication* when two-digit numerals are encountered. Now you are ready to culminate these efforts in the *standard algorithm*. Study the following progression which begins with two-digit times one-digit numerals with regrouping.

CONTINUE TO M–24.

(M–20)

$$
\begin{array}{llll}
6 \times 16 & 16 \;=\; 10 + 6 & 16 \\
6(10 + 6) & \underline{\times\; 6} \quad\; \underline{\times\; 6} & \underline{\times\; 6} \\
(6 \times 10) + (6 \times 6) & \qquad\;\; 60 + 36 & 36 \\
60 + 36 & \qquad\quad\;\; 96 & 60 \\
60 + (30 + 6) & & \overline{96} \\
(60 + 30) + 6 \\
90 + 6 \\
96
\end{array}
$$

Each of these is an algorithm. Each algorithm is more *efficient* than the one before.

CONTINUE TO M–21.

(M–21)

$$
\begin{array}{c}
12 \times 13 \\
12(10 + 3) \\
(12 \times 10) + (12 \times 3) \\
(10 + 2)10 + (10 + 2)3 \\
[(10 \times 10) + (2 \times 10)] + [(10 \times 3) + (2 \times 3)] \\
(100 + 20) + (30 + 6) \\
100 + [20 + (30 + 6)] \\
100 + [(20 + 30) + 6)] \\
100 \;\;+\;\; 50 \;\;+\;\; 6 \\
156
\end{array}
$$

Least efficient

$$
\begin{array}{ll}
13 \;=\; \quad 10 + 3 & \quad 13 \\
\underline{\times 12} \qquad \underline{10 + 2} & \underline{\times 12} \\
\quad\; 100 + 30 + 20 + 6 & \quad\;\; 6 \\
\qquad\quad 156 & \quad 20 \\
& \quad 30 \\
& \underline{100} \\
\text{More efficient} & \quad 156
\end{array}
$$

More efficient

CONTINUE TO M–22.

(M–22)

$$62 \times 47$$
$$62(40 + 7)$$
$$(62 \times 40) + (62 \times 7)$$
$$(60 + 2)40 + (60 + 2)7$$
$$2400 + 80 + 420 + 14$$
$$2914$$

$$\begin{array}{r} 47 \\ +62 \\ \hline 14 \\ 80 \\ 420 \\ \underline{2400} \\ 2914 \end{array}$$

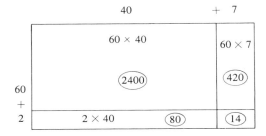

CONTINUE TO M–23.

M–24

Horizontal-Expanded Notation	*Vertical-Expanded Notation*

(a) 4×37

$4 \times (30 + 7)$

$(4 \times 30) + (4 \times 7)$

$120 + 28$

$120 + (20 + 8)$

$(120 + 20) + 8$

$[(100 + 20) + 20] + 8$

$[100 + (20 + 20)] + 8$

$100 + 40 + 8$

148

(b) $\begin{array}{r} 37 \\ \times\ 4 \\ \hline \end{array}$ $\begin{array}{r} 30 + 7 \\ \times\ 4 \\ \hline 120 + 28 \\ 148 \end{array}$

Partial Products	*Standard*		*Step 1*	*Step 2*

(c) $\begin{array}{r} 37 \\ \times\ 4 \\ \hline 28 \\ 120 \\ \hline 148 \end{array}$

(d) $\begin{array}{r} 37 \\ \times\ 4 \\ \hline 148 \end{array}$

(e) $\begin{array}{r} 37 \\ \times 24 \\ \hline 148 \\ 740 \\ \hline 888 \end{array}$ — *Step 3* $\begin{array}{r} 37 \\ \times\ 4 \\ \hline 148 \end{array}$ $\begin{array}{r} 37 \\ \times 20 \\ \hline 740 \end{array}$

(f) $\begin{array}{r} 37 \\ \times 24 \\ \hline 148 \\ 740 \\ \hline 888 \end{array}$

(g) $\begin{array}{r} 37 \\ \times 24 \\ \hline 148 \\ 74 \\ \hline 888 \end{array}$

Notice how each step is built upon the preceding steps.

THE END.

Division Algorithms

Objectives

When you have completed this unit, you will be able to:

(1) Estimate quotients using place value.

(2) Find quotients of two-digit by one-digit numerals by using the distributive property.

(3) Find quotients by repeated subtraction utilizing the *scaffolding* algorithm.

(4) Compute quotients utilizing the "round-up—round-down" method.

(5) Relate the steps of simple division problems to manipulation of objects.

Materials Needed

Objects for counting, about 50: paper clips, thumb tacks, hair pins, coins, etc.

Assumptions

A. Youngsters know all division facts through $81 \div 9 = 9$.

B. Teachers have used sets and have developed understandings in addition, subtraction, and multiplication, particularly in place value concepts and regrouping.

C. A readiness program has been followed in K–3 in developing understanding of estimation.

D–1

As noted in the chapter on developmental concepts of multiplication and division, the measurement concept of division is the one which lends itself more readily to an understanding of a division algorithm because

(1) It relates easily to a subtractive approach, and
(2) It does not require familiarity with fractional concepts.

Thus: $8 \div 2$ means, in the measurement concept, how many sets of two are there in eight?

$$8 - 2 = 6, \quad 6 - 2 = 4, \quad 4 - 2 = 2, \quad 2 - 2 = 0$$
$$1 \quad + \quad 1 \quad + \quad 1 \quad + \quad 1 \quad = 4$$

There are 4 sets of two in eight. Use the counters to show this. It is, as usual, imperative that the child be provided some kind of counters to gain concrete experiences with the operation of division.

SEE ANSWER FRAME (D–1).

D–2

Since division is the inverse operation of multiplication, the statement could be restated.

$$8 \div 2 = \square \quad \text{means} \quad \square \times 2 = 8$$
$$\square = 4 \quad \text{so there are 4 twos in eight.}$$

There exist many circumstances in which the answer is not so obvious.

For example: $7 \div 2$ $7 - 2 = 5, \quad 5 - 2 = 3, \quad 3 - 2 = 1$
$$1 \quad + \quad 1 \quad + \quad 1 \quad = 3$$

You get 3 twos and 1 left over which is written: 3R1.

Use the counters to show this.

SEE ANSWER FRAME (D–2).

D–3

Hence, $7 \div 2 = 3R1$
$\quad 7 = 3 \times 2 + 1$ There are 3 twos and 1 left over in 7.
$\quad 8 = 4 \times 2$ There are 4 twos in 8.

Examine how you can use the *distributive property* to help solve a division question:

$$42 \div 3 = \square$$

Suppose you know that $8 \times 3 = 24$,
then $42 = (8 \times 3) + 18$ *but* $3 \times 6 = 18$, so now by the distributive property,
$\quad 42 = (8 \times 3) + (6 \times 3)$
$\quad 42 = (8 + 6)3$ or
$\quad 42 = 14 \times 3$.
So, $42 \div 3 = 14$.

CONTINUE TO D–4.

Notice how the distributive property was utilized. Now, $57 \div 6$ implies that there exists a $\triangle$ and $\square$ such that

$$\boxed{57 = \triangle \times 6 + \square \text{ where } \square \text{ is less than 6.}}$$

You remember that $7 \times 6 = 42$.

Then $57 = (7 \times 6) + 15$. You remember that $2 \times 6 = 12$.

$57 = (7 \times 6) + [(2 \times 6) + 3]$
$57 = [(7 \times 6) + (2 \times 6)] + 3$ ⟶ Distributive Property
$57 = (7 + 2) \times 6 + 3$
$57 = 9 \times 6 + 3$ ⟶ $57 \div 6 = 9R3$
$57 = \triangle \times 6 + \square$
$57 = 9 \times 6 + 3$ Thus: $\triangle = 9$ and $\square = 3$

Try this one using $7 \times 7 = 49$: $69 \div 7$

SEE ANSWER FRAME (D–4).

In actual practice, this approach is seldom used with youngsters because the *scaffolding* algorithm is easy to use and easy to understand:

$27 \div 6$ is 6)27

		count out 27 objects:
6	1×6 (1 six)	remove 6
21		
6	1×6 (1 six)	remove 6
15		
6	1×6 (1 six)	remove 6
9		
6	1×6 (1 six)	remove 6
3		⟶ you have 3 left

Altogether: 4 sixes and 3 left over: 4R3

You think of having 27 pieces of candy and passing them out 6 at a time and then count to see how many children received candy. Four children received 6 pieces of candy and there were three pieces left.

CONTINUE TO D–6.

Another: $44 \div 9$.   *Count out 44 objects* (supply the missing numerals).

9 is called the *divisor*.
44 is called the *dividend*.
The result is called the *quotient*.

9)44

9	$1 \times 9 \rightarrow$	remove *one* set of 9
35		
(a)	$1 \times 9 \rightarrow$	remove *one* set of 9
26		
18	$2 \times 9 \rightarrow$	remove *two* sets of 9
(b)		

4 nines and (c) left over: 4R(d)

Use your objects and write the steps for $41 \div 6$ taking two sets of 6 each time.

SEE ANSWER FRAME (D–6).

(D–1)

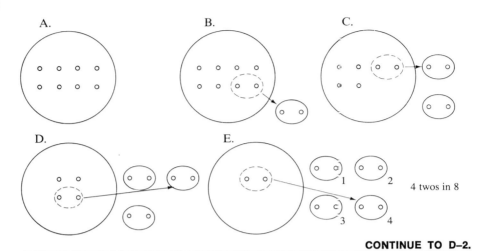

CONTINUE TO D–2.

(D–2)

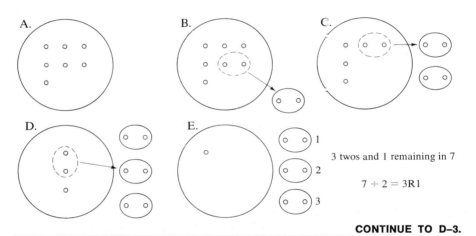

CONTINUE TO D–3.

D–7

The sum is usually totaled and written at the top with the remainder:

$$37 \div 8 \qquad 8\overline{)37} \quad \overset{4R5}{}$$

$$\begin{array}{r|l} \underline{8} & 1 \times 8 \\ 29 & \\ \underline{8} & 1 \times 8 \\ 21 & \\ \underline{8} & 1 \times 8 \\ 13 & \\ \underline{8} & 1 \times 8 \\ 5 & 4 \times 8 \end{array}$$

4 eights and 5 left over

(a) Divide 15 by 4 by removing one set of four each time. Use your objects.

(b) Divide 62 by 7 by removing four sets of seven each time.

SEE ANSWER FRAME (D–7).

(D–4)

$69 = \triangle \times 7 + \square$

$7 \times 7 = 49$

$69 = 7 \times 7 + 20$

$69 = (7 \times 7) + [(2 \times 7) + 6]$

$\left.\begin{array}{l} 69 = [(7 \times 7) + (2 \times 7)] + 6 \\ 69 = [(7 + 2) \times 7] + 6 \end{array}\right\}$ Distributive Property

$69 = 9 \times 7 + 6$

or

$69 \div 7 = 9R6$

$\triangle = 9$ and $\square = 6$

CONTINUE TO D–5.

D–8

The divisor name can be omitted after you are sure that the child no longer needs it as a reminder.

$$
\begin{array}{r}
3R7 \\
8)\overline{31} \\
\underline{8} \quad \\
23 \\
\underline{8} \quad \\
15 \\
\underline{8} \quad \\
7
\end{array}
\begin{array}{l}
\\
\text{1 eight} \\
\\
\text{1 eight} \\
\\
\text{1 eight} \\
\text{3 eights}
\end{array}
\qquad \text{or simply:} \qquad
\begin{array}{r}
3R7 \\
8)\overline{31} \\
\underline{8} \quad \\
23 \\
\underline{8} \quad \\
15 \\
\underline{8} \quad \\
7
\end{array}
\begin{array}{l}
\\
1 \\
\\
1 \\
\\
1 \\
3
\end{array}
$$

CONTINUE TO D–9.

(D–6)

(a) 9

(b) 8

(c) 8

(d) 8

$$
\begin{array}{r}
6)\overline{41} \\
\underline{12} \\
29 \\
\underline{12} \\
17 \\
\underline{12} \\
5
\end{array}
\begin{array}{l}
\\
\text{2 sixes} \\
\\
\text{2 sixes} \\
\\
\text{2 sixes} \\
\text{6 sixes}
\end{array}
$$

6 sets of six and 5 left: 6R5

CONTINUE TO D–7.

D–9

The child will be able to work this method easily by removing one set each time, but it *is* inefficient. The efficiency can be increased by removing more than one set.

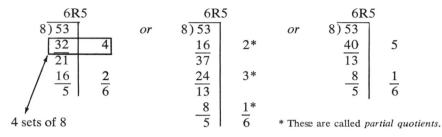

4 sets of 8

* These are called *partial quotients.*

Notice how this algorithm takes on clarity through examples related to the *measurement* concept of division, i.e., removing subsets of a given size.

The result can be found several ways. The child can choose his own unique way. As his understanding and skill increase, he will become more sophisticated and efficient.

CONTINUE TO D–10.

D–10

For quotients involving many sets, the teacher should *help children discover the use of multiple groupings as they are ready.* Ten groups will greatly increase efficiency.

$$
\begin{array}{r}
14R1 \\
4)\overline{57} \\
20 \quad\; 5 \\
\overline{37} \\
20 \quad\; 5 \\
\overline{17} \\
16 \quad\; 4 \\
\overline{1} \quad 14
\end{array}
\qquad\qquad
\begin{array}{r}
14R1 \\
4)\overline{57} \\
40 \quad 10 \\
\overline{17} \\
16 \quad\; 4 \\
\overline{1} \quad 14
\end{array}
$$

Try this one both ways: $47 \div 3$ use 7, 7 on the first method as partial quotients.

SEE ANSWER FRAME (D–10).

(D–7)

$$
\begin{array}{r}
3R3 \\
4)\overline{15} \\
4 \quad 1 \times 4 \\
\overline{11} \\
4 \quad 1 \times 4 \\
\overline{7} \\
4 \quad 1 \times 4 \\
\overline{3} \quad 3 \times 4
\end{array}
\qquad\qquad
\begin{array}{r}
8R6 \\
7)\overline{62} \\
28 \quad \text{4 sevens} \\
\overline{34} \\
28 \quad \text{4 sevens} \\
\overline{6} \quad \text{8 sevens} \\
\\
\text{8 sevens and 6}
\end{array}
$$

CONTINUE TO D–8.

Use ten-set groupings and other groupings as indicated:

$$\text{(a) } 8\overline{)91} \qquad\qquad \text{(b) } 4\overline{)67}$$
$$\text{(use 4, 4)} \qquad\qquad\quad \text{(use 5, 5, 5)}$$

Use only grouping by 10s:

$$\text{(c) } 9\overline{)112} \qquad\qquad \text{(d) } 4\overline{)92}$$

SEE ANSWER FRAME (D–11).

As the degree of problem complexity increases, children need to become more sophisticated in their problem-solving approaches. There are two basic knowledges which are essential.

(1) Rounding up and down to the nearest ten or hundred.
(2) Ability to think in flexible terms with respect to number names.

1 hundred is 10 tens ($\underline{1}00 = 1\underline{0}0$)
7 hundred is 70 tens ($\underline{7}00 = 7\underline{0}0$)
tens times tens is hundreds
ones times tens is tens
tens times ones is tens

CONTINUE TO D–13.

Handy rule for scaffolding: Round divisor *up* and round dividend *down*.

Problem	Round	Think
(1) $43\overline{)344}$	(a) $50\overline{)340}$	"What is 34 tens divided by 5 tens?"

(2)
$$\begin{array}{r} 43\overline{)344} \\ \underline{258} \quad 6 \\ 86 \end{array}$$

(b) $50\overline{)80}$ — "What is 8 tens divided by 5 tens?"

(3)
$$\begin{array}{r} 43\overline{)344} \\ \underline{258} \quad 6 \\ 86 \\ \underline{43} \quad 1 \\ 43 \end{array}$$

$$\overset{1}{43\overline{)43}}$$

Notice that the rounding is always done in such a way that it will yield a division question within the basic facts range.

(a) 34 tens ÷ $\underline{5}$ tens   Always round the divisor to a
(b) 8 tens ÷ $\underline{5}$ tens $\Rightarrow$ *single non-zero digit.*

Also round the dividend to one non-zero digit. If this digit is smaller than the non-zero digit in the divisor, retain *two* digits.

STUDY THIS CAREFULLY; THEN LOOK AT FRAME D–14.

D–14

$$
\begin{array}{r}
6 \\
21\overline{)126} \\
84 \\
\overline{42} \\
21 \\
\overline{21} \\
21 \\
\overline{0} \\
\end{array}
\begin{array}{l}
\\
4 \\
\\
1 \\
\\
1 \\
6 \\
\end{array}
$$

Round

(1) $30\overline{)120}$

(2) $30\overline{)40}$

(3) Not necessary

Think

"What is 12 tens divided by 3 tens"

"What is 4 tens divided by 3 tens?"

"$21 \div 21 = 1$"

(a) 21 is rounded *up* to a single non-zero digit: 3 tens.

(b) 126 is rounded *down* until rounding places the problem within the basic facts range. Since there are 3 tens, the dividend range must be between 2 and 30. The single non-zero digit in the dividend is *one*. Since one is less than 3, the single non-zero digit in the rounded divisor, two digits are retained: 12 tens.

Try this one: $434 \div 62$

SEE ANSWER FRAME (D–14).

(D–10)

$$
\begin{array}{r}
15R2 \\
3\overline{)47} \\
21 \\
\overline{26} \\
21 \\
\overline{5} \\
3 \\
\overline{2} \\
\end{array}
\begin{array}{l}
\\
7 \\
\\
7 \\
\\
1 \\
15 \\
\end{array}
\qquad
\begin{array}{r}
15R2 \\
3\overline{)47} \\
30 \\
\overline{17} \\
15 \\
\overline{2} \\
\end{array}
\begin{array}{l}
\\
10 \\
\\
5 \\
15 \\
\end{array}
$$

IF YOU GOT THESE CORRECT, SKIP THE NEXT FRAME, D–11.

D–15

Remember to round the divisor *up* and the dividend *down*.

Round   *Verbalize*

$32\overline{)329} \longrightarrow 40\overline{)320}$ $\dfrac{32 \text{ tens}}{4 \text{ tens}} = 8 \text{ ones}$

Round: up   down

Round these and indicate the first partial quotient:

(a) $21\overline{)148}$ (b) $65\overline{)552}$ (c) $49\overline{)398}$ (d) $26\overline{)29741}$

SEE ANSWER FRAME (D–15).

(D–11)

(a)
```
      11R3            11R3
    8)91           8)91
      32   4         80   10
      59             11
      32   4          8    1
      27              3   11
      24   3
       3  11
```

(b)
```
      16R3            16R3
    4)67           4)67
      20   5         40   10
      47             27
      20   5         24    6
      27              3   16
      20   5
       7
       4    1
       3   16
```

(c)
```
      12R4
    9)112
      90   10
      22
      18    2
       4   12
```

(d)
```
        23
    4)92
      40   10
      52
      40   10
      12
      12    3
       0   23
```

CONTINUE TO D–12.

D–16

Study this:

```
      7R5
   84)593
     504   6   (1)
      89
      84   1   (2)
       5   7
```

(1) $590 \div 90$; $\dfrac{59 \text{ tens}}{9 \text{ tens}}$ is about 6 ones.

(2) Not necessary

Try these: (a) $62\overline{)302}$ (b) $77\overline{)500}$ (c) $35\overline{)214}$

SEE ANSWER FRAME (D–16).

D–17

The same technique can be extended to divisions involving larger numbers.

Verbalize

```
      168R25
   37)6241
     3700   100   (a)
     2541
     2220    60   (b)
      321
      296     8   (c)
       25    168
```

(a) $\dfrac{6 \text{ thousands}}{4 \text{ tens}}$ is about 1 hundred

(b) $\dfrac{25 \text{ hundreds}}{4 \text{ tens}}$ is about 6 tens

(c) $\dfrac{32 \text{ tens}}{4 \text{ tens}}$ is about 8 ones

Notice that the rounding is always done in such a way as to yield the range of *basic division facts*.   [$6 \div 4$, $25 \div 4$, $32 \div 4$]   Children are not asked to remember $4\overline{)62}$ or $4\overline{)254}$ or $4\overline{)321}$ but they are asked to remember $4\overline{)6}$, $4\overline{)25}$ and $4\overline{)32}$.

CONTINUE TO D–18.

(D–14)

$$
\begin{array}{r}
7 \\
62\overline{)434} \\
372 \\
\overline{62} \\
62 \\
\overline{0}
\end{array}
\quad
\begin{array}{c}
\\
6 \\
\\
\\
1 \\
\overline{7}
\end{array}
\qquad
70\overline{)430}*
\qquad
\begin{array}{c}
43 \text{ tens} \\
\overline{7 \text{ tens}}
\end{array}
$$

The key is to round the divisor *up* to a single non-zero digit: 7 tens. Then round the dividend *down* to a basic facts range which for sevens is 7 through 69. Hence, 434 is too much but 43 tens is just right because 43 ÷ 7 is within the range of basic facts. The child will be able to say "What is the largest multiple of 7 in 43?" It is 42 so 6 × 7 is the answer.

$$7\overline{)43} \text{ is 6 and tens} \div \text{tens} = \text{ones.}$$

* 4 < 7 so the second digit, 3, is retained.

CONTINUE TO D–15.

D–18

How were these rounded?

$$
\begin{array}{r}
98R17 \\
47\overline{)4623} \\
4230 \\
\overline{393} \\
329 \\
\overline{64} \\
47 \\
\overline{17}
\end{array}
\quad
\begin{array}{c}
\\
\\
90 \\
\\
7 \\
\\
1 \\
\overline{98}
\end{array}
$$

	Round	*Verbalize*
(a)		
(b)		
(c)		

SEE ANSWER FRAME (D–18).

(D–15)

Verbalize

(a) $\dfrac{14 \text{ tens}}{3 \text{ tens}}$ is about 4 ones

(b) $\dfrac{55 \text{ tens}}{7 \text{ tens}}$ is about 7 ones

(c) $\dfrac{39 \text{ tens}}{5 \text{ tens}}$ is about 7 ones

(d) $\dfrac{29 \text{ thousands}}{3 \text{ tens}}$ is about 9 hundreds

CONTINUE TO D–16.

Try this one:

	Round	*Verbalize*
72)6741	?	?
?		

SEE ANSWER FRAME (D–19).

(a)   4R54
62)302
   248   4*
    54

(b)   6R38
77)500
   462   6*
    38

(c)   6R4
35)214
   175   5*
    39
    35    $\frac{1}{6}$
     4

*300 ÷ 70

$\frac{30 \text{ tens}}{7 \text{ tens}}$ is about 4 ones

*500 ÷ 80

$\frac{50 \text{ tens}}{8 \text{ tens}}$

*210 ÷ 40

$\frac{21 \text{ tens}}{4 \text{ tens}}$

CONTINUE TO D–17.

Try this one, too.

	Round	*Verbalize*
81)8649	?	?
?		

SEE ANSWER FRAME (D–20).

D–21

You will notice that you have been rounding the divisor so that it has only *one* non-zero digit, and you have been rounding the dividend to two digits if doing so yields a basic fact. Otherwise, you have been rounding the dividend to one non-zero digit also. The objective is to end up within the range of basic facts, i.e., a number between zero and 89 divided by a single digit.

CONTINUE TO D–22.

(D–18)

Round	*Verbalize*
(a) $50\overline{)4600}$	$\dfrac{46\ \text{hundreds}}{5\ \text{tens}}$ is about 9 tens $= 90$
(b) $50\overline{)390}$	$\dfrac{39\ \text{tens}}{5\ \text{tens}}$ is about 7 ones $= 7$
(c) $50\overline{)60}$	$\dfrac{6\ \text{tens}}{5\ \text{tens}}$ is about 1 one $= 1$

CONTINUE TO D–19.

D–22

Quotients can be estimated before beginning to determine the "reasonableness" of the derived result.

$$62\overline{)4827}$$

Before beginning this problem, the child can do the following:

$$
\begin{aligned}
62 \times 1 &= 62 \\
62 \times 10 &= 620 \\
62 \times 100 &= 6200
\end{aligned}
\quad -\!\!\boxed{4827}
$$

Since 4827 is between 620 and 6200, the quotient will be between 10 and 100.

CONTINUE TO D–23.

(D–19)

		Round	*Verbalize*

```
        93R45
     72)6741
        5760      80      80)6700
         981
         720      10      80)900
         261
         216       3      80)260
          45       93
```

$\dfrac{67 \text{ hundreds}}{8 \text{ tens}}$ is about 8 tens

$\dfrac{9 \text{ hundreds}}{8 \text{ tens}}$ is about 1 ten

$\dfrac{26 \text{ tens}}{8 \text{ tens}}$ is about 3 ones

CONTINUE TO D–20.

D–23

If every child could use the method just described (scaffolding) many teachers would be content. With this method, because of the rounding technique, *no erasures* are necessary because the system has *under-estimates* built in. Further, this method allows children to proceed *at a rate and at a level of understanding* which are consonant with their growth in mathematics. However, all people are not of this opinion. What now must be done to get to the standard algorithm?

CONTINUE TO D–24.

(D–20)

		Round	*Verbalize*

```
       106R63
    81)8649
       7290      90      90)8600
       1359
        810      10      90)1300
        549
        486       6      90)540
         63      106
```

$\dfrac{86 \text{ hundreds}}{9 \text{ tens}}$ is about 9 tens

$\dfrac{13 \text{ hundreds}}{9 \text{ tens}}$ is about 1 ten

$\dfrac{54 \text{ tens}}{9 \text{ tens}}$ is about 6 ones

CONTINUE TO D–21.

D–24

First, a new rounding-off technique must be introduced which will enable the child to get more accurate estimates. In other words, you need to help the child reduce the degree of *under* estimating without at the same time *over* estimating.

To do this, you can round the divisor *up or down* and the dividend *up or down* depending upon the size of adjacent digits. These are the usual rounding techniques. This is the way you learned to do it.

46 rounds up to 50	567 rounds up to 570 or 600
42 rounds down to 40	537 rounds up to 540 or down to 500

CONTINUE TO D–25.

D–25

Examine this: 3261 ÷ 47. The usual rounding rules will be used.

The estimated quotient:

$$47 \times 1 = 47$$
$$47 \times 10 = 470$$
$$47 \times 100 = 4700 \quad \boxed{3261}$$

3261 is between 470 and 4700 so the quotient will be between 10 and 100.

```
47)3261
   2820 | 60  (a)
   ----
    441
    376 |  8  (b)
    ---
     65
```

Round

(a) 50)3300 is about 6 tens

(b) 50)440
     This is close on 8 *or* 9.

The remainder is too big so you go back and use 9. *Familiar?!*

CONTINUE TO D–26.

D–26

Look at another one with the common rounding rules:

```
52)7642
   5200 | 100
   ----
   2442
   2080 |  40
   ----
    362
    364 |   7
    ---
    (-2)
```

50)8000

50)2400

50)360

$\dfrac{8 \text{ thousands}}{5 \text{ tens}}$ is about 100

$\dfrac{24 \text{ hundreds}}{5 \text{ tens}}$ is about 40

$\dfrac{36 \text{ tens}}{5 \text{ tens}}$ is about 7

No remainder so you have to erase and try 6.

Clearly, this method is harder and more frustrating for students. Try this one:
74)6741

SEE ANSWER FRAME (D–26).

D–27

Try this one, too

$$37\overline{)7731}$$

?

Round

?

SEE ANSWER FRAME (D–27).

D–28

The next step toward the *standard algorithm* would be to eliminate the scaffolding. To take a small step, it can be placed on top.

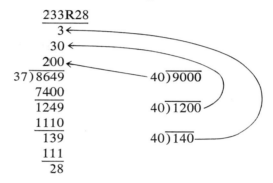

CONTINUE TO D–29.

D–29

Taking the previous problem, all you have to do is get rid of the "mountain."

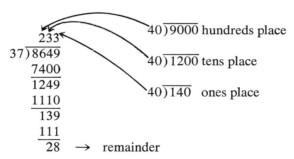

Compare these last two frames. Notice that, rather than omitting the zeros and bringing down" as in the traditional or standard algorithm (e.g., 74<u>00</u>, 111<u>0</u>), the zeros are retained in the subtraction process.

CONTINUE TO D–30.

(D–27)

$$
\begin{array}{r}
208\text{R}35 \\
37\overline{)7731} \\
7400 \\
\hline
331 \\
296 \\
\hline
35
\end{array}
\qquad
\begin{array}{r}
200 \\[2ex]
8 \\
\hline
208
\end{array}
$$

$$40\overline{)8000}$$

$$40\overline{)330}$$

$$\frac{8\text{ thousands}}{4\text{ tens}} \text{ is about 2 hundreds}$$

$$\frac{33\text{ tens}}{4\text{ tens}} \text{ is about 8 ones}$$

See, it *does* work! (sometimes)

CONTINUE TO D–28.

D–30

Summary of rounding procedures for the "round-up—round-down" method.

1. Round the divisors up to a single non-zero digit.
2. Round the dividend down to a single non-zero digit.
3. If the digit in step 2 is smaller than the digit in step 1, keep two digits in step 2.

Examples

(a) $27\overline{)681}$

$$\frac{6\text{ hundreds}}{3\text{ tens}}$$

(b) $31\overline{)176}$

$$\frac{1\text{ hundred}}{4\text{ tens}}$$

$$\frac{17\text{ tens}}{4\text{ tens}}$$

(c) $84\overline{)736}$

$$\frac{7\text{ hundreds}}{9\text{ tens}}$$

$$\frac{73\text{ tens}}{9\text{ tens}}$$

THE END.

(D–26)

$$
\begin{array}{r}
91\text{R}7 \\
74\overline{)6741} \\
6660 \\
\hline
81 \\
74 \\
\hline
7
\end{array}
\qquad
\begin{array}{r}
90 \\[2ex]
1 \\
\hline
91
\end{array}
$$

$$70\overline{)6700}$$

$$\frac{67\text{ hundreds}}{7\text{ tens}} \text{ is about 9 tens}$$

CONTINUE TO D–27.

Multiplication-Division Self-Test

Part I. Multiplication

1. Include all steps of the horizontal form to determine this product: 4×16. Show the steps with paper strips.
2. Multiply 27×32 by
   A. Horizontal-short form, expand 27 first
   B. Vertical
      (1) Expanded Notation
      (2) Partial Products
      (3) Traditional Algorithm
   Show the partial products on a rectangular region.

Part II. Division

1. Estimate the quotient of $26781 \div 39$ using place value.
2. Divide 67 by 9 using the distributive property starting with 4×9.
3. Divide 84 by 7 using 5, 5, 2.
4. Divide 521 by 23 using ten groups each time.
5. Divide 1397 by 21 using the "round-up–round-down" method.

Answers to Multiplication-Division Self-Test

Part I. Multiplication

1.　　　　　4 × 16
　　　　　4 × (10 + 6)
　　　　(4 × 10) + (4 × 6)
　　　　　40 + 24
　　　　40 + (20 + 4)
　　　　(40 + 20) + 4
　　　　　　60 + 4
　　　　　　　64
　　　See (M–8) for strips.

2. Rectangular Region

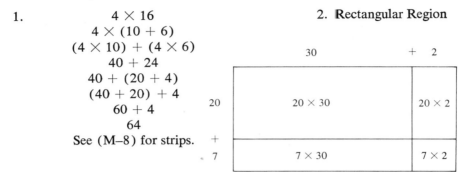

2A. Horizontal-short form

$$27 × 32$$
$$(20 + 7) × 32$$
$$(20 × 32) + (7 × 32)$$
$$[20 × (30 + 2)] + [7 × (30 + 2)]$$
$$(20 × 30) + (20 × 2) + (7 × 30) + (7 × 2)$$
$$600 \quad + \quad 40 \quad + \quad 210 \quad + \quad 14$$
$$864$$

2B1. Expanded Notation

$$27 \quad = \quad 20 + 7$$
$$×32 \qquad 30 + 2$$
$$\overline{} \qquad \overline{600 + 210 + 40 + 14}$$
$$864$$

2B2.　Partial Products

$$27$$
$$×32$$
$$\overline{14}$$
$$40$$
$$210$$
$$600$$
$$\overline{864}$$

2B3.　Traditional Algorithm

$$27$$
$$×32$$
$$\overline{54}$$
$$81$$
$$\overline{864}$$

Part II. Division

1. $39 \times \quad 10 = 390$
   $39 \times \quad 100 = 3900$
   $39 \times 1000 = 39000$ $\boxed{26781}$
   Thus:
   $100 < x < 1000$

2. $67 = 36 + 31$
   $\quad = (4 \times 9) + 31$
   $\quad = (4 \times 9) + [(3 \times 9) + 4]$
   $\quad = [(4 \times 9) + (3 \times 9)] + 4$
   $\quad = (4 + 3) \times 9 + 4$
   $\quad = 7 \times 9 + 4$
   Thus, $67 \div 9 = 7R4$

3.
```
        12
    7)84
        35     5
        49
        35     5
        14
        14     2
         0    12
```

4.
```
            22R15
     23)521
        230     10
        291
        230     10
         61
         46      2
         15     22
```

5.
```
            66R11
    21)1397            13 hundreds
       840     40       3 tens
       557             5 hundreds
       210     10       3 tens
       347             3 hundreds
       210     10       3 tens
       137             13 tens
        84      4        3 tens
        53             5 tens
        21      1       3 tens
        32             3 tens
        21      1       3 tens
        11     66
```

General Methods and Specific Materials of Instruction

Multiplication.   Probably the single most important idea in developing students' understanding of multiplication of numerals with more than one digit is a thorough familiarity with the distributive property. Exploratory experiences such as those described in the previous chapter help children observe its nature. Its *use* may not be so obvious.

You observed that place value played a very important role in addition and subtraction computational procedures. Its fundamental role in multiplication can also be observed through manipulatory experiences.

Start with simple problems of one-digit and two-digit numerals such as 3×12. Relate this product to repeated addition by having children arrange 3 sets of twelve objects and then count them.

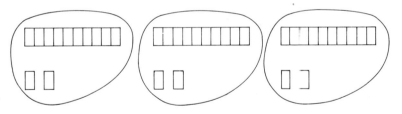

$$\begin{array}{r} 12 \\ \times\ 3 \\ \hline 36 \end{array} \qquad \begin{array}{r} 12 \\ 12 \\ 12 \\ \hline 36 \end{array}$$

They can work several such problem-pairs. Many will discover the relations $3 \times 2 = 6$ and $3 \times 1 = 3$. After a short time, the repeated addition notion can be used by renaming 12 as 1 ten and 2 ones.

3 tens and 6 ones

Children can be asked to relate such solutions to previous experiences with place value and the distributive property:

$$3 \times 8 = 3 \times (6 + 2) = (3 \times 6) + (3 \times 2) = 18 + 6 = 24$$
$$3 \times 12 = 3 \times (10 + 2) = (3 \times 10) + (3 \times 2) = 30 + 6 = 36$$

Special Notation:

$$3 \times 12 = 3 \times (\textcircled{1} + 2) = (3 \times \textcircled{1}) + (3 \times 2) = \textcircled{3} + 6 = 36$$

On the SRA Bead Frame or with colored objects, the relations can be seen with one color at first:

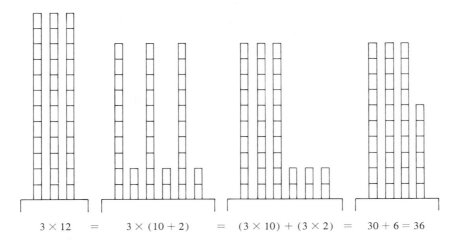

$$3 \times 12 \quad = \quad 3 \times (10 + 2) \quad = \quad (3 \times 10) + (3 \times 2) \quad = \quad 30 + 6 = 36$$

Then the role of the distributive property can be demonstrated with *two* colors: one color for tens and another color for ones.

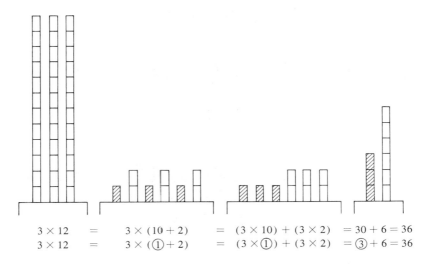

$$3 \times 12 \quad = \quad 3 \times (10 + 2) \quad = \quad (3 \times 10) + (3 \times 2) \quad = 30 + 6 = 36$$
$$3 \times 12 \quad = \quad 3 \times (①+ 2) \quad = \quad (3 \times ①) + (3 \times 2) \quad = ③+ 6 = 36$$

As always, children need opportunities for individualized manipulative experiences. These can be provided through the same materials originally used to teach place value concepts: popsicle sticks, straws, tickets, or other objects which can be bundled with rubber bands, or paper strips for tens, or Cuisenaire Rods.

Other usable teacher aids are abaci of various types, large arrays, a pocket chart, poker chips, poppit beads and perhaps pennies and dimes.

As with addition and subtraction, regrouping in multiplication is a most crucial step.

Standard Notation	Steps	Special Notation
3 × 24	1	3 × 24
3 × (20 + 4)	2	3 × (②) + 4)
(3 × 20) + (3 × 4)	3	(3 × ②) + (3 × 4)
60 + 12	4	⑥ + 12
60 + (10 + 2)	5	⑥ + (10 + 2)
(60 + 10) + 2	6	(⑥ + ①) + 2
70 + 2	7	⑦ + 2
72	8	72

In step 4, there are 6 tens and 12 ones. The child must learn to break 12 ones down into 10 ones and 2 ones as in step 5 and then change 10 ones to 1 ten as in step 6. Objects are "bundled" going from step 5 to step 6. Here is how it looks with Cuisenaire Rods:

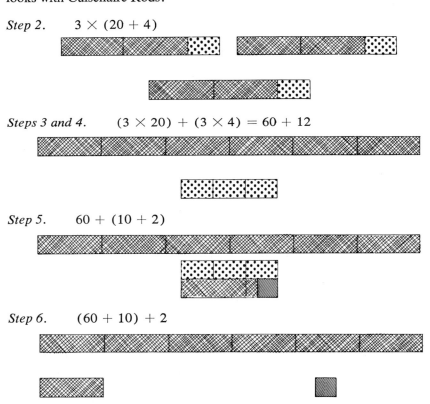

Step 2.   3 × (20 + 4)

Steps 3 and 4.   (3 × 20) + (3 × 4) = 60 + 12

Step 5.   60 + (10 + 2)

Step 6.   (60 + 10) + 2

Manipulative experiences with a variety of objects and teaching aids will help the child *believe in* the distributive property. It will become meaningful and, hence, a *usable* concept.

The usual concrete, semi-concrete, abstract sequence of developmental activities should be followed. Forget the book at the beginning; allow children to use objects in groups of ten and ones to answer such questions as, "How many cookies will be needed for twenty-four children if each child gets three cookies?" Class discussion will help clarify the use of ten-groupings and establish the inefficiency of counting.

After such informal explorations, symbols can be written in conjunction with the manipulations, and the use of the distributive property can be examined. Finally, children who are ready can draw pictures or simply carry out numerical computations. Encourage children to use objects as long as they feel a need for them.

To facilitate pupil growth through meaningful discovery, provide bundles of ten tickets and ask children to determine the answers to questions such as, "A total of how many tickets were sold by Bill, Tom and Jack if each one sold 18 tickets?" What are some possible ways in which children might answer this question? Jot them down and compare your list with the ones on the top of the next page.

Undoubtedly, there are ways other than those listed, but those listed are representative of the procedures children will use. After the children arrive at a solution, discuss the solutions with the class and write some form of algorithm for each one on the board. *Do not place evaluative judgments on the merit of various algorithms.* Try another problem. Many children will use an approach different from and more efficient than the first trial. They have discovered a way to get an answer on the first trial and have used self-selection to increase their efficiency on the second trial: they are proceeding through stages which have meaning. As the children continue to work, you can move about the room and use guided questioning to facilitate advancement of children to increasingly efficient and meaningful procedures.

The algorithms presented in the programmed section are used in many texts, and they will help you grasp the notion of continuous growth in efficiency. You can utilize them in relation to the children's work (the algorithms which they discover), and they will help you relate pupil-discovered algorithms to the distributive property.

Division. Paper strips and squares or tickets or ten-rods such as Dienes Blocks can be used to help children increase their efficiency in division. The subtractive method, you will recall, was easily translated in measurement questions such as, "How many boys receive marbles if Bill has twelve marbles and gives three marbles to each boy?" Twelve objects can be removed in sets of three to determine that there are four sets.

When solving division problems such as 39 ÷ 3, children can first take 39 objects (39 ones) and divide them into 13 sets of three. After a couple problems of this type, they can be asked to work the same or similar problems with objects which are grouped in tens. Make up a problem for solution: "Harriet has some strings of lollipops. There are ten in each string. She bought four strings and ate one lollipop. She took the remaining lollipops and wrapped them in orange tissue in groups of three for her party. How many

---

Possible Solutions:

A. Unbundle, count three groups of 18 and count again.
B. Same as A but add: $18 + 18 + 18 = 54$
C. Place one bundle and eight for each boy and add:
   $(10 + 8) + (10 + 8) + (10 + 8) = 54$
D. Same as C but count bundles and add:
   $30 + 8 + 8 + 8 = 54$
E. Same as D but count bundles, multiply 3×8 and add:
   $30 + 24 = 54$

---

children are coming to the party?" What are some possible solutions? Jot them down and compare them with the list on the next page. The solutions can be explored as they were with multiplication to help children begin to work with ten groups each time.

Research. The algorithm stressed in this chapter is referred to as the *subtractive approach* or *scaffolding algorithm*. The traditional algorithm is referred to as the *distributive approach*. Example:

$$
\left.
\begin{array}{r}
24\text{R}10 \\
16\overline{)394} \\
32 \\
\overline{74} \\
64 \\
\overline{10}
\end{array}
\right\} \text{Long Division}
$$

Dawson and Ruddell (1) found that children using the subtractive approach do better on both immediate and delayed testing. They also reported that when children use this approach and manipulative aids, they achieve a greater understanding of division and its relation to other operations than when they are taught the distributive approach. Scott (7) suggested that both algorithms should be taught since the children in his study who learned both had greater understanding of division than those who learned only one.

Research of Olander and Sharp (6), Grossnickle (2, 3), and John (4) supports the use of long division over short division.[1] Children tend to be more accurate with the long division form.

Accommodation of Individual Differences

Objectives. Behavioral objectives in multiplication and division should take into account the increasing complexity of the subject matter and the levels of abstraction. Multiplication is presented first.

---

[1] *Short division* is the name given to the computational procedure in which one does all work mentally, i.e., there is no "bringing down" or subtracting shown.

Possible Solutions:

A. Take the objects and place them in sets of three; count the sets.
B. Take one from each set of 10 for three children; group the rest in sets of 3.
$$3 + 3 + 3 + 1 + 1 + 1 + 1 = 13$$
$$9 + 9 + 9 + 3 + 3 + 3 + 3 = 39$$
C. Same as B but recognize the fourth group of 9:
$$3 + 3 + 3 + 3 + 1 = 13$$
$$9 + 9 + 9 + 9 + 3 = 39$$
D. Recognize the three groups of 10 as enough for 10 children; sets of 3
$$10 + 1 + 1 + 1 = 13$$
$$30 + 3 + 3 + 3 = 39$$
E. Same as D; recognize the 9 as enough for 3:
$$10 + 3 = 13$$
$$30 + 9 = 39$$

Concept	*Levels*

A. The product of a one-digit numeral and a two-digit numeral without regrouping, e.g., $3 \times 12 = 36$	I. Concrete
	  A. Without symbols
	  B. With symbols

B. The product of a one-digit numeral and a two-digit numeral with regrouping, e.g., $4 \times 13 = 52$	II. Semi-concrete III. Abstract
C. The product of two two-digit numerals without regrouping, e.g., $12 \times 23 = 276$	
D. The product of two two-digit numerals with regrouping, e.g., $16 \times 48 = 768$	

Children should be able to perform the sixteen possible tasks (four concepts at four levels). Several concrete materials have been suggested. Semi-concrete materials include items with pictures or diagrams: pictures of sets, arrays, number lines. Abstract levels cover the use of numerals and operational symbols solely. Following are some sample objectives:

A.II. The child will be able to circle pictures of ten-rods and units to find products of one- and two-digit numerals without regrouping.

D.II. The child will be able to fold an array to find the product of two two-digit numerals with regrouping by finding the sum of the partial products and labeling them on the array.

B.I. The child will be able to determine the products of one- and two-digit numerals with regrouping by using bundles of ten objects.

Objectives for division can be written similarly using the same levels of abstraction.

Concepts

A. Division by a one-digit divisor as repeated subtraction using only one set or group each time, e.g., $18 \div 6$:

$$18 - 6 = 12, 12 - 6 = 6, 6 - 6 = 0$$
$$1 \quad\quad + \quad 1 \quad\quad + 1 \quad = 3$$

B. Division by a one-digit divisor using multiples of sets which correspond to basic facts, e.g., $24 \div 3$:

$$24 - 15 = 9, 9 - 9 = 0 \quad\quad\quad 24 - 12 = 12, 12 - 12 = 0$$
$$5 \quad\quad + 3 \quad = 8 \quad\quad\quad \text{or} \quad\quad 4 \quad\quad + \quad 4 \quad\quad = 8$$

C. Division by a one-digit divisor using ten sets or groups each time, e.g., $63 \div 3$:

$$63 - 30 = 33, 33 - 30 = 3, 3 - 3 = 0$$
$$10 \quad\quad + \quad 10 \quad\quad + 1 \quad = 21$$

D. Division by a one-digit divisor using a round-down method on the dividend, e.g., $7021 \div 7 \longrightarrow \dfrac{7 \text{ thousand}}{7}$

E. Division by two-digit divisors using a "round-up–round-down" procedure, e.g., $3496 \div 42 \longrightarrow \dfrac{34 \text{ hundreds}}{5 \text{ tens}}$

If teaching strategies are used which are similar to the ones described, preassessment can be done informally by noting at what level students are functioning. Those who are already operating at stage III (abstract) can be channeled into enrichment work.

Diagnosis. After several days of large- or small-group work, you can administer a diagnostic test. The test will cover the objectives of the unit which will usually include one or two of the major concepts above at all levels of abstraction. On the basis of the diagnostic test you will regroup the students into enrichment, practice and reteach groups. The latter group will almost certainly need additional work with concrete materials. They may also need additional work on place value.

Children who have mastered the concept(s) but need additional practice can work on story problems, make up their own story problems and trade them, play game-like activities as listed in the Chapter 6 bibliography, work a page of text or workbook problems now and then, or rename factors to discover relationships about distributivity and associativity and short-cut procedures: $4 \times 32 = 4 \times (30 + 2) = 4 \times (40 - 8) = 4 \times (4 \times 8) = (4 \times 4) \times 8$, etc.

Children who have mastered the concepts of the unit need lateral enrichment materials for use while the remainder of the class is attaining greater mastery of the concepts. Appropriate topics for these units include multiplication and division in other systems of numeration (Egyptian, Roman, base 2, 3, 4, 5, 6), multiplying and dividing measures where regrouping is necessary, modular arithmetic, helping other students, reading biographies of great mathematicians and scientists, etc. Each of these can become boring if over-used. Provide variety and choice whenever possible. Some children may enjoy some of the activities for the practice group.

Readiness.   Place value, addition and subtraction experiences provide readiness for multiplication and division algorithms since these concepts can be related to expanded notation and regrouping. Naming powers of ten is also of great importance in facilitating pupil understanding of these algorithms.

Teachers in grades one and two should work very diligently to develop flexibility in the child's perception of two- and three-place numerals, e.g., 213 ones = 21 tens and 3 ones = 2 hundreds and 13 ones. This concept greatly enhances understanding of addition and subtraction algorithms and provides a base upon which third- and fourth-grade teachers can build.

In multiplication, the third-grade teacher, particularly, should constantly reinforce 5×513 as "5 times 3 is 15," "5 times 1 ten is 5 tens," and "5 times 5 hundreds is 25 hundreds." This is then extended in two-place multiplication in 45×513 to "4 tens times 3 is 12 tens," "4 tens times 1 ten is 4 hundreds," and "4 tens times 5 hundreds is 20 thousands." Reinforcement of this concept is *critically* needed for the division algorithm in which the child must say "13 hundreds divided by 4 tens is about 3 tens." Each teacher has a readiness job. Vocabulary, skills and teaching aids all play crucial roles in the developmental sequence.

Suggested Discussion Questions and Projects

1. What other commercial or homemade materials can be used to teach multiplication and division algorithms?
2. Demonstrate multiplication and division with regrouping on aids mentioned in this chapter or others available to you.
3. Outline a guided discovery lesson on multiplication with regrouping. Pose some questions to be answered. What pupil answers can be expected?
4. Outline a guided discovery lesson on division with regrouping. Pose some questions to be answered. What pupil answers can be expected?
5. Write some behavioral objectives on multiplication and division algorithms which cover all levels of abstraction. Write questions which evaluate progress.
6. Locate specific references which can be used as source materials for enrichment.
7. Discuss ways the teacher can formally or informally evaluate pupil understanding at the concrete level individually and in a large-group setting.
8. How can an overhead projector be utilized in teaching these algorithms to third, fourth- and fifth-graders?
9. If the teacher decided to spend some time with the enrichment group, what are some activities which could be used for the practice and reteach groups?

Additional Resources

Filmstrips

   Renaming Numbers for Multiplication, Popular Science (3H–6)
   Estimation in Division, Popular Science (5H–4)

Films

   Multiplication and the Distributive Property, National Council of Teachers of Mathematics

   Division Algorithms, National Council of Teachers of Mathematics

Elementary School Textbooks

   Silver Burdett (1970), Grade 3, *Modern Mathematics Through Discovery,* by R. Morton, M. Ross, H. S. More, M. Gray, E. Sage, W. Collins.
     Student Text: pp. 231–47, 252–55, 270–77, 296–305.

   Silver Burdett (1970), Grade 4, *Modern Mathematics Through Discovery,* by R. Morton, M. Ross, H. S. More, M. Gray, E. Sage, W. Collins.
     Student Text: pp. 88–96, 113–23, 154–56, 186–204, 254–60.

   Addison-Wesley (1968), Grade 4, *Elementary School Mathematics,* by R. Eicholz, P. O'Daffer, C. Brumfiel, M. Shanks, N. Hildebrand.
     Student Text: pp. 134–42, 156–62, 168–84, 202–27.

   Addison-Wesley (1968), Grade 5, *Elementary School Mathematics,* by R. Eicholz, P. O'Daffer, C. Brumfiel, M. Shanks, N. Hildebrand.
     Student Text: pp. 208–24, 262–74.

Bibliography

1. Dawson, Dan T. and Arden K. Ruddell. "An Experimental Approach to the Division Idea." *The Arithmetic Teacher* (February 1955), 2:6–9.

2. Grossnickle, Foster E. "An Experiment with a One-Figure Divisor in Short and Long Division," I. *Elementary School Journal* (March 1934), 34:496–506.

3. Grossnickle, Foster E. "An Experiment with a One-Figure Divisor in Short and Long Division," II. *Elementary School Journal* (April 1934), 34:590–99.

4. John, Lenore. "The Effect of Using the Long Division Form in Teaching Division by One-Digit Numbers." *Elementary School Journal* (May 1930), 30:675–92.

5. *Mathematics for Elementary School Teachers.* Washington, D.C.: National Council of Teachers of Mathematics, 1966.

6. Olander, Herbert T. and E. Preston Sharpe. "Long Division Versus Short Division." *Journal of Educational Research* (September 1932), 26:6–11.

7. Scott, Lloyd. "A Study of Teaching Division Through the Use of Two Algorisms." *School Science and Mathematics* (December 1963), 63:739–52.

B

Rational
Numbers

13

Teaching Structure and Basic Concepts of Rational Numbers

The whole numbers are closed with respect to addition and multiplication. When you add two whole numbers, the sum is a whole number, and when you multiply two whole numbers, the product is a whole number. The difference of two whole numbers is not always a whole number, and the quotient of two whole numbers is not always a whole number. The set of whole numbers is *not* closed with respect to subtraction and division.

Subtraction *is* closed on the set of integers, $\{0, \pm1, \pm2, \dots \}$. The difference of two integers is an integer. Every integer is a whole number or the additive inverse of a whole number. At the present time, negative integers, $\{-1, -2, -3, \dots \}$, are not commonly used in elementary school mathematics programs except as enrichment topics.

Division is closed on the set of rational numbers; that is, the quotient of two rational numbers is a rational number. A rational number is defined as a number which can be represented by the quotient of two integers, $\frac{a}{b}$, where the denominator, b, is not zero. The common name for a rational number is "fraction." *Fraction* generally refers to a rational number which is not negative since negative rationals are not usually included in elementary school mathematics.

A rational number is an abstract idea just as a whole number is an abstract idea. The terms *rational numbers* and *rationals* are used interchangeably in this and succeeding chapters to refer to *numbers*.

Whole numbers are named by numerals. In this and succeeding chapters, numerals which name non-negative rational numbers will be referred to as *fractions* or *fractional numerals*. A fraction has the form $\frac{a}{b}$ where a is a whole number and b is a natural number. Fractions have numerators and denominators; rational numbers do not. Non-negative rational numbers can also be named by decimals and percents.

Non-negative rational numbers can be added, subtracted, multiplied and divided. In order to carry out these operations, the numbers are represented by fractions. It is technically improper to say, "Add these two fractions." It is also technically improper to say, "Compute the sum of these two rational numbers with like denominators." However, the correct statements are wordy:

Add the rational numbers named by these fractions.

Compute the sums of the two rational numbers named by these fractions with like denominators.

The approach used in this and succeeding chapters is to use *rational number* whenever number, solely, is being discussed; *fraction* will be used whenever numeral, solely, is being discussed or when wordiness is a problem because number and numeral are both referents.

The main topic of this chapter is an analysis of basic concepts of non-negative rational numbers. The analysis includes a discussion of properties and simple relationships. Techniques for developing pupil understanding and facilitating discovery of these concepts are included.

Rational Number Concepts and the Spiraling Curriculum

How do children develop rational number concepts? They are acquired over a long period. Most pre-schoolers become familiar with verbal names for common rational numbers in the home. They receive a half-glass of milk or half an apple. They encounter experiences in which money or candy or game objects are distributed equally to two, three, or four children. Such experiences provide readiness for formal instruction on rational numbers.

After the child begins formal schooling, he encounters rational number concepts at each grade level. If you examine an elementary school mathematics textbook series such as those listed at the end of the chapter, you will find a development similar to the following:

Grade 1: Objects or groups of objects are divided into two, three, or four equal parts and numerals are introduced:

Grade 2: Halves, thirds and fourths are extended to fifths and sixths. Usually only unit fractions are introduced, i.e., fractions which have a numerator of "1." Names for "1" are introduced: 1, $\frac{2}{2}$, $\frac{3}{3}$, etc.

Grade 3: Grade-two rational number concepts are reviewed and extended. Non-unit fractions are introduced; elementary equivalent fractions may be explored such as $\frac{1}{2} = \frac{2}{4}$ or $\frac{1}{3} = \frac{2}{6}$. Simple addition and subtraction problems are presented using fractions with the same denominator and sums and differences less than or equal to one. Vocabulary is introduced; numerator and denominator, and elementary concepts of inequality are explored, e.g., $\frac{1}{3} < \frac{1}{2}$.

Grade 4: Grade-three concepts are reviewed and extended. New topics usually include inequalities of fractions with the same numerator or same denominator, generation of equivalent fractions, addition and subtraction with sums and differences greater than one, and addition and subtraction of simple fractions with different denominators.

Grade 5: Extension of grade-four concepts and introduction of multiplication and division of rational numbers are the main topics.

Grade 6: Grade-five concepts are extended, and introductory experiences with decimals and percents are provided.

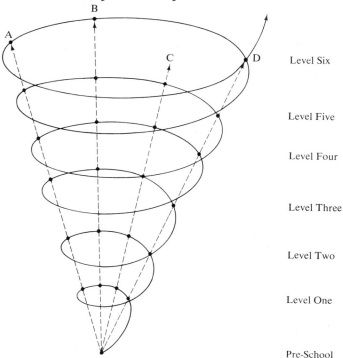

If you think of each dotted line in the preceding figure as a concept core and each loop in the spiral as a grade level, you can begin to conceptualize the concept of the spiraling curriculum as it is embodied in rational number concepts. Let line A denote the concept core of rational number concepts. As indicated in the previous paragraphs, children begin formal schooling with certain ideas related to rational numbers. These constitute the readiness foundation upon which systematic instruction builds. Each year, the concepts of the previous year are reviewed and extended. Rational number experiences become more complex and sophisticated each year.

Lines B, C, and D represent other curriculum concept cores such as whole numbers, measurement and geometry. Beginning with a core of knowledge possessed by pre-schoolers, each child progresses through the curriculum through a set of experiences designed to reinforce and elaborate previously acquired concepts and skills.

Development of Rational Number Concepts*

Objectives

After completing this unit you will be able to:

(1) Select from a list of given numerals those which name natural numbers, whole numbers, integers, rational numbers and real numbers.
(2) Determine what rational number is represented by a given repeating decimal.
(3) Explain how to help children "discover" that $\frac{1}{a} > \frac{1}{b}$ or $\frac{1}{a} < \frac{1}{b}$ or $\frac{1}{a} = \frac{1}{b}$ (a,b $\neq$ 0) with concrete materials.
(4) Demonstrate equivalent fractions with a fraction kit.
(5) Determine whether $\frac{c}{a} > \frac{d}{b}$, $\frac{c}{a} < \frac{d}{b}$, or $\frac{c}{a} = \frac{d}{b}$ with
   a. Sets of equivalent fractions
   b. Sets of multiples

Materials needed

A fraction kit. Trace several circles on paper. You can use the bottom of a jar. Make sixteen circular regions and cut them as follows:

3 regions intact—units
2 regions in two parts—halves
2 regions in three parts—thirds
2 regions in four parts—fourths
2 regions in five parts—fifths

---

* *When questions are asked, answers are located in the same page section (top, middle, bottom) on the second page following.*

2 regions in six parts—sixths
2 regions in eight parts—eighths
1 region in twelve parts—twelfths

Place an appropriate numeral on each section: $\frac{1}{2}$, $\frac{1}{8}$, $\frac{1}{4}$, etc.

Assumptions

A. Children have a good understanding of the properties of *whole* numbers.

B. Children are accustomed to giving numbers many names.

Subsets of Real Numbers

There are many sets of numbers. Some sets are encountered so frequently that they have names. You are undoubtedly familiar with elements of the following sets of numbers.

    A. Natural Numbers or Counting Numbers: $\{1,2,3,4,5, \ldots\}$
    B. Whole Numbers: $\{0,1,2,3,4, \ldots\}$
    C. Integers: $\{\ldots, -3,-2,-1,0,1,2,3,4, \ldots\}$
    D. Rational Numbers: $\{0,1,-1, \frac{1}{2}, -\frac{1}{2}, \frac{2}{1}, -\frac{2}{1}, \frac{3}{1}, -\frac{3}{1}, \frac{1}{3}, -\frac{1}{3}, \ldots\}$

Three dots within a set mean "continue with this pattern."

CONTINUE TO THE NEXT FRAME.

Here is a schematic representation of the sets:

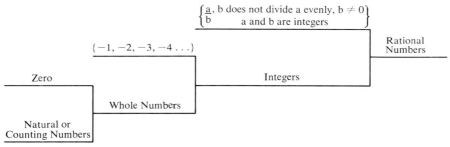

In grades K–3, most textbook series use the whole numbers almost exclusively. In grades 3–6 the non-negative rationals are utilized. The set is referred to as "non-negative" because it includes all rational numbers which are *not negative,* i.e., all positive rational numbers and zero. The *positive rational numbers* do not include zero since zero is neither positive nor negative.

CONTINUE TO THE NEXT FRAME.

Another schematic representation:

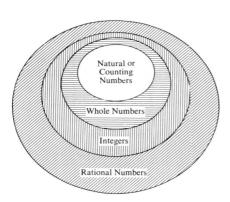

This diagram says that Natural Numbers can loosely be thought of as a subset of Whole Numbers; Whole Numbers can loosely be thought of as a subset of Integers and so on.

Describe the elements in each shaded area. Refer to the previous two frames for help.

SEE ANSWER FRAME (F–3).

F–4

Draw three number lines and indicate each of the following sets:

    A. Natural or Counting Numbers
    B. Whole Numbers
    C. Integers

SEE ANSWER FRAME (F–4).

F–5

Most number experiences in K–3 are with Whole Numbers. However, in the future you can expect to see negative numbers appear in the K–3 curriculum with greater frequency. At that time, the K–3 curriculum will be centered about the *Integers*.

As negative numbers are introduced into the K–6 curriculum, $\{-1, -2, -3, \ldots\}$, the *Non-Negative Rational Numbers* which are presently studied will be expanded to include all *Rational Numbers*.

CONTINUE TO F–6.

F–6

Each of these names a rational number:

$$\tfrac{1}{2}, \quad \tfrac{3}{7}, \quad -\tfrac{26}{93}, \quad \tfrac{4126}{9999}, \quad .614, \quad .9132741$$

Also, any repeating decimal names a rational number.

Consider this repeating decimal: .33333 . . . (the three dots indicate there is an endless series of threes); such decimals are referred to as *nonterminating decimals*. .3333 . . . names a rational number. That is, .3333 . . . can be represented by

$$\tfrac{a}{b} \text{ where } a, b \text{ are integers and } b \neq 0.$$

The rational number named by this repeating decimal is $\tfrac{1}{3}$. "1" and "3" are integers; $3 \neq 0$.

.614 can be considered a *terminating decimal* or as a nonterminating decimal with repeating zeros: .614000. . . .

CONTINUE TO F–7.

Remember that if $x = 4$,

then $2x = 8$

and $10x = 40$ (equals multiplied by equals)

Further, recall that if $10x = 40$

and $x = 4$

then $\overline{10x - x = 40 - 4}$ (equals subtracted from equals)

so $9x = 36$

There exists an $x = .33333 \ldots = \frac{a}{b}$ where a, b are integers and $b \neq 0$.

Study this:
$$10x = 3.3333 \ldots$$
$$\underline{x = .3333 \ldots}$$
$$9x = 3.0000 \ldots$$
$$9x = 3$$
$$x = \tfrac{3}{9} = \tfrac{1}{3} = \tfrac{a}{b}, \quad b \neq 0!$$

Hence, $.3333 \ldots$ names a rational number.

Can you use a similar strategy to find the rational number named by this decimal: $.6666 \ldots$?

SEE ANSWER FRAME (F–7).

Each repeating decimal has a *period*. The period of a repeating decimal tells how often the decimal repeats.

Repeating Decimal	Period	Repeating Decimal	Period
$.\overset{2}{1}\overset{2}{3}1313 \ldots$	2	$.3333 \ldots$	1
		$.143261432614326 \ldots$	5
		$.71717171 \ldots$	2
$.25312531253\overset{4}{1}2531 \ldots$	4	$.444 \ldots$	1

Each repeated sequence must contain the same *digits* in the same *order* or *sequence*. The following are *not* repeating decimals:

$.232324232424 \ldots$ $.213423142413 \ldots$ $.21211211121111 \ldots$

CONTINUE TO F–9.

Zero: $\{0\}$ = {Whole Numbers which are not Natural Numbers}

Negative Integers: $\{-1, -2, -3, \ldots\}$ = {Integers which are not Whole Numbers}

{Rationals which are not integers} = $\{\frac{a}{b}$ where a and b are integers, $b \neq 0$ and b does not divide a evenly} = $\{\frac{a}{b} \mid a, b \in I, b \neq 0, b$ does not divide $a\}$

CONTINUE TO F–4.

(F–4)

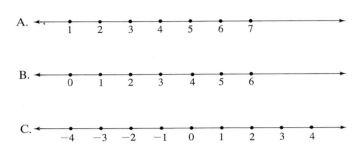

A.

B.

C.

CONTINUE TO F–5.

F–9

To determine a and b, multiply both sides of the equation by the power of ten which equals the period.

$$x = .\overset{3}{\widehat{141}}141141 \ldots \qquad \text{The period is } \underline{3}.$$

$$10^3(x) = 10^3 (.141141 \ldots)$$
$$1000x = 1000 (.141141 \ldots)$$

$$\begin{array}{rcl} 1000x &=& 141.141141 \ldots \\ x &=& .141141 \ldots \\ \hline 999x &=& 141.00000 \ldots \end{array}$$

Subtract the equations.

so $\quad x = \dfrac{141}{999}$

The reason you multiply both sides by ten raised to the power of the period is that through subsequent subtraction the infinite sequence of repeating digits disappears. Try a couple more. Find a and b for these decimal numerals:

$$.78787878 \ldots$$
$$.236142361423614 \ldots$$

SEE ANSWER FRAME (F–9).

F–10

By definition, non-repeating nonterminating decimals have no period.

For example: .13113111311113 . . . There is a *pattern* but there is no *period*.

No non-repeating nonterminating decimal is a *Rational Number* because it can not be represented by $\frac{a}{b}$ as noted. Non-repeating nonterminating decimals are *Real Numbers*. Numbers which are Real Numbers but are *not* Rational Numbers are called *Irrational Numbers*.

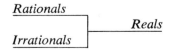

CONTINUE TO F–11.

F–10

$$10x = 6.6666\ldots$$
$$\underline{x = .6666\ldots}$$
$$9x = 6.0000.\ldots$$

$$9x = 6$$
$$x = \tfrac{6}{9} = \tfrac{2}{3} = \tfrac{a}{b}, b \neq 0$$

Note that if   x = 2.3146   Similarly, if   x = .461446144614 ...
then   10x = 23.146   then   10x = 4.61446144614 ...
and   100x = 231.46   and   100x = 46.1446144614 ...
                       and   1000x = 461.446144614 ...

CONTINUE TO F–8.

F–11

The set of Rational Numbers can loosely be thought of as a subset of the Real Numbers.

Every point on the number line is the location or position of a Real Number.

There are many points on the number line which are not locations of Rational Numbers; all such points are locations of Real Numbers. You may think there are no such points! There are infinitely many. Every non-repeating nonterminating decimal names an *Irrational Number.*

CONTINUE TO F–12.

F–12

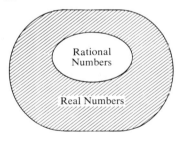

The shaded area represents the *Irrational Numbers.*

{Rationals} ∩ {Irrationals} = ∅

There is no number which is both Rational *and* Irrational.

{Reals} ∩ {Rationals} = {Rationals}

Rational Numbers can loosely be thought of as Real Numbers.

{Rationals} ∪ {Irrationals} = {Reals}

Rationals and Irrationals together constitute the Reals.

CONTINUE TO F–13.

F–13

Few *Irrational Numbers* are encountered in K–6. Pi is such a number. Use of the Pythagorean Theorem in right triangles frequently yields irrationals since square roots of all numbers which are not perfect squares are irrational.

Pythagorean Theorem: *Example:*

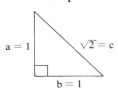

$$a^2 + b^2 = c^2$$

$a = 1$ $\sqrt{2} = c$

$b = 1$

$$a^2 + b^2 = \qquad c^2$$
$$1^2 + 1^2 = 1 + 1 = 2$$
$$c^2 = 2$$

Hypotenuse: $c = \sqrt{2}$

CONTINUE TO F–14.

(F–9)

$$100,000x = 23614.2361423614 \ldots$$
$$\underline{x = \qquad\quad .2361423614 \ldots}$$
$$99,999x = 23614.0000000000 \ldots$$

$$x = \frac{23614}{99999}$$

$$100x = 78.7878 \ldots$$
$$\underline{x = \quad .7878 \ldots}$$
$$99x = 78.0000. \ldots$$

$$x = \frac{78}{99}$$

CONTINUE TO F–10.

F–14

Here is a short proof that $\sqrt{2}$ is not rational. It is a proof by contradiction (*reductio ad absurdem*); you assume $\sqrt{2}$ is rational and show that your assumption cannot be true.

Statement	Reason
(1) *Assume* $\sqrt{2}$ is rational	(1) *Assumption*
(2) Then $\sqrt{2} = \frac{a}{b}$ where a, b are integers, $b \neq 0$	(2) Definition of a rational number
(3) *Assume* a and b have no common factors	(3) *Assumption*
(4) $a = b\sqrt{2}$	(4) Multiply both sides by b
(5) $a^2 = 2b^2 = 2(b^2)$	(5) Square both sides
(6) a^2 is even	(6) 2 times any number yields an even number
(7) a is even so 2 is a factor of a	(7) Odd $\times$ odd = odd; even $\times$ even = even
(8) $a = 2c$	(8) Every even number is the product of 2 and some other number

(CONTINUED ON NEXT FRAME, F–15).

F–15

(9) $a^2 = 4c^2$	(9) Square both sides
(10) $a^2 = 2b^2$ so $4c^2 = 2b^2$	(10) Substitution of $4c^2$ for a^2
(11) $2c^2 = b^2$	(11) Divide both sides by 2
(12) b is even so 2 is a factor of b	(12) Same reasoning as steps (5), (6), and (7)
(13) 2 is a factor of a and b	(13) Steps (7) and (12)
(14) $\sqrt{2} \neq \frac{a}{b}$	(14) Step (13) contradicts step (3)
(15) $\sqrt{2}$ is not rational	(15) Does not satisfy the definition.

CONTINUE TO F–16.

F–16

Properties of Whole Numbers and of Rational Numbers

Whole Numbers	Rational Numbers
1. Addition is closed	?
2. Multiplication is closed	?
3. Addition is commutative	?
4. Multiplication is commutative	?
5. Addition is associative	?
6. Multiplication is associative	?
7. Addition has an identity element	?
8. Multiplication has an identity element	?
9. Addition has no inverse element	?
10. Multiplication has no inverse element	?
11. Multiplication is distributive over addition	?

Make statements about these eleven properties relative to rational numbers.

SEE ANSWER FRAME (F–16).

F–17

Elementary Rational Number Concepts

Youngsters' earliest experiences with rational number concepts are designed to acquaint them with elementary relationships indicating the total number of parts in a single object or group of objects. Models commonly used may be solids such as pieces of fruit or containers with contents. Other models are two-dimensional such as pictures and geometric regions, e.g., square, circular or rectangular regions. First contacts are based upon items the parts of which are congruent, that is, the parts have the *same size and shape*. Draw a picture of an apple to show $\frac{1}{2}$ as two congruent parts.

Draw three rectangles and show $\frac{1}{2}$ as congruent parts three different ways.

SEE ANSWER FRAME (F–17).

F–18

The concept of fractional parts can be related to *area* after children have encountered the concept of area in grade three or grade four. Make several rectangular regions and divide them into six equal parts which are *not* congruent.

Similarly, $\frac{1}{2}$ can be represented as one of two.

Hence, $\frac{1}{2}$ the stars are shaded.

Draw stars to show $\frac{2}{3}$ and $\frac{4}{6}$.

SEE ANSWER FRAME (F–18).

F–19

A concept which is usually touched upon in grade two and elaborated upon in grade three is order of rational numbers. Inequalities can easily be explored with flannel board pieces of pie-shaped materials for the teacher and fraction kits for desk work. Working first only with unit fractions, fractions with "1" in the numerator, you can place several pieces on the flannel board such as $\frac{1}{2}$, $\frac{1}{3}$, $\frac{1}{4}$ and let children use their kits.

Ask them to arrange the pieces by size, assuming that all pieces have been cut from unit circles. Then ask them to write fractional numerals and place them in order, smallest to largest. Use notation to write $\frac{1}{2} > \frac{1}{3} > \frac{1}{4}$ and $\frac{1}{4} < \frac{1}{3} < \frac{1}{2}$. Ask if someone can see a pattern. To avoid giving it away, ask, "What do you think is the next number in the sequence?" It should be $\frac{1}{5}$, of course. Then use the $\frac{1}{5}$ piece to show that $\frac{1}{4} > \frac{1}{5}$ and $\frac{1}{5} < \frac{1}{4}$. Now write $\frac{1}{5} < \frac{1}{4} < \frac{1}{3} < \frac{1}{2}$ and $\frac{1}{2} > \frac{1}{3} > \frac{1}{4} > \frac{1}{5}$.

Place your four pieces on a sheet of paper and write the appropriate symbols.

SEE ANSWER FRAME (F–19).

F–20

After $\frac{1}{5}$ has been examined, examine $\frac{1}{6}$; most children will notice the denominator pattern: $\frac{1}{2} > \frac{1}{3} > \frac{1}{4} > \frac{1}{5} > \frac{1}{6}$. To practice, give other unit fractions such as $\frac{1}{31}$ and ask for the unit fraction or piece of pie which is a little larger, $\frac{1}{30}$, or a little smaller, $\frac{1}{32}$, and give practice with appropriate notation:

$$\frac{1}{31} > \frac{1}{32}, \quad \frac{1}{31} < \frac{1}{30}, \quad \frac{1}{32} < \frac{1}{31}, \quad \frac{1}{30} > \frac{1}{31}$$

Locate several positions on a number line. Also, locate some whole numbers on the number line to reinforce that $<$ means "is to the left of" and $>$ means "is to the right of."

CONTINUE TO F–21.

Notice that the pattern used in this development has been based on the *sizes* of concrete materials rather than on any symbolic manipulation which will come later. Since children are accustomed to encountering $1 < 2 < 3 < 4$ . . . , the teacher will do well to give many concrete experiences to help children see that $\frac{1}{2} > \frac{1}{3} > \frac{1}{4} > \frac{1}{5}$ . . . Simple parts of a group can be utilized in this sequence if the fractions are chosen with care. Example:

$\frac{1}{2}$ the set is 6 $\frac{1}{3}$ the set is 4 $\frac{1}{4}$ the set is 3

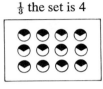

Hence, $\frac{1}{2} > \frac{1}{3} > \frac{1}{4}$ whether you compare *parts of a whole* or *parts of a set*.

CONTINUE TO F–22.

Rational Numbers

1. Addition is closed, e.g., $\frac{3}{4} + \frac{2}{3} = \frac{17}{12}$
2. Multiplication is closed, e.g., $\frac{3}{4} \times \frac{5}{7} = \frac{15}{28}$
3. Addition is commutative, e.g., $\frac{2}{3} + \frac{3}{4} = \frac{3}{4} + \frac{2}{3}$
4. Multiplication is commutative, e.g., $\frac{3}{4} \times \frac{5}{7} = \frac{5}{7} \times \frac{3}{4}$
5. Addition is associative, e.g., $\frac{1}{2} + (\frac{2}{3} + \frac{3}{4}) = (\frac{1}{2} + \frac{2}{3}) + \frac{3}{4}$
6. Multiplication is associative, e.g., $\frac{1}{2} \times (\frac{2}{3} \times \frac{3}{4}) = (\frac{1}{2} \times \frac{2}{3}) \times \frac{3}{4}$
7. Addition has an identity element, zero, e.g., $\frac{2}{3} + \frac{0}{3} = \frac{2}{3}$
8. Multiplication has an identity element, one, e.g., $\frac{2}{3} \times \frac{1}{1} = \frac{2}{3}$
9. Addition has inverse elements, e.g., $\frac{2}{3} + (-\frac{2}{3}) = \frac{0}{3}$
10. Multiplication has inverse elements (except zero), e.g., $\frac{3}{4} \times \frac{4}{3} = \frac{1}{1}$
11. Multiplication is distributive over addition, e.g., $\frac{2}{3} \times (\frac{3}{4} + \frac{5}{7}) = (\frac{2}{3} \times \frac{3}{4})$
    $+ (\frac{2}{3} \times \frac{5}{7})$

CONTINUE TO F–17.

Cut it vertically through the stem end.

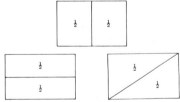

Congruence can be emphasized by having children fold and tear paper to show how the parts "match."

CONTINUE TO F–18.

(F–18)

Examples:

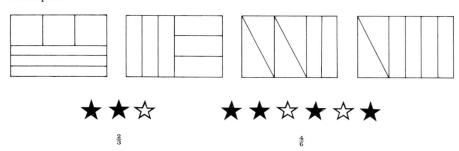

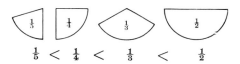

$$\tfrac{2}{3} \qquad\qquad\qquad \tfrac{4}{6}$$

CONTINUE TO F–19.

(F–19)

$$\tfrac{1}{5} < \tfrac{1}{4} < \tfrac{1}{3} < \tfrac{1}{2}$$

Your order may be reversed.

CONTINUE TO F–20.

F–22

The clarity of visual models is of utmost importance in the development of rational number concepts. If circular regions are used to teach relationships, you will do well always to back parts by a whole.

(b) is more easily discriminated as $\tfrac{1}{3}$ than (a).

Further, it is desirable for you to keep an *extra* unit circle in plain sight as a constant reminder that it represents *one*.

CONTINUE TO F–23.

The presence of a unit region is of special importance when working with *rectangular* regions. The $\frac{1}{3}$ circular region can easily be imagined a "part" of something. The child will "fill in" the circular region because the arc gives a mental clue towards closure. However, this certainly is *not* the case with rectangular regions.

This region could be 1, $\frac{1}{2}$, $\frac{1}{3}$, $\frac{1}{4}$, or any other fractional part depending on the size of the *unit rectangle*. Hence, it is of special importance to have the unit rectangle visually present.

CONTINUE TO F–24.

After extensive exploration of unit fractions, you can provide children with experiences related to fractions with identical *denominators* but different numerators. With the help of flannel board circular regions and other devices children learn that $\frac{a}{b} < \frac{c}{b}$ when a $<$ c and $\frac{a}{b} > \frac{c}{b}$ when a $>$ c.

A number line can be used. Children cannot explore comparison or ordering of fractions with different numerators *and* different denominators such as $\frac{2}{7}$, $\frac{3}{14}$ until they learn how to find many names for a rational number.

CONTINUE TO F–25.

Fractions which name the same rational number are called *equivalent fractions*.

The mathematical nature of equivalent fractions is seen in this illustration:

$$\frac{2}{3} = \frac{2}{3} \times 1$$ multiplicative identity element

$$= \frac{2}{3} \times \frac{4}{4}$$ another name for 1

$$= \frac{2 \times 4}{3 \times 4}$$ definition of multiplication of rational numbers

$$= \frac{8}{12}$$ multiply

CONTINUE TO F–26.

F–26

You cannot use this mathematical approach with third-graders because it utilizes an unfamiliar concept, multiplication of rational numbers. What you do instead is to develop the notion of equivalent fractions deductively or intuitively through patterns by using fraction kits and number lines. Place a unit circular region on your desk and place a half-unit circular region on top of it.

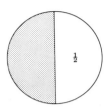

CONTINUE TO F–27.

F–27

Now take thirds, fourths, fifths and so on to determine what sets of identical pieces will *exactly cover* one-half. You will find 2 fourths, 3 sixths, 4 eighths; $\frac{1}{2}$ a circular region, $\frac{2}{4}$ a circular region, $\frac{3}{6}$ a circular region and $\frac{4}{8}$ a circular region all name the same amount, i.e., $\frac{1}{2} = \frac{2}{4} = \frac{3}{6} = \frac{4}{8}$

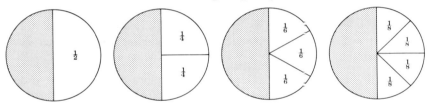

Ask "How many tenths do you think it will take to cover $\frac{1}{2}$?" Children will begin to notice denominator patterns (2, 4, 6, 8, *10*) and numerator patterns (1, 2, 3, 4, 5). Encourage them.

CONTINUE TO F–28.

F–28

These patterns can easily be generalized to sums: add one to the numerator and two to the denominator of this name for one-half to get the next one, e.g.,
$\frac{4}{8} = \frac{4 + 1}{8 + 2} = \frac{5}{10}$

For thirds, add 1 and 3, e.g., $\frac{2}{6} = \frac{2 + 1}{6 + 3} = \frac{3}{9}$

Quickly, they will learn that names can be generated by sums to yield *sets of equivalent fractions:*

$$\{\tfrac{3}{7}, \tfrac{3 + 3}{7 + 7} = \tfrac{6}{14}, \tfrac{6 + 3}{14 + 7} = \tfrac{9}{21}, \tfrac{9 + 3}{21 + 7} = \tfrac{12}{28}, \ldots\}$$
$$\{\tfrac{3}{7}, \qquad \tfrac{6}{14}, \qquad \tfrac{9}{21}, \qquad \tfrac{12}{28}, \ldots\}$$

Skip counting can be used, too:

$\{3, 6, 9, 12, \ldots\} \quad \rightarrow$
$\{7, 14, 21, 28 \ldots\} \quad \rightarrow \quad \{\tfrac{3}{7}, \tfrac{6}{14}, \tfrac{9}{21}, \tfrac{12}{28}, \ldots\}$ Use these two methods to find the first five names in the set of names for $\frac{4}{9}$.

SEE ANSWER FRAME (F–28).

Now children can order fractions such as $\frac{1}{2}$ and $\frac{2}{3}$.

To begin, you can ask children to make various comparisons with desk materials.

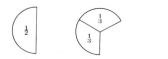

Certainly $\frac{1}{2} < \frac{2}{3}$ or $\frac{2}{3} > \frac{1}{2}$

Other comparisons can be easily made: $\frac{1}{2} < \frac{3}{4}; \frac{1}{8} < \frac{3}{4}; \frac{1}{5} < \frac{2}{5}; \frac{3}{5} < \frac{2}{3}$ and so on.

After children develop skill with these materials, choose an example which cannot be done because there are no pieces the right size. For example, if you have pieces for $\frac{1}{2}, \frac{1}{3}, \frac{1}{4}, \frac{1}{5}$ then ask, $\frac{3}{7} \bigcirc \frac{4}{9}$.

CONTINUE TO F–30.

It would be most desirable to let children "invent" ways to solve some problems of this type before continuing. Some would probably cut new pieces.

Some children will relate this experience to sets of equivalent fractions, especially with a little encouragement from you.

Write the two sets for $\frac{2}{3}$ and $\frac{3}{4}$ to decide whether $\frac{2}{3} < \frac{3}{4}$ or $\frac{2}{3} > \frac{3}{4}$.

SEE ANSWER FRAME (F–30).

After considerable experience with generation and verification of sets, new problems can be posed.

"What is another name for $\frac{4}{7}$ which has 28 in the denominator?" $\frac{4}{7} = \frac{?}{28}$

$$\{\frac{4}{7}, \frac{8}{14}, \frac{12}{21}, \frac{16}{28}\} \quad thus, \quad \frac{4}{7} = \frac{16}{28}$$

You will help them notice that $7 \times 4 = 28$ and $4 \times 4 = 16$.

$$\frac{4}{7} = \frac{4 \times 4}{7 \times 4} = \frac{16}{28}$$

Children should be provided opportunities to calculate equivalent fractions by choosing some n for $\frac{a \times n}{b \times n}$ and then verifying their calculations with a fraction kit. This will develop intuitive understanding of this concept which can be made more mathematically meaningful after they have encountered *multiplication* of rational numbers.

CONTINUE TO F–32.

F–32

After some experience with questions of the type in the previous frame, children will begin to realize that they can find common denominators by examining only multiples of denominators. They can build *sets of multiples*. For the following inequality, they can determine the first few multiples of 5 and 3.

$$\tfrac{3}{5} \bigcirc \tfrac{2}{3}$$

$$\{3,6,9,12, \textcircled{15}, 18, \ldots\}$$

$$\{5, 10, \textcircled{15}, \ldots\}$$

$$\frac{2}{3} = \frac{2 \times \textcircled{5}}{3 \times \textcircled{5}} = \frac{10}{\textcircled{15}}$$

$$\frac{3}{5} = \frac{3 \times \textcircled{3}}{5 \times \textcircled{3}} = \frac{9}{\textcircled{15}}$$

15 is a multiple of 3, and 15 is a multiple of 5. 15 is called the *Least Common Multiple* of 3 and 5 because it is the smallest whole number which is a multiple of *both* 3 and 5. After the child finds the Least Common Multiple, he uses the generalization discovered earlier that $\frac{a}{b} = \frac{a \times n}{b \times n}$.

In this case, the child looks for two numbers which satisfy $5 \times \square = 15$ and $3 \times \square = 15$.

CONTINUE TO F–33.

F–33

Finish this one using the method described in the previous frame:

$$(a) \quad \tfrac{2}{5} \bigcirc \tfrac{3}{10}$$

$$\{5, \textcircled{10}, 15, 20, 25, 30, \ldots\}$$

$$\{ \textcircled{10} \ldots \} \quad 10 \text{ is the Least Common Multiple of 5 and 10.}$$

Find the Least Common Multiple of 6 and 18 to complete this problem:

$$(b) \quad \tfrac{5}{6} \bigcirc \tfrac{11}{18}$$

SEE ANSWER FRAME (F–33).

(F–28)

$$\left\{ \frac{4}{9}, \; \frac{4+4}{9+9} = \frac{8}{18}, \; \frac{8+4}{18+9} = \frac{12}{27}, \; \frac{12+4}{27+9} = \frac{16}{36}, \; \frac{16+4}{36+9} = \frac{20}{45} \right\}$$

$$\left\{ \frac{4}{9}, \quad \frac{8}{18}, \quad \frac{12}{27}, \quad \frac{16}{36}, \quad \frac{20}{45} \right\}$$

$$\{4,8,12,16,20\} \longrightarrow$$
$$\{9,18,27,36,45\} \longrightarrow \left\{ \frac{4}{9}, \; \frac{8}{18}, \; \frac{12}{27}, \; \frac{16}{36}, \; \frac{20}{45} \right\}$$

Further *verification* of these abstractly generated patterns should be carried out by students to establish pattern validity. Children should be provided *many* manipulative experiences to relate patterns to objects. They must believe or understand that the patterns are short-cuts for generating sets of names which could be found, but less efficiently, by using the objects.

CONTINUE TO F–29.

$$\{\tfrac{5}{8},\ \tfrac{10}{16},\ \boxed{\tfrac{15}{24}},\ \tfrac{20}{32},\ \tfrac{25}{40},\ \tfrac{30}{48},\ \tfrac{35}{56},\ \tfrac{40}{64},\ \tfrac{45}{72},\ \tfrac{50}{80},\ \tfrac{55}{88},\ \boxed{\tfrac{60}{96}}\}$$
$$\{\tfrac{11}{12},\ \boxed{\tfrac{22}{24}},\ \tfrac{33}{36},\ \tfrac{44}{48},\ \tfrac{55}{60},\ \tfrac{66}{72},\ \tfrac{77}{84},\ \boxed{\tfrac{88}{96}}\}$$

Since you have the notion that $\tfrac{4}{5} = \tfrac{4 \times n}{5 \times n}$ for some integer n, you cut down on the work by using only the denominators of the sets of equivalent fractions listed above:

$$\{8, 16, \boxed{24}, 32, 40, 48, 56, 64, 72, 80, 88, \boxed{96}\}$$
$$\{12, \boxed{24}, 36, 48, 60, 72, 84, \boxed{96}\}$$

Then you ask $8 \times \square = 24$. It is 3, so $\tfrac{5 \times 3}{8 \times 3} = \tfrac{15}{24}$.

Similarly, $12 \times \square = 24$ $\tfrac{11 \times 2}{12 \times 2} = \tfrac{22}{24}$
$$\square = 2$$

Try this one: $\tfrac{7}{8} \; \boxed{?} \; \tfrac{9}{10}$

SEE ANSWER FRAME (F–34).

Write elements of the $\tfrac{2}{3}$ set and write names for $\tfrac{3}{4}$ until you find one in each set with the same denominator.

Step 1. $\tfrac{2}{3} \; \boxed{?} \; \tfrac{3}{4}$ $\{\tfrac{2}{3},\ \tfrac{4}{6},\ \tfrac{6}{9},\ \tfrac{8}{12}, \ldots\}$

Step 2. $\tfrac{8}{12} \; \boxed{?} \; \tfrac{9}{12}$ $\{\tfrac{3}{4},\ \tfrac{6}{8},\ \tfrac{9}{12}, \ldots\}$

Step 3. $\tfrac{8}{12} \; \boxed{<} \; \tfrac{9}{12}$

Step 4. $\tfrac{2}{3} \; \boxed{<} \; \tfrac{3}{4}$

CONTINUE TO F–31.

Try one more: Is $\tfrac{6}{11} > \tfrac{7}{9}$ or $\tfrac{6}{11} < \tfrac{7}{9}$?

You are wise if you reinforce these concepts with other materials such as the number line, Sterns blocks, fraction charts and so on.

Now students have the prerequisites for studying standard operations on the set of rational numbers.

SEE ANSWER FRAME (F–35).

(F–34)

$$\frac{7}{8}\,\textcircled{?}\,\frac{9}{10}$$

$$\{10, 20, 30, \textcircled{40}, 50, 60, 70, 80, \ldots\}$$

$$\{8, 16, 24, 32, \textcircled{40}, 48, 56, 64, 72, 8C, \ldots\}$$

Now 80 is in both sets but 40 is the *first* one in both sets

$$8 \times \boxed{5} = 40 \quad so \quad \frac{7 \times 5}{8 \times 5} = \frac{35}{40} \quad and$$

$$10 \times \boxed{4} = 40 \quad so \quad \frac{9 \times 4}{10 \times 4} = \frac{36}{40} \qquad \frac{35}{40} < \frac{4C}{3\epsilon} \quad so \quad \frac{7}{8} < \frac{9}{10}.$$

CONTINUE TO F–35.

(F–33)

(a) $\{5, 10, 15, \ldots\}$ $\{10, 20, \ldots\}$

$$5 \times \square = 10$$
$$\square = 2$$

$$\frac{2}{5} = \frac{2 \times 2}{5 \times 2} = \frac{4}{10}$$

(1) $\frac{2}{5}\,\textcircled{?}\,\frac{3}{10}$

(2) $\frac{4}{10}\,\textcircled{?}\,\frac{3}{10}$

(3) $\frac{4}{10} > \frac{3}{10}$

(4) $\frac{2}{5} > \frac{3}{10}$

(b) $\{6, 12, \underline{18}, 24, 30, 36, \ldots\}$
$\{\underline{18}, 36, \ldots\}$

$6 \times \square = \underline{1}8$

$\square = 3$

$\frac{5}{6} = \frac{5 \times \textcircled{3}}{6 \times \textcircled{3}} = \frac{15}{\underline{1}8}$

(1) $\frac{5}{6}\,\textcircled{?}\,\frac{11}{18}$

(2) $\frac{15}{18}\,\textcircled{?}\,\frac{11}{18}$

(3) $\frac{15}{18} > \frac{11}{18}$

(4) $\frac{5}{6} > \frac{11}{18}$

IF YOU GOT THIS CORRECT, YOU ARE FINISHED.
IF YOU WANT MORE PRACTICE, GO TO F–34.

(F–35)

Multiples of 11: $\{11, 22, 33, 44, 55, 66, 77, 88, \underline{99}, \ldots\}$
Multiples of 9: $\{9, 18, 27, 36, 45, 54, 63, 72, 81, 90, \underline{99}, \ldots\}$
99 is the Least Common Multiple of 11 and 9.

$$\frac{6}{11} = \frac{\square}{99} \text{ and } \frac{7}{9} = \frac{\square}{99}.$$

Now $11 \times \underline{9} = 99$ so $\frac{6}{11} = \frac{6 \times 9}{11 \times 9} = \frac{54}{99}$

and $9 \times \underline{11} = 99$ so $\frac{7}{9} = \frac{7 \times 11}{9 \times 11} = \frac{77}{99}.$

Thus $\frac{6}{11}\,\textcircled{?}\,\frac{7}{9}$ is the same as $\frac{54}{99}\,\textcircled{?}\,\frac{77}{99}.$

THE END.

Development of Rational Numbers Self-Test

1. Select from the list on the right the smallest set to which each element on the left belongs:

a. 2	f. .616616661 . . .	1—Rational Numbers
b. −5	g. 0	2—Integers
c. $\sqrt{2}$	h. $\frac{9}{14}$	3—Natural Numbers
d. π	i. $\sqrt{\frac{3}{4}}$	4—Real Numbers
e. .333 . . .	j. .61286128 . . .	5—Whole Numbers

2. Find the rational number whose decimal value is .616161 . . . .

3. Use sets of equivalent fractions to determine whether

$\frac{3}{5} < \frac{5}{7}$ or $\frac{3}{5} > \frac{5}{7}$

4. Use sets of multiples to determine whether $\frac{5}{8} > \frac{4}{7}$ or $\frac{5}{8} < \frac{4}{7}$

Answers to Development of Rational Numbers Self-Test

1. a. 3   f. 4
   b. 2   g. 5
   c. 4   h. 1
   d. 4   i. 4
   e. 1   j. 1

2. $100x = 61.6161\ldots$
   $\underline{\quad x = \quad .6161\ldots}$
   $99x = 61$
   $x = \frac{61}{99}$

3. $\{\frac{3}{5}, \frac{6}{10}, \frac{9}{15}, \frac{12}{20}, \frac{15}{25}, \frac{18}{30}, \frac{21}{35}, \ldots\}$ $\frac{21}{35} < \frac{25}{35}$ so $\frac{3}{5} < \frac{5}{7}$
   $\{\frac{5}{7}, \frac{10}{14}, \frac{15}{21}, \frac{20}{28}, \frac{25}{35}, \ldots\}$

4. $\{8, 16, 24, 32, 40, 48, 56, \ldots\}$
   $\{7, 14, 21, 28, 35, 42, 49, 56, \ldots\}$
   $\frac{5}{8} = \frac{5 \times 7}{8 \times 7} = \frac{35}{56}$
   $\frac{4}{7} = \frac{4 \times 8}{7 \times 8} = \frac{32}{56}$ $\frac{35}{56} > \frac{32}{56}$ so $\frac{5}{8} > \frac{4}{7}$

Specific Materials and Discovery Strategies

The use of concrete materials in early pupil contacts with rational number concepts cannot be overemphasized. Fractions must *make sense*. To the child, this means in particular that new ideas must agree with perceptions of the real world about him. Manipulation of concrete materials will help the child accommodate new ideas into his own structure of reality. *Parts of wholes* can be taught with objects that can be taken apart and put back together again, and *parts of groups* can be taught with sets of objects students can move about on their desks.

In kindergarten, first and second grades, concrete materials such as plaster of paris models of fruit can be made; they are also available commercially. Children can *see and manipulate* apples cut in half, pears cut in thirds, and peaches cut in fourths. *Real* fruit can be used, too. If each child has one, two, three, or four of several objects, he can place various combinations on his desk top to explore simple unit fractions and names for one.

An appropriate step to follow concrete materials is use of pictures of objects. Children can be encouraged to bring pictures of various objects from magazines at home. The pictures can be cut into two, three or four pieces as desired for discussion and pupil exploration. Following many experiences with concrete materials and pictures, children in grades two and three can begin to examine relative positions of fractions on a number line, and they can make their own fraction kits similar to the one you have constructed.

When children begin exploration of renaming rational numbers by finding equivalent fractions, two aids which are particularly useful are flannel board kits and fraction charts. The flannel board kit can be color-coordinated with the youngsters' fraction kits.

A fraction chart can be used to demonstrate equivalent fractions and simple addition and subtraction problems. The most versatile fraction chart is one which has movable parts. You can easily show that $\frac{1}{2} = \frac{2}{4} = \frac{3}{6} = \frac{4}{8} = \frac{6}{12}$ or $\frac{1}{3} + \frac{1}{2} = \frac{5}{6}$.

1											
$\frac{1}{2}$						$\frac{1}{2}$					
$\frac{1}{3}$				$\frac{1}{3}$				$\frac{1}{3}$			
$\frac{1}{4}$			$\frac{1}{4}$			$\frac{1}{4}$			$\frac{1}{4}$		
$\frac{1}{6}$		$\frac{1}{6}$		$\frac{1}{6}$		$\frac{1}{6}$		$\frac{1}{6}$		$\frac{1}{6}$	
$\frac{1}{8}$	$\frac{1}{8}$		$\frac{1}{8}$		$\frac{1}{8}$	$\frac{1}{8}$		$\frac{1}{8}$		$\frac{1}{8}$	$\frac{1}{8}$
$\frac{1}{12}$	$\frac{1}{12}$	$\frac{1}{12}$	$\frac{1}{12}$	$\frac{1}{12}$	$\frac{1}{12}$	$\frac{1}{12}$	$\frac{1}{12}$	$\frac{1}{12}$	$\frac{1}{12}$	$\frac{1}{12}$	$\frac{1}{12}$

A fraction chart can be made with seven 24-inch strips of tagboard. The strips can be placed in a pocket chart or place value chart.

Paper folding can be another valuable aid in your repertoire. Children can fold rectangular regions to develop understanding of $\frac{1}{2}$, $\frac{1}{3}$, $\frac{1}{4}$, and so on. Paper folding can also be used to demonstrate or practice finding equivalent fractions. First, fold three pieces of paper, mark the creases, and write "$\frac{1}{2}$" on each section. Then fold the pieces so that a single "$\frac{1}{2}$" is showing; fold one

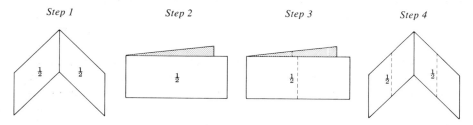

Step 1   Step 2   Step 3   Step 4

piece in half again, one in thirds and one in fourths. You can use these three strips to show $\frac{1}{2} = \frac{2}{4} = \frac{3}{6} = \frac{4}{8}$.

Discovery.   The two most appropriate uses of directed discovery strategies in the concepts of this chapter are in instruction of inequalities and equivalent fractions. General approaches for the development of these concepts were discussed in the programmed section.

Ask the students to take one fractional part of each size and order them in a stack by placing the largest on the bottom and the smallest on top. Then ask them to write the numerals on small pieces of paper and place them in order left to right, largest to smallest.

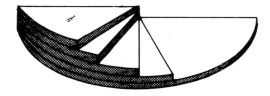

Name other unit fractions for which sections are not available and see if they can place the numeral cards in proper position. Walk around the room and help. Follow up this exercise with a discussion of the generalization. This

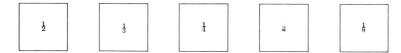

approach could be modified by couching the problem in a socially relevant situation.

To discover generalizations for generating sets of equivalent fractions, ask children to start with one fractional part and see how many ways they can "cover it up" exactly by using pieces of one size. For one-half they might try thirds and find they did not work, try fourths and determine two will work, and so on. Encourage them to guess what the next one will be: $\frac{1}{2} = \frac{2}{4} = ?$ They might guess $\frac{4}{6}$. They try fifths and find no suitable result. Then they try sixths and find that 3 will cover one-half. Now they should hypothesize again. They will begin to notice patterns: $\frac{1}{2} = \frac{2}{4} = \frac{3}{6} = ?$; 1, 2, 3, and 2, 4, 6. After one-half, they can repeat the activity with other parts. Another approach which is probably a bit more difficult is to give children a set of twelve objects and have them determine different names for subsets:

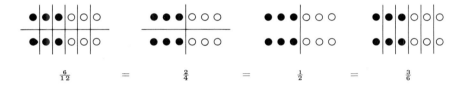

$$\frac{6}{12} \quad = \quad \frac{2}{4} \quad = \quad \frac{1}{2} \quad = \quad \frac{3}{6}$$

Guide them to analyze sequences through rearrangement of numerals: $\frac{1}{2} = \frac{2}{4} = \frac{3}{6} = \frac{6}{12}$. Ask them to use objects for determining other names for one half.

Establishing Appropriate Objectives

Objectives which cover elementary rational number concepts extend over a three- or four-year period. In relation to the typical curriculum outlined in section one of this chapter, the following concepts and levels are appropriate.

Grade 1:
1. Simple unit fractions as part of a whole and part of a group: concrete and semi-concrete levels.

Grade 2:
2. Simple fractions as part of a whole and part of a group: concrete and semi-concrete levels.
3. Names for one: concrete and semi-concrete.

Grade 3:
4. Order and inequalities: all three levels.
5. Equivalent fractions: all three levels.

The following are some sample objectives.
The child will be able to:
1. *concrete:* hold up a numeral card which says "$\frac{1}{2}$", "$\frac{1}{3}$" or "$\frac{1}{4}$" when shown a fractional part of an object such as an apple.

1. *semi-concrete:* circle the appropriate numeral when he sees $\frac{1}{2}$, $\frac{1}{3}$ or $\frac{1}{4}$ of a shaded circle or rectangle.

4. *concrete:* place sections of his fraction kit in order, largest to smallest.

4. *semi-concrete:* circle the fraction which names the smallest rational number by locating the positions on a number line which has the positions and numerals indicated.

5. *concrete:* write another name for a given fraction by placing pieces of equal size on top of the piece representing the given number.

5. *semi-concrete:* rename fractions by superimposing number lines.

5. *semi-concrete:* rename fractions by drawing rectangular regions and partitioning them.

5. *abstract:* rename fractions by generating sets of equivalent fractions without the use of aids.

At the risk of becoming monotonous, notice again that all objectives should be mastered *concretely*. Books are, by their very nature, semi-concrete and abstract. Meaningful learning does not begin with the textbook. Teachers who conscientiously seek to develop total mastery use books in phase two, semi-concrete, *after* they have explored concrete manifestations of concepts.

Discussion and Projects

1. What other materials, commercial or homemade, can be used to teach developmental concepts of rational numbers such as unit and equivalent fractions?

2. What are some social situations which can be used in a discovery lesson on equivalent fractions?

3. Write other objectives for developmental concepts.

4. Write some test questions which evaluate pupil progress towards the objectives listed in this chapter and/or the ones which you wrote in the previous item.

5. What are some concepts on each level of the spiraling curriculum which are geometric? Measurement? Whole numbers?

6. Write a number sentence which has all elements, including the correct response, in the set of natural numbers. Then write other number sentences which "show a need for" enlarged number systems including whole numbers, integers, rationals and reals.

Additional Resources

Filmstrips

    Least Common Multiples, Popular Science (6H–4)
    Using One to Rename Fractions, Filmstrip-of-the-Month (1213)

Films

> *Beyond the Whole Numbers,* National Council of Teachers of Mathematics.
>
> *Fractions and Rational Numbers,* National Council of Teachers of Mathematics.

Elementary School Textbooks

> Silver Burdett (1970), Grade 1, *Modern Mathematics Through Discovery,* by R. Morton, M. Ross, H. S. More, M. Gray, E. Sage, W. Collins.
>> Student Text: pp. 87–88.
>
> Silver Burdett (1970), Grade 2, *Modern Mathematics Through Discovery,* by R. Morton, M. Ross, H. S. More, M. Gray, E. Sage, W. Collins.
>> Student Text: pp. 116, 223–24.
>
> Silver Burdett (1970), Grade 3, *Modern Mathematics Through Discovery,* by R. Morton, M. Ross, H. S. More, M. Gray, E. Sage, W. Collins.
>> Student Text: pp. 68–71, 209–13, 263–68.
>
> Harper & Row (1970), Grade 1, *New Dimensions in Mathematics,* by C. D'Augustine, F. Brown, H. Heddens, C. Howard.
>> Student Text: pp. 127–28, 193–94.
>
> Harper & Row (1970), Grade 2, *New Dimensions in Mathematics,* by C. D'Augustine, F. Brown, H. Heddens, C. Howard.
>> Student Text: pp. 119–25, 185–88.
>
> Harper & Row (1970), Grade 3, *New Dimensions in Mathematics,* by C. D'Augustine, F. Brown, H. Heddens, C. Howard.
>> Student Text: pp. 198–221, 302–03.

14

Teaching Addition and Subtraction of Rational Numbers

Section one of this chapter teaches you various ways to add and subtract rational numbers. A careful analysis is made of the mathematical rationale supporting the development, and appropriate pedagogical concepts are related to the presentation. The section has behaviorally stated objectives and a self-test.

Section two relates addition and subtraction of rational numbers more specifically to the general treatment in this text on discovery strategies and materials of instruction.

Section three relates the mathematical content of the chapter to the individualization model presented in detail earlier. Ideas relative to readiness and psychological concepts are briefly explored.

Content and Specific Methodology

After you have read the following list of behavioral objectives, you may wish to take the self-test at the end of the section. If you perform satisfactorily, you may wish to skim the programmed auto-tutorial section quickly or to omit it entirely.

Addition and Subtraction of Non-Negative Rational Numbers

Objectives

After you complete this unit, you will be able to:

(1) Use the numberline, paper strips and pie-wedges to find sums and differences of fractions with like denominators with and without regrouping of units and parts.
(2) Use the associative property and regrouping of units and parts to compute sums and differences of fractions with like denominators.
(3) Determine the unique set of prime factors which yield a given number.
(4) Compute least common multiples by the sets of multiples method.
(5) Reduce terms of fractions by finding the greatest common factor with sets of factors and by prime factorization.

Materials Needed

Fractional parts made of paper which you used in the previous unit. Make some strips of paper:

Length	Number	Fractional Part
12 inches	3	1 unit
6 inches	4	$\frac{1}{2}$
4 inches	6	$\frac{1}{3}$
3 inches	8	$\frac{1}{4}$
2 inches	12	$\frac{1}{6}$
$1\frac{1}{2}$ inches	12	$\frac{1}{8}$
1 inch	18	$\frac{1}{12}$

Assumptions

A. Children understand the concepts of numerator and denominator.
B. Children are thoroughly familiar with many names for each rational number.
C. Children can find sets of equivalent fractions.

A. *Addition and Subtraction With Like Denominators*

Readiness activities in grades one and two should provide experiences with concrete materials which help children gradually develop the idea that

> one-half placed with one-half is two halves,
> one-third placed with one-third is two thirds,
> one-fourth placed with two-fourths is three fourths, etc.

The teacher in grade three can build upon such experiences by using paper strips, pie-wedges, number lines and other familiar materials.

Make a number line with intervals of one-sixth and show $\frac{3}{6} + \frac{1}{6} = n$.

Show it also with paper strips.

SEE ANSWER FRAME (AS–1).

AS–2

Now use the pie-wedges. Place the unit region in front of you and place 6 sixths next to it. Position 3 sixths and 1 sixth nearby.

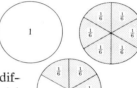

Now place the 3-sixths and one-sixth *on top of* a different unit circle. This also provides a good visual model for $\frac{3}{6} + \frac{1}{6} = \frac{4}{6}$.

The use of different colors helps because of the visual contrast it provides.

Repeat the number line, wedges and strips for other combinations which have sums less than 1:

$$\tfrac{1}{4} + \tfrac{2}{4}, \ \tfrac{1}{3} + \tfrac{1}{3}, \ \tfrac{3}{8} + \tfrac{4}{8}, \text{ etc.}$$

CONTINUE TO AS–3.

AS–3

(a) How can you show one and two-sixths, $1\frac{2}{6}$, with strips? wedges? How many sixths would this be altogether?

(b) How can you show two and one-third, $2\frac{1}{3}$, with strips? wedges? How many thirds are there altogether?

You need to relate an explanation to $\frac{3}{3} = 1$, $\frac{6}{6} = 1$, etc

SEE ANSWER FRAME (AS–3).

$\frac{4}{6} + \frac{3}{6} = n$

(a) Place the pieces: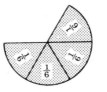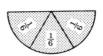

(b) Count them: $\frac{7}{6}$

(c) Place them one-at-a-
time *on a unit region:*

(d) Place a unit region *on
top of* the 6-sixths.

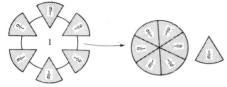

The corresponding steps: $\underbrace{\frac{4}{6} + \frac{3}{6}}_{(a)} = \underbrace{\frac{7}{6}}_{(b)} = \underbrace{\frac{6}{6} + \frac{1}{6}}_{(c)} = \underbrace{1 + \frac{1}{6}}_{(d)} = 1\frac{1}{6}$

You try this one: $\frac{3}{8} + \frac{7}{8} = n$

SEE ANSWER FRAME (AS–4).

Find this sum with strips in steps which are clear:

(a) $\frac{2}{3} + \frac{2}{3} = n$

Find this sum with a number line in steps which are clear:

(b) $\frac{3}{4} + \frac{3}{4} = n$

(Note that *horizontal* lines are being used in fractions, e.g., $\frac{3}{4}$. Diagonals tend
to be more confusing for children, e.g., 3/4.)

SEE ANSWER FRAME (AS–5).

The procedure for subtraction is similar:

$\frac{4}{5} - \frac{3}{5} = n$

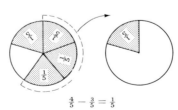

$\frac{4}{5} - \frac{3}{5} = \frac{1}{5}$

Place $\frac{4}{5}$ on a unit region and remove three of them.

Show these: $\frac{3}{4} - \frac{1}{4} = n$ and $\frac{7}{8} - \frac{4}{8} = n$

CONTINUE TO AS–7.

(AS–1)

$\frac{3}{6} + \frac{1}{6} = \frac{4}{6}$

To relate the strips to the number line and to prepare children for regrouping, use the strips with a unit and sixths. Keep the unit strip visibly present to

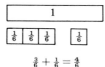

serve as a reminder of size in relation to the pieces which are one-sixth of the unit. Each fractional part should be labeled. Later you can turn them over if you do not wish to use the numeral.

$\frac{3}{6} + \frac{1}{6} = \frac{4}{6}$

CONTINUE TO AS–2.

AS–7

$1\frac{1}{4} - \frac{3}{4} = n$

(a) Place one unit region and a quarter region.

$1 + \frac{1}{4}$

(b) Place four quarters on the unit region.

$\frac{4}{4} + \frac{1}{4}$

(c) Count them.

(d) Remove three quarter regions.

$\frac{5}{4} - \frac{3}{4} = \frac{2}{4}$

Try these with strips and circular regions: (a) $1\frac{3}{8} - \frac{5}{8} = n$ (b) $1\frac{1}{3} - \frac{2}{3} = n$

SEE ANSWER FRAME (AS–7).

(AS–3)

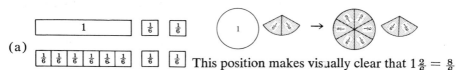

(a)

This position makes visually clear that $1\frac{2}{6} = \frac{8}{6}$
One unit region and 2 one-sixth regions. Eight-sixths—
Place strips or wedges *on top of a unit* or *next to it in* close proximity.

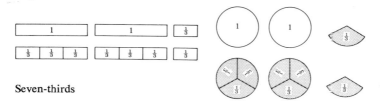

Seven-thirds

Place 3 thirds on each unit region or next to it to reinforce $\frac{3}{3} = 1$.

CONTINUE TO AS–4.

(AS–4)

$$\tfrac{3}{8} + \tfrac{7}{8} = n$$

(a) Place the pieces:

(b) Count them: $\tfrac{10}{8}$

(c) Place 8 of them *on top of* a unit region.

$$\tfrac{10}{8} = \tfrac{8}{8} + \tfrac{2}{8}$$

(d) Place another unit on top of the $\tfrac{8}{8}$ to get

$$\tfrac{8}{8} + \tfrac{2}{8} = 1 + \tfrac{2}{8} = 1\tfrac{2}{8}$$

CONTINUE TO AS–5.

(AS–5)

(a)

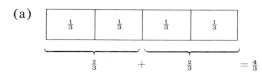

Place a unit strip *on top of* three-thirds to get $1 + \tfrac{1}{3} = 1\tfrac{1}{3}$.

(b)

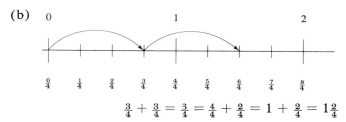

$$\tfrac{3}{4} + \tfrac{3}{4} = \tfrac{3}{4} = \tfrac{4}{4} + \tfrac{2}{4} = 1 + \tfrac{2}{4} = 1\tfrac{2}{4}$$

CONTINUE TO AS–6.

AS–8

After *children* have had an opportunity to do these at their desks or in groups (concrete stage of operations), let them begin to *draw pictures* of circular regions, number lines or strips (semi-concrete stage of operations). Finally move to the abstract stage of operations.

$$\tfrac{3}{4} + \tfrac{2}{4} = n$$

$\tfrac{5}{4}$ Add

$\tfrac{4}{4} + \tfrac{1}{4}$ Rename   *Do this one:*

$1 + \tfrac{1}{4}$ Rename $\tfrac{3}{7} + \tfrac{6}{7} = n$

$1\tfrac{1}{4}$ Rename

Note that you start with *concrete materials* (wedges, strips) and then use *pictures* (semi-concrete) before manipulating symbols by themselves.

SEE ANSWER FRAME (AS–8).

AS–9

Example:

		Try these:
$\frac{2}{3} + \frac{2}{3} = n$		(a) $\frac{1}{2} + \frac{1}{2} + \frac{1}{2} = n$
$\frac{4}{3}$	Add	(b) $\frac{5}{6} + \frac{2}{6} = n$
$\frac{3}{3} + \frac{1}{3}$	Rename	(c) $\frac{5}{9} + \frac{8}{9} = n$
$1 + \frac{1}{3}$	Rename	
$1\frac{1}{3}$	Rename	

Try one or two of these with strips, number lines or wedges.

SEE ANSWER FRAME (AS–9).

(AS–7)

(a)

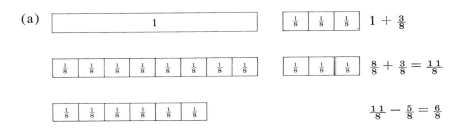

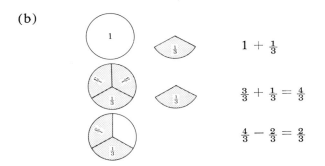

$1 + \frac{3}{8}$

$\frac{8}{8} + \frac{3}{8} = \frac{11}{8}$

$\frac{11}{8} - \frac{5}{8} = \frac{6}{8}$

(b)

$1 + \frac{1}{3}$

$\frac{3}{3} + \frac{1}{3} = \frac{4}{3}$

$\frac{4}{3} - \frac{2}{3} = \frac{2}{3}$

CONTINUE TO AS–8.

AS–10

B. *Addition and Subtraction With Different Denominators*

After extensive work with sums and differences of the previous type, children should explore sums and differences of fractional numbers whose numerals have different denominators. Use the wedge-shapes and paper strips to find this sum: $\frac{1}{2} + \frac{1}{3} = n$

Place the $\frac{1}{2}$- and $\frac{1}{3}$-regions on a unit region. Now, using pieces of only *one* size, determine the size which will cover $\frac{1}{2} + \frac{1}{3}$ *exactly.* Children might try halves, thirds, fourths, and then sixths. They will, of course, find that $\frac{1}{2} + \frac{1}{3}$ can be covered by 5 sixths.

Try this one: $\frac{1}{4} + \frac{2}{3}$

SEE ANSWER FRAME (AS–10).

AS–11

After some experimentation children can be lead to notice that when $\frac{1}{2} + \frac{1}{3} = \frac{5}{6}$ there are 3 sixths on the $\frac{1}{2}$ so $\frac{1}{2} = \frac{3}{6}$ and there are 2 sixths on the $\frac{1}{3}$ so $\frac{1}{3} = \frac{2}{6}$. This should be acceptable to them because of their previous work on ordering of fractions with different denominators.

After discussing this development, allow them to do a couple more, and then give them one for which they have no appropriate pieces.

CONTINUE TO AS–12.

AS–12

Suppose they have no *ninths*. Divide the class into small groups and ask them to find $\frac{1}{6} + \frac{2}{9} = n$. Hopefully some students will remember their work with sets of equivalent fractions:

$$\{ \tfrac{1}{6}, \tfrac{2}{12}, \boxed{\tfrac{3}{18}}, \tfrac{4}{24}, \tfrac{5}{30}, \cdots \}$$
$$\{ \tfrac{2}{9}, \boxed{\tfrac{4}{18}}, \cdots \}$$
$$\frac{1}{6} - \frac{2}{9} = \frac{3}{18} + \frac{4}{18} = \frac{7}{18}$$

Try one utilizing this method: $\frac{2}{3} + \frac{3}{4}$

SEE ANSWER FRAME (AS–12).

(AS–8)

$\frac{3}{7} + \frac{6}{7} = n$	Problem
$\frac{9}{7}$	Add
$\frac{7}{7} + \frac{2}{7}$	Rename
$1 + \frac{2}{7}$	Rename
$1\frac{2}{7}$	Rename

Do the next frame if you need more practice.

CONTINUE TO AS–9 OR AS–10.

(AS–9)

(a) $\frac{1}{2} + \frac{1}{2} + \frac{1}{2}$ (b) $\frac{5}{6} + \frac{2}{6}$ (c) $\frac{5}{9} + \frac{8}{9}$

$\frac{3}{2}$ $\frac{7}{6}$ $\frac{13}{9}$

$\frac{2}{2} + \frac{1}{2}$ $\frac{6}{6} + \frac{1}{6}$ $\frac{9}{9} + \frac{4}{9}$

$1 + \frac{1}{2}$ $1 + \frac{1}{6}$ $1 + \frac{4}{9}$

$1\frac{1}{2}$ $1\frac{1}{6}$ $1\frac{4}{9}$

CONTINUE TO AS–10.

AS–13

Using sets of equivalent fractions enables you to find a "better name" or a more "appropriate" name for a fractional number.

$$\frac{3}{8} = \frac{27}{72} \qquad \left\{\frac{3}{8}, \frac{6}{16}, \frac{9}{24}, \frac{12}{32}, \frac{15}{40}, \frac{18}{48}, \frac{21}{56}, \frac{24}{64}, \boxed{\frac{27}{72}}, \ldots\right\}$$

$$+\; \frac{5}{9} = \frac{40}{72} \qquad \left\{\frac{5}{9}, \frac{10}{18}, \frac{15}{27}, \frac{20}{36}, \frac{25}{45}, \frac{30}{54}, \frac{35}{63}, \boxed{\frac{40}{72}}, \ldots\right\}$$

Using this approach required *30* different products, 15 numerators and 15 denominators. You would need only a fourth as many products if you used only denominators.

$$\frac{3}{8} = \frac{}{72} \qquad \text{(Proceed to find multiples of 9 and ask each time if it is a multiple of 8.)}$$

$$+\; \frac{5}{9} = \frac{}{72} \qquad \{9, 18, 27, 36, 45, 54, 63, \underline{72}, \ldots\}$$

After you decide that 72 is the name for the denominator, rename the fractions.

$$\frac{3}{8} = \frac{3 \times 9}{8 \times 9} = \frac{27}{72} \quad and \quad \frac{5}{9} = \frac{5 \times 8}{9 \times 8} = \frac{40}{72}$$

Study this carefully.

CONTINUE TO AS–14.

(AS–10)

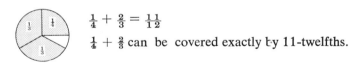

$\frac{1}{4} + \frac{2}{3} = \frac{11}{12}$

$\frac{1}{4} + \frac{2}{3}$ can be covered exactly by 11-twelfths.

Children usually begin explorations with fractions in which one denominator is a multiple of the other, e.g., $\frac{1}{2} + \frac{1}{4}$, $\frac{1}{3} + \frac{2}{6}$, $\frac{5}{8} + \frac{1}{4}$. Some children may notice that $\frac{1}{4} + \frac{2}{3} = \frac{1 \times 3 + 4 \times 2}{4 \times 3} = \frac{3 + 8}{12}$. This is the definition of rational number addition, $\frac{a}{b} + \frac{c}{d} = \frac{ad + bc}{bd}$. This definition is inefficient in many cases and is often memorized without understanding.

CONTINUE TO FRAME AS–11.

The steps are as follows:

(a) $\frac{3}{8}$

$+ \frac{5}{9}$ $\{9, 18, 27, 36, 45, 54, 63, (72), \ldots\}$

(b) $\frac{3}{8} = \frac{}{72}$ ⟶ What do I multiply times 8 to get 72? $\underline{9}$

$+ \frac{5}{9} = \frac{}{72}$ ⟶ What do I multiply times 9 to get 72? $\underline{8}$

(c) $\frac{3 \times 9}{8 \times 9}$ (d) $\frac{27}{72}$

$\frac{5 \times 8}{9 \times 8}$ $+ \frac{40}{72}$ Try this one: $\frac{2}{15} + \frac{3}{10} = n$

$\frac{67}{72}$

SEE ANSWER FRAME (AS–14).

$\frac{2}{3} + \frac{3}{4}$

$\{\frac{2}{3}, \frac{4}{6}, \frac{6}{9}, (\frac{8}{12}), \frac{10}{15}, \ldots\}$

$\{\frac{3}{4}, \frac{6}{8}, (\frac{9}{12}), \ldots\}$

$\frac{2}{3} + \frac{3}{4} = \frac{8}{12} + \frac{9}{12} = \frac{17}{12} = \frac{12}{12} + \frac{5}{12} = 1\frac{5}{12}$

CONTINUE TO AS–13.

2, 4, 10, 38 are *multiples* of 2. That is, each is $2 \times a$ where a is some whole number.

5, 15, 100, 625 are multiples of 5.

$\{2, 4, 6, 8, 10, 12, 14, 16, 18, 20, 22, \ldots\}$ This is the *set of multiples* of 2.

$\{5, 10, 15, 20, 25, 30, \ldots\}$ This is the *set of multiples* of 5.

Notice that 10 is a multiple of 2, and 10 is a multiple of 5. Notice that 20 is, too. 10 and 20 are called *common multiples* of 2 and 5. In adding fractions with different denominators, you can use any common multiple. Example:

$\frac{2}{3}$ $\{3, 6, 9, \underline{12}, 15, 18, \boxed{24}, 27, 30, 33, \textcircled{36}, \ldots\}$

$+\frac{3}{4}$ $\{4, 8, \underline{12}, 16, 20, \boxed{24}, 28, 32, \textcircled{36}, 40, \ldots\}$

(a) $\frac{2}{3} = \frac{}{12}$ (b) $\frac{2}{3} = \frac{}{24}$ (c) $\frac{2}{3} = \frac{}{36}$

$+ \frac{3}{4} = \frac{}{12}$ $+ \frac{3}{4} = \frac{}{24}$ $+ \frac{3}{4} = \frac{}{36}$

Finish these.

SEE ANSWER FRAME (AS–15).

AS–16

The *first* common multiple in the sets is called the *Least Common Multiple* (LCM). It is the number which is the *Lowest Common Denominator* (LCD) when adding fractions.

What is the *Least Common Multiple* of each of the following?

    (a) 3 and 10
    (b) 6 and 20
    (c) 4 and 6
    (d) 8 and 18

SEE ANSWER FRAME (AS–16).

AS–17

The sets of multiples method works well for simple problems, but what if you wanted to find the sum of $\frac{1}{2}$, $\frac{1}{5}$, $\frac{1}{48}$, and $\frac{1}{39}$? To make sets of multiples of these denominators would entail considerable labor. Try it! A new technique is needed.

First you must become acquainted with some new terms:
    (1) Factor
    (2) Prime number
    (3) Composite number

CONTINUE TO AS–18.

AS–18

A *factor* is any whole number which will divide another whole number evenly. The factors of 6 are 1, 2, 3 and 6 because $6 \div 1 = 6$, $6 \div 2 = 3$, $6 \div 3 = 2$ and $6 \div 6 = 1$.

$\{1, 2, 3, 6\}$ is called the *set of factors* of 6. Factors are commonly grouped in pairs $\{(1,6), (2,3)\}$. Six has two factor pairs.

Find the factors of the following numbers:

    (a) 4
    (b) 8
    (c) 7
    (d) 12
    (e) 13
    (f) 100

Now write the sets of *factor pairs*.

SEE ANSWER FRAME (AS–18).

(AS–14)

$$\frac{2}{15} = \frac{2 \times 2}{15 \times 2} = \frac{4}{30}$$

$$\frac{3}{10} = \frac{3 \times 3}{10 \times 3} = \frac{9}{30}$$

$$\frac{13}{30}$$

$\{15, \textcircled{30}, 45, 60, \ldots\}$

$\{10, 20, \textcircled{30}, 40, \ldots\}$

Either of these sets of multiples can be calculated, but you will save time if you use the largest denominator.

30 is a multiple of 10, and 30 is a multiple of 15. 30 is a *common multiple* of 10 and 15.

CONTINUE TO AS–15.

AS–19

A natural number is *composite* if it has at least three distinct factors. A natural number is *prime* if it has *exactly two* distinct factors: itself and one. Natural numbers which are not prime are composite numbers. *By definition,* "1" is neither prime nor composite.

2 is prime because 2 is divisible only by 2 and 1.
3 is prime because 3 is divisible only by 3 and 1.
4 is *not* prime because 4 is divisible by 4, 1 and 2.
5 is prime because 5 is divisible only by 5 and 1.

What numbers less than 40 are prime?

SEE ANSWER FRAME (AS–19).

(AS–15)

(a) $\frac{2}{3} = \frac{2 \times 4}{3 \times 4} = \frac{8}{12}$

$\frac{3}{4} = \frac{3 \times 3}{4 \times 3} = \frac{9}{12}$

$\frac{17}{12}$

(b) $\frac{2 \times 8}{3 \times 8} = \frac{16}{24}$

$\frac{3 \times 6}{4 \times 6} = \frac{18}{24}$

$\frac{34}{24}$

(c) $\frac{2 \times 12}{3 \times 12} = \frac{24}{36}$

$\frac{3 \times 9}{4 \times 9} = \frac{27}{36}$

$\frac{51}{36}$

$\frac{17}{12}$, $\frac{34}{24}$ and $\frac{51}{36}$ name the same number since

$$\frac{17 \times 2}{12 \times 2} = \frac{34}{24}, \qquad \frac{17 \times 3}{12 \times 3} = \frac{51}{36}$$

CONTINUE TO AS–16.

(AS–16)

(a) $\{10, 20, \underline{30}, \ldots\}$

(b) $\{20, 40, \underline{60}, \ldots\}$

(c) $\{6, \underline{12}, \ldots\}$

(d) $\{18, 36, 54, \underline{72}, \ldots\}$

CONTINUE TO AS–17.

AS–20

The *Fundamental Theorem of Arithmetic* states that every natural number can be represented as a *unique* product of a certain set of prime factors. The Theorem says that every natural number can be expressed by only *one* set of prime numbers multiplied together when order is not considered.

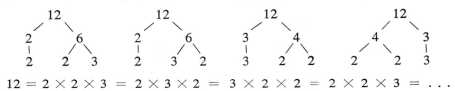

$12 = 2 \times 2 \times 3 = 2 \times 3 \times 2 = 3 \times 2 \times 2 = 2 \times 2 \times 3 = \ldots$

The product of two twos and one three is twelve; there is no other set of primes whose product is twelve.

CONTINUE TO AS–21.

(AS–18)

(a)   4: $\{1, 2, 4\}$ (a) $\{(1,4),(2,2)\}$

(b)   8: $\{1, 2, 4, 8\}$ (b) $\{(1,8),(2,4)\}$

(c)   7: $\{1, 7\}$ (c) $\{(1,7)\}$

(d)   12: $\{1, 2, 3, 4, 6, 12\}$ (d) $\{(1,12),(2,6),(3,4)\}$

(e)   13: $\{1, 13\}$ (e) $\{(1,13)\}$

(f)   100: $\{1, 2, 4, 5, 10, 20, 25,$ (f) $\{(1,100),(2,50),(4,25),$
           $50, 100\}$ $(5,20),(10,10)\}$

A *factor* divides a number evenly.

CONTINUE TO AS–19.

The previous frame contains what is frequently called a "factor tree." When using the tree with children, the teacher can carry all primes along on each step or circle the primes.

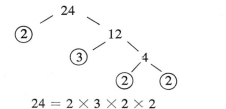

$$24 = 2 \times 3 \times 2 \times 2$$

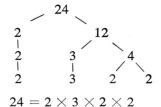

$$24 = 2 \times 3 \times 2 \times 2$$

CONTINUE TO AS–22.

2	17
3	19
5	23
7	29
11	31
13	37

CONTINUE TO AS–20.

Make a factor tree for each of these:

(a) 36—start with 4 × 9

(b) 49

(c) 32—start with 2 × 16

SEE ANSWER FRAME (AS–22).

AS–23

    (a) What is a factor?

    (b) What is a prime number?

    (c) Which of the following are prime: 2, 3, 4, 5, 6, 7, 8, 9?

    (d) How many prime numbers are there between 10 and 20?

    (e) How many even numbers are prime?

SEE ANSWER FRAME (AS–23).

AS–24

The number 10 has *four* factors

        {1, 2, 5, 10}

The number 25 has *three* factors

        {1, 5, 25}

"1" is a common factor of 10 and 25. "5" is a common factor of 10 and 25. There is no common factor of 10 and 25 which is larger than 5, so 5 is called the *Greatest Common Factor* (GCF) of 10 and 25.

What are the sets of factors of

    (a) 15   (b) 32   (c) 36   (d) 18   (e) 97

    (f) What is the GCF of 36 and 18?   15 and 18?   15 and 32?

SEE ANSWER FRAME (AS–24).

AS–25

Another way to find prime factors is to keep dividing by primes:

Step 1	*Step 2*	*Step 3*	*Step 4*	*Step 5*
		9	③)9̄	
	18	2)18̄	②)18̄	
36	2)36̄	2)36̄	②)36̄	$36 = 2 \times 2 \times 3 \times 3$

Try these: (a) 24

          (b) 100

          (c) List the factor pairs of 100

SEE ANSWER FRAME (AS–25).

AS–26

Now, how can the *Fundamental Theorem of Arithmetic* be utilized to find lowest common denominators?

You know that the lowest common denominator is the *least common multiple* of all the denominators under consideration. That is, for $\frac{1}{2} + \frac{1}{3}$ the lowest common denominator, 6, is the smallest number which is a multiple of 2, $\{2, 4, \textcircled{6}, 8, \ldots\}$, which is at the same time a multiple of 3, $\{3, \textcircled{6}, 9, \ldots\}$.

CONTINUE TO AS–27.

AS–27

Another example:

$$\frac{1}{6} + \frac{1}{14}$$
$$\{14, 28, \textcircled{42}, 56, 70, \textcircled{84}, \ldots\}$$

Now 42 is the LCD because it is the LCM or the smallest number which can be divided evenly by both 6 and 14.

By the *Fundamental Theorem of Arithmetic:*

$$6 = 2 \times 3$$
$$14 = 2 \times 7$$
$$42 = 2 \times 3 \times 7$$

I. Notice that $\frac{42}{6} = \dfrac{\textcircled{2} \times \textcircled{3} \times 7}{\textcircled{2} \times \textcircled{3}} = 7$

II. and $\frac{42}{14} = \dfrac{\textcircled{2} \times 3 \times \textcircled{7}}{\textcircled{2} \times \textcircled{7}} = 3$

Observe: Statements I and II indicate that 6 and 14 divide the LCD, 42, as required. Every prime factor of 42 was "needed," i.e., every factor was needed to enable you to divide evenly by 6 and 14 and there were no prime factors *not* needed.

CONTINUE TO AS–28.

(AS–22)

(a)
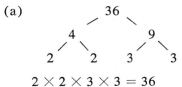

$2 \times 2 \times 3 \times 3 = 36$

(b)
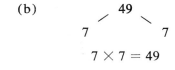

(c)
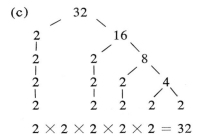

$2 \times 2 \times 2 \times 2 \times 2 = 32$

(c)
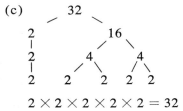

$2 \times 2 \times 2 \times 2 \times 2 = 32$

CONTINUE TO AS–23.

(AS–23)

(a) If *a* and *b* are natural numbers, *a* is a factor of *b* if *a* divides *b* and has no remainder.

(b) A prime number has *exactly* two factors (*1* and *itself*)

(c) 2, 3, 5, 7

(d) 4; {11, 13, 17, 19}

(e) *One:* {2}. All others have at least three factors: If *n* is an even number and n > 2 then n is divisible by 1; n is divisible by n, and n is divisible by 2.

CONTINUE TO AS–24.

(AS–24)

(a) 15 {1, 3, 5, 15}

(b) 32 {1, 2, 4, 8, 16, 32}

(c) 36 {1, 36, 2, 18, 3, 12, 4, 9, 6}

(d) 18 {1, 18, 2, 9, 3, 6}

(e) 97 is prime. How do you know when to stop looking? You try 2, 3, 5, 7 and so on, but when do you decide there are no other factors?

(f) 18; 3; 1

CONTINUE TO AS–25.

(AS–25)

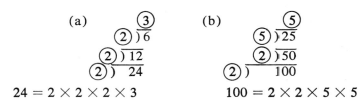

(a)　24 = 2 × 2 × 2 × 3

(b)　100 = 2 × 2 × 5 × 5

(c) Try 1: (1,100)
Try 2: (2,50)
Try 3: (3,　) No
Try 4: (4,25)
Try 5: (5,20)

When do you stop trying numbers?

CONTINUE TO AS–26.

Another example. The smallest denominator for $\frac{1}{8} + \frac{1}{12}$ is twenty-fourths.

Notice: $8 = 2 \times 2 \times 2$ $\frac{24}{8} = \frac{2 \times 2 \times 2 \times 3}{2 \times 2 \times 2} = 3$

$12 = 2 \times 2 \times 3$ $\frac{24}{12} = \frac{2 \times 2 \times 2 \times 3}{2 \times 2 \times 3} = 2$

$24 = 2 \times 2 \times 2 \times 3$

There were only twos and threes as factors of 8 and 12 so there were only twos and threes in the LCD.

8 has three twos so the LCD must have three twos.

12 has two twos and one three so the LCD must have two twos and one three.

CONTINUE TO AS–29.

(a) Find the prime factors of these denominators:

$$\tfrac{1}{6} + \tfrac{1}{5} + \tfrac{1}{15} + \tfrac{1}{4}$$

(b) What prime factors must occur in the LCD?

(c) The LCD is 60; factor it.

SEE ANSWER FRAME (AS–29).

Since $6 = 2 \times 3$	there must be *one 2* and *one 3* to divide evenly	$\frac{LCD}{6} = \frac{LCD}{2 \times 3} = a$
Since $5 = 5$	there must be *one 5* to divide evenly	$\frac{LCD}{5} = b$
Since $15 = 3 \times 5$	there must be *one 3* and *one 5* to divide evenly	$\frac{LCD}{15} = \frac{LCD}{3 \times 5} = c$
Since $4 = 2 \times 2$	there must be *two 2s* to divide evenly	$\frac{LCD}{4} = \frac{LCD}{2 \times 2} = d$

Checking all four of these conditions at once, you see there must be two 2s, one 3 and one 5: $2 \times 2 \times 3 \times 5 = 60$!

CONTINUE TO AS–31.

AS–31

$$\tfrac{1}{8} + \tfrac{1}{6} + \tfrac{1}{12} + \tfrac{1}{15} + \tfrac{1}{24}$$

$8 = 2 \times 2 \times 2$	Three 2s
$6 = 2 \times 3$	One 2 and one 3
$12 = 2 \times 2 \times 3$	Two 2s and one 3
$15 = 3 \times 5$	One 3 and one 5
$24 = 2 \times 2 \times 2 \times 3$	Three 2s and one 3

What is the LCD which will satisfy all these conditions as found by the *Fundamental Theorem?*

SEE ANSWER FRAME (AS–31).

AS–32

Find the LCD by the prime factor method:

$$\tfrac{1}{24} + \tfrac{1}{42}$$

Now verify this by using the sets of multiples method.

SEE ANSWER FRAME (AS–32).

AS–33

The LCD is the smallest number which can be divided by all the denominators of a problem. When you add $\tfrac{1}{2} + \tfrac{1}{3}$, 6 is the LCD because it is the smallest number which is divisible by *both* 2 and 3. Notice that $\tfrac{6}{2} = \tfrac{\cancel{2} \times 3}{\cancel{2}} = 3$ and $\tfrac{6}{3} = \tfrac{2 \times \cancel{3}}{\cancel{3}} = 2$.

6 is a *multiple* of both 2 and 3.
6 is three 2s, and 6 is two 3s.

$6 = 2 + 2 + 2 \quad 6 = 3 + 3$

CONTINUE TO AS–34.

Similarly, for $\frac{1}{8} + \frac{1}{6}$ the LCD is 24.

$24 = (2 \times 2 \times 2) \times 3 = 8 \times 3 \longrightarrow$ three 8s and
$24 = 2 \times 2 \times (2 \times 3) = 4 \times 6 \longrightarrow$ four 6s. Hence, 24 is a multiple of
both 6 and 8. How do you know it is the *least* or *smallest* multiple?

Study the next frame.

CONTINUE TO AS–35.

(a) $6 = 2 \times 3$
        $5 = 5$
      $15 = 3 \times 5$
        $4 = 2 \times 2$

(b)   twos, threes, fives

(c) $60 = 2 \times 2 \times 3 \times 5$

Why were there two 2s but only one 3 and one 5?

CONTINUE TO AS–30.

Since the LCD must be divisible by 6 and 8, you know the LCD must be
divisible by 2×3 and by $2 \times 2 \times 2$.

Thus, $\frac{\text{LCD}}{6} = \frac{\cancel{2} \times \cancel{3} \times (?)}{\cancel{2} \times \cancel{3}}$ *and* $\frac{\text{LCD}}{8} = \frac{\cancel{2} \times \cancel{2} \times \cancel{2} \times (*)}{\cancel{2} \times \cancel{2} \times \cancel{2}}$

Now it should be clear that you have the smallest combination of factors when
$2 \times 3 \times (?) = 2 \times 2 \times 2 \times (*)$. Obviously this is true when (?) is 2×2
and (*) is 3. So LCD $= 2 \times 2 \times 2 \times 3 = 24$.

CONTINUE TO AS–36.

(AS–31)

2s, 3s and 5s are needed. If you check your factor trees, you will find that you need

$$\left.\begin{array}{l}\text{three 2s}\\\text{one 3}\\\text{one 5}\end{array}\right\} \quad 2 \times 2 \times 2 \times 3 \times 5 = 120$$

CONTINUE TO AS–32.

(AS–32)

$$24 = 2 \times 2 \times 2 \times \boxed{3}$$
$$42 = 2 \times 3 \times \textcircled{7}$$
$$\text{LCD} = 2 \times 2 \times 2 \times \boxed{3} \times \textcircled{7} = 168$$
$$\{24, 48, 72, 96, 120, 144, \textcircled{168}, \ldots\}$$
$$\{42, 84, 126, \textcircled{168}, \ldots\}$$

If you feel you have grasped this concept of LCD by prime factorization, skip to frame AS–39. Otherwise continue to the next frame.

CONTINUE TO AS–33 OR AS–39.

AS–36

Study the previous frame very carefully.

Now if you have $\frac{1}{12} + \frac{1}{18}$, $\begin{array}{l}12 = 2 \times 2 \times 3\\18 = 2 \times 3 \times 3\end{array}$

What is the smallest collection of factors?

$$\underline{} \times \underline{} \times \underline{} \times \underline{}$$

CONTINUE TO AS–37.

AS–37

$$2 \times 2 \times 3 \times 3 = 36$$

Now find the LCD for $\frac{1}{9} + \frac{1}{24}$

SEE ANSWER FRAME (AS–37).

AS–38

You should now be able to do the following:

Find the LCD for $\{\frac{1}{2}, \frac{1}{3}, \frac{1}{4}, \frac{1}{12}, \frac{1}{15}\}$

Find the LCD for $\{\frac{1}{50}, \frac{1}{36}, \frac{1}{20}\}$

SEE ANSWER FRAME (AS–38).

AS–39

After you have attained pupil understanding of this concept, you can incorporate it with previous ideas:

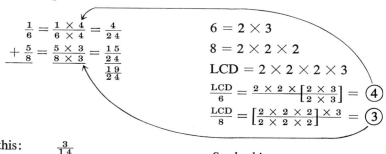

Try this: $\frac{3}{14}$

    $+ \frac{5}{21}$ *Study this.*

SEE ANSWER FRAME (AS–39).

AS–40

Do *not* find the value of x and y to answer this question.

If x = 2 × 2 × 3 × 5 × 7 and
    y = 2 × 5 × 7

What is x ÷ y?

SEE ANSWER FRAME (AS–40).

AS–41

Try one more: $\frac{5}{12}$

$\frac{2}{9}$

$+ \frac{7}{18}$

SEE ANSWER FRAME (AS–41).

AS–42

As you have probably surmised, factoring makes renaming easier. What you have traditionally called *reducing* is simply renaming in the most common name.

$$\frac{8}{42} = \frac{2 \times 2 \times 2}{2 \times 3 \times 7} = \frac{2 \times 2 \times 2 \div 2}{2 \times 3 \times 7 \div 2} = \frac{2 \times 2}{3 \times 7} = \frac{4}{21}$$

Later, when multiplication is explored, another way to rename will be examined which uses the multiplicative identity element, one.

The Greatest Common Factor can also be used to determine the standard numeral or common name. Simply write the sets of factors and divide the numerator and denominator by the GCF.

8: {1, 2, 4, 8}

42: {1, 2, 3, 7, 6, 14, 21, 42}

$$\frac{8}{42} = \frac{8 \div 2}{42 \div 2} = \frac{4}{21}$$

CONTINUE TO AS–43.

$$9 = 3 \times 3$$
$$24 = 2 \times 2 \times 2 \times 3$$
$$\text{LCD} = 2 \times 2 \times 2 \times 3 \times 3 = 72$$
$$\frac{72}{9} = \frac{2 \times 2 \times 2 \times \left[3 \times 3\right]}{\left[3 \times 3\right]} = 8$$
$$\frac{72}{24} = \left[\frac{2 \times 2 \times 2 \times 3}{2 \times 2 \times 2 \times 3}\right] \times 3 = 3$$

Notice that $\frac{72}{24} = 3$ can be cetermined by using the prime factors rather than dividing $24\overline{)72}$.

CONTINUE TO AS–38.

$2 = 2$

$3 = 3$ LCD must have 2s, 3s, 5s

$4 = 2 \times 2$

$12 = 2 \times 2 \times 3$ LCD $= 2 \times 2 \times 3 \times 5 = 60$

$15 = 3 \times 5$

$50 = 2 \times 5 \times 5$ LCD must have 2s, 3s, 5s

$36 = 2 \times 2 \times 3 \times 3$ LCD $= 2 \times 2 \times 3 \times 3 \times 5 \times 5 = 900$

$20 = 2 \times 2 \times 5$

CONTINUE TO AS–39.

$$14 = 2 \times 7$$
$$21 = 3 \times 7$$
$$\text{LCD} = 2 \times 3 \times 7$$

$$\frac{3}{14} = \frac{3 \times 3^*}{14 \times 3^*} = \frac{9}{42}$$
$$+\frac{5}{21} = \frac{5 \times 2^{**}}{21 \times 2^{**}} = \frac{10}{42}$$
$$\frac{19}{42}$$

* Notice that you don't need to multiply the factors of the LCD. Just notice that $14 = 2 \times 7$. Cover up the 2 and 7 in the LCD to see what's left: 3.

** Similarly $\frac{\text{LCD}}{21}$ is $\frac{2 \times 3 \times 7}{3 \times 2}$ or 2.

CONTINUE TO AS–40.

(AS–40)

$$\left(\tfrac{2}{2}\right)\frac{\times\,2\,\times\,3\,\times}{\times}\left(\tfrac{5}{5}\right)\frac{\times}{\times}\left(\tfrac{7}{7}\right) = 2 \times 3 = 6$$

Skip the next frame if you are breezing along.

CONTINUE TO AS–41 OR AS–42.

(AS–41)

$$12 = 2 \times 2 \times 3$$
$$9 = 3 \times 3$$
$$18 = 2 \times 3 \times 3$$

$$\text{LCD} = 2 \times 2 \times 3 \times 3$$

$$\frac{5}{12} = \frac{5 \times 3}{12 \times 3} = \frac{15}{36}$$

$$\frac{2}{9} = \frac{2 \times 4}{9 \times 4} = \frac{8}{36}$$

$$+\,\frac{7}{18} = \frac{7 \times 2}{18 \times 2} = \frac{14}{36}$$

$$\frac{37}{36} = \frac{36}{36} + \frac{1}{36} = 1\tfrac{1}{36}$$

CONTINUE TO AS–42.

AS–43

Addition with regrouping: whole numbers and rational numbers. Notice the parallel between rational and whole number addition with regrouping.

$$2\tfrac{4}{7} = 2 + \tfrac{4}{7}$$
$$+3\tfrac{5}{7} = 3 + \tfrac{5}{7}$$
$$\overline{\phantom{+3\tfrac{5}{7}} \; 5 + \tfrac{9}{7}}$$
$$5 + \left(\tfrac{7}{7} + \tfrac{2}{7}\right)$$
$$(5 + 1) + \tfrac{2}{7}$$
$$6 \;+\; \tfrac{2}{7}$$
$$6\tfrac{2}{7}$$

$$46 \;=\; 40 + 6$$
$$+37 \;=\; 30 + 7$$
$$\overline{ 70 + 13}$$
$$70 + (10 + 3)$$
$$(70 + 10) + 3$$
$$80 + 3$$
$$83$$

Try these: (a) $4\tfrac{6}{11} + 5\tfrac{8}{11}$ (b) $6\tfrac{2}{7} + 5\tfrac{1}{4}$

SEE ANSWER FRAME (AS–43).

The same ideas are used in subtraction. Note the use of the associative property.

Step 1	*Step 2*	*Step 3*	*Step 4*
$5\frac{1}{3}$	$5 + \frac{1 \times 4}{3 \times 4}$	$5 + \frac{4}{12}$	$(4+1) + \frac{4}{12}$
$-1\frac{7}{12}$	$1 + \frac{7}{12}$	$1 + \frac{7}{12}$	$1 + \frac{7}{12}$

Step 5

$4 + \left(\frac{12}{12} + \frac{4}{12}\right)$

$1 + \frac{7}{12}$

Step 6

$4 + \frac{16}{12}$

$1 + \frac{7}{12}$

$3 + \frac{9}{12} = 3 + \frac{3 \times 3}{3 \times 4} = 3\frac{3}{4}$

CONTINUE TO AS–45.

If you can handle these, you graduate!

Rename in common names (reduce the terms):

(a) $\frac{2}{6}$

(b) $\frac{75}{100}$

Use both methods to reduce: greatest common factor and prime factorization in (a) and (b).

(c) Subtract:

$6\frac{3}{8}$

$-2\frac{9}{10}$

Be sure to use the associative property and to rename 1.

SEE ANSWER FRAME (AS–45).

Observe the relation in regrouping rational and whole numbers in subtraction.

$5\frac{1}{6} = 5 + \frac{1}{6} = (4+1) + \frac{1}{6} = 4 + \left(\frac{6}{6} + \frac{1}{6}\right) = 4 + \frac{7}{6}$

$-2\frac{5}{6} \quad\quad 2 + \frac{5}{6} \quad\quad\quad 2 + \frac{5}{6} \quad\quad 2 + \frac{5}{6} \quad\quad\quad 2 + \frac{5}{6}$

$2 + \frac{2}{6} = 2\frac{1}{3}$

$42 = 40 + 2 = (30 + 10) + 2 = 30 + (10 + 2) = 30 + 12$

$-25 \quad\quad 20 + 5 \quad\quad\quad 20 \quad\quad + 5 \quad\quad 20 + \quad 5 \quad\quad\quad 20 + 5$

$10 + 7 = 17$

THE END.

(AS–45)

Greatest Common Factor Method:

(a)   Factors of 2: $\{1, 2\}$
     Factors of 6: $\{1, 2, 3, 6\}$ $\frac{2}{6} = \frac{2 \div 2}{6 \div 2} = \frac{1}{3}$
     The GCF of 2 and 6 is 2.

(b)   Factors of 75: $\{1, 3, 5, 15, \underline{25}, 75\}$
     Factors of 100: $\{1, 2, 4, 5, 10, 20, \underline{25}, 50, 100\}$
     The GCF of 75 and 100 is 25.

$$\frac{75}{100} = \frac{75 \div 25}{100 \div 25} = \frac{3}{4}$$

Prime Factorization Method:

(a) $\frac{2}{6} = \frac{2 \times 1}{2 \times 3} = \frac{2 \times 1 \div 2}{2 \times 3 \div 2} = \frac{1}{3}$

(b) $\frac{75}{100} = \frac{3 \times 5 \times 5}{2 \times 2 \times 5 \times 5} = \frac{3 \times 5 \times 5 \div (5 \times 5)}{2 \times 2 \times 5 \times 5 \div (5 \times 5)} = \frac{3}{4}$

(c) $8 = 2 \times 2 \times 2$
        $10 = 2 \times 5$
     $\text{LCD} = 2 \times 2 \times 2 \times 5$

$$
\begin{array}{ccccc}
6\frac{3}{8} & 6 + \frac{3}{8} & 6 + \frac{3 \times 5}{8 \times 5} & 6 + \frac{15}{40} & (5 + 1) + \frac{15}{40} \\
-2\frac{9}{10} & 2 + \frac{9}{10} & 2 + \frac{9 \times 4}{10 \times 4} & 2 + \frac{36}{40} & 2 \quad + \frac{36}{40}
\end{array}
$$

$$
\begin{array}{cc}
5 + \left(\frac{40}{40} + \frac{15}{40}\right) & 5 + \frac{55}{40} \\
2 + \frac{36}{40} & 2 + \frac{36}{40} \\
& 3 + \frac{19}{40} = 3\frac{19}{40}
\end{array}
$$

CONTINUE TO AS–46.

(AS–43)

(a) $\begin{aligned} 4\frac{6}{11} &= 4 + \frac{6}{11} \\ +5\frac{8}{11} &= 5 + \frac{8}{11} \\ \hline & 9 + \frac{14}{11} \\ & 9 + \left(\frac{11}{11} + \frac{3}{11}\right) \\ & (9 + 1) + \frac{3}{11} \\ & 10 + \frac{3}{11} \\ & 10\frac{3}{11} \end{aligned}$

(b) $\begin{aligned} 6\frac{2}{7} &= 6 + \frac{2 \times 4}{7 \times 4} = 6 + \frac{8}{28} \\ +5\frac{1}{4} &= 5 + \frac{1 \times 7}{4 \times 7} = 5 + \frac{7}{28} \\ \hline & 11 + \frac{15}{28} \\ & 11\frac{15}{28} \end{aligned}$

CONTINUE TO AS–44.

Addition and Subtraction of Rationals Self-Test

1. Show these sums and differences on the number line, with paper strips and with pie-shaped regions:

   (a) $\frac{1}{4} + \frac{2}{4} = n$ (c) $\frac{2}{3} - \frac{1}{3} = n$

   (b) $\frac{3}{8} + \frac{6}{8} = n$ (d) $1\frac{1}{4} - \frac{2}{4} = n$

2. *Compute* the sums of B and D above using renaming and associativity.

3. Determine the unique set of prime factors whose product is 27; 60.

4. Use sets of multiples to find the least common multiple of 9 and 15.

5. Reduce $\frac{60}{84}$ to lowest terms by

   (a) finding the greatest common factor
   (b) using prime factorization

Answers to Addition and Subtraction of Rationals Self-Test

1. Review these in frames AS–1 through AS–7 if you are uncertain.

2. $\frac{3}{8} + \frac{6}{8}$ $1\frac{1}{4} - \frac{2}{4}$

     $\frac{9}{8}$ $(1 + \frac{1}{4}) - \frac{2}{4}$

     $\frac{8}{8} + \frac{1}{8}$ $(\frac{4}{4} + \frac{1}{4}) - \frac{2}{4}$

     $1 + \frac{1}{8}$ $\frac{5}{4} - \frac{2}{4}$

     $1\frac{1}{8}$ $\frac{3}{4}$

3. $27 = 3 \times 3 \times 3$
   $60 = 2 \times 2 \times 3 \times 5$

4. $\{9, 18, 27, 36, \underline{45}, \ldots\}$
   $\{15, 30, \underline{45}, \ldots\}$

5. (a) Factors of 60: $\{1, 2, 3, 4, 5, 6, 10, \underline{12}, 15, 20, 30, 60\}$
   Factors of 84: $\{1, 2, 3, 4, 6, 7, \underline{12}, 14, 21, 28, 42, 84\}$
   $$\frac{60}{84} = \frac{60 \div 12}{84 \div 12} = \frac{5}{7}$$

   (b) $60 = 2 \times 2 \times 3 \times 5$
   $84 = 2 \times 2 \times 3 \times 7$
   $$\frac{60}{84} = \frac{(2 \times 2 \times 3 \times 5) \div (2 \times 2 \times 3)}{(2 \times 2 \times 3 \times 7) \div (2 \times 2 \times 3)} = \frac{5}{7}$$

General Methods and Specific Materials of Instruction

In my judgment the coordinated use of flannel board circular regions and region sections coupled with color-coordinated construction paper kits for pupils constitutes the best visual and manipulative aid for teaching addition and subtraction of rational numbers. Rectangular regions can also be used but they have a disadvantage not characteristic of circular regions: the shape does not reinforce the rational number it represents. The one-fourth circular region is more easily visually discriminated as one-fourth than is the rectangular

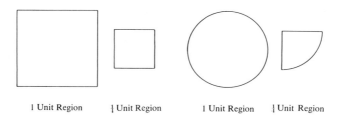

1 Unit Region   ¼ Unit Region   1 Unit Region   ¼ Unit Region

one-fourth region in the absence of the unit region. There is an exception. If students use rectangular regions which have pictures (such as candy bar wrappers), halves, thirds, and quarters can be easily discriminated.

Sterns Blocks can be used for addition and subtraction of rational numbers with like denominators. If you wish to add $\frac{2}{7} + \frac{6}{7}$, let the seven-rod be the unit length; the one-rod is one-seventh.

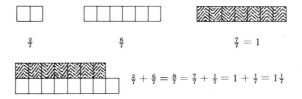

$$\frac{2}{7} \qquad \frac{6}{7} \qquad \frac{7}{7} = 1$$

$$\frac{2}{7} + \frac{6}{7} = \frac{8}{7} = \frac{7}{7} + \frac{1}{7} = 1 + \frac{1}{7} = 1\frac{1}{7}$$

Cuisenaire Rods can be used similarly. The primary drawback with them, however, is that they are unmarked; you cannot tell by looking if the rod represents 5 or 6 or 7. In introductory stages, especially, it is important for the visual image to reinforce the rational number concept. This can be accomplished with the Cuisenaire Rods by keeping a visual model always present. If you are working with thirds, you can have a three-rod and three unit-rods visually present as a reminder. An interesting characteristic of the Cuisenaire Rods and Sterns Blocks is that the nine-rod can be the unit-rod, the three-rod thirds, and the unit-rod ninths. This enables you to add thirds and ninths. Other combinations are possible, too.

A reasonable approach is to begin with aids to add and subtract rational numbers whose sums and differences are less than one at the *verbal-manipulative level*. After skill has begun to develop, move to a *manipulative-symbolic* level of development. That is, write equations to represent the manipulations. When concrete materials are no longer needed, children can draw pictures to find sums or use number lines, and, finally, they can write equations without representations either concrete or pictorial. The same stages can be followed for sums and differences greater than one.

Discovery. How can teachers in grades three and four help children discover strategies for adding and subtracting rational numbers? This question was handled in the programmed materials, but some additional comments will be added here.

Assuming that third graders have already solved number sentences such as $4 + 5 = \Box$, $27 - 13 = \Box$, $9 \times 8 = \Box$, and that the children already know how to write fractional numerals, a dittoed sheet can be distributed. Working in small groups of two, three, or four, they can *use fraction kits* to find sums such as these:

$$\frac{1}{3} + \frac{1}{3} = \Box \qquad\qquad \frac{6}{8} - \frac{1}{8} = \Box$$
$$\frac{2}{5} + \frac{1}{5} = \Box \qquad\qquad \frac{3}{4} - \frac{2}{4} = \Box$$
$$\frac{3}{8} + \frac{4}{8} = \Box \qquad\qquad \frac{4}{5} - \frac{1}{5} = \Box$$

The groups can quickly discover the pattern.

At a later time, when rational number concepts are encountered again in the spiraling curriculum, another sheet can be distributed. Children can be presented with such problems as these:

A. Bill, John and Gary each ate three pieces of pie. If the pies were cut in fifths, how many pies did they eat?

B. Sue wanted to put some trim on her new skirt. She needed two strips; each one was $\frac{3}{4}$-yard. How much did she need altogether?

C. There were $1\frac{1}{4}$ pies on the counter. Kim and Jerry each ate $\frac{1}{4}$ pie. How much pie was left?

D. Beth had $1\frac{1}{3}$ yards of material. She used $\frac{2}{3}$-yard for a skirt. How much was left to make a blouse?

Children can explore solutions in small groups and then discuss the alternatives with their classmates.

In the fourth grade or early fifth grade, students usually begin to add and subtract rational numbers whose numerals have different denominators. With the aid of fractional parts kits, they can use a trial-and-error approach by covering sums with pieces of equal size.

$$\frac{1}{2} + \frac{1}{3} = \Box$$
$$\frac{1}{4} + \frac{3}{8} = \Box$$
$$\frac{2}{3} + \frac{1}{6} = \Box$$

With teacher guidance they will begin to notice that $\frac{1}{2}$ is covered with $\frac{3}{6}$, $\frac{1}{3}$ is covered with $\frac{2}{6}$ and so on. They should already be familiar with the concept of *equivalent fractions* from grades 2, 3 and 4.

Through small group interactions similar to these, children can find meaningful ways to perform operations on rational numbers. The concept of many numerals for each rational number will acquire meaning and significance as each child through manipulative experiences actively searches for the right names to do the job!

Accommodation of Individual Differences

As you have undoubtedly observed, there are several stages in the development of meaningful mastery of addition and subtraction of rational numbers. A complete list of objectives should account for all the stages at all levels of abstraction:

> I. Concrete
>> A. Without symbols
>> B. With symbols
> II. Semi-concrete
> III. Abstract (mathematical symbols)

Major Concepts

Addition and subtraction of rational numbers

> A. With like denominators; all elements of the equation less than one (without regrouping), e.g., $\frac{1}{4} + \frac{2}{4} = \frac{3}{4}$; $\frac{4}{5} - \frac{1}{5} = \frac{3}{5}$.
> B. With like denominators; two elements of the equation less than one and one element between one and two (with regrouping); e.g., $\frac{3}{4} + \frac{2}{4} = 1\frac{1}{4}$; $1\frac{1}{3} - \frac{2}{3} = \frac{2}{3}$.
> C. Like A above but with unlike denominators, e.g., $\frac{1}{8} + \frac{1}{4} = \frac{3}{8}$; $\frac{5}{6} - \frac{1}{3} = \frac{3}{6}$.
> D. Like B above but with unlike denominators, e.g., $\frac{3}{4} + \frac{5}{8} = 1\frac{3}{8}$; $1\frac{1}{3} - \frac{5}{6} = \frac{3}{6}$.
> E. With mixed numerals, e.g., $1\frac{1}{3} + 3\frac{4}{5}$ or $6\frac{1}{8} - 2\frac{3}{7}$.

The last three can be subdivided into method of solution desired: (1) simple, known rational numbers, (2) sets of equivalent fractions, (3) sets of multiples (least common multiple), and (4) prime factorization.

For *concept A,* the following objectives would be suitable. The child will be able to:

> 1. State the sum by using his fractional number kit.
> 2. Write an equation with the aid of his fractional number kit.
> 3. Write an equation or number sentence by using a number line.
> 4. Solve equations without the use of manipulative aids or diagrams.

As the child increases his ability at the abstract level, you may wish to place decreasing emphasis on concrete manipulations and rely more on diagrams and symbolic manipulations.

Preassessment and Instruction.   As each new major concept is introduced, you can usually preassess informally by observing youngsters in small-group interaction. Those who demonstrate mastery can be channeled into enrichment activities rather than left with the class for unnecessary instruction. Specific activities are suggested later. After these students have been identified and directed, instruction on the major concept can commence.

Instruction may continue through small groups with further directed exploration. If you need to present material on notation or explain a process, large-group instruction might be more expedient. Or, if you have appropriate materials, you may wish to have children work individually or in pairs on unipacs or individually prescribed materials.

Diagnosis.   After the instructional phase has run its course as determined by your judgment that several children have attained complete mastery of the concept, regrouping should take place. If you feel you know well enough the level of mastery of the children, you can assign them to groups informally. You can also ask children to go to the group which they feel will best meet their needs. Or, you can administer a formal diagnostic test based on your behavioral objectives and regroup the class according to the results.

The reteach group needs additional developmental experiences. They should be taught by a different strategy; the first one did not work! Use different teaching aids if you can. Give as much individual attention as possible. Use individualized diagnostic procedures as outlined in Chapter 5 for particularly difficult cases. Place particular emphasis on mastery of concepts in level one (concrete) before allowing these children to move on to more abstract modes. Slow children are likely to move too quickly into meaningless computational procedures just to keep up with their peers. They do not realize, as you do, that mastery of the concept in level one will nearly always enhance mastery of the abstract relations.

The practice group can carry on activities similar to those mentioned in previous chapters. Game-like activities should especially be sought since practice can be very boring unless camouflaged in an interesting experience. Refer to the bibliography in Chapter 6 for specific sources.

Children who have mastered the concept might enjoy exploring rational numbers in non-decimal systems. By this time they also have the mathematical background to study simple statistical concepts such as mean, median, mode and range. They can carry out computations on sets of data and learn how to make histograms and frequency distributions. They might also enjoy studying some elementary logic and learning how to make truth tables or determining simple probabilities such as related to rolling a number with one die, two dice or three dice. Other general activities described in previous chapters can also be utilized.

Readiness and Psychological Principles. Notice the extensive opportunities for utilizing small group interactions to promote pupil growth and the great use of concrete exploratory experiences by individual pupils. Children need opportunities to learn from experience and to have their ideas challenged. Their own thinking is clarified through explaining beliefs and positions to peers in a relaxed and non-threatening atmosphere.

Addition and subtraction of whole numbers are readiness building blocks for addition and subtraction of rational numbers. Use of sets and number lines have also aided pupil growth and provided continuity in content and method. The similarity between associative and regrouping steps in addition and subtraction of whole and rational numbers was pointed out in the programmed section of the chapter but deserves special mention here once again.

Whole Numbers		*Steps*	*Rational Numbers*
Special Notation	Standard Notation		
34	34	1	$3\frac{1}{5}$
$③ + 4$	$30 + 4$	2	$3 + \frac{1}{5}$
$(② + ①) + 4$	$(20 + 10) + 4$	3	$(2 + 1) + \frac{1}{5}$
$② + (10 + 4)$	$20 + (10 + 4)$	4	$2 + \left(\frac{5}{5} + \frac{1}{5}\right)$
$② + 14$	$20 + 14$	5	$2 + \frac{6}{5}$

Moving *down* through these steps, you can see the steps involved in regrouping for subtraction. Moving *up* through these steps, you can see the steps involved in regrouping for addition.

Finally, it should be mentioned that these experiences provide readiness for addition of decimal numerals. Work with decimals will be related to operations performed with fractional numerals.

Topics for Discussion and Projects

1. What other homemade or commercial materials can be used to teach addition and subtraction of rational numbers?

2. Demonstrate addition and subtraction of rational numbers on aids mentioned in this chapter or on others available to you.

3. Outline a discovery lesson on a phase of addition or subtraction of rational numbers. What results can you anticipate? Include some problem situations.

4. Write some behavioral objectives for this unit which cover all three levels of abstraction.

5. Write evaluation items which test pupil performance of the objectives in the preceding item.

6. Locate specific enrichment materials.

7. How could you use pure discovery in this unit?

Additional Resources

Filmstrips

> *Greatest Common Factor,* Popular Science (7H–3)
> *Least Common Multiples,* Popular Science (6H–4)
> *Adding With Fractions,* Filmstrip-of-the-Month (1203)
> *Common Denominators: Addition and Subtraction,* Popular Science (5H–6)
> *Fundamental Theorem of Arithmetic,* Filmstrip-of-the-Month (1240)

Films

> *Addition of Rational Numbers,* National Council of Teachers of Mathematics.
> *Subtraction of Rational Numbers,* National Council of Teachers of Mathematics.

Elmentary School Textbooks

> Harper & Row (1970), Grade 4, *New Dimensions in Mathematics,* by C. D'Augustine, F. Brown, J. Heddens, C. Howard
> > Student Text: pp. 232–57.
> Harper & Row (1970), Grade 5, *New Dimensions in Mathematics,* by C. D'Augustine, F. Brown, J. Heddens, C. Howard.
> > Student Text: pp. 150–60, 180–200.
> Harper & Row (1970), Grade 6, *New Dimensions in Mathematics,* by C. D'Augustine, F. Brown, J. Heddens, C. Howard.
> > Student Text: pp. 66–80.
> Houghton-Mifflin (1970), Grade 4, *Modern School Mathematics,* by E. Duncan, L. Capps, M. Dolciani, W. Quast, M. Zweng.
> > Student Text: pp. 134–37, 288–315.
> Houghton-Mifflin (1970), Grade 5, *Modern School Mathematics,* by E. Duncan, L. Capps, M. Dolciani, W. Quast, M. Zweng.
> > Student Text: pp. 164–78, 228–51.
> Houghton-Mifflin (1970), Grade 6, *Modern School Mathematics,* by E. Duncan, L. Capps, M. Dolciani, W. Quast, M. Zweng.
> > Student Text: pp. 164–75, 212–24.

15

Teaching Multiplication and Division of Rational Numbers

Section one has the usual programmed, auto-tutorial format. There is a self-test at the end of the section on which you can evaluate your performance on the behaviorally stated objectives.

Section two contains a discussion of other teaching aids which can be used to determine products and quotients of rational numbers. Specific suggestions are made relative to appropriate uses of discovery strategies.

Section three relates the chapter topics to the individualization model. In particular, behavioral objectives, major concepts, diagnosis and appropriate group activities are presented and explored.

Content and Specific Methodology

After you have read through the following list of behavioral objectives, you may wish to examine Part I of the self-test at the conclusion of the section. If you feel you can satisfactorily exhibit the desired behaviors, you may wish to omit the multiplication section or skim through it quickly. Then proceed to Part II of this section which covers division of rational numbers and follow a similar pattern.

Multiplication and Division of Non-Negative Rational Numbers

Objectives

At the completion of this unit, you will be able to:

(1) List a sequence of four stages in the development of multiplication of non-negative rational numbers and give an example of each.

(2) Name three ways to divide non-negative rational numbers and give an example of each.

(3) Relate multiplication and division of non-negative rational numbers to similar operations on whole numbers.

(4) Show multiplication and division of non-negative rational numbers on the number line.

(5) Show multiplication and division of non-negative rational numbers with fractional parts of circular regions.

(6) Draw a picture or diagram to show the product or quotient of two non-negative rational numbers.

(7) Show simple products and quotients of non-negative rational numbers by folding paper.

Materials Needed

1. Rectangular-shaped pieces of paper (6 or 8 pieces)
2. Narrow strips of paper (6 or 8 pieces)
3. The pie-wedges used in the addition and subtraction unit
4. Several number lines marked off in halves, thirds, fourths and fifths.

Assumptions

For the work in this unit, it is assumed that youngsters:

A. Were taught multiplication on the number line, as the union of equivalent disjoint sets and as repeated addition.

B. Were taught division as repeated subtraction.

C. Have used number sentences.

D. Know multiplication and division are inverse operations.

E. Have worked with the associative and commutative properties.

F. Have worked with equivalent fractions.

The work which follows will capitalize on children's experiences with multiplication and division of whole numbers. First, a developmental sequence for teaching multiplication of non-negative rationals (hereafter referred to as *rationals*) will be presented and then three strategies for working with division of rationals will be presented.

CONTINUE TO MD–2.

The sequence for development of multiplication of rationals is as follows:

    A. Product of a whole number and a unit fraction, e.g., $3 \times \frac{1}{2}$

    B. Product of a whole number and a non-unit fraction, e.g., $4 \times \frac{2}{3}$

    C. Product of two unit fractions, e.g., $\frac{1}{2} \times \frac{1}{3}$

    D. Product of two non-unit fractions, e.g., $\frac{2}{3} \times \frac{3}{4}$

CONTINUE TO MD–3.

A. *Product of a Whole Number and a Unit Fraction*

Since good instruction attempts to relate new learning experiences to previously acquired concepts, you should attempt to relate an introduction to multiplication of rationals to multiplication of whole numbers.

2×3 was interpreted as

    1. two jumps of three on the number line
    2. two sets of three
    3. three used as an addend two times
    4. a two-by-three array
    5. a cross-product

You can easily relate the new work to one, two, and three.

Social problems such as the following can be used to introduce this concept:

"Bill, John and Al each had one-fourth of a pie; how much did they eat altogether?"

"Four teachers needed one-fourth yard of burlap each for bulletin boards; how much material was needed altogether?"

CONTINUE TO MD–4.

MD–4

(a) Since 2×3 means two jumps of three on the number line, $2 \times \frac{1}{3}$ can be translated as two jumps of one-third on the number line.

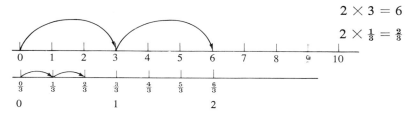

$$2 \times 3 = 6$$
$$2 \times \tfrac{1}{3} = \tfrac{2}{3}$$

(b) Since 2×3 means two sets of three, $2 \times \frac{1}{3}$ translates as two sets of one-third.

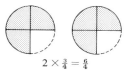

$$2 \times 3 = 6$$

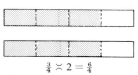

$$2 \times \tfrac{1}{3} = \tfrac{2}{3}$$

(c) Since $2 \times 3 = 3 + 3 = 6$, then $2 \times \frac{1}{3} = \frac{1}{3} + \frac{1}{3} = \frac{2}{3}$. Use your number line and pie-wedges to show this product all three ways: $3 \times \frac{1}{4}$

TURN THE PAGE TO ANSWER FRAME (MD–4).

MD–5

B. *Product of a Whole Number and a Non-unit Fraction*

An approach similar to the one described for unit fractions can be used. Use the number line, fractional parts of a whole and repeated addition to show $3 \times \frac{2}{5}$. Can you use a name for "one" to show the result as a mixed numeral?

SEE ANSWER FRAME (MD–5).

MD–6

Even though the commutative property is true on the set of rational numbers, everyday use makes a distinction between $2 \times \frac{3}{4}$ and $\frac{3}{4} \times 2$. The former is "two times three-fourths" as when a measure is doubled in a recipe. However, $\frac{3}{4} \times 2$ is usually read "three-fourths of two." Of course, the two products are the same, but the schematic or pictorial representations differ.

$2 \times \tfrac{3}{4} = \tfrac{6}{4}$

"Two three-fourths are six fourths."

This one is additive:

$$\tfrac{3}{4} + \tfrac{3}{4} = \tfrac{6}{4}$$

$\tfrac{3}{4} \times 2 = \tfrac{6}{4}$

"Three-fourths of two is six fourths."

This one is partitive; a set of 2 is partitioned into four equal parts and three are retained.

Work with both types will help children realize that "of" is related to multiplication of rational numbers.

CONTINUE TO MD–7.

The mathematical relation between products of whole numbers and unit fractions and whole numbers and non-unit fractions can be emphasized with the help of renaming and the associative property of multiplication.

Recall that $\frac{3}{4} = 3 \times \frac{1}{4}$; then $3 \times \frac{1}{4} = \frac{3}{4}$.

Thus: $2 \times \frac{3}{4}$

$2 \times (3 \times \frac{1}{4})$ Renaming

$(2 \times 3) \times \frac{1}{4}$ Associative Property

$6 \times \frac{1}{4}$

$\frac{6}{4}$

$\frac{4}{4} + \frac{2}{4}$

$1\frac{2}{4}$

Write the corresponding steps for $3 \times \frac{4}{5}$ and $5 \times \frac{2}{7}$.

SEE ANSWER FRAME (MD–7).

C. Product of Two Unit Fractions

Children can use pie-wedges to show that

$\frac{1}{2} \times \frac{1}{2} = \frac{1}{4}$ "One-half *of* one-half is one-fourth."

$\frac{1}{2} \times \frac{1}{3} = \frac{1}{6}$ "One-half *of* one-third is one-sixth."

Manipulation and verification will help the child discover a pattern. The question is simply, "What can you place on $\frac{1}{2}$ twice which will exactly cover it?"

CONTINUE TO MD–9.

Another approach is to relate multiplication of unit-fractions to multiplication of whole numbers:

6×8 is "6 eights"

$\frac{1}{2} \times \frac{1}{2}$ is "$\frac{1}{2}$ one-half"

To show this, use one of your rectangular-shaped pieces of paper.

Step 1. Fold it in half; open it and mark the crease. Write the numeral "$\frac{1}{2}$" on each side.

Step 2. Fold it so you are looking at "$\frac{1}{2}$".

Step 3. Fold the visible half in half again to get $\frac{1}{2}$ one-half. While folded, scribble on it.

Step 4. Open one crease to verify that you marked $\frac{1}{2}$ one-half.

Step 5. Open it completely and decide on a name for the marked portion. $\frac{1}{2}$ one-half is $\frac{1}{4}$.

CONTINUE TO MD–10.

(MD–4)

(a) Number line: $3 \times \frac{1}{4} = \frac{3}{4}$

$\frac{0}{4}$ $\frac{1}{4}$ $\frac{2}{4}$ $\frac{3}{4}$ $\frac{4}{4}$

0   1

(b) Sets: $3 \times \frac{1}{4} = \frac{3}{4}$

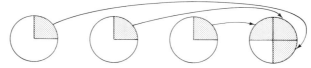

It is best to use *four* unit circles to help the child see the relationships as indicated by the curves.

(c) Repeated addition: $3 \times \frac{1}{4} = \frac{1}{4} + \frac{1}{4} + \frac{1}{4} = \frac{3}{4}$

RETURN TO MD–5.

(MD–5)

(a) Number line: $3 \times \frac{2}{5} = \frac{6}{5}$

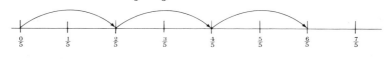

$\frac{0}{5}$ $\frac{1}{5}$ $\frac{2}{5}$ $\frac{3}{5}$ $\frac{4}{5}$ $\frac{5}{5}$ $\frac{6}{5}$ $\frac{7}{5}$

0   1

(b) Fractional parts: $3 \times \frac{2}{5} = \frac{6}{5} = \frac{5}{5} + \frac{1}{5} = 1\frac{1}{5}$

(c) Repeated addition:

$$3 \times \frac{2}{5} = \frac{2}{5} + \frac{2}{5} + \frac{2}{5} = \frac{6}{5} = \frac{5+1}{5} = \frac{5}{5} + \frac{1}{5} = 1 + \frac{1}{5} = 1\frac{1}{5}$$

RETURN TO MD–6.

MD–10

Try the preceding sequence of steps for $\frac{1}{2} \times \frac{1}{4}$.

Appropriate social situations from which such problems arise would be similar to these:

"Mary made one-half a recipe which called for the following ingredients: $\frac{1}{3}$ cup shortening, $\frac{1}{4}$ cup sugar, $\frac{1}{2}$ teaspoon salt. How much of each did she put in her recipe?"

"Jim was able to complete only half the half-mile track. How far did he run?"

SEE ANSWER FRAME (MD–10).

$$3 \times \tfrac{4}{5}$$
$$3 \times (4 \times \tfrac{1}{5})$$ Renaming
$$(3 \times 4) \times \tfrac{1}{5}$$ Associative Property
$$12 \times \tfrac{1}{5}$$
$$\tfrac{12}{5}$$
$$\tfrac{10}{5} + \tfrac{2}{5}$$
$$2\tfrac{2}{5}$$

$$5 \times \tfrac{2}{7}$$
$$5 \times (2 \times \tfrac{1}{7})$$
$$(5 \times 2) \times \tfrac{1}{7}$$
$$10 \times \tfrac{1}{7}$$
$$\tfrac{10}{7}$$
$$\tfrac{7}{7} + \tfrac{3}{7}$$
$$1\tfrac{3}{7}$$

CONTINUE TO MD–8.

Try one more:

$\tfrac{1}{4} \times \tfrac{1}{3}$ or $\tfrac{1}{4}$ one-third

You can divide your piece of paper into thirds by making an S-shape.

    Mash it!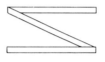

SEE ANSWER FRAME (MD–11).

Children can work several such problems to discover the following pattern:

$\tfrac{1}{2} \times \tfrac{1}{3} = \tfrac{1}{6}$
$\tfrac{1}{4} \times \tfrac{1}{3} = \tfrac{1}{12}$
$\tfrac{1}{3} \times \tfrac{1}{5} = \tfrac{1}{15}$
$\tfrac{1}{2} \times \tfrac{1}{4} = \tfrac{1}{8}$
$\tfrac{1}{2} \times \tfrac{1}{2} = \tfrac{1}{4}$
etc.

$$\frac{1}{a} \times \frac{1}{b} = \frac{1}{a \times b}$$

The child might think, "Keep the one in the numerator and multiply the denominators."

Or, the child might think, "1 × 1 and a × b."

The latter is, of course, correct but he will find out in due time.

CONTINUE TO MD–13.

D. *Product of Two Non-unit Fractions*

Finally, a problem such as $\frac{2}{3} \times \frac{3}{4}$ can be worked similar to the previous type.

 three-fourths

Step 1

Step 2

Step 3

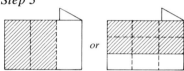

or

Step 4

$\frac{2}{3}$ three-fourths is one-half

$$\frac{2}{3} \times \frac{3}{4} = \frac{1}{2} \text{ or } \frac{2}{4}$$

Also, $\frac{2}{3} \times \frac{3}{4} = \frac{6}{12}$

Accept all three as correct responses: $\frac{1}{2}$, $\frac{2}{4}$, $\frac{6}{12}$

Try this one: $\frac{1}{2} \times \frac{3}{4}$

SEE ANSWER FRAME (MD–13).

After several such exercises, children can be lead to discover this pattern:

$\frac{2}{3} \times \frac{3}{4} = \frac{6}{12}$*
$\frac{1}{2} \times \frac{3}{4} = \frac{3}{8}$
$\frac{2}{3} \times \frac{4}{5} = \frac{8}{15}$
etc.

Hence,

$$\frac{a}{b} \times \frac{c}{d} = \frac{a \times c}{b \times d}$$

* Sample problem: "Mary used only two thirds of the three-fourths yard of material she bought. How much did she have left?"

CONTINUE TO MD–15.

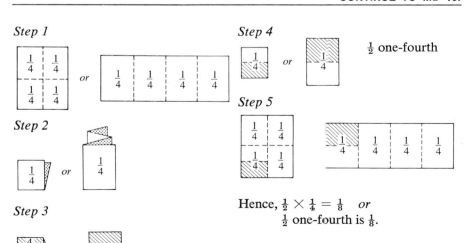

Step 1

or

Step 2

$\frac{1}{4}$ *or* $\frac{1}{4}$

Step 3

or

Step 4

or $\frac{1}{2}$ one-fourth

Step 5

Hence, $\frac{1}{2} \times \frac{1}{4} = \frac{1}{8}$ or
$\frac{1}{2}$ one-fourth is $\frac{1}{8}$.

CONTINUE TO MD–11.

Products of this type can be computed with the aid of commutative and associative properties and renaming.

$$\frac{2}{3} \times \frac{3}{4}$$
$$(2 \times \tfrac{1}{3}) \times (3 \times \tfrac{1}{4})$$
$$(2 \times 3) \times (\tfrac{1}{3} \times \tfrac{1}{4})$$
$$6 \times \tfrac{1}{12}$$
$$\tfrac{6}{12}$$

Then:

$$\left[\frac{6}{12} = \frac{2 \times 3}{2 \times 2 \times 3} = \frac{1}{2} \times \frac{2 \times 3}{2 \times 3} * \right]$$

Note the use of prime factorization.

* This is now possible because children know that
$$\frac{a \times c}{b \times d} = \frac{a}{b} \times \frac{c}{d} .$$

Work this one: $\frac{3}{5} \times \frac{4}{9}$

SEE ANSWER FRAME (MD–15).

Step 1

Step 2

Step 3

Step 4

$\frac{1}{4}$ one-third

Step 5

$\frac{1}{4}$ one-third is one-twelfth

$$\tfrac{1}{4} \times \tfrac{1}{3} = \tfrac{1}{12}$$

The sequence of steps is important to facilitate good visual reinforcement.

CONTINUE TO MD–12.

Acquisition of some or all of these skills allows the child to work with mixed numerals. Two methods can be used.

A. Change to improper fractions.　　B. Use the distributive property.

A.　　$2 \times 4\frac{2}{3}$
　　$2 \times (4 + \frac{2}{3})$　　Renaming
　　$2 \times (\frac{12}{3} + \frac{2}{3})$　　Renaming
　　$\frac{2}{1} \times \frac{14}{3}$　　Renaming
　　　$\frac{28}{3}$
　$\frac{72}{3} + \frac{1}{3} = 9\frac{1}{3}$

What is the difference between A
and B on the number line? Try this
one both ways: $5 \times 2\frac{3}{4}$

B.　$2 \times 4\frac{2}{3}$
　$2 \times (4 + \frac{2}{3})$
　$(2 \times 4) + (2 \times \frac{2}{3})$　　Distributive Property
　$(2 \times 4) + (\frac{2}{1} \times \frac{2}{3})$　　Renaming
　$8 + \frac{4}{3}$
　$8 + \frac{3}{3} + \frac{1}{3}$
　$8 + 1 + \frac{1}{3} = 9\frac{1}{3}$

SEE ANSWER FRAME (MD–16).

(MD–13)

Step 1

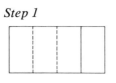

Step 3

Step 2

Step 4

$\frac{1}{2}$ three-fourths is three-eights

Try a couple more such as $\frac{3}{4} \times \frac{3}{8}$ or $\frac{2}{3} \times \frac{5}{8}$.

$\frac{1}{2} \times \frac{3}{4} = \frac{3}{8}$

CONTINUE TO MD–14.

MD–17

When two mixed numerals are multiplied, the distributive property is frequently clumsy because the addition requires you to find lowest common denominators; however, it does permit you to relate multiplication of whole numbers and rationals through use of rectangular regions.

A. (1) $2\frac{2}{3} \times 3\frac{5}{8}$

(2) $(2 + \frac{2}{3}) \times (3 + \frac{5}{8})$

(3) $(\frac{6}{3} + \frac{2}{3}) \times (\frac{24}{8} + \frac{5}{8})$

(4) $\frac{8}{3} \times \frac{29}{8}$

(5) $\frac{232}{24}$

(6) $*\frac{2 \times 2 \times 2 \times 29}{2 \times 2 \times 2 \times 3}$

(7) $*\left(\frac{2 \times 2 \times 2}{2 \times 2 \times 2}\right) \times \frac{29}{3}$

(8) $1 \times \frac{29}{3}$

(9) * This is now possible because children know that $\frac{a \times c}{b \times d} = \frac{a}{b} \times \frac{c}{d}$.

B. (1) $2\frac{2}{3} \times 3\frac{5}{8}$

(2) $(2\frac{2}{3}) \times (3 + \frac{5}{8})$

(3) $(2\frac{2}{3} \times 3) + (2\frac{2}{3} \times \frac{5}{8})$

(4) $(2 + \frac{2}{3}) \times 3 + (2 + \frac{2}{3}) \times \frac{5}{8}$
Renaming

(5) $(2 \times 3) + (\frac{2}{3} \times 3) + (2 \times \frac{5}{8}) + (\frac{2}{3} \times \frac{5}{8})$

(6) $6 + \frac{6}{3} + \frac{10}{8} + \frac{10}{24}$

(7) $6 + 2 + 1 + \frac{1}{4} + \frac{5}{12}$

(8) $9 + \frac{1}{4} + \frac{5}{12}$

(9) $9 + \frac{3}{12} + \frac{5}{12} =$
$9 + \frac{8}{12} = 9\frac{2}{3}$

CONTINUE TO MD–18.

MD–18

You may be asking, "Should I go through all those steps with children?" That is a difficult question. The answer depends on the students' background, the way the material is presented, and the sequence followed in your students' textbook. Look at the example in the previous frame, left side. Steps two and three can be omitted after children have attained an understanding of these steps. A good practice is to allow them to move to the generalization $2\frac{2}{3} = \frac{8}{3}$ when they *discover through experience* that it is true. Further, steps seven and eight can be omitted after children understand the role of one.

$$2\frac{2}{3} \times 3\frac{5}{8} = \frac{8}{3} \times \frac{29}{8} = \frac{232}{24} = \frac{2 \times 2 \times 2 \times 29}{2 \times 2 \times 2 \times 3} = \frac{29}{3} = 9\frac{2}{3}$$

CONTINUE TO MD–19.

$$\overset{\frac{3}{5} \times \frac{4}{9}}{\left(3 \times \tfrac{1}{5}\right) \times \left(4 \times \tfrac{1}{9}\right)}$$
$$(3 \times 4) \times \left(\tfrac{1}{5} \times \tfrac{1}{9}\right)$$
$$12 \times \tfrac{1}{45}$$
$$\tfrac{12}{45}$$

$$\tfrac{12}{45} = \tfrac{2 \times 2}{3 \times 3} \times \tfrac{3}{3} = \tfrac{4}{15}$$

Try a few more.

CONTINUE TO MD–16.

Since problems of this type have several steps, you may wish to eliminate sequences before looking at the total process. Children can work first with concrete materials to learn that $2\tfrac{2}{3} = 1 + 1 + \tfrac{2}{3} = \tfrac{3}{3} + \tfrac{3}{3} + \tfrac{2}{3} = \tfrac{8}{3}$.

Several experiences with concrete materials will enable children to move to the generalization as stated above. Then most children can rather quickly and easily move to $2\tfrac{2}{3} = \tfrac{8}{3}$.

Previous work with reducing answers in addition and subtraction can be reviewed and reinforced to facilitate omission of other steps.

CONTINUE TO MD–20.

A is 2 jumps of $4\tfrac{2}{3}$ or 2 jumps of $\tfrac{14}{3}$.
B is 2 jumps of 4 followed by 2 jumps of $\tfrac{2}{3}$.

A.

$5 \times 2\tfrac{3}{4}$	
$5 \times (2 + \tfrac{3}{4})$	Renaming
$5 \times (\tfrac{8}{4} + \tfrac{3}{4})$	Renaming
$5 \times \tfrac{11}{4}$*	Renaming
$\tfrac{5}{1} \times \tfrac{11}{4}$	Renaming
$\tfrac{55}{4}$	
$\tfrac{52}{4} + \tfrac{3}{4}$	
$13 + \tfrac{3}{4}$	
$13\tfrac{3}{4}$	

B.

$5 \times 2\tfrac{3}{4}$	
$5 \times (2 + \tfrac{3}{4})$	Renaming
$(5 \times 2) + (5 \times \tfrac{3}{4})$	Dist. Prop.
$(5 \times 2) + (\tfrac{5}{1} \times \tfrac{3}{4})$**	
$10 + \tfrac{15}{4}$	
$10 + \tfrac{12}{4} + \tfrac{3}{4}$	
$10 + 3 + \tfrac{3}{4}$	
$13\tfrac{3}{4}$	

** 5 jumps of two and 5 jumps of $\tfrac{3}{4}$.

* 5 jumps of $\tfrac{11}{4}$.

Try this too: $2\tfrac{2}{3} \times 3\tfrac{5}{8}$.

CONTINUE TO MD–17.

MD–20

Due to previous experiences with multiplication of whole numbers, children believe a product will always be greater than or equal to the factors used, e.g., $6 \times 8 = 48$ and 48 is larger than either six or eight. Two helpful procedures are both based upon a relation between whole number and rational number multiplications.

I. *Use words and concrete materials* II. *Use a deductive sequence*

3×2 means "3 twos": 6 $8 \times 4 = 32$
4×6 means "4 sixes": 24 $4 \times 4 = 16$
$\frac{1}{2} \times 8$ means "$\frac{1}{2}$ eight": 4 $2 \times 4 = 8$ Note the
$\frac{1}{2} \times \frac{1}{4}$ means "$\frac{1}{2}$ one-fourth": $\frac{1}{8}$ $1 \times 4 = 4$ patterns.
                                         $\frac{1}{2} \times 4 = 2$
                                         $\frac{1}{4} \times 4 = 1$

CONTINUE TO MD–21.

MD–22

DIVISION

A. *The Unit-Division Approach*

Division of rational numbers should also be related to division of whole numbers as was done with multiplication. You will recall that division was related to subtraction at the intuitive level and partitive cases were explored later.

$12 \div 4 = \square$ says "How many 4s in 12?"
$12 \div 4 = 3$

$1 \div \frac{1}{3} = \square$ says "How many $\frac{1}{3}$s in 1?"
$1 \div \frac{1}{3} = 3$

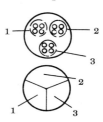

CONTINUE TO MD–22.

MD–21

Similarly, on the number line or with subtraction:

$12 \div 4 = \square$ says "How many jumps of 4 in 12?" $12 - 4 = 8$ 1
$12 \div 4 = 3$ $8 - 4 = 4$ 1
                                                           $4 - 4 = 0$ $\frac{1}{3}$

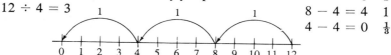

$1 \div \frac{1}{3} = \square$ says "How many jumps of $\frac{1}{3}$ in 1?" $1 - \frac{1}{3} = \frac{2}{3}$ 1
$1 \div \frac{1}{3} = 3$ $\frac{2}{3} - \frac{1}{3} = \frac{1}{3}$ 1
                                                                             $\frac{1}{3} - \frac{1}{3} = 0$ $\frac{1}{3}$

Cover a unit circular region to show $1 \div \frac{1}{4}$, $1 \div \frac{2}{3}$. Also use a number line.

SEE ANSWER FRAME (MD–22).

Paper strips can be used to help children relate intuitively to division with a manipulative experience. Take a strip of paper. Its length will be considered 1 unit. To find $1 \div \frac{1}{2} = \square$, you must answer the question: "How many $\frac{1}{2}$s in 1?" Fold the strip lengthwise; tear off $\frac{1}{2}$. You now have two one-half strips, so $1 \div \frac{1}{2} = \boxed{2}$

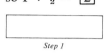   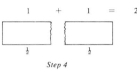

Step 1   Step 2   Step 3   Step 4

Try these with strips: $1 \div \frac{1}{3}$ $1 \div \frac{1}{4}$ $1 \div \frac{2}{3}$

SEE ANSWER FRAME (MD–23).

In a discussion of $1 \div \frac{2}{3}$, you will do well to avoid wordiness. After the initial question, avoid the use of "two-thirds" until the conclusion. To the class, say the following:

"How many two-thirds are in one? First you fold your paper strips into thirds. Then you find this one and tear it off. Compare the strip to the strip which is left. The short one is half as long so here is one and here is one-half. There are $1\frac{1}{2}$. Let's write on the board $1 \div \frac{2}{3} = 1\frac{1}{2}$ which says 'There are $1\frac{1}{2}$ two-thirds in 1.'"

Having introduced several problems of the type $1 \div \frac{1}{a}$ will allow children to make this transition rather smoothly.

Try these: $1 \div \frac{3}{4} = \square$ and $1 \div \frac{2}{5} = \square$

SEE ANSWER FRAME (MD–24).

You can say $14 \div 3 = 4R2$
    or $14 \div 3 = 4\frac{2}{3}$.

Similarly, you can say $1 \div \frac{2}{3} = 1R\frac{1}{3}$
    or $1 \div \frac{2}{3} = 1\frac{1}{2}$.

When you divide 5 by 3, you get one group of 3 and two remaining:

$$5 = (\underline{1} \times 3) + \underline{2} \text{ or } 5 \div 3 = 1R2.$$

When you divide 1 by $\frac{3}{4}$, you get one $\frac{3}{4}$ and $\frac{1}{4}$ remaining:

$$1 = (\underline{1} \times \frac{3}{4}) + \frac{1}{4} \text{ or } 1 \div \frac{3}{4} = 1R\frac{1}{4}$$

1 three–fourth

The desired method is to say 2 is $\frac{2}{3}$ of 3 and $\frac{1}{4}$ is $\frac{1}{3}$ of $\frac{3}{4}$, i.e., represent the remainder as a fractional part of the divisor.

CONTINUE TO MD–26.

MD–26

Now write the answers to these questions:

$$1 \div \tfrac{1}{2} = \square$$
$$1 \div \tfrac{1}{3} = \square$$
$$1 \div \tfrac{1}{4} = \square$$
$$1 \div \tfrac{1}{8} = \square$$
$$1 \div \tfrac{1}{a} = \square$$

Write these responses as improper fractions, e.g., $1\tfrac{6}{7} = \tfrac{13}{7}$

$$1 \div \tfrac{2}{3} = \square$$
$$1 - \tfrac{3}{4} = \square$$
$$1 - \tfrac{2}{5} = \square$$
$$1 - \tfrac{3}{5} = \square$$
$$1 \div \tfrac{a}{b} = \square$$

SEE ANSWER FRAME (MD–26).

MD–27

Now if $24 \div 6 = 4$, then $24 = 6 \times 4$. Hence

$$1 \div \tfrac{2}{3} = \tfrac{3}{2} \quad so \quad 1 = \tfrac{2}{3} \times \tfrac{3}{2}$$
$$1 \div \tfrac{3}{5} = \tfrac{5}{3} \quad so \quad 1 = \tfrac{3}{5} \times \tfrac{5}{3}$$
$$1 \div \tfrac{3}{4} = \tfrac{4}{3} \quad so \quad 1 = \tfrac{3}{4} \times \tfrac{4}{3}$$
$$1 \div \tfrac{a}{b} = \tfrac{b}{a} \quad so \quad 1 = \tfrac{a}{b} \times \tfrac{b}{a}$$

$\tfrac{2}{3}$ and $\tfrac{3}{2}$ are reciprocals

$\tfrac{5}{3}$ and $\tfrac{3}{5}$ are reciprocals

$\tfrac{a}{b}$ and $\tfrac{b}{a}$ are reciprocals

One number is a *reciprocal* of another if their product is 1, i.e., M is a reciprocal of N and N is a reciprocal of M if $M \times N = 1$.

CONTINUE TO MD–28.

(MD–22)

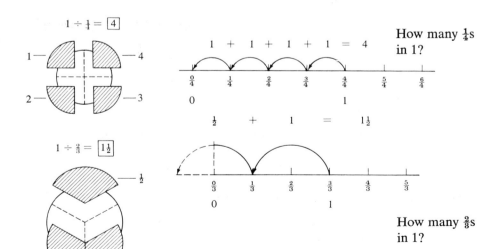

How many $\tfrac{1}{4}$s in 1?

$$1 + 1 + 1 + 1 = 4$$

How many $\tfrac{2}{3}$s in 1?

CONTINUE TO MD–23.

(MD–23)

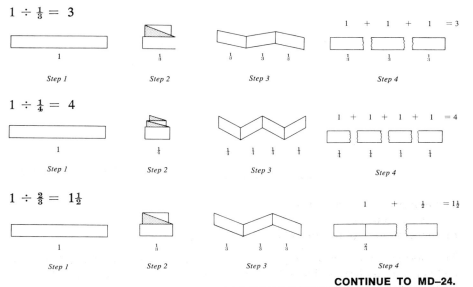

$1 \div \frac{1}{3} = 3$

$1 \div \frac{1}{4} = 4$

$1 \div \frac{2}{3} = 1\frac{1}{2}$

CONTINUE TO MD–24.

(MD–24)

If each apron takes $\frac{3}{4}$ yard of material, each yard of material will be enough for $1\frac{1}{3}$ aprons.

$1 \div \frac{3}{4} = 1\frac{1}{3}$

$1 + \frac{1}{3} = 1\frac{1}{3}$ three-fourths

Step 3   *Step 4*

If each boy eats two one-fifth pieces of pie, each pie will serve $2\frac{1}{2}$ boys.

$1 \div \frac{2}{5} = 2\frac{1}{2}$

$1 + 1 + \frac{1}{2} = 2\frac{1}{2}$ two-fifths

Step 3   *Step 4*

If this is clear, skip the next frame.

CONTINUE TO MD–25 OR MD–26.

MD–28

You have divided one by a unit fraction: $1 \div \frac{1}{a} = a$. You have divided one by a non-unit fraction: $1 \div \frac{b}{a} = \frac{a}{b}$. How can these patterns be extended to other possibilities? Give the students several problems of whole numbers greater than one divided by unit fractions and help them generate a generalization by using a number line.

$$2 \div \frac{1}{4} = 8 \qquad 3 \div \frac{1}{3} = 9 \qquad 6 \div \frac{1}{5} = 30$$

A short cut will quickly become obvious. How can it be "justified"? Since the number of fourths in two is twice the number of fourths in one, the previous generalization $1 \div \frac{1}{a} = a$ can be used.

CONTINUE TO MD–29.

(MD–26)

$$1 \div \tfrac{1}{2} = 2 \qquad\qquad 1 \div \tfrac{2}{3} = \tfrac{3}{2}$$
$$1 \div \tfrac{1}{3} = 3 \qquad\qquad 1 \div \tfrac{3}{4} = \tfrac{4}{3}$$
$$1 \div \tfrac{1}{4} = 4 \qquad\qquad 1 \div \tfrac{2}{5} = \tfrac{5}{2}$$
$$1 \div \tfrac{1}{8} = 8 \qquad\qquad 1 \div \tfrac{3}{5} = \tfrac{5}{3}$$
$$1 \div \tfrac{1}{a} = a \qquad\qquad 1 \div \tfrac{a}{b} = \tfrac{b}{a}$$

CONTINUE TO MD–27.

MD–29

The number of fourths in *two*, $2 \div \tfrac{1}{4}$,

     is the same as

twice the number of fourths in *one*, $2 \times (1 \div \tfrac{1}{4})$.

This notion should be developed *intuitively* through the use of number lines and concrete materials. The rationale is based on the right-hand distributivity of division over addition.

Whole Numbers	*Rational Numbers*
$(36 + 12) \div 4 = (36 \div 4) + (12 \div 4)$	$(1 + 1) \div \tfrac{1}{4} = (1 \div \tfrac{1}{4}) + (1 \div \tfrac{1}{4})$
$48 \div 4 = 9 + 3$	$2 \div \tfrac{1}{4} = 4 + 4$
$12 = 12$	$8 = 8$

CONTINUE TO MD–30.

MD–30

You can quickly handle whole numbers divided by non-unit fractions once the previous generalization is established.

$$2 \div \tfrac{3}{8}$$
$$2 \times (1 \div \tfrac{3}{8})$$
$$2 \times \tfrac{8}{3}$$
$$\tfrac{16}{3}$$
$$5\tfrac{1}{3}$$

Relate many such questions to the number line. Also have children continue to determine $1 \div \tfrac{3}{8}$ with paper strips or some similar aid. Relate problems to the question form: How many $\tfrac{3}{8}$s are in 2?

You try these: $6 \div \tfrac{1}{5}$

$$3 \div \tfrac{3}{4}$$
$$5 \div \tfrac{2}{7}$$

SEE ANSWER FRAME (MD–30).

More difficult cases can be handled similarly:

$$\frac{3}{4} \div \frac{1}{2}$$

$$\frac{3}{4} \times (1 \div \frac{1}{2})$$

$$\frac{3}{4} \times 2$$

$$\frac{6}{4} = 1\frac{1}{2}$$

Question: How many half-mile lengths will a boy run who completes a $\frac{3}{4}$-mile track?

Be sure to allow and to encourage children to do many such problems using concrete materials.

"How many halves in three-fourths?"

How many halves can you "put on top of" three-fourths? $1\frac{1}{2}$

Try these:

$$\frac{2}{5} \div \frac{3}{8}, \quad 1\frac{1}{4} \div 6\frac{5}{7}$$

SEE ANSWER FRAME (MD–31).

One more case which deserves special mention is a rational number divided by a whole number such as $\frac{2}{3} \div 4$.

The same reasoning as before can be used:

$$\frac{2}{3} \div 4 = \frac{2}{3} \times (1 \div 4) = \frac{2}{3} \times \frac{1}{4}$$

The child may grasp the relation more readily simply by saying

"$\frac{2}{3} \div 4$ is like $12 \div 4$"

"One-fourth of 12 is 3, so what is one-fourth of $\frac{2}{3}$?"

This relates it immediately to the whole numbers

$$12 \div 4 = \frac{12}{4} = 12 \times \frac{1}{4} \text{ so } \frac{2}{3} \div 4 = \frac{2}{3} \times \frac{1}{4}.$$

CONTINUE TO MD–33.

There are two other methods with which you should be familiar. The next one is more difficult to develop intuitively but is found in many elementary school textbooks.

B. *Identity Element Approach*

One is the multiplicative identity element: $1 \times a = a \times 1 = a$. It has many names: $1, \frac{2}{2}, \frac{19}{19}, \frac{9-4}{5}, \frac{2}{\frac{3}{2}\frac{}{3}}$

Now:

$$6 \div \frac{1}{4} = \frac{6}{\frac{1}{4}} = \frac{6}{\frac{1}{4}} \times 1$$

A name for "1" will be chosen in such a way that the "$\frac{1}{4}$" will "disappear."
A name for "1" which will do the job in this case is $\frac{4}{4}$.

CONTINUE TO MD–34.

MD–34

Now:

$$\frac{6}{\frac{1}{4}} \times 1 = \frac{6}{\frac{1}{4}} \times \frac{4}{4}$$

Since the children already know how to multiply rational numbers, this can be written:

$$\frac{6}{\frac{1}{4}} \times \frac{4}{4} = \frac{6 \times 4}{\frac{1}{4} \times 4}$$

$\frac{1}{4}$ and 4 are reciprocals so the product can be replaced by "1"

$$\frac{6 \times 4}{\frac{1}{4} \times 4} = \frac{24}{1} = 24$$

Try these: $6 \div \frac{1}{5}$, $\frac{2}{3} \div \frac{1}{4}$

SEE ANSWER FRAME (MD–34).

MD–35

The key is to choose the reciprocal of the denominator. Thus:

$$\frac{2}{3} \div \frac{1}{6} = \frac{\frac{2}{3}}{\frac{1}{6}} \times 1 = \frac{\frac{2}{3}}{\frac{1}{6}} \times \frac{\frac{6}{1}}{\frac{6}{1}} = \frac{\frac{2}{3} \times \frac{6}{1}}{\frac{1}{6} \times \frac{6}{1}} = \frac{\frac{12}{3}}{1} = 4$$

and

$$\frac{2}{3} \div \frac{5}{7} = \frac{\frac{2}{3}}{\frac{5}{7}} \times 1 = \frac{\frac{2}{3}}{\frac{5}{7}} \times \left(\frac{\frac{7}{5}}{\frac{7}{5}} \right) = \frac{\frac{2}{3} \times \frac{7}{5}}{\frac{5}{7} \times \frac{7}{5}} = \frac{\frac{14}{15}}{\frac{35}{35}} = \frac{14}{15}$$

Try these: $\frac{3}{5} \div \frac{6}{7}$ $1\frac{1}{2} \div 2\frac{3}{8}$

SEE ANSWER FRAME (MD–35).

(MD–30)

$6 \div \frac{1}{5}$	$3 \div \frac{3}{4}$**	$5 \div \frac{2}{7}$
$6 \times (1 \div \frac{1}{5})$*	$3 \times (1 \div \frac{3}{4})$*	$5 \times (1 \div \frac{2}{7})$*
6×5	$3 \times \frac{4}{3}$	$5 \times \frac{7}{2}$
30	$\frac{12}{3}$	$\frac{35}{2}$
	4**	$17\frac{1}{2}$

    * Use paper folding to clarify this. Work many problems on a fractional number line.
    ** In 3 there are 4 three-fourths. Four pies can be made with 3 cups of sugar if each pie requires $\frac{3}{4}$-cup sugar.

CONTINUE TO MD–31.

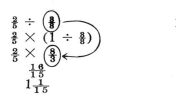

$$1\tfrac{1}{4} \div 6\tfrac{5}{7}$$
$$\tfrac{5}{4} \div \tfrac{47}{7}$$
$$\tfrac{5}{4} \times (1 \div \tfrac{47}{7})$$
$$\tfrac{5}{4} \times \tfrac{7}{47}$$
$$\tfrac{35}{168}$$

{ Encourage children to continue to include this step until you are certain they understand its role.

Notice how "reasonable" this makes the old "invert and multiply" rule.

CONTINUE TO MD–32.

C. Common Denominator Approach

Another approach is to find the common denominator. Consider this question: How many $\tfrac{1}{4}$-pound hamburgers can Jim's mother make from $1\tfrac{1}{2}$ pounds of ground beef?

$$1\tfrac{1}{2} \div \tfrac{1}{4} = \square$$
$$\tfrac{3}{2} \div \tfrac{1}{4} = \square$$
$$\tfrac{6}{4} \div \tfrac{1}{4} = \boxed{6}$$

One way to answer the question is to change $1\tfrac{1}{2}$ to $\tfrac{1}{4}$s.

Read, "How many 1 fourths are in 6 fourths?"

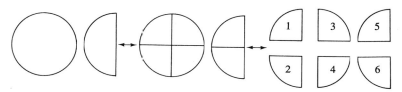

Draw a diagram and perform the computations to answer this question: Mary and Alice want strips of crepe paper $\tfrac{3}{8}$-yard in length. How many can be cut from $1\tfrac{1}{2}$ yards?

SEE ANSWER FRAME (MD–36).

The strength of the common denominator approach is in the ease with which it can be interpreted concretely, as was the case with the unit-fraction approach. The number of $\tfrac{2}{3}$ in $3\tfrac{1}{2}$ can be related to the number of 40 in 280. By using the common denominators, the statements are: $\dfrac{28 \text{ tens}}{4 \text{ tens}}$ and $\dfrac{21 \text{ sixths}}{4 \text{ sixths}}$.

Work these and write similar statements; make a diagram for the first one:

$$2\tfrac{1}{2} \div \tfrac{3}{4} = \square \qquad 4\tfrac{1}{2} \div 1\tfrac{5}{8} = \square$$

SEE ANSWER FRAME (MD–37).

(MD–34)

$$6 \div \frac{1}{5} = \frac{6}{\frac{1}{5}} \times 1 = \frac{6}{\frac{1}{5}} \times \frac{5}{5} = \frac{30}{1} = 30$$

$$\frac{2}{3} \div \frac{1}{4} = \frac{\frac{2}{3}}{\frac{1}{4}} \times 1 = \frac{\frac{2}{3}}{\frac{1}{4}} \times \frac{4}{4} = \frac{\frac{2}{3} \times 4}{1} = \frac{2}{3} \times \frac{4}{1} = \frac{8}{3}$$

CONTINUE TO MD–35.

(MD–35)

$$\frac{3}{5} \div \frac{6}{7} = \frac{\frac{3}{5}}{\frac{6}{7}} \times 1 = \frac{\frac{3}{5}}{\frac{6}{7}} \times \frac{\frac{7}{6}}{\frac{7}{6}} = \frac{\frac{21}{30}}{\frac{42}{42}} = \frac{\frac{21}{30}}{1} = \frac{21}{30} = \frac{7}{10}$$

$$1\frac{1}{2} \div 2\frac{3}{8} = \frac{\frac{3}{2}}{\frac{19}{8}} \times 1 = \frac{\frac{3}{2}}{\frac{19}{8}} \times \frac{\frac{8}{19}}{\frac{8}{19}} = \frac{\frac{24}{38}}{1} = \frac{24}{38} = \frac{12}{19}$$

CONTINUE TO MD–36.

MD–38

Nearly all the examples of this chapter are *measurement* division; division has been related primarily to repeated subtraction. This has been done intentionally because it is the division concept to which children most readily relate. Measurement division is best for introductory work, but after children begin to develop rational number division skills partitive questions should be pursued.

Measurement:

> Whole numbers: Bill had eight marbles and gave two to each of his friends; how many boys received marbles?
>
> Rational numbers: Mrs. Adams had three pounds of hamburger and froze it in $\frac{3}{4}$-pound packages; how many packages of meat did she freeze?

Partition:

> Whole numbers: Forty-eight cookies were given to eight children; how many cookies did each child receive?
>
> Rational numbers: A candy box is half full when it has 12 candy bars; how many candy bars are in a full box?

The measurement questions can be meaningfully answered by removing two marbles at a time or $\frac{3}{4}$-pounds of meat each time. The partition questions cannot be meaningfully answered this same way. The candy bar question implies that $12 \div \frac{1}{2} = \square$ or, with a proportion $\dfrac{12 \text{ candy bars}}{\frac{1}{2} \text{ box}} = \dfrac{\square \text{ candy bars}}{1 \text{ box}}$. As an inverse statement, $12 \div \frac{1}{2} = \square$ says that $\square \times \frac{1}{2} = 12$. The illustration on the right can be used.

Make diagrams and solve these problems:

> A. A bucket contains $1\frac{1}{2}$ gallons when it is $\frac{1}{3}$ full; what is its capacity when full?
>
> B. Jane told Sally that the $2\frac{1}{2}$ yards of material she had left was only $\frac{3}{4}$ what she needed to make another jumper. How much material is needed to make a jumper?

SEE ANSWER FRAME (MD–38).

(MD–38)

Diagrams are needed which reflect a proportional situation:

A.

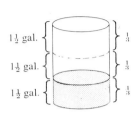

B.

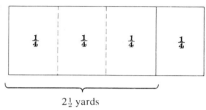

$$1\tfrac{1}{2} \div \tfrac{1}{3} = \square$$
$$\tfrac{1}{3} \times \square = 1\tfrac{1}{2}$$
$$\tfrac{3}{2} \div \tfrac{1}{3} = \square$$
$$\tfrac{9}{6} \div \tfrac{2}{6} = \tfrac{9}{2} = 4\tfrac{1}{2}$$

$$2\tfrac{1}{2} \div \tfrac{3}{4} = \square$$
$$\tfrac{3}{4} \times \square = 2\tfrac{1}{2}$$
$$\tfrac{5}{2} \div \tfrac{3}{4} = \square$$
$$\tfrac{10}{4} \div \tfrac{3}{4} = \tfrac{10}{3} = 3\tfrac{1}{3}$$

THE END.

(MD–36)

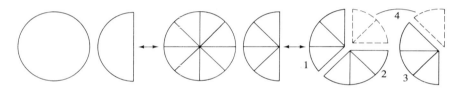

Question: How many $\tfrac{3}{8}$ in $1\tfrac{1}{2}$?

$$1\tfrac{1}{2} \div \tfrac{3}{8} = \square$$
$$\tfrac{3}{2} \div \tfrac{3}{8} = \square$$
$$\tfrac{12}{8} \div \tfrac{3}{8} = \boxed{4}$$

"How many 3 eighths in 12 eighths? $\underline{4}$

CONTINUE TO MD–37.

(MD–37)

$$2\tfrac{1}{2} \div \tfrac{3}{4} = \square$$
$$\tfrac{5}{2} \div \tfrac{3}{4} = \square$$
$$\tfrac{10}{4} \div \tfrac{3}{4} = \square$$
$$\square = 3\tfrac{1}{3}$$

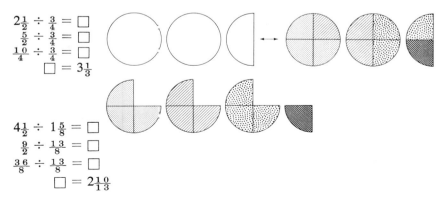

$$4\tfrac{1}{2} \div 1\tfrac{5}{8} = \square$$
$$\tfrac{9}{2} \div \tfrac{13}{8} = \square$$
$$\tfrac{36}{8} \div \tfrac{13}{8} = \square$$
$$\square = 2\tfrac{10}{13}$$

CONTINUE TO MD–38.

Multiplication and Division of Rationals Self-Test

1. List the four-stage sequence of problem-types in multiplication and give an example of each.

2. List three ways to divide rationals. Work $\frac{1}{3} \div \frac{4}{5} = $ n all three ways.

3. Write the corresponding verbal statements for A and B:

         A. $3 \times 2 = 6$ B. $12 \div 3 = 4$

           $\frac{1}{3} \times 6 = 2$ $1 \div \frac{1}{3} = 3$

4. Show A and B on the number line and with circular regions:

         A. $4 \times \frac{2}{3} = $ n   B. $1 \div \frac{3}{8} = $ n

5. Show A and B with paper folding:

         A. $\frac{1}{3} \times \frac{1}{4} = $ n   B. $1 \div \frac{3}{4} = $ n

Answers to Multiplication and Division of Rationals Self-Test

1. A. Whole $\times$ unit fraction $6 \times \frac{1}{2} = n$
    B. Whole $\times$ non-unit fraction $4 \times \frac{3}{5} = n$
    C. Unit fraction $\times$ unit fraction $\frac{1}{3} \times \frac{1}{2} = n$
    D. Non-unit fraction $\times$ non-unit fraction $\frac{2}{3} \times \frac{3}{9} = n$

2. A. Unit Division: $\frac{1}{3} \div \frac{4}{5} = \frac{1}{3} \times (1 \div \frac{4}{5}) = \frac{1}{3} \times \frac{5}{4} = \frac{5}{12}$
    B. Identity Element:

$$\frac{\frac{1}{3}}{\frac{4}{5}} \times 1 = \frac{\frac{1}{3}}{\frac{4}{5}} \times \frac{\frac{5}{4}}{\frac{5}{4}} = \frac{\frac{1}{3} \times \frac{5}{4}}{\frac{4}{5} \times \frac{5}{4}} = \frac{\frac{1}{3} \times \frac{5}{4}}{1} = \frac{5}{12}$$

    C. Common Denominator:

$$\frac{1}{3} \div \frac{4}{5} = \frac{5}{15} \div \frac{12}{15} = \frac{5 \div 12}{15 \div 15} = \frac{5 \div 12}{1} = \frac{5}{12}$$

3. 3 twos are 6   There are 4 threes in 12.
    $\frac{1}{3}$ six is 2   There are 3 thirds in 1.

4A.

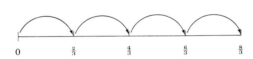

4B.

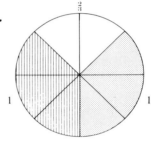

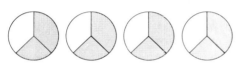

5A.

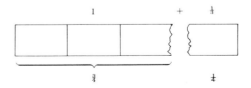

5B.

General Methods and Specific Materials of Instruction

Multiplication.   Number lines and paper folding were used extensively in the programmed materials. Sterns Blocks can also be used rather easily to demonstrate products of whole numbers and rational numbers. To multiply $6 \times \frac{1}{3}$, use the three-block as the unit. Then each subdivision is one-third.

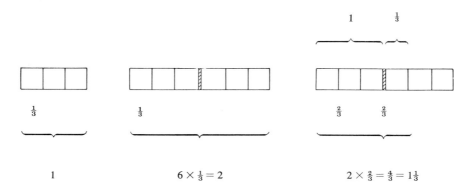

Measuring cups can be used to work with simple products, too. To multiply $5 \times \frac{1}{3}$, use the one-third cup or spoon measure five times.

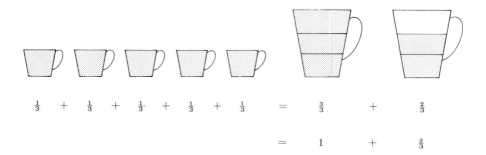

To find $\frac{1}{2} \times \frac{1}{2}$ or $\frac{1}{2} \times \frac{1}{4}$ simply measure out $\frac{1}{2}$ and divide it equally so $\frac{1}{2} \times \frac{1}{2} = \frac{1}{4}$, and measure $\frac{1}{4}$ and divide it equally, $\frac{1}{2} \times \frac{1}{4} = \frac{1}{8}$.

You can easily think of several ways in which whole number-rational number products can be demonstrated because of the repeated addition relationship. Another way to show products of two rational numbers is to have students draw square regions.

Problem: $\frac{3}{5} \times \frac{3}{4} = n$. Draw a unit square and estimate fourths on one side; shade in three-fourths with diagonal lines.

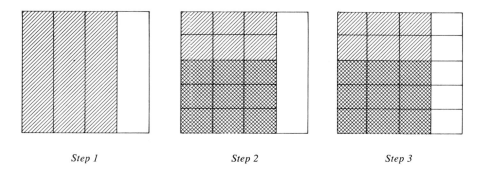

Step 1   *Step 2*   *Step 3*

On the adjacent side, estimate fifths and draw in fifths on the shaded three-fourths. Shade in three-fifths in the opposite direction. You now have double-diagonals on three-fifths of three-fourths which is $\frac{3}{5} \times \frac{3}{4} = $ n. To find the value of n, extend the "fifth lines." This will enable you to determine the fractional part of the area which has double shading. There are twenty small units and nine have double shading so

$$\frac{3}{5} \times \frac{3}{4} = \frac{9}{20}$$

Problems of this type can be done in a similar manner on the overhead projector.

Division.   The number line and paper folding were suggested for demonstrating division of rational numbers. Number line-type teaching aids can be set up just as with multiplication by using Sterns Blocks or some similar home-made aid, especially for unit-division. To find $1 \div \frac{1}{3} = $ n or $1 \div \frac{1}{4} = $ n, use the three- and four-blocks, respectively.

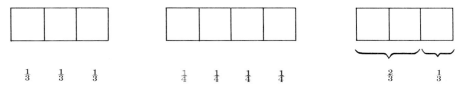

$$1 \div \tfrac{1}{3} = 3 \qquad\qquad 1 \div \tfrac{1}{4} = 4 \qquad\qquad 1 \div \tfrac{2}{3} = 1\tfrac{1}{2}$$

To show $1 \div \frac{2}{3} = $ n, you could use the two-blocks to show there are $1\frac{1}{2}$ two-thirds. The three-block is the defined unit.

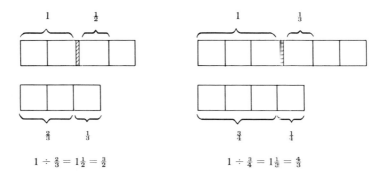

$$1 \div \tfrac{2}{3} = 1\tfrac{1}{2} = \tfrac{3}{2} \qquad 1 \div \tfrac{3}{4} = 1\tfrac{1}{3} = \tfrac{4}{3}$$

If examples are planned ahead of time, division problems can be worked with measurements, too. Remember, $1 \div \tfrac{1}{2} = n$ asks. "How many halves in one?" and $1 \div \tfrac{1}{3} = n$ asks, "How many thirds in ɔne ?" With measuring cups children can quickly demonstrate the $1 \div \tfrac{1}{2} = 2$ and $1 \div \tfrac{1}{3} = 3$. Similarly, $\tfrac{2}{3} \div \tfrac{1}{2} = n$ asks, "How many halves in two-thirds?" and $\tfrac{3}{4} \div \tfrac{1}{2} = n$ asks, "How many halves in three-fourths?"

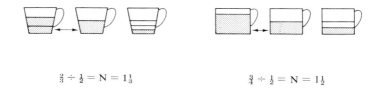

$$\tfrac{2}{3} \div \tfrac{1}{2} = N = 1\tfrac{1}{3} \qquad \tfrac{3}{4} \div \tfrac{1}{2} = N = 1\tfrac{1}{2}$$

The models suggested here for pupil manipulation will help children gain an intuitive grasp of the concepts. They will be able to *accept the results as reasonable*. The importance of this objective in elemenʇary school mathematics instruction cannot be overemphasized.

If it is your objective that children relate mathematɩcs learnings to an overall structural pattern, then you must make a consciɑus effort to build many bridges between previous learnings and new learnings. Ϲapitalize upon previous experiences; take advantage of readiness experiences; ƀuild a continuous strand of relatedness. Simple ideas such as the following are ∨ery important in achieving your goal:

A. 3×2 is 3 twos
$3 \times \tfrac{1}{2}$ is 3 halves
$\tfrac{1}{2} \times \tfrac{1}{2}$ is $\tfrac{1}{2}$ one-half

B. Multiplication of whole numbers and of certain rational numbers can be demonstrated on the number line.

C. Arrays relate intuitively to the square-region approach.

D. Multiplication of whole numbers and of certain rational numbers can be related to repeated addition.

E. Union of equivalent disjoint sets is intuitively related to the additivity of regions.
F. Knowledge of whole number products can be used through deductive sequences in helping establish the "reasonableness" of product sizes.
G. $12 \div 3$ asks, "How many threes in twelve?"
   $3 \div \frac{1}{2}$ asks, "How many halves in three?"
   $\frac{3}{4} \div \frac{1}{3}$ asks, "How many thirds in three-fourths?"
H. Division of whole numbers and of certain rational numbers can be related to the number line.
I. Division of whole numbers and of certain rational numbers can be related to repeated subtraction.
J. Knowledge of whole number quotients can be used through deductive sequences to help establish the "reasonableness" of rational number quotients:

1. $8 \div 4 = 2$	4. $8 \div \frac{1}{2} = 16$
2. $8 \div 2 = 4$	5. $8 \div \frac{1}{4} = 32$
3. $8 \div 1 = 8$	6. $8 \div \frac{1}{8} = 64$

Discovery. The preceding list can be used in providing direction on discovery strategies in working with products and quotients of rational numbers. Children can be divided into groups to solve problems the solutions of which can be based on the relationships listed above. You can review or remind them of one or more of the generalizations or you can give them hints as you guide and direct the discovery process in each small group. Give several problems of one type and suggest that they look for a generalization. Instruct them to guess the result before tackling each new problem. Instruct them also to keep the "secret" so that each child may have an opportunity to make the discovery.

A. For the first type of multiplication, whole $\times$ unit-fraction, this would be an example: "Mary, Cora and Beth each had $\frac{1}{4}$-yard ribbon; how much ribbon had they altogether?"
B. Whole $\times$ non-unit: "After the ball game, 8 boys went to a restaurant for pie and milk. Each boy had two pieces and the pies were cut in sevenths. How many pies did they eat?"
C. Unit $\times$ unit: "There was half a pie on the counter and Jim ate half of it. How much pie was left?"
D. Non-unit $\times$ non-unit: "Esther had $\frac{3}{4}$-yard of material and used $\frac{2}{3}$ of it for a blouse. How much should she buy next time if she wants to use the pattern again for a different color?"
E. One divided by a unit-fraction. "How many boys get pie if there is one pie and each boy gets one-fifth of a pie?"
F. One divided by a non-unit-fraction: "How many strips of ribbon $\frac{2}{5}$-yard long can be cut from each yard of ribbon?"

With encouragement to use number lines, paper folding and other aids suggested, students should be able to make meaningful discoveries relative to computational short cuts for finding products and quotients of rational numbers. The discovery of generalizations can be greatly facilitated by providing a set format for writing number sentences. This increases the likelihood that the youngsters will begin to observe an emerging pattern in their work.

Accommodation of Individual Differences

The individualization model presented in an earlier chapter suggested the following sequence for meeting student needs: state objectives; preassess; instruct and provide enrichment; diagnose; regroup into enrichment, practice and reteach groups; continue to the next major concept. Each item in the sequence will now be explored with attention fixed on multiplication and division of rational numbers.

Objectives

The usual levels of concrete, semi-concrete and abstract learning experiences should be followed. If the elementary school mathematics curriculum has provided readiness experiences in number sentences and elementary rational number concepts, concrete experiences can probably be related immediately to number sentences which describe them.

Here is a list of major concepts for multiplication; other lists could be made, but they would be similar. This list is *typical* rather than rigidly fixed.

A. Product of a whole number and a unit-fraction, e.g., $4 \times \frac{1}{3} = n$
B. Product of a whole number and a non-unit-fraction, e.g., $5 \times \frac{3}{4} = n$
C. Product of two unit-fractions, e.g., $\frac{1}{2} \times \frac{1}{3} = n$
D. Product of two non-unit-fractions, e.g., $\frac{2}{3} \times \frac{3}{4} = n$
E. Product of mixed numerals, e.g., $2\frac{1}{2} \times 3\frac{1}{4} = n$

Following is a similar list for division of rational numbers.

A. Quotient of one and a unit-fraction, e.g., $1 \div \frac{1}{3} = n$
B. Quotient of a whole number and a unit-fraction, e.g., $4 \div \frac{1}{3} = n$
C. Quotient of one and a non-unit-fraction, e.g., $1 \div \frac{2}{5} = n$
D. Quotient of a whole number and a non-unit-fraction, e.g., $5 \div \frac{3}{4} = n$
E. Quotient of two fractions, e.g., $\frac{2}{3} \div \frac{7}{9} = n$
F. Quotient of mixed numerals, e.g., $2\frac{1}{3} \div 3\frac{2}{7} = n$

The following objectives are representative of ones which could be written on "C" in the multiplication and division concept lists.

Concrete: The child will be able to:

1. Determine products of unit-fractions with the use of a fraction kit or paper folding and write the appropriate number sentence.

    2. Determine quotients of one and non-unit-fractions with the use of a fraction kit or paper folding and write the appropriate number sentence.

Semi-Concrete: The child will be able to:
    1. Draw and shade a gridded region to determine the product of two unit fractions.
    2. Construct a number line or draw a unit region diagram to determine quotients of one and non-unit-fractions.

Abstract: The child will be able to:
    1. Calculate products of unit-fractions without the use of concrete materials or diagrams.
    2. Compute quotients of one and non-unit-fractions without the use of concrete or semi-concrete aids.

Preassessment. Special care should be observed in preassessment to determine whether or not children who can compute products and quotients of rational numbers can do so meaningfully. Since products and quotients are relatively easy to compute, you must seek to determine if mastery of the concepts is *only* at the abstract level. If a child can calculate answers but cannot relate the calculations meaningfully to concrete materials or diagrammatic forms, you can hardly feel he has *total mastery*. Such children may benefit greatly from the instructional phase of the concept development which relies heavily upon concrete materials. Those who can compute *and* relate their computations meaningfully should not proceed through the instructional phase but, rather, should be channeled into lateral enrichment activities. Specific activities are suggested below and can be found in the sources cited in Chapter 5.

Instructional Phase. Children can work as an entire class carrying out manipulations at their seats with the teacher leading the class, or the class can be divided into small groups to carry out activities similar to those suggested in the previous section. If individualization materials, either programmed or unipacs, are available, they can be used, and the teacher can spend some time with the enrichment group and serve as a troubleshooter.

Diagnosis. When the teacher feels that several children have attained high levels of mastery, a diagnostic test can be administered. The test should cover the behavioral objectives of the unit and should cover concept development in at least the semi-concrete and abstract levels of the concepts.

    Children who do poorly can be placed in a reteach group. These children need more concrete experiences. They need to manipulate materials to gain mastery at this level. New strategies should be tried if at all possible since the strategies just completed were not successful. A small number of students (up to four or five) may need special diagnostic testing as described in Chapter 5 to find deficiencies in subconcepts similar to the structural aspects of readiness proposed by Gagné.

The children who can perform concept tasks concretely, and to some extent semi-concretely and abstractly, should be placed in or elect to join a practice group in which they can explore additional experiences designed to continue and reinforce total mastery. This group should have *interesting* activities. They can become quite bored with overuse of worksheet materials. Consult bibliographic references in Chapter 6 for books which describe such activities.

Children who demonstrate a high level of mastery can work on enrichment activities. Activities appropriate for children at this level would include work in other bases related to rational number operations, study of historical methods of computation, extension of elementary notions of probability and statistics, introduction to logic, reading selected bibliographic references, writing reports, giving oral reports, constructing demonstration models, making a bulletin board, studying topology and elementary notions of spherical geometry and exploring operations on integers. Children should be given a *choice* whenever possible to maintain interest, motivation and enthusiasm.

Discussion and Project Ideas

1. What other homemade and commercial aids can be used to teach multiplication and division of rational numbers?

2. Demonstrate multiplication and division of rational numbers on aids either mentioned in this chapter or on others available to you.

3. Outline a discovery lesson on a phase of multiplication or division of rational numbers. What results can you anticipate? Write some story problems to be solved in small groups.

4. Write some other behavioral objectives for this unit. Include all three levels of abstraction.

5. Write evaluation items for the objectives in this chapter or for the ones you wrote in the preceding item.

6. Locate some specific enrichment materials.

7. Write a unipac on one or more of the major concepts in this unit.

8. Suggest some specific activities for a multiplication and/or division practice group.

Additional Resources

Filmstrips

> *Using One to Rename—Fractions,* Filmstrip-of-the-Month (1213)
> *Multiplication with Fractions,* Filmstrip-of-the-Month (1215)
> *Products of Fractional Numbers,* Popular Science (5H–8)
> *Modern Mathematics: Division of Fractional Numbers,* Society for Visual Education (A532–17)

Films

Multiplication of Rational Numbers, National Council of Teachers of Mathematics.

Division of Rational Numbers, National Council of Teachers of Mathematics.

Elementary School Textbooks

Harper & Row (1970), Grade 5, *New Dimensions in Mathematics,* by C. D'Augustine, F. Brown, J. Heddens, C. Howard.

Student Text: pp. 161–75, 201–11.

Harper & Row (1970), Grade 6, *New Dimensions in Mathematics,* by C. D'Augustine, F. Brown, J. Heddens, C. Howard.

Student Text: pp. 150–66.

Houghton-Mifflin (1970), Grade 5, *Modern School Mathematics,* by E. Duncan, L. Capps, M. Dolciani, W. Quast, M. Zweng.

Student Text: pp. 198–207, 290–313, 234–267.

16

Teaching Decimals and Percents

Rational numbers take on several forms when expressed as numerals. The previous three chapters explored in some detail the fractional notation and procedures for operating on rational numbers expressed in that form.

This chapter presents two additional ways of expressing names for rational numbers: decimal fractions and percents. Many relations of fractions can be used to make these two forms meaningful for children. The next section of this chapter explores in a programmed format some of the many ways that experiences with rational numbers can be built upon to enhance youngsters' understanding of and ability to work with decimals and percents.

Slow down! The next section is designed to stimulate your imagination by presenting opportunities to discover generalizations implicit in operations you have performed but have not, perhaps, fully understood. Allow yourself the time to do some reflective thinking about the questions posed.

Decimals and Percents

Objectives

At the completion of this unit, you will be able to do each of the following:

(1) Demonstrate inequalities of decimal fractions with graph paper and by converting to fractions.

(2) Demonstrate with graph paper and a pocket chart sums and differences of decimal fractions.

(3) Demonstrate with a pocket chart the product of a whole number and a decimal fraction.

(4) Estimate quotients by using place value names.

(5) Demonstrate with a pocket chart the quotient of a decimal fraction and a whole number.

(6) Describe strategies for helping children discover how to operate on decimal fractions with particular emphasis on the placement of the decimal point.

(7) Demonstrate with graph paper that $1 = 100\%$ and for any whole numbers less than 100, $n\% = \frac{n}{100}$.

(8) Solve problems involving the three cases of percent.

Materials Needed

1. Graph paper cut into single squares, strips with ten squares each and large squares with 100 squares each.

2. Sheet of paper with *ones, tenths, hundredths* written across the top and some small objects such as paper clips.

Ones	Tenths	Hundredths

Assumptions

The children have:

A. Learned to find equivalent names for fractions.

B. Learned to add, subtract, multiply and divide fractions.

C. Worked with place value charts or groups of objects in relation to place value concepts.

D. Estimated whole number quotients by using place value names.

NOTE

Many frames in the following programmed section ask you to respond to questions. Carry out the activities and work the problems. Take your time; the material is condensed. Answers to questions are located on the second page following in the same relative position as the question (same third of a page).

A *decimal fraction* is simply a numeral for a rational number. Initial pupil experiences with decimal fractions should build upon relationships between decimal fractions and fractional forms previously encountered utilizing numerators and denominators to name rational numbers. As is the usual convention, "decimal fractions" may be called simply "decimals." "Fraction" refers in this chapter to numerals of the form $\frac{a}{b}$ where a and b are whole numbers and $b \neq 0$.

To help children learn proper notation, you can ask them to write a column of fractions with denominators of ten and one-hundred. In a second column they can write the decimal equivalents after you have explained the proper notation.

Fraction	*Decimal*
$\frac{3}{10}$	.3
$\frac{14}{100}$	.14
$\frac{2}{100}$	.02

CONTINUE TO D–2.

Such renaming should lead immediately into an extension of place value concepts. First, a brief tangent.

Look at the following numerals. Write down the four which you "like the best"; which four are most esthetically pleasing or balanced or symmetric?

6.4	81.4	48.72	26.39
26.2	161.4	2.368	43.2
	3.89		324.617

SEE ANSWER FRAME (D–2).

Most people choose numerals which are symmetric with respect to the decimal point. People have been conditioned to view the decimal point as the focal point of a numeral.

6.4   48.72   324.617

This is not good. Why?

SEE ANSWER FRAME (D–3).

Decimal numerals *do* have place value matchings or symmetry with respect to *ones* if the decimal point is simply treated as a marker.

↓

thousands   hundreds   tens   ones   tenths   hundredths   thousandths

Do you have an idea how you might promote this feeling or point of view?

SEE ANSWER FRAME (D–4).

Decimal Fraction Inequalities

Graph paper can be used to show the relation between tens and ones:

10   1

Then one small square can be introduced as $\frac{1}{10}$: □ .

The objective in working with such materials is to develop an intuitive feel for the "ten times as big as the one to the right" relation. The concept is an extension to the right of the 1, 10, 100, 1000 relationship.

Uses your pieces of graph paper to decide if 1.23 > 1.3 or 1.23 < 1.3.

SEE ANSWER FRAME (D–5).

Addition and Subtraction

Operations with decimal fractions can easily be related to operations on fractions. Allow children to discover generalizations by providing structured sequences of activities. For example, to find .2 + .3, change to $\frac{2}{10} + \frac{3}{10}$; find the sum, $\frac{5}{10}$ and write the result as a decimal fraction: .2 + .3 = .5.

Change each of the following to fractions and solve:

Add: .3   .7   .04   .06   *Subtract:*   .8   .09   .14   1.2
        +.4   +.5   +.05   −.07   −.2   −.04   −.06   − .5

Example   *Example*

$$.2 = \tfrac{2}{10} \atop +.3 = \tfrac{3}{10}\Big\} \text{Step 1}$$
$$.5 \leftarrow \tfrac{5}{10}\} \text{Step 2}$$
Step 3

$$.9 = \tfrac{9}{10} \atop -.1 = \tfrac{1}{10}\Big\} \text{Step 1}$$
$$.8 \leftarrow \tfrac{8}{10}\} \text{Step 2}$$
Step 3

SEE ANSWER FRAME (D–6).

D–7

In working with whole numbers, children are provided many instructional activities to develop an understanding of place value. Graph paper and place value charts are two of many aids to help children learn

$$123 = 100 + 20 + 3 = 12 \text{ tens } 3 \text{ ones } \textit{and } 13 \text{ ones } = 1 \text{ ten } 3 \text{ ones.}$$

The same instructional aids can be used to help children learn that:

    (A) $.123 = .1 + .02 + .003 = 12$ hundredths 3 thousandths
    (B)   13 hundredths $= 1$ tenth 3 hundredths

Show with your graph paper and place value sheet that (A) and (B) are true.

SEE ANSWER FRAME (D–7).

(D–2)

Most people will choose: Most people will *not* choose:

Most people will choose:	Most people will *not* choose:
6.4	26.2
48.72	81.4
26.39	161.4
324.617	3.89
	43.2
	2.368

Study the list on the left. Can you see a common characteristic?

CONTINUE TO D–3.

(D–3)

This is not good because numerals *do not* have place value matching or symmetry with respect to the decimal point. This focus can be misleading.

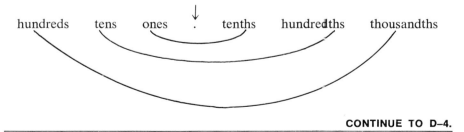

hundreds   tens   ones   .   tenths   hundredths   thousandths

CONTINUE TO D–4.

(a) Encourage children to determine place value by always starting with the *ones'* position:

8263.419

"ones, tens, hundreds, thousands"

"ones, tenths, hundredths, thousandths"

(b) In introducing work with decimals, place a zero in the ones' place:

$\left. \begin{array}{l} 10. \longrightarrow \text{one ten} \\ 0.1 \longrightarrow \text{one tenth} \end{array} \right\}$ *Tens and Tenths* each have *two* digits.

$\left. \begin{array}{l} 613 \text{ is six hundred thirteen} \\ 6.13 \text{ is six and thirteen hundredths} \\ 410 \text{ is four hundred ten} \\ 0.41 \text{ is forty-one hundredths} \end{array} \right\}$ *Hundreds* and *Hundredths* each have *three* digits.

CONTINUE TO D–5.

1.23   1.3

| 1. | 2 | 3 | | 1. | 3 |
| one | tenths | hundredths | | one | tenths |

1.23 < 1.3

If the pieces of graph paper are left unmarked, their values can be changed. You may begin with 10, 1, $\frac{1}{10}$ and then use 1, $\frac{1}{10}$, $\frac{1}{100}$, or you can label one side "one one," "one tenth," "one hundredth" and label the other side "one ten," "one one," "one tenth," and use the side desired.

CONTINUE TO D–6.

Add

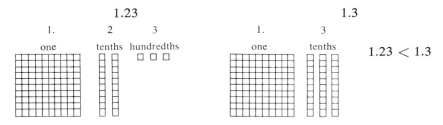

$$.3 = \frac{3}{10}$$
$$+ .4 = \frac{4}{10}$$
$$\overline{.7} \leftarrow \frac{7}{10}$$

$$.7 = \frac{7}{10}$$
$$+.5 = \frac{5}{10}$$
$$\overline{1.2} \quad \frac{12}{10} = 1\frac{2}{10}$$

$$.04 = \frac{4}{100}$$
$$+.05 = \frac{5}{100}$$
$$\overline{.09} \leftarrow \frac{9}{100}$$

$$.06 = \frac{6}{100}$$
$$+.07 = \frac{7}{100}$$
$$\overline{.13} \leftarrow \frac{13}{100}$$

Subtract

$$.8 = \frac{8}{10}$$
$$-.2 \quad \frac{2}{10}$$
$$\overline{.6} \leftarrow \frac{6}{10}$$

$$.09 = \frac{9}{100}$$
$$-.04 \quad \frac{4}{100}$$
$$\overline{.05} \leftarrow \frac{5}{100}$$

$$.14 = \frac{14}{100}$$
$$-.06 \quad \frac{6}{100}$$
$$\overline{.08} \leftarrow \frac{8}{100}$$

$$1.2 = 1\frac{2}{10} = \frac{12}{10}$$
$$- .5 \quad \frac{5}{10}$$
$$\overline{.7} \leftarrow \frac{7}{10}$$

Sequences similar to these can be used to help children discover generalizations for adding and subtracting decimal fractions.

CONTINUE TO D–7.

(D–7)

(A)

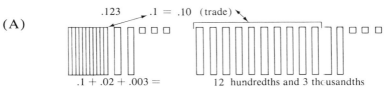

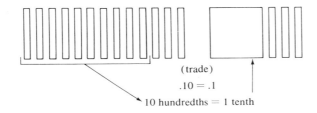

.1 + .02 + .003 =   12 hundredths and 3 thousandths

tenths	hundredths	thousandths
X	XX	XXX

tenths	hundredths	thousandths
	XXXXX	
	XXXXX	XXX
	XX	

Change .1 to .10;

1 tenth = 10 hundredths $\frac{1}{10} = \frac{10}{100}$

(trade)

.10 = .1

10 hundredths = 1 tenth

You are using the relation: $.1 = \frac{1}{10} = \frac{1}{10} \times 1 = \frac{1}{10} \times \frac{10}{10} = \frac{10}{100} = .10$

CONTINUE TO D–8.

D–8

Similarly, these aids can be used for addition and subtraction

$.67 = \frac{6}{10} + \frac{7}{100}$
$+.58 = \frac{5}{10} + \frac{8}{100}$

Step 1 $\frac{11}{10} + \frac{15}{100}$

$\frac{11}{10} + \left(\frac{10}{100} + \frac{5}{100}\right)$

Step 2 $\left(\frac{11}{10} + \frac{1}{10}\right) + \frac{5}{100}$

$\frac{12}{10} + \frac{5}{100}$

Step 3 $\left(\frac{10}{10} + \frac{2}{10}\right) + \frac{5}{100}$

$1 + \frac{2}{10} + \frac{5}{100}$

Show this problem with your graph paper.

SEE ANSWER FRAME (D–8).

D–9

Ragged decimals can be troublesome for youngsters One satisfactory approach is to change the problem to one which involves only fractions. Do so for this question; it is started for you:

$$2.4 \quad = \quad 2\frac{4}{10}$$
$$.613 \quad = \quad \frac{613}{1000}$$
$$+42.89 \quad = \quad 42\frac{89}{100}$$

SEE ANSWER FRAME (D–9).

Multiplication

Children can also discover generalizations for multiplication of decimal fractions through structured sequences. Solve these problems by changing them to fractions and see if you can discover the generalization relative to the decimal point. The first one is done for you.

$$
\begin{array}{r} .6 \\ \times .2 \\ \hline .12 \end{array}
\qquad
\boxed{Step\ 1} \quad \frac{6}{10} \times \frac{2}{10} \; = \; \boxed{Step\ 2} \quad \frac{12}{100}
$$

Step 3

Try these:

(a)	$\begin{array}{r}.5\\ \times .3\end{array}$	(b)	$\begin{array}{r}.81\\ \times .4\end{array}$	(c)	$\begin{array}{r}.06\\ \times .3\end{array}$	(d)	$\begin{array}{r}1.6\\ \times\ .3\end{array}$

Reinforce previous place value products:

tens $\times$ tens = hundreds
tenths $\times$ tenths = hundredths

SEE ANSWER FRAME (D–10).

To reinforce the place value characteristics of decimal fractions and the concept of multiplication as repeated addition, a place value or pocket chart can be used to find products of decimal fractions and whole numbers. Answers can be compared with fraction products. Draw a diagram or use your place value sheet to find this product: $4 \times .36 = \square$. Then determine the product by changing .36 to a fraction. (Remember that .36 is used as an addend 4 times.)

$$
\begin{aligned}
4 \times .36 &= 4 \times (.3 + .06) \\
&= (4 \times .3) + (4 \times .06) \\
&= 4\ (3\ \text{tenths}) + 4\ (6\ \text{hundredths})
\end{aligned}
$$

SEE ANSWER FRAME (D–11).

Division

Change the following problems to fractions. See if you can see a pattern which determines the placement of the decimal point in the answers.

(a) $3\overline{)\,.6}$	(c) $.2\overline{)\,.628}$
(b) $4\overline{)\,.12}$	(d) $.4\overline{)\,.8}$

SEE ANSWER FRAME (D–12).

D–13

	Dividend	Divisor	Quot'ent
a	1	0	1
b	2	0	2
c	3	1	2
d	1	1	0
e	2	1	1
f	2	2	0
y	minus	x	is	z

Thus $\dfrac{6.1482}{3.69}$ will have $4 - 2 = 2$ decimal places in the quotient *if 3.69 divides 6.1482 evenly*. This generalization is inadequate when the division is not even and when the difference is negative, as in $\dfrac{61.2}{.03}$ which yields -1. Hence, the generalization is useful but does not include all possibilities.

CONTINUE TO D–14.

(D–8)

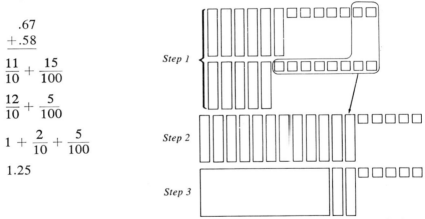

.67
+.58

$\dfrac{11}{10} + \dfrac{15}{100}$

$\dfrac{12}{10} + \dfrac{5}{100}$

$1 + \dfrac{2}{10} + \dfrac{5}{100}$

1.25

Step 1

Step 2

Step 3

Subtraction is of course similarly done; make up your own problem and show the regrouping to the *right*. You can easily see the great similarity to the whole number sum, $67 + 58 = \square$.

CONTINUE TO D–9.

(D–9)

$2 + \dfrac{4}{10} \times \dfrac{100}{100} = \qquad 2\dfrac{400}{1000}$

$\dfrac{613}{1000} \times \dfrac{1}{1} = \qquad \dfrac{613}{1000}$

$+\ 42 + \dfrac{89}{100} \times \dfrac{10}{10} = 42\dfrac{890}{1000}$

Hence, 2.4 and 2.400 name the same number, and 42.89 and 42.890 name the same number.

$\qquad 44\dfrac{1903}{1000} = 45\dfrac{903}{1000} = 45.903$

CONTINUE TO D–10.

(D–10)

(a) $\begin{array}{r}.5 \\ \times .3 \\ \hline .15\end{array}$ $\boxed{\begin{array}{c} \text{Step 1} \\ \dfrac{5}{10} \times \dfrac{3}{10}\end{array}} = \boxed{\begin{array}{c} \text{Step 2} \\ \dfrac{15}{100}\end{array}}$ $\boxed{\text{Step 3}}$

(b) $\begin{array}{r}.81 \\ \times .4 \\ \hline .324\end{array}$ $\dfrac{81}{100} \times \dfrac{4}{10} = \dfrac{324}{1000}$

(c) $\begin{array}{r}.06 \\ \times .3 \\ \hline .018\end{array}$ $\dfrac{6}{100} \times \dfrac{3}{10} = \dfrac{18}{1000}$

(d) $\begin{array}{r}1.6 \\ \times .3 \\ \hline .48\end{array}$ $1\dfrac{6}{10} \times \dfrac{3}{10} =$

$\dfrac{16}{10} \times \dfrac{3}{10} = \dfrac{48}{100}$

The old rule of "count the number of decimal places" makes sense!

CONTINUE TO D–11.

(D–11)

$$4(3 \text{ tenths}) + 4(6 \text{ hundredths})$$

Step 1

Rename

$\dfrac{20}{100}$ as $\dfrac{2}{10}$

$\begin{array}{r}.36 \\ .36 \\ .36 \\ .36 \\ \hline 1.44\end{array}$

Ones	Tenths	Hundredths
	XXX←	(XXXXXX)
	XXX←	XXXXXX
	XXX	XXXXXX
	XXX	(XXXXXX)

$\begin{array}{r}.36 \\ \times 4 \\ \hline 1.44\end{array}$

Step 2

Rename

$\dfrac{10}{10}$ as 1

Ones	Tenths	Hundredths
←	(XXXX)	
	XXXX	XX
	XXX	XX
	XXX	

$\dfrac{36}{100} \times \dfrac{4}{1} =$

$\dfrac{144}{100} = \dfrac{144}{100}$

Step 3

Ones	Tenths	Hundredths
X		
		XX
	X	XX
	XXX	

$$1 \text{ one} + 4 \text{ tenths} + 4 \text{ hundredths}$$
$$1.44$$

CONTINUE TO D–12.

(D–12)

(a) $\dfrac{6}{10} \div 3 = \dfrac{2}{10}$ so $3\overline{)\,.6}^{\,.2}$

(c) $\dfrac{628}{1000} \div \dfrac{2}{10} = \dfrac{314}{100}$ so $.2\overline{)\,.628}^{\,3.14}$

(b) $\dfrac{12}{100} \div 4 = \dfrac{3}{100}$ so $4\overline{)\,.12}^{\,.03}$

(d) $\dfrac{8}{10} \div \dfrac{4}{10} = 2$ so $.4\overline{)\,.8}^{\,2}$

Hint: What was the pattern for multiplication? Since division is the inverse operation, there should be a relation. Write three columns of decimal places and look for the relation. (Dividend ÷ Divisor = Quotient)

CONTINUE TO D–13.

D–14

The usual procedure is to "change" the divisor to a whole number. Can you justify this from your knowledge of fractions?

$$.4\overline{)\,.68} \quad \longrightarrow \quad 4\overline{)\,6.8}$$

Hint: Change to fraction form with a decimal fraction in the numerator and denominator and use an appropriate name for the multiplicative identity element.

SEE ANSWER FRAME (D–14).

D–15

With the following procedure, the approximate value of the quotient can be estimated without regard for the number of decimal places in the answer. First, use the generalization which you just verified with the multiplicative identity element.

$$6.14\overline{)\,.0061} \quad \longrightarrow \quad 614\overline{)\,.61}$$

Then treat the divisor as *ones*. Retain enough digits in the numerator to make it larger than the divisor. Determine its place value.

$$\frac{6100 \text{ ten-thousandths}}{614 \text{ ones}} \longrightarrow 9 \text{ ten-thousandths}$$

Try these:

    (a) $6.23 \div .048$

    (b) $.0012 \div 3.6$

    (c) $1.2 \div .068$

Ask, "6100 what?"

.6100
tenths
hundredths
thousandths
ten thousandths

$6 < 614$
$61 < 614$
$610 < 614$
$\boxed{6100 > 614}$

SEE ANSWER FRAME (D–15).

D–16

You can demonstrate division on a pocket chart to reinforce the relationship between place value on the left and right of the ones' position. Use an example which is the quotient of a decimal fraction and a natural number. If you distribute 6.28 into four sets of equal size, how much will be in each set?

$$6.28 \div 4 = \square$$

Step 1

$$6 + .2 + .08$$

Step 2   Separate the ones into four equal subsets and convert the "extras" to tenths.

$$4 + 2.2 + .08$$

Try this one: $7.02 \div 3 = \square$.

Step 3   Separate the tenths into four equal subsets and convert the "extras" to hundredths.

$$4 + 2.0 + .28$$

Step 4   Separate the hundredths into four separate subsets of equal size.

$$4 \times (1 + .5 + .07)$$
$$6.28 \div 4 = 1.57$$

In 6.28 there are 4 sets of 1.57.

SEE ANSWER FRAME (D–16).

Summary Exercises

Decimal fractions are numerals for rational numbers. Answer each of the following questions by changing the problem to fractional form.

(a) $1.34 \bigcirc 1.4$ (c) $\begin{array}{r} 4.24 \\ -1.05 \\ \hline \end{array}$ (e) $\begin{array}{r} 1.29 \\ \times .03 \\ \hline \end{array}$

(b) $\begin{array}{r} 1.3 \\ .28 \\ +.05 \\ \hline \end{array}$ (d) $.8\overline{)\,.64}$

SEE ANSWER FRAME (D–17).

Regrouping occurs in addition, subtraction, multiplication and division. Use your chart and paper strips to demonstrate each of the following and write the mathematical steps involved:

(a) 1.2 is 12 tenths

(b) $5 \times 1.3 = 6.5$

SEE ANSWER FRAME (D–18).

When you estimated whole number quotients, you rounded both numbers:

$$\frac{6247}{241} \longrightarrow \frac{7\ \text{thousand}}{2\ \text{hundred}} \longrightarrow 3\ \text{tens.}$$

You had to know that thousands $\div$ hundreds $=$ tens. To ease the load, the denominator in the decimal fraction was left intact and called *ones* after the decimal point was moved:

$$\frac{.04923}{.34} = \frac{.04923}{.34} \times \frac{100}{100} = \frac{4.923}{34} \longrightarrow \frac{49(?)}{34\ ones}$$

Digits were retained until the numerator was greater than the denominator. Finally, the appropriate name was determined: 4 ones, 49 *tenths*. Then $49 \div 34$ is about 1 and tenths $\div$ ones is tenths so the estimated quotient is 49 tenths or 4.9. Thus for $\dfrac{.06238}{1.34}$ you follow these steps:

$$\frac{.06238}{1.34} \times \frac{100}{100} = \frac{6.238}{134} \longrightarrow \frac{623\ \text{hundredths}}{134\ \text{ones}} \longrightarrow 4\ \text{hundredths}$$

You try these:

(a) $18 \div .061$
(b) $.0021 \div .9$
(c) $6.841 \div .239$

SEE ANSWER FRAME (D–19).

Multiplicative Identity

$.4\overline{)\,.68}$

$$\frac{.68}{.4} = \frac{.68}{.4} \times \left(1\right) = \frac{.68}{.4} \times \left(\frac{10}{10}\right) = \frac{6.8}{4}$$

or

$$\frac{\dfrac{68}{100}}{\dfrac{4}{10}} \times 1 = \frac{\dfrac{68}{100}}{\dfrac{4}{10}} \times \frac{10}{10} = \frac{\dfrac{68}{10}}{4} = \frac{6.8}{4}$$

CONTINUE TO D–15.

　　　　"Move" the Decimal　　　　　　　*Estimate the Quotient*

(a) $\dfrac{6.23}{.048} \times \dfrac{1000}{1000} = \dfrac{6230}{48}$　　$\dfrac{62 \text{ hundreds}}{48 \text{ ones}} \longrightarrow 1 \text{ hundred} = 100$

(b) $\dfrac{.0012}{3.6} \times \dfrac{10}{10} = \dfrac{.012}{36}$　　$\dfrac{120 \text{ ten-thousandths}}{36 \text{ ones}} \longrightarrow 3 \text{ ten-thousandths} = .0003$

(c) $\dfrac{1.2}{.068} \times \dfrac{1000}{1000} = \dfrac{1200}{68}$　　$\dfrac{120 \text{ tens}}{68 \text{ ones}} \longrightarrow 1 \text{ ten} = 10$

This type of estimate yields the place value of the first digit of the quotient.

CONTINUE TO D–16.

Step 1　　　$7.02 \div 3 = \square$　　　　　*Step 3*

　　　$7 \quad + \quad .0 \quad + \quad .02$　　　　　　$6 + \quad .9 \ + \quad\quad .12$

Ones	Tenths	Hundredths
XXXXXX(X) ↘		XX

Ones	Tenths	Hundredths
XX	XXX	XX
XX	XXX	XXXXXXXXXX
XX	XXX	

Step 2　　　　　　　　　　　　　　　*Step 4*

　$6 \ + \quad\quad 1.0 \quad\quad + \quad .02$　　　$3 \times (2 + \ .3 \ + \quad .04)$

Ones	Tenths	Hundredths
XX	XXXXXXXXX(X) ↘	XX
XX		
XX		

Ones	Tenths	Hundredths
XX	XXX	XXXX
XX	XXX	XXXX
XX	XXX	XXXX

In 7.02 there are 3 sets of 2.34.

CONTINUE TO D–17.

(a) $1.34 \bigcirc 1.4$

$1\dfrac{34}{100} \bigcirc 1\dfrac{4}{10}$

$\dfrac{134}{100} \bigcirc \dfrac{14}{10}$

$\dfrac{134}{100} \enclose{circle}{<} \dfrac{140}{100}$

(b) $1.3 = 1\dfrac{3}{10} = 1\dfrac{30}{100}$

$.28 = \dfrac{28}{100} = \dfrac{28}{100}$

$.05 = \dfrac{5}{100} = \dfrac{5}{100}$

$1.63 \longleftarrow 1\dfrac{63}{100}$

(c) $\quad 4.24 = 4\dfrac{24}{100}$

$\quad -1.05 \quad\quad 1\dfrac{5}{100}$

$\quad\quad \overline{3.19} \longleftarrow 3\dfrac{19}{100}$

(d) $1.29 \quad 1\dfrac{29}{100} \times \dfrac{3}{100}$

$.03 \quad \dfrac{129}{100} \times \dfrac{3}{100}$

$\overline{.0387} \longleftarrow \dfrac{387}{10000}$

(e) $.8\overline{)\,.64}$ $\quad \dfrac{64}{100} \div \dfrac{8}{10} = \dfrac{64}{80} = \dfrac{8}{10} = .8$

CONTINUE TO D–18.

(a) 1.2 is 12 tenths

Ones	Tenths
/	//

Ones	Tenths
	// //////////

(b)

Ones	Tenths
/	///
/	///
/	///
/	///
/	///

Ones	Tenths
/	///
/	//
/	
/	
/	

$5 \times (1.3) = 6.5$

1.3
$\times 5$
6.5

CONTINUE TO D–19.

(a) $\dfrac{18}{.061} \times \dfrac{1000}{1000} = \dfrac{18000}{61} \longrightarrow \dfrac{180 \text{ hundreds}}{61 \text{ ones}} \longrightarrow 2 \text{ hundreds} = 200$

(b) $\dfrac{.0021}{.9} \times \dfrac{10}{10} = \dfrac{.021}{9} \longrightarrow \dfrac{21 \text{ thousandths}}{9} \longrightarrow 2 \text{ thousandths} = .002$

(c) $\dfrac{6.841}{.239} \times \dfrac{1000}{1000} = \dfrac{6841}{239} \longrightarrow \dfrac{684 \text{ tens}}{239 \text{ ones}} \longrightarrow 2 \text{ tens} = 20$

CONTINUE TO D–20.

D–20

Percent

A percent is another name for a rational number. Rational numbers can be named in many ways; you have already observed that they can be named by fractions and decimals.

Rational Number	Fraction	Decimal	Percent
One-half	$\frac{1}{2}$	.5	50%
One-fourth	$\frac{1}{4}$	.25	25%
One-eighth	$\frac{1}{8}$	.125	12.5%

A percent describes how many parts of one-hundred. Twenty-five percent is 25 parts of one-hundred. 100% is 100 parts of one-hundred, $\frac{100}{100}$.

CONTINUE TO D–21.

D–21

Percents can be introduced through paper folding of graph paper. A piece of graph paper with one-hundred squares can be used. The relation between percents and fractions with denominators of 100 can be established by counting squares:

Fraction Name	Percent Name	Fraction Name	Percent Name
$\frac{1}{100}$	1%	$\frac{13}{100}$	13%
$\frac{2}{100}$	2%	$\frac{71}{100}$	71%

How could you use pieces of graph paper to establish percent names for 1, $\frac{1}{2}$, $\frac{1}{4}$, $\frac{1}{8}$?

CONTINUE TO D–22.

D–22

Fraction	Fraction in Hundredths	Percent	Fraction	Fraction in Hundredths	Percent
1	$\frac{100}{100}$	100%	$\frac{1}{10}$	$\frac{?}{100}$	?
$\frac{1}{2}$	$\frac{50}{100}$	50%	$\frac{3}{10}$	$\frac{?}{100}$	?
$\frac{1}{4}$	$\frac{25}{100}$	25%	$\frac{3}{4}$	$\frac{?}{100}$	?
$\frac{1}{8}$	$\frac{12\frac{1}{2}}{100}$	$12\frac{1}{2}$%			

Remind youngsters that the first two columns are equivalent fractions. Do *you* remember how to find equivalent fractions? (*Hint:* Use the multiplicative identity element.)

SEE ANSWER FRAME (D–22).

Children learn that two fractions name the same number when their cross-products are equal, e.g., $\frac{2}{3} = \frac{14}{21}$ because $2 \times 21 = 3 \times 14$.

$$\frac{a}{b} = \frac{c}{d} \; when \; a \times d = b \times c.$$

Thus, $\frac{2}{3} = \frac{m}{100}$ is the equation which must be solved to find the percent which names two-thirds.

Since $m \times 3 = 2 \times 100$ then $3 \times m = 200$ so $m = \frac{200}{3} = 66\frac{2}{3}$.

$$\frac{2}{3} = \frac{66\frac{2}{3}}{100} = 66\frac{2}{3}\%$$

Use this relation to find the percent names for $\frac{5}{8}$ and $\frac{7}{9}$.

SEE ANSWER FRAME (D–23).

All problems related to percent involve the statement between equivalent fractions in the form $\frac{p}{b} = \frac{c}{100}$. Since there are three variables, p, b and c, there are three problem types.
Unknown

p   What is 16% of 39? $\frac{p}{39} = \frac{16}{100}$

b   25 is 10% of what number? $\frac{25}{b} = \frac{10}{100}$

c   What percent of 27 is 2? $\frac{2}{27} = \frac{c}{100}$

CONTINUE TO D–25.

The equation $\frac{p}{b} = \frac{c}{100}$ is usually stated in a different form. Since $\frac{c}{100}$ is the percent, it is usually referred to as the rate, r. Thus, $r = 3\% = \frac{3}{100}$.

In this form, $\frac{b}{p} = r$ or $p = b \times r$.

"p" represents *percentage* which is the answer to the question, "What is r% of b?" Thus, 6% of 10 is .6, so .6 is the percentage. Many people confuse *percent* and *percentage*. Percentage is the product of a percent and a given number.

All percent problems relate to "r% of b is p" $r \times b = p$.

Problems can be represented by one of these three equations:
    A. r% of *some number* is p, $r \times \square = p$
    B. *some* % of b is p, $\square \times b = p$
    C. r% of b is *some number*, $r \times b = \square$

CONTINUE TO D–26.

D–26

Decide in each of the following whether you are looking for the percentage (p), the base (b) or the rate (r). Write the equation and calculate the result.

(a) Athens won 8 games and lost 2. What percent did they win?

(b) Bill had 90% on his mathematics quiz. There were 40 questions. How many did he get right?

(c) Lamps were marked "50% off." How much must you pay for a $13 lamp?

(d) Meat prices went up 6%. What will be the price of hamburger which was formerly $1 for each pound?

(e) Floor covering was discounted 10%. If you paid $8.10 for each square yard, what was the pre-sale price?

SEE ANSWER FRAME (D–26).

D–27

Solve the following problems by setting up a proportion in the form $\dfrac{p}{b} = \dfrac{c}{100}$.

(a) 40% of the class were boys. How big was the class if there were 24 boys?

(b) What percent of Joe's marbles are red if he has 20 red marbles and 16 blue marbles?

(c) A $30 swim suit was discounted 40%. What was the sale price?

SEE ANSWER FRAME (D–27).

(D–22)

$$\frac{1}{2} \times \frac{50}{50} = \frac{50}{100}$$

$$\frac{1}{10} \times \frac{10}{10} = \frac{10}{100}$$

$$\frac{3}{10} \times \frac{10}{10} = \frac{30}{100}$$

$$\frac{3}{4} \times \frac{25}{25} = \frac{75}{100}$$

When you help children discover this relationship, choose denominators which are factors of 100, i.e., 1, 2, 4, 5, 10, 20, 25, 50, 100.

The relation 1 = 100% is a particularly important concept. Any entity can be described in terms of its "wholeness," i.e., there is *exactly one*. A car is *one car*. A dog is *one dog*. $\dfrac{100}{100}$ is another name for 1 so any entity is 100% of itself!

Do you have an idea what can be done for $\dfrac{2}{3}$?

CONTINUE TO D–23.

$$\frac{5}{8} = \frac{m}{100}$$

$$8 \times m = 5 \times 100$$

$$8 \times m = 500$$

$$m = \frac{500}{8}$$

$$m = 62\frac{1}{2}$$

$$\frac{5}{8} = \frac{62\frac{1}{2}}{100} = 62\frac{1}{2}\%$$

$$\frac{7}{9} = \frac{m}{100}$$

$$9 \times m = 7 \times 100$$

$$9 \times m = 700$$

$$m = \frac{700}{9}$$

$$m = 77\frac{7}{9}$$

$$\frac{7}{9} = \frac{77\frac{7}{9}}{100} = 77\frac{7}{9}\%$$

CONTINUE TO D–24.

D–28

The crucial decision is always related to "given" and "unknown." Since percent means "parts of 100," translation of questions involving percent to these words will often help decide what is known and what is unknown. Substitution of "parts of 100" or "hundredths" for "%" will sometimes help.

Examples:

    A. What is 20% of 30?

        What is 20 hundredths of 30? $\frac{20}{100} \times 30 = \square$

    B. 9 is what percent of 36?

        9 is how many hundredths of 36? $\frac{9}{36} = \frac{x}{100}$ or $9 = \frac{x}{100} \times 36$

    C. 18 is 40% of what number?

        18 is 40 hundredths of what number? $\frac{40}{100} \times \square = 18$

CONTINUE TO D–29.

D–29

Translate the questions in frames D–26 and D–27 and write an appropriate equation; the first one is done for you:

    8 games is what percent of 10 games?

    8 is how many hundredths of 10?

$$8 = \frac{\square}{100} \times 10$$

SEE ANSWER FRAME (D–29).

(D–26)

(a) You are looking for r, the percent.

$$r\% \text{ of } 10 \text{ is } 8, \square \times 10 = 8, so \square = \frac{8}{10} = 80\%.$$

(b) You are looking for the percentage, p.
90% of 40 is p, $.9 \times 40 = \square$ so $\square = 36.$

(c) You are looking for the percentage, p.
50% of $13 is p, $.5 \times 13 = \square$ so $\square = 6.50.$

(d) You are looking for the percentage, p.
6% of $1 is p, $.06 \times 1 = \square$ so $\square = 6¢.$ The new price is $1.06.

(e) You are looking for the base, b.
90% of b is $8.10, $.9 \times \square = \$8.10$ so $\square = \$9.00.$

CONTINUE TO D–27.

(D–27)

(a) $\dfrac{24}{x} = \dfrac{40}{100}, \quad \begin{array}{l} 40x = 2400 \\ x = 60 \end{array}$

(b) $\dfrac{20}{36} = \dfrac{x}{100}, \quad \begin{array}{l} 36x = 2000 \\ x = 55\frac{5}{9}\% \end{array}$

(c) *Sale Price*

$$\frac{x}{30} = \frac{60}{100}, \quad \begin{array}{l} 100x = 1800 \\ x = \$18 \end{array}$$

or Discount

$$\frac{x}{30} = \frac{40}{100}, \quad \begin{array}{ll} 100x = 1200 & 30 - 12 = \$18 \\ x = \$12 \end{array}$$

CONTINUE TO D–28.

(D–29)

D–26, (b) What is 90% of 40?
What is 90 hundredths of 40?

$\square = \dfrac{90}{100} \times 40$

D–26, (c) What is 50% of 13?
What is 50 hundredths of 13?

$\square = \dfrac{50}{100} \times 13$

D–26, (d) What is 106% of 1?
What is 106 hundredths of 1?

$\square = \dfrac{106}{100} \times 1$

D–26, (e) $8.10 is 90% of what?
$8.10 is 90 hundredths of what?

$\$8.10 = \dfrac{90}{100} \times \square$

D–27, (a) 40% of what is 24?
40 hundredths of what is 24?

$\dfrac{40}{100} \times \square = 24$

D–27, (b) 20 is what percent of 36?
20 is how many hundredths of 36?

$20 = \dfrac{\square}{100} \times 36$

D–27, (c) What is 60% of $30?
What is 60 hundredths of $30?

$\square = \dfrac{60}{100} \times 30$

THE END.

Decimals and Percents Self-Test

1. Determine whether $1.34 > 1.9$ or $1.34 < 1.9$ by converting to fractions and by using your graph paper.

2. A. Demonstrate with graph paper: $1.8 + 2.54$
   B. Demonstrate with your pocket chart: $3.5 - 1.67$

3. Demonstrate with your pocket chart: 3×3.57

4. Estimate these quotients by using place value names:
   A. $6.23 \div .41$ B. $.00689 \div 2.31$

5. Demonstrate with your pocket chart $7.41 \div 3$

6. How could you help children discover where to place the decimal point in addition of decimal fractions? in multiplication?

7. Demonstrate with graph paper that $1 = 100\%$ and that $\frac{75}{100} = 75\%$.

8. Solve these problems:
   A. Bill ate three pieces of pie and Gary ate two. What percent of the total pie eaten was consumed by Bill?
   B. Ten percent of the 80 drivers failed their driving test. How many failed?

Answers to Decimals and Percents Self-Test

1. $1.34 = 1\frac{34}{100} = \frac{134}{100}$

   $1.9 = 1\frac{9}{10} = \frac{19}{10} = \frac{190}{100}$

   $\frac{134}{100} < \frac{190}{100}$ *so* $1.34 < 1.9$

   If you are unsure of the use of graph paper, see frame (D–5).

2. See (D–7), D–8 and (D–8) if you are unsure.

3. See frame (D–11).

4. A. $\frac{6.23}{.41} \times \frac{100}{100} = \frac{623}{41} \longrightarrow \frac{62 \text{ tens}}{41 \text{ ones}} \longrightarrow 1 \text{ ten} = 10$

   B. $\frac{.00689}{2.31} \times \frac{100}{100} = \frac{.689}{231} \longrightarrow \frac{689 \text{ thousandths}}{231 \text{ ones}} \longrightarrow 2 \text{ thousandths} = .002$

5. See frame (D–16).

6. Addition: See frames D–6 and (D–6).
   Multiplication: See frames D–10 and (D–10).

7. By definition, $1\% = \frac{1}{100}$ so a unit square region which is divided into 100 equal sub-regions has $1 = \frac{100}{100} = 100\%$; $1\% = \frac{1}{100}$ so $75\% = \frac{75}{100}$.

8. A. Bill ate 3 pieces; 5 were eaten altogether:

   $\frac{3}{5} = \frac{60}{100} = 60\%$

   B. 10% of 80 failed.

   10 hundredths of 80 failed. $\frac{10}{100} \times 80 = \square = 8$

Other Instructional Materials

Beware! Do not assume transfer! *Obviously,* decimal fractions are very much like whole numbers in many operational respects. Obvious to whom? Yes, to you. It is probably *not* obvious to a child.

The place value properties of decimal fractions should be stressed. Children need experiences which help them realize that 10 tenths = 1 one and 10 hundredths = 1 tenth just as they learned that 10 tens = 1 hundred and 10 ones = 1 ten. Transfer can be facilitated by using aids similar to those used in primary grades relative to whole numbers and by relating decimal fraction concepts to fraction concepts.

Two useful aids are graph paper and an abacus. Combined use of decimal fraction and fraction examples with aids will help build bridges, i.e., promote transfer. Suppose you have two abaci or two pocket charts or two sets of graph paper of different color. With one, you can work a whole number problem and with the other, you can use the *same digits* as decimal fractions. The "agreement" of procedures can be demonstrated with fractions. Here is an illustration:

24	$.24$	$\dfrac{24}{100} + \dfrac{39}{100}$	
$+39$	$+.39$		

Tens	Ones		Tenths	Hundredths
XX	XXXX		XX	XXXX
XXX	XXXXX		XXX	XXXXX
	XXXX			XXXX

$$\frac{63}{100}$$

$$\frac{50}{100} + \frac{13}{100}$$

$$\frac{5}{10} + \frac{13}{100}$$

Familiarity with instructional aids will help children relate to operational procedures more readily. (Graph paper can be dittoed in sections of 100 squares and placed under an acetate sheet for children's repeated use.)

Other environmental objects which can be used to build decimal number concepts are odometers (mileage indicators), rain gauges, number lines (especially centimeter rulers) and pegboards.

Odometers are particularly good in that they reinforce the place value relatedness between tenths and ones, ones and tens, etc. Instruction with decimal fractions should usually begin with tenths.

Many pegboards have exactly ten rows of ten (100 pegs). A row is one tenth and a single peg is one hundredth. Such a board is particularly useful as a percent board since each peg represents one percent.

Money can be used but you should be aware that children do not generally think of a dime as a fractional part of a dollar. They usually think of it as a single entity, *one dime,* or as a group, *ten cents.* The relationship between dimes and dollars must be established before money can be used as a meaningful aid. Even though children can add $3.84 and $1.67, their backgrounds lead them to think of 384¢ and 167¢ rather than decimal fractions. Just do not assume that the relation is obvious to children.

In *some* schools, references to stock market reports are interesting and meaningful. If you are teaching in such an environment, the daily newspaper is a rich source of teaching material.

Instructional Strategies

Children can build upon previous experiences with fractions, but concrete materials should still be used. The progression of developmental stages indicated that many children will still be functioning at the level of concrete operations. Decimal fractions should be introduced concretely; slow learners, especially, need considerable concrete experiences. Faster learners may need *less* but they should definitely have *some*.

The following are some of the concepts of this unit:

A. Relation between decimal fractions and fractions, and notation for decimal fractions

B. Writing decimal fraction numerals as fractions for computing sums and differences of tenths, hundredths, and tenths and hundredths

C. Addition and subtraction of tenths and hundredths *without* regrouping

D. Addition and subtraction of tenths and hundredths *with* regrouping

E. Addition and subtraction of "ragged decimals" with tenths and hundredths

F. Extension of addition and subtraction of decimals beyond hundredths

G. Writing decimal fraction numerals as fractions for computing products

H. Multiplication of tenths, hundredths, and tenths and hundredths

I. Extension of multiplication

J. Writing decimal fraction numerals as fractions to compute quotients

K. Computing quotients involving ones, tenths and hundredths

L. Estimating quotients and extending division

M. Relation between fractions, decimals and percents

N. Computing percents

O. Use of the p = br relation

Sample Objectives.   The child will be able to:

D. Show sums and differences of tenths and hundredths with regrouping on a pocket chart (concrete).

D. Show sums and differences of tenths and hundredths with regrouping by drawing pictures or diagrams to represent place value groupings (semi-concrete).

D. Compute sums and differences of tenths and hundredths with regrouping without the use of aids (abstract).

N. Determine a percent when given a fraction by using a 100 peg-board (concrete).

N. Determine a percent when given a fraction by using graph paper with 100 unit-square regions (semi-concrete).

N. Determine a percent without the use of aids when given a fraction (abstract).

As was mentioned in Chapter 4, the curriculum is similar to a musical score. In the three-beat measure, beat one is concrete, beat two is semi-concrete and beat three is abstract. In primary grades the emphasis is on beat one. In the intermediate grades, the emphasis is lessened on beat one and is shifted to beats two and three. However, beat one is still sounded!

Topics for Discussion and Projects

1. Suggest other aids for teaching decimals and percents.

2. Demonstrate some of the concepts of this chapter with aids available to you.

3. Write other behavioral objectives for the concrete, semi-concrete and abstract levels.

4. Write evaluation items for the objectives listed in the last section of this chapter or on the objectives you wrote for the previous item.

Other Teacher Education Resources

Filmstrip

Using Per Cent, Popular Science (7H–6)

Films

T7 Decimals: Addition and Subtraction, National Council of Teachers of Mathematics (Silver Burdett Company)

T8 Decimals: Multiplication and Division, National Council of Teachers of Mathematics (Silver Burdett Company)

C

Metric
and
Non-Metric
Geometry

17

Understanding and Teaching Measurement Concepts

Since maturation plays an important role in the child's development of number concepts, you probably will not be surprised to learn that maturational considerations are also important in the child's conception of measurement.

Section one of this chapter presents the major maturational and experiential considerations relative to measurement instruction, and section two is a programmed section designed to help you understand measurement concepts and generate instructional strategies. The last section of the chapter discusses measurement objectives.

Measurement: Maturational Readiness

Conservation of number (quantity) was a necessary prerequisite for total understanding of number and addition. Similarly, conservation of length is necessary for total understanding of linear measurement, and conservation of area is a necessary prerequisite for total understanding of two-dimensional measurement.

Very few children in grade one and few children in grade two are conservers of length and area. Here are two illustrations of my daughter's work which will help you comprehend lack of conservation. Her age is $4\frac{1}{2}$ years.

Length. Amy, here are two trains which are getting ready to leave the station. Is this one (A) longer or this one (B) or are they the same length?

A
B

They are the same length.
This train (B) is ready to leave so he begins to pull out of the station. Choo-choo, choo-choo, choo-choo. Now is this train (A) longer or is this one (B) or are they the same length?

A
B

This one is longer. (B)
Most six-year-olds and many seven-year-olds will give such responses. They are still perception bound and tend to focus on a single attribute. Since the movement is eye-catching, they tend to focus on the movement at the extremity and notice that the end of one is past the end of the other. They do not compensate for the corresponding difference at the opposite end.

Area. Amy, will you place this stick across the middle of this page and pretend we have equal pastures for our cows to eat grass?
Yes, Daddy. (She places the stick).

Now whose cows have more grass to eat, yours or mine or are they both the same?
They're the same.
Let's each build a house. (Houses are placed.) Now whose cows have more grass, yours or mine or are they the same?

They're the same.
Here, Amy, you build this addition on your house and I'll build an addition on my house. Now whose cows have more grass to eat, or are they the same?

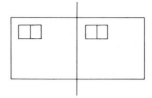

They're the same.
Now you build a big addition onto your house and my mother-in-law is coming to live with me so I will build her a house on the other side of the pasture. Now whose cows have more grass to eat, yours or mine or are they the same?
My cows have more grass, Daddy. (B)

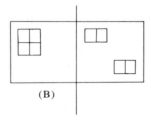

(B)

Again, most six-year-olds and many seven-year-olds will give such responses. They do not conserve area so they cannot fully comprehend two-dimensional measurement. In a given third-grade class, it is quite possible that about a quarter of the children *will not conserve* length and area.

Another mental skill which is requisite to total comprehension of measurement is transitivity. When you measure a room with a yardstick, you place the rule on the floor several times, A, B, C, D. The repeated use of the ruler is called *iteration,* which simply means that you use the unit of measure repeatedly. When you do so, you must *believe* that the first time you place the ruler on the floor, A, measures the same length as the second, B, and so on. Consider the relation "has the same measure as" which can be represented by "$\underset{=}{m}$". Now A $\underset{=}{m}$ B and B $\underset{=}{m}$ C so A $\underset{=}{m}$ C. This is the use of the transitive property relative to the measuring relation. The child must believe in this property with respect to measures if the results of measuring are to make sense! Smedslund's (4) research supports the development of transitivity of length at about the same age as conservation acquisitions. They both occur at an average age of eight years. As Lovell says,

> For true measurement of distances and lengths, the child must be able to recognize that any length may be decomposed into a series of intervals

which are known to be equal, and that one of them may be applied to each of the others in turn (2:106).

The movement of a non-conserver to conservation brings the child to a new stage.

> This last development involves two new operations in logic. The first operation is the arbitrary *division* of the object to be measured into sub-units the same length as the measuring rod, realizing that the whole is the sum of its parts. The second operation; *displacement* or *substitution,* allows him to apply or substitute one part (the measuring rod) upon another (the object being measured) an appropriate number of times, thereby building a system of units (1:191).

Conservation of length and conservation of area occur about the same time. Seventy-five percent of all children conserve length and area by about 8 or $8\frac{1}{2}$ years of age.

Measurement: Readiness Experiences

What are the implications for teaching measurement concepts of the maturational factors described in the previous section?

First and foremost, teachers must take cognizance of developmental differences. Some children conserve as early as six years of age and others do not conserve until nine years of age. However, the factors cited do not imply complete absence of measurement instruction for pre-conservers.

The following concepts can be developed intuitively with pre-conservers. Pre-conservers probably *will not* totally grasp the concepts; this is the nature of nearly all intuitive knowledge:

A. Objects can be compared by
   1. superposition or "bringing together," or
   2. by relating them to a third object which is movable.
B. Objects can be described in terms of other objects with greater movability or of general acquaintance of a given audience.
C. Objects can be compared and described with other objects which are continuous or discrete (iterative).
D. Comparisons and descriptions are approximate.
E. Objects used to describe or compare can be arbitrarily chosen.

Experiences in grades one and two focus on problem situations. Standard units are *not* used. Children work in small groups and create their own solutions. Then they carry out the solutions and present them to the rest of the class. You can make comments which direct their attention to the five generalizations above without being wordy or sophisticated. Sample problems and alternative solutions are presented in the programmed section of this chapter.

Teachers in grades three, four and five can build upon generalizations and intuitive concepts by extending them to standard units. Return to the five generalizations after you have gone through the programmed section; they should be clarified by the materials which follow.

In this programmed section, you are asked to respond to questions. They are designed to engage your active participation and to stimulate your imagination. Respond to all questions. Each answer is located on the second page following.

Measurement

Objectives

At the completion of this unit, you will be able to

(1) Describe activities which develop the concept of precision relative to a given type of measure, e.g., length, area, volume, angle measure.

(2) Describe realistic problem situations for children to solve without the aid of standard units of measure and suggest alternate solution schemes.

(3) Describe activities designed to develop the concept of approximation of length, area, volume and angle measures.

(4) Suggest several non-standard units of measure which can be used for descriptive purposes to communicate length, area and volume.

(5) Determine perimeters of given figures.

(6) Determine areas of given figures made up of circles, rectangles, triangles, or portions of them.

(7) Describe activities for developing concepts of perimeter and congruence.

(8) Determine the area of a given geoboard figure.

(9) Describe activities designed to help children discover common perimeter, area and volume formulas.

Materials Needed

Geoboard or Graph Paper
Lots of imagination!

Assumptions

Children will encounter measurement concepts as they are maturationally and experientially ready as outlined in the first section of this chapter.

Note

Proceed slowly. Take time to consider the questions raised. The time spent now will help you become aware of some more facets and challenges of good mathematics instruction.

Exploratory Problem Situations Which Teach
Basic Characteristics of Measurement

Basically, people measure for two reasons. Either they want to *compare two or more items* for which measurement is a *means,* or they wish to *describe an item* in which case measurement is an *end.* You obviously notice that both cases involve comparisons either of two items through measurement or of an item to a measure. In the former, the measure is used to carry out a task but in the latter the measurement is an end in itself. Thus, most measures are used to *compare* or to *describe.*

In teaching measurement concepts, "real" problem situations should be used, i.e., problems of a nature similar to those encountered at home or in a business. Since transfer of problem-solving approaches is desired, you must learn to teach for transfer. Transfer is maximized when instruction closely approximates the "real" conditions in which the learner will need to call upon the generalization or concept to solve a new problem. Contrived problems may allow you to teach a concept, but they will not greatly help the child recognize appropriate uses. You will now explore some problem-types through which characteristics of measurement can be taught.

CONTINUE TO MS–2.

A. Measurement and Comparison

Example

> *Scene:*   Second-grade Classroom
>
> *Problem:* "Will this table fit under the window?"
>
> > This is a "real" question related to height. List several solutions children might suggest. Check your list with the list of ideas in the answer frame. No rulers allowed!

SEE ANSWER FRAME (MS–2).

Two objects, the window and the table, were compared. The measurement was a *means* of answering the question. Consider this area problem situation:

> *Scene:*   Third-grade Classroom
>
> *Problem:* "Do we have enough contact paper to cover this table?" (The table has an irregular shape.)

This, too, is a "real" problem. You encounter problems like this one often. You don't want to ruin the paper unless you know you have enough to do the job. What are some solutions small groups of children might suggest? Check the list in the answer frame. No common measuring tools and no formulas allowed!

SEE ANSWER FRAME (MS–3).

MS–4

Activities such as those just described help children learn that various objects and various strategies can be utilized to compare length and area. Try one more:

> *Scene:*   Fourth-grade Social Studies Class
>
> *Problem:* "Which of the two lakes on this map would have the most room for skating, fishing, and water skiing?"

How could small groups answer this? Check your ideas with those listed on the answer frame. Think first! Prove your ingenuity!

SEE ANSWER FRAME (MS–4).

MS–5

Each of the problems and solution types suggested are designed to teach three basic characteristics of measurement:

> I. Measurements *compare.*
>
> II. *Units* of measure can be *arbitrarily* chosen.
>
> III. Measurements are *approximate*.

Explain what is meant by each. Check your ideas against those in the answer frame.

SEE ANSWER FRAME (MS–5).

MS–6

B. *Measurement and Description*

The problem situations cited involve instances of measurement as a *means*. Measures are taken as intermediary steps in the solution of a question which is more extensive than, "How big is it?" Situations of this type help children readily observe that they can arbitrarily choose a unit, that their measures are "off," i.e., approximate, and that they can compare objects by using units of measure.

Many instances occur in everyday experiences in which you wish to know, "How big is it?" Such questions involve measurements in a *descriptive* sense. They allow you to compare a given object with a general population or class of objects as the height of a person related to the height of most people, or they allow you to compare one object with another not physically present, as when you decide how tall a door to buy to fit a given doorway. In the latter case, measures are often needed which can be readily communicated as through a phone conversation.

CONTINUE TO MS–7.

Most of the objectives used in previous problems can be used to explore descriptive cases as well. You can ask youngsters, "How tall is John?" or "How long is the desk?" Divide the children into groups of two, three or four. Give each group a dittoed sheet with the following headings:

Object Measured	Object Used to Measure	Number in Length	
		Estimate (Guess)	Measure
Desk			
John			

As the groups begin, a question will likely arise. Think! What is the question?

SEE ANSWER FRAME (MS–7).

   A. Choose an object such as a pencil, book, shoe, hand, or eraser. See how many of a given unit can be used to measure the table and window heights.

   B. Choose several objects of a type and stack them, e.g., books, shoe boxes, erasers, etc.

   C. Choose several different kinds of objects which when stacked are about the same height as the table, e.g., 1 box, 4 books, and an eraser.

   D. Choose a long object such as a piece of string, a stick, a rope, a board, or one's body to mark the height of the window or the desk and compare that length to the other.

   E. Move the desk to the window.

As you can see, there are many ways to answer the question. Each *object* suggested by the child represents an alternative solution.

CONTINUE TO MS–3.

This is an area question. Children will suggest small or large units or a large, continuous "replacement."

   A. The replacement idea is inherent in the suggestion that newspaper be cut the shape of the table and then cut in pieces to see if all the newspaper can be placed on the sheet of contact paper; construction paper or cloth could also be used.

   B. Large units could include books, sheets of paper, shoes and so on.

   C. Small units could include playing cards, hands, dominoes, milk cartons, etc.

   D. Combination of units: books, cards, erasers, coins, dominoes, and so on.

CONTINUE TO MS–4.

(MS–4)

This is another "real" situation. Here are some alternatives; perhaps you thought of several others:

  A. Trace one lake on onionskin paper and cut it out. See if it can be cut into pieces which will fit inside the untraced lake.

  B. Use rice, macaroni, lima beans, coins, or some other small objects. See if all the ones which fit in one will fit in the other.

  C. Like B, above, only fill both and count.

  D. Use objects of more than one size to try to fill one up. See if the objects will then fit into the other.

CONTINUE TO MS–5.

(MS–5)

  I. Compare—When you measure, you compare the object being measured with the selected unit of measure to find the relationship between them or between two given objects whose relation is desired.

  II. Arbitrary—Any object which allows you to make the desired comparison can be used as the unit of measure; you can arbitrarily choose an appropriate unit of measure.

  III. Approximate—Objects chosen for making comparisons rarely even *appear* to be in exact "fit." When you measure, there is nearly always a visible shortage or excess regardless of the unit selected.

CONTINUE TO MS–6.

MS–8

Assume these answers were obtained by a group:

Object Measured	Objects Used to Measure	Number in Length		
		Estimate	At Least	Not Quite
1. John	1. Math Book	3	4	5
	2. Pencil	10	8	9
	3. Block of wood	2	2	3
	4. Cement blocks on wall	9	6	7
	5. Chalkboard eraser	10	8	9
2. Door	1. Geography book	6	6	7

Group decisions should be presented to the class and discussed. From this work children should begin to realize that small units of measure have smaller margins of error than large units. This is the concept of *precision*. Define *precision* in your own words. See if your definition agrees in general respects with the one in the answer frame.

SEE ANSWER FRAME (MS–8).

(MS–7)

"What should we do when it doesn't come out exact?"

Suggest that they write *two* numerals under the "Number in Length" column. The first can say "A little more than" and the other "A little less than," or "At least" and "Not quite" as in the next frame, MS–8.

When a group has finished, ask the members to decide which of the numeral pairs under the "Number in Length" column is the "best" piece of information in the sense that it communicates to other people most exactly the lengths measured.

CONTINUE TO MS–8.

MS–9

The activities described are particularly relevant for first- and second-graders who may be pre-conservers. For them, they may well serve as readiness experiences. If, on the other hand, these activities are used in grade three or four then, after two or three or four days of exploratory activities of the type described so far, children can be confronted with a problem that creates a need for standard measures. Feet, inches and pounds are standard measures. What are standard measures? Why are they needed? Compare your ideas with those listed in the answer frame. Think!

SEE ANSWER FRAME (MS–9).

MS–10

Children can be guided to adopt their own standard units. First they can agree to use a cement block on the wall or a reading book or a pencil. They can discuss the problems associated with each. What are some problems associated with the reading book? Compare your list with the answer frame.

SEE ANSWER FRAME (MS–10).

After the class has adopted a standard unit, explore possible ways of overcoming items B, C and D of the previous answer frame. A possible alternative is to use the reading book but then cut pieces of paper to the appropriate length. The paper strips will be easier to carry around and easier to use. To increase precision, they can be subdivided. Children can use their own units and subunits to measure and to learn conversion principles by renaming measures.

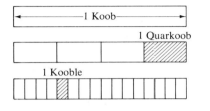

4 Quarkoobs $\underset{=}{m}$ * 1 Koob

4 Koobles $\underset{=}{m}$ 1 Quarkoob

* Read, "Has the same measure as" or "Is equal in measure to."

Answer these:
- A. 1 Koob $\underset{=}{m}$ _____ Koobles
- B. 3 Koobs $\underset{=}{m}$ _____ Quarkoobs $\underset{=}{m}$ _____ Koobles
- C. 82 Koobles $\underset{=}{m}$ _____ Koobs _____ Koobles (This last one has several answers!)

SEE ANSWER FRAME (MS–11).

Problems necessitating telephone communications can establish a need for *standard units of measure* for populations outside the class. Ordering floor covering or a new door or enough crepe paper to trim the bulletin board are just a few examples which can be used. At this time foot rulers can be introduced, followed by inches and yards. Through activities similar to these, children can learn that measures allow one to compare and describe, and that they are approximate and in varying degrees of precision. Standards are needed. Local, limited standards can be created but generalized standards are also necessary.

CONTINUE TO MS–13.

Precision refers to the degree of exactness of a measure. Small units communicate more precision than large units. A measure which is between 2 and 3 book lengths does not communicate a given length as well as the same length reported by the number of small erasers, between 9 and 10, or the number of pencils placed side-by-side, say between 62 and 63. The margins of error are one book, one eraser and one pencil diameter, respectively.

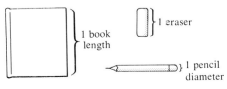

Erasers are smaller than books so erasers yield a more precise measure than books.

The pencil is smaller than the eraser so pencil diameters yield a more precise measure than erasers.

CONTINUE TO MS–9.

MS–13

In the exploratory work with length, children were asked to solve problems. Some solutions involved continuous quantities such as a piece of string, part of a board, piece of rope, etc. With such quantities a simple "more than" or "less than" was used to answer the question. Other solutions involved units which were used repeatedly. They could be counted although counting certainly was not necessary. Such measures are called *iterative* measures; a unit is used several times. Name some iterative measures and continuous-type quantities which could be used for deciding (a) which of two jars holds more, and (b) whether a given plastic or metal garbage can holds more.

SEE ANSWER FRAME (MS–13).

(MS–9)

A *standard measure* or *standard unit of measure* is a quantity agreed upon by a group of people to which other quantities can be compared or by which other quantities can be described. For example the *meter* is accepted by people who live in Europe as a *standard measure of length*. They use it to measure length for purposes of comparison and description. Standard measures are needed to *facilitate communication* about length, weight, volume and so on.

CONTINUE TO MS–10.

(MS–10)

 A. People outside the school will probably not have one.

 B. It is bulky to use.

 C. It is cumbersome to carry around.

 D. It is not a very precise measure.

CONTINUE TO MS–11.

(MS–11)

A. 16 Koobles

B. 12 Quarkoobs and 48 Koobles

C. 1 Koob 66 Koobles
2 Koobs 50 Koobles
3 Koobs 34 Koobles
4 Koobs 18 Koobles
5 Koobs 2 Koobles

CONTINUE TO MS–12.

MS–14

Estimation.   Throughout all the experiences with length, area, volume, and other measures, youngsters should be encouraged to "guess" before carrying out the activities. Through such experiences they will learn to estimate and there will be, hopefully, transfer of the estimation concept to work with number operations.

When children work in small groups have each child write down his estimate and compare it with estimates of team members. Try to place a column for estimations on all dittoed group and individual materials.

CONTINUE TO MS–15.

MS–15

When third-grade children have one-dimensional measurement skills (length), they can study the concept of *perimeter*. The perimeter of a polygon is the *sum of the measures of the sides*. Rooms, book covers, and other square, rectangular and triangular shapes can be measured by children to determine perimeter. Thin wire or heavy string can be used to determine the perimeter of objects or figures of unusual shape. Get your geoboard or use graph paper for the following activities.

Make several rectangles and record the following information:

Length	*Width*	*Perimeter*
1.		
2.		

What is the relation between the columns of numbers?
Make some squares. What is this relation?

SEE ANSWER FRAME (MS–15).

(MS–13)

(A) *Two Jars*

Continuous—water, sand, sugar, various liquids, shortening, paste, etc.

Iterative—Discrete–navy beans, lima beans, rice, macaroni, stones, marbles, bottle caps, etc.

(B) *Two Garbage Cans*

Continuous—water, sand, gravel, dirt, etc.

Iterative—Discrete–tin cans, baseballs, stones, books, pop bottles, ping pong balls, bricks, etc.

CONTINUE TO MS–14.

MS–16

After third- and fourth-grade children have explored the concept of area with non-standard, irregularly shaped units, square units can be introduced. The geoboard or graph paper can be used. As with length, the distance between two pegs on the geoboard or the length of one square on the graph paper is arbitrarily defined as one unit. The unit length must be the *horizontal* or *vertical* distance between two pegs; the diagonal distance may create problems. Find the area of the following figures with your geoboard or graph paper.

A. 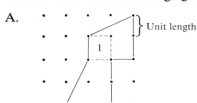   B.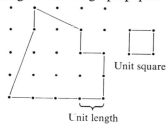

(*Hint:* Break the figures up into squares, rectangles and triangles.)

Note: 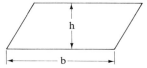 Area of triangle is $\frac{1}{2} \times 3 = 1\frac{1}{2}$.

These are appropriate fourth-grade activities.

SEE ANSWER FRAME (MS–16).

MS–17

On your geoboard or graph paper make several rectangles and describe the pattern:

Length   Width   Area

Now repeat for parallelograms*:

Length of bottom (b)   Distance from top to bottom (h)   Area

Compare your results with those on the answer frame. Be sure to keep *b* parallel to one side of your geoboard.

* A *parallelogram* is a four-sided polygon whose opposite sides are parallel.

SEE ANSWER FRAME (MS–17).

MS–18

Now make several triangles. Record this information and see if you can see a pattern.

Length of base (b)   *Distance from base to top (h)*   *Area*

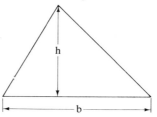

Note: Keep *b* on a line or row of nails.

SEE ANSWER FRAME (MS–18).

MS–19

A *trapezoid* is a four-sided polygon two sides of which are parallel.

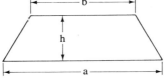

Make several trapezoids on your geoboard or graph paper. Record the following information and see if you can discover the pattern:

Length of one parallel side (a)   *Length of the other parallel side (b)*   *Distance between the parallel sides (h)*   *Area*

SEE ANSWER FRAME (M–19).

(MS–15)

	Rectangles			Squares	
Length	Width	Perimeter	Length	Perimeter	
3	1	8	1	4	
4	1	10	2	8	
4	2	12	3	12	

$$2L + 2W = 2 \times (L + W) = P \qquad 4 \times L = P$$

Fourth-grade children can be lead to discover these simple perimeter patterns which yield formulas.

CONTINUE TO MS–16.

MS–20

Through many such experiences, formulas for perimeter and area become meaningful. Similar strategies can be used with building blocks to discover simple volume formulas.

Each of the units for length, area or volume used repeatedly is called an *iterative* measure. Iterative measures involve the concept of congruence. When objects or figures are *congruent,* they have *identical size and shape.* When a ruler is used for linear measures, each iteration is assumed to be congruent, i.e., each foot is congruent (the same size as) with every other foot. When an inch square is iterated to measure area, each inch square is assumed to be congruent (same size *and* shape) to every other inch square. Lack of congruence is one reason why more crude measures yield results with more error. How can children check linear and area congruence?

SEE ANSWER FRAME (MS–20).

(MS–16)

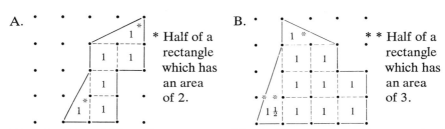

A. * Half of a rectangle which has an area of 2.

B. ** Half of a rectangle which has an area of 3.

Note that B could have been computed by finding the *external* area and subtracting: $16 - 3 - 2\frac{1}{2} = 10\frac{1}{2}$.

A. A = 6   B. A = $10\frac{1}{2}$

CONTINUE TO MS–17.

(MS–17)

| *Rectangles* | | | | *Parallelograms* | | |
Length	Width	Area		Length	Heighth	Area
3	2	6		4	2	8
4	2	8		3	2	6
5	1	5		4	1	4
5	2	10		5	2	10

L × W = A   L × H = A

2 [diagram]   [diagram] H = 2
   3   L = 3

2 × 3 = 6   The shaded areas are the same.

Discovering area formulas is an appropriate fifth- and sixth-grade activity.

CONTINUE TO MS–18.

(MS–18)

Length of base (b)	Distance from base to top (h)	Area
4*	2	4
3	3	$4\frac{1}{2}$
5**	1	$2\frac{1}{2}$
4	4	8
$\frac{1}{2} \times$ b $\times$	h $=$	A

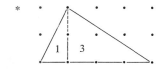

CONTINUE TO MS–19.

(MS–19)

a	b	h	A
3	2	1	$2\frac{1}{2}$*
4	2	1	3
4	2	2	6**
5	2	1	$3\frac{1}{2}$
5	2	2	7
(a $+$ b) $\times \frac{1}{2} \times$ h $=$			A

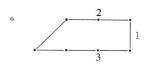

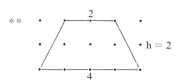

CONTINUE TO MS–20.

MS–21

Children can also discover the approximate value of π. How could you help children make this discovery?

(*Hint:* Think of an activity which uses the relation C $= \pi$D. Solve this for π.)

SEE ANSWER FRAME (MS–21).

(MS–20)

Through *superposition,* i.e. placing one on top of the other. Straight lines can simply be measured since shape is no factor. Non-straight lines must have shape checked, however.

CONTINUE TO MS–21.

MS–22

With knowledge of perimeter, area and simple formulas, children in grades five and six can determine perimeters and areas of various shapes. Try this one. Find the perimeter *and* area. The ends are semi-circles.

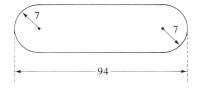

Remember:

Circumference = Pi × Diameter
$$C = \pi D$$

Area = Pi × Radius × Radius
$$A = \pi r^2$$

Use $\pi = \frac{22}{7}$

Hint: How long are the "straight stretches"?

SEE ANSWER FRAME (MS–22).

MS–23

Catching on? Try this one:

Use $\pi = \frac{22}{7}$

Compute the perimeter and area.

SEE ANSWER FRAME (MS–23)

Angle Measure. Activities related to those of linear measure can be used. Rough approximations can be made by superposition methods. One angle can be placed upon another to determine whether the first is smaller than, equal to, or larger than the second.

When superposition is not possible, measurement units must be used. Any arbitrarily chosen angle can be used as a unit angle. One can simply be cut from a piece of paper and used repeatedly. The usual characteristics can be developed through appropriate activities.

    (a) What are some sources of right (90°) angles?

    (b) How can children easily make a 45° angle? $22\frac{1}{2}°$?

    (c) How could children make some unit angles which are not 90° or 45° or $22\frac{1}{2}°$?

SEE ANSWER FRAME (MS–24).

Similar Figures. Work with angles is different in at least one major respect. The units for length, area and volume were *congruent,* but for angle measure they need only be *similar.* Similar figures have the same shape but only *proportionate* size. For area the following units could *not* be used interchangeably:

For angle measure, the following *can* be used interchangeably:

The angles are the same size, but the figures need not be the same size. Enlarged (various sizes) photos are excellent for teaching similarity.

THE END.

Since $C = \pi D$, then $\pi = \dfrac{C}{D}$.

Pi is the ratio of the circumference to the diameter.

Supply flexible rulers, or rigid rulers and string, several round objects such as bicycle tires, wood discs, cups, and tin cans. Ask youngsters to keep a record of the circumferences and diameters and to look for a relation between them. Some will notice that the relation is about 3:1.

CONTINUE TO MS–22.

(MS–24)

    a. Right angles (90°)—Corners of many objects: books, record albums, blocks of wood, a strip of paper folded in half, etc.

    b. 45° (half a right angle)—Fold a right angle in half; $22\frac{1}{2}°$ (one-fourth a right angle)—Fold a right angle in half *twice*.

    c. Others—Fold a rectangular sheet of paper diagonally, cut on the diagonal. Draw an angle on a piece of paper and cut it out; trace it if duplicates are needed.

CONTINUE TO MS–25.

(MS–22)

The perimeter is the distance around the outside.

The total distance is two semi-circles and two line segments or a circle of radius 7 and two line segments of length 80.

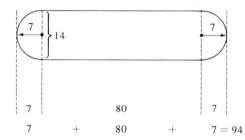

$$P = 80 + 80 + \pi D$$
$$P = 80 + 80 + \tfrac{22}{7} \times 14$$
$$P = 80 + 80 + 44$$

7   +   80   +   7 = 94 $P = 204$

The area is a circle and a rectangle.

    Circle: $A = \pi r^2 = \tfrac{22}{7} \times 7^2 = \tfrac{22}{7} \times 49 = 154$

    Rectangle: $A = L \times W = 80 \times 14 = 1120$

    Total Area $= 154 + 1120 = 1274$

CONTINUE TO MS–23.

(MS–23)

Perimeter	*Area*
3 sides of a rectangle and a semi-circle	Rectangle and semi-circle
$(14 + 14 + 28) + \tfrac{1}{2}(\tfrac{22}{7} \times 28)$	$(14 \times 28) + \tfrac{1}{2} \times (\tfrac{22}{7} \times 196)$
56 + 44	392 + 308
100	700

CONTINUE TO MS–24.

Measurement Self-Test

1. Describe an activity designed to develop the concept of precision relative to *area*.

2. Describe a realistic problem situation for children to solve related to *area*. Suggest some continuous and iterative units which might be used.

3. Describe an activity designed to develop the concept of approximation of volume.

4. Suggest several non-standard units for measuring the volume of a quart jar.

5. Find the perimeter of this figure:

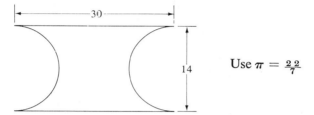

Use $\pi = \frac{22}{7}$

Find the area.

6. Describe an activity for developing the concept of congruence of area.

7. Determine the area of this geoboard figure:

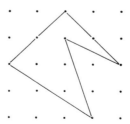

8. Describe activities designed to allow children to discover the formula for the perimeter of a rectangle; the area of a rectangle.

Answers to Measurement Self-Test

1. Example: Explain to the class that you want to buy some contact paper to fit an irregularly-shaped table in the room. Ask them to take turns measuring the table in groups. They can use any objects they wish. From this can ensue a discussion which will bring out that (1) the smallest units of measure give the most precise description, or (2) when large objects were used, small objects had to be used to fill in the left over space on the table top.

2. See the example above. Another example: Which of these two tables shall we use for our display to have the most room for projects?

     Continuous units: large sheets of paper or
                        material cut to an approximate fit
     Iterative units: books, sheets of paper, shoes,
                        hands, milk cartons

3. Ask children to decide which of three or four containers will hold the most beverage. Provide several objects of various size which can be used iteratively. Ask them to keep a record. Examine responses of groups which used the same container. Small containers which had to be used (iterated) many times will yield different results for groups. Explore the basis for this discrepancy.

4. Various kinds of dried beans and cereals, macaroni, marbles, pebbles, pop bottle caps, paper clips, night crawlers.

5. $P = 2l + 2\pi r = 2 \times 30 + 2 \times \frac{22}{7} \times 7$
$$= 60 + 44 = 104$$
$A = l \times w - \pi r^2 = 30 \times 14 - \frac{22}{7} \times 7 \times 7$
$$= 420 - 154 = 266$$

6. Bring a picture puzzle to class which has two or three pieces missing. Ask the children to replace them by using some cardboard provided.

   Bring "shapes" puzzles in which shapes must be matched to holes.

7.

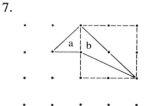

$$a = \tfrac{1}{2}, \quad b = 4 - 1 - 2 = 1$$

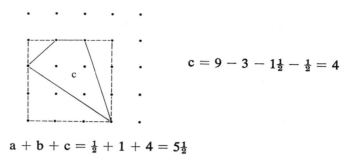

$$c = 9 - 3 - 1\tfrac{1}{2} - \tfrac{1}{2} = 4$$

$$a + b + c = \tfrac{1}{2} + 1 + 4 = 5\tfrac{1}{2}$$

8. See frames MS–15, (MS–15), MS–17 and (MS–17).

A Review of Intuitive Relationships

When readiness experiences were discussed at the beginning of the chapter, five generalizations were made relative to intuitively developed measurement concepts. Review them now.

A. *Objects can be compared (1) by superposition, or (2) by relating them to a third object which is movable.*

Children learn that linear measurement questions can be answered by actual comparison of lengths or by using a piece of string or some object which can be iterated.

B. *Objects can be described in terms of other objects with greater movability, or in terms of general acquaintance of a given audience.*

Children learn that lengths, areas and volumes can be described by using shoes, books, marbles, rice and so on. Objects which cannot be moved can be compared by using a third object which can. Problem situations creating a communication problem may be used to help children become aware of the need for standard units of measure.

C. *Objects can be compared and described with other objects which are continuous or discrete (iterative).*

When children want to compare two lengths or areas, or when they want to describe an object, they can use measures such as string or rope or paper which are used only once (are not iterated) or they can use objects which *can* be iterated. Here are some continuous measures:
Length—rope, string, body parts
Area—single piece of paper cut to approximate size and shape, or burlap or other fabric
Volume—water, sand, paste
Iterative measures could be a piece of string, book, rice, macaroni, coins and other objects *which can be counted* to describe the measure.

D. *Comparisons and descriptions are approximate.*

Children learn that measures of length, volume and angle size are never exact.

E. *Objects used to describe or compare can be arbitrarily chosen.*

Any object which helps a person answer a comparison question or describe an object satisfactorily can be used as a unit of measure.

A K-6 Summary

Measurement activities in kindergarten, first and second grade should focus on simple problem-solving situations without reference to standard measures.

Children should be allowed and encouraged to "invent" solution strategies. Such activities are readiness experiences for more formal work and develop intuitive understandings of measurement characteristics as noted earlier.

Children begin to conserve length and area at about the same time. Nearly all children are conservers by the end of grade three. During the latter part of grade three, children can be led to discover a need for standard measures. At that time foot, yard and inch rulers can be introduced and children can discover the relationships 3:1:36, respectively. After considerable experience with *actual measuring,* children can use *scaled strips of paper* with appropriate scales of 3:1:36 to interchange or convert real measures of scale drawings from one unit to another. Finally, they can work with *tables* of relations such as "1 foot $\overset{m}{=}$ 12 inches," "1 yard $\overset{m}{=}$ 3 feet," and so on.

Third- and fourth-graders can also use geoboards or graph paper to *count* areas and perimeters of figures. This should, of course, be preceded by actual measuring of length and area with non-standard units. Most fourth-graders can also discover simple perimeter formulas.

Work with *area formulas* should, in general, be delayed until at least grade five. According to Piaget *et al.* (3), children cannot fully understand the relationship between linear measures and calculation of area until they achieve formal operational thought; this does not occur for most children, as you recall, until the age of eleven or twelve.

Readiness work with volume can begin in grades four and five. Formal work, as with formulas, should follow area topics in grades five and six.

The use of formulas is an example of *indirect measurement.* Instead of measuring directly with objects, certain measurements (usually linear) are made and results calculated. Another example of indirect measurement is the use of proportions as you have probably done with shadows.

$$\frac{6}{4} = \frac{x}{16}$$

$$x = 24 \text{ ft.}$$

Objectives

Concrete, semi-concrete and abstract forms can roughly be compared to actual measures, scaled or representative models and tables of relationships. Here is an illustration from liquid measures.

Concrete. In accordance with procedures outlined in this chapter, children should be provided opportunities to discover relations among various standard measures of cup, pint, quart, half-gallon and gallon. They can fill containers with pints, quarts and cups and then try to find proportional relations among them. After such experiences with water or sand, they can move to semi-concrete experiences.

Semi-concrete. You can ditto proportional pieces of paper so that children can continue to manipulate relations as they seek to solve problems and make conversions. A whole page can be dittoed as a gallon, half-pages as half-gallons, quarter-pages as quarts, etc. Notice the *proportional sizes*. Children can manipulate pieces of paper to solve problems.

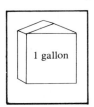 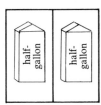 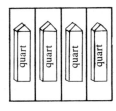  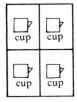

Abstract. After work with dittoed materials, children can work from tables or charts of equivalent measures. Now there is no referent, only number manipulations.

Many fine lab-type measurement activities for individuals and small groups in grades two through six can be found in the Measurement Mathset listed in the bibliography.

Additional Teacher Education Resources

Filmstrips

　　Introduction to Measurement, Popular Science (3H–8)
　　Measurement—Precision, Filmstrip-of-the-Month (1238)
　　Areas of Geometric Figures, Popular Science (7H–9)
　　Areas of Triangular Regions, Popular Science (6H–11)

Films

　　An Introduction to Geometry Via Nail-Boards, Madison Project

Kit

　　Mathset—Measurement, Scott Foresman

Bibliography

1. Copeland, Richard W. *How Children Learn Mathematics.* New York: The Macmillan Company, 1970.

2. Lovell, Kenneth. *The Growth of Understanding in Mathematics*. New York: Holt, Rinehart and Winston, Inc., 1971.

3. Piaget, J., B. Inhelder, and A. Szeminska. *The Child's Conception of Geometry*. New York: Basic Books, 1960.

4. Smedslund, Jan. "Development of Concrete Transitivity of Lengths in Children." *Child Development* (June 1963), Vol. 34, pp. 389–405.

18

Elementary School Geometry: Non-Metric

Curriculum *evolves*. During the past two decades "modern math" has been incorporated into the elementary school mathematics curriculum. The curriculum is not stagnant. It continues to change as it responds to pressures and needs of learners, mathematicians and society. Geometry is in a state of flux; it is evolving into a new, more dominant position in the elementary school curriculum. Analysis of trends in geometry provides an excellent opportunity to observe the evolutionary nature of curriculum.

The nature of the learner and the influence of mathematicians have been strong in the determination of geometric concepts in the curriculum since the late fifties and early sixties. Geometry was formerly reserved for high school at which time concepts of Euclidean geometry were formally and extensively explored. Now the number and variety of geometric experiences for youngsters has increased considerably.

Increased awareness and emphasis is cited by Vigilante who noted that,

Between the years 1954 and 1960 it [*The Arithmetic Teacher*] contains one article on the topic 'elementary school geometry.' In contrast, approximately twenty-five such articles appear between the years 1961 and 1966 (6:453).

One of the most significant factors influencing greater attention given to geometry is the Report of the Cambridge Conference on School Mathematicics, *Goals for School Mathematics*. The report of the 1963 conference says, "The task of the conference, as we conceived it, was exploratory thinking with a view to a long-range future" (3:3). A major concern was a reorganization of the mathematics curriculum which would have ". . . as its principal aspect the parallel development of geometry and arithmetic (or algebra in later years) from kindergarten on" (3:8). Some of the specific suggestions are listed here:

1. Identifying and naming various geometric configurations (3:33)
2. Visualization, such as cutting out cardboard to construct three-dimensional figures, where the child is shown the three-dimensional figure and asked to find his own way to cut the two-dimensional paper or cardboard (3:33)
3. Symmetry and other transformations leaving geometrical figures invariant. The fact that a line or circle can be slid into itself. The symmetries of squares and rectangles, circles, ellipses, etc., and solid figures like spheres, cubes, tetrahedra, etc. This study could be facilitated with mirrors, paper folding, etc. (3:33)
4. Use of straightedge and compass to do the standard geometric constructions such as comparing segments or angles, bisecting a segment or angle, etc. (3:34)
5. Similar figures, both plane and solid, starting from small and enlarged photographs, etc. (3:34)
6. Conic sections (3:38)
7. Equation determining a straight line (3:38)
8. Cartesian coordinates in three dimensions (3:38)

The recommendations received considerable attention and were widely discussed, debated and explored. Today there is little agreement as to the exact nature and extent of geometry experiences for children; however, the influence of Bruner and Piaget, especially, has given strength to certain points of view relative to content and methodology. According to Moredock (5) and Vigilante (6), there are several reasons for introducing many geometry concepts into the elementary school curriculum:

1. Students can gain a better understanding of their environment; they can see position, shape, and size in space as something they can understand, use, control, and manipulate to explore their environment.
2. Geometry strengthens the arithmetic program by providing geometric models for the arithmetic processes, so it can help children develop other mathematical insights.
3. In a practical sense, children can explore applications and learn that geometry is useful.

4. Children can learn to appreciate the aesthetic qualities of geometry.
5. Study of geometric concepts can help children grasp concepts of measurement.
6. Children can see a closer relation between mathematics and science.
7. Early study of geometry will enable children to acquire insights and will promote and develop creativity and inquiry.

A fundamental characteristic of the evolving geometry curriculum which seems to be accepted by nearly all mathematicians and educators is that elementary school experience will begin with exploratory, intuitive experiences.

> The geometry studied in the K–6 grades is often called 'informal geometry.' The 'informal' is not to be taken in any casual or sloppy sense but to indicate that the geometry is *not* formal or deductive (5:167).

Or, in the words of the Report,

> At the first stage an intuitive or pre-mathematics approach offers the opportunity of an early introduction of important concepts. There is time for each of these concepts, first drawn from the student's general experience, to be made more familiar and more precise, and time to develop the concept further. The concept can be used by the student from the beginning in appropriate simple contexts.
> The intuitive discussion should not be wrong or misleading, as it often is, but incomplete structurally (3:13–14).

As in previous chapters, informal and intuitive mathematics implies emphasis on pupil manipulation with a minimum of pupil verbalization. Concepts are developed through many experiences in which the child must discriminate differences *nonverbally*. Many positive examples can be encountered, as may many counterexamples; then the child can distinguish the attributes of the concept without being able to give a verbal description of the attributes. For example, six-year-olds can distinguish "square" from "not square" but they cannot define "squareness."

In this chapter special attention will be given to the problems of content and cognition. If you wish to explore some of the concepts in greater detail, study the references cited at the end of the chapter.

Sequential Treatment of Geometry in the Elementary School Curriculum

The child's concept of space proceeds through developmental stages. First the child is aware of very general notions such as "inside," "outside," order, and nearness. Gradually, he becomes more aware of shape and begins to notice that shape is an attribute by which objects differ and by which they can be classified. He develops the ability to internalize actions on objects at which time he can use his imagination to distort and change objects. Finally, at the stage of formal or logical operations, he understands the concept of point and can conceptualize infinite sets of points. In this section will be presented the development of concepts of geometry consistent with the child's ability to comprehend them.

Nursery School, Kindergarten—Topology

Some states will not allow citizens to drive if they have sight in only one eye. The reason is that depth-perception is limited. Visual cues of size and distance come, in general, from a set of experiences in living with objects and from sensory-motor cues from the eyes to the brain, i.e., the brain "computes" distance from readings sent from the eyes. The smaller the angle of focus, the farther the object and vice versa.

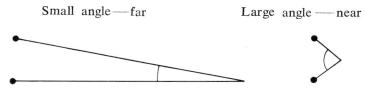

Small angle—far   Large angle—near

If you have had occasion to observe an infant, you probably noticed that eye-coordination is weak. The ability to focus comes with development and experience, and the interpretation of visual stimuli is probably a learned behavior. The very small child lacks good depth perception and the necessary skills to interpret visual stimuli, so what does the world look like to him?

The work of Piaget helps answer this question. The child does not appear to be aware of the constancy of size and shape, so the child does not readily accommodate changes of position and distance. Mama's coming and going is not associated with nearness and farness. Rather, Mama's face is small (far) or large (near) in the child's field of vision. Similarly, since the child does not possess the "habit" of believing in a single shape for objects, Mama's face has many shapes. Sometimes her eyes are high on her head and sometimes they are in the middle; sometimes she has two ears and sometimes one; sometimes she has two nostrils and sometimes none. These statements may seem odd to you but imagine how a friend's face changes in shape and visual composition when the head is lowered or raised, turned to the left or right or positioned straight ahead. You have a mental image of your friend's face which you consider a "given"; it is fixed in your mind. The infant probably has no such "given." You are willing to accommodate the changes as functions of your perspective rather than attributing the changes to physical distortion. The child is probably unable to do this because no *fixed* image exists. "Mama" is the sum total of many distortions with perhaps a familiar sound, her voice.

Hence, reality as the infant interprets it is akin to a piece of elastic material which is stretched. Mama does not turn her head; her face distorts. Her ear moves to the middle of the visual image. Mama does not simply come near; she gets bigger. The door does not simply open; it gets narrower. While recent studies indicate that young children have depth perception in the first few months of life, the inability to *interpret* it precisely as in the preceding paragraphs gives rise to a distorted concept of space. This distorted view will serve as the model for the discussion which follows.

Distortions similar to those cited are studied by a branch of mathematics called *topology*. Topological properties of space do not accommodate nearness and farness (no meaning to length). Neither do they accommodate shape. If one object can be distorted (transformed) into another, the two objects are *topologically equivalent*.

Imagine that you have a piece of rubber on which is drawn a circle. You could stretch the rubber in such a way as to form an ellipse, a square, a rectangle, a parallelogram or any other polygon. All these shapes are said to be *topologically equivalent* because one can be distorted to make the other. You might wonder if there are any characteristics which are constant when distortions are made. Yes, there are. Can you think of any?

Proximity.   Things which were "close" will remain close in a relative sense. For example, if you place three paper clips on a rubber band so that the middle one is not equally spaced, it will remain unequally spaced in the same sense when the rubber band is stretched, i.e., it will retain the same relative position.

Separation.   Two figures which are touching or separated will continue to touch or be separated, respectively, when they are distorted.

Order.   "Betweenness" or seriation will remain constant through the transformation or change.

Enclosure.   "Inside," "outside" or "on" will remain constant.

Copeland has studied Piaget's research and the development of geometric concepts in children. From his study and extensive work with children, he concludes:

> Geometrically the emphasis at the nursery level should be topological. At the kindergarten and first grade levels the transition from topology to Euclidean geometry can be made (1:176).

Nursery, kindergarten and first-grade teachers should emphasize the topological invariants mentioned above by constructing models such as village scenes in which buildings may be attached or separated (separation), animals fenced (enclosure), positions noted (order), and nearness of objects discussed (proximity). Children should construct their own scenes and study them from different vantage points (perspectives) and through manipulations be lead to conceptualize the invariant nature of topological characteristics.

The Mr. "O" materials of the Science Curriculum Improvement Project (SCIS) can be used to develop certain topological concepts. These materials, developed under the direction of Robert Karplus of the University of California at Berkeley, use a very egocentric observer (Mr. "O") to help children conceptualize nearness, farness, left, right and other perspectives.

Topological distortions are reflections of the child's perception boundedness. Try to create activities in which perceptual cues can be shown to give erroneous data relative to "reality." Examples:

Proximity. Create a situation in which objects nearer *appear to look farther.* Have three children stand on the playground as indicated below at A, B and C. Have the children stand at X and ask, "Who is closer to B, A or C?" It appears

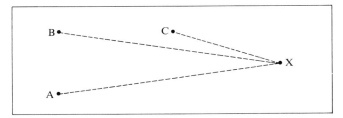

from X that C is closer than A. On a signal have A and C run to B. A will arrive first. Such activities will help children see that A is closer to B than C even though C appears to be closer than A.

Separation.   Have children observe two objects, A and B, from C. They are not touching. Then have them observe A and B from D. They now appear to be joined. Ask, "Are they touching?" Pass your hand between them (dotted

line) or place a stick or ruler between them. This will help children see that perception can be tricky relative to joining and separation of objects.

Order.   Have children copy orders of objects placed cn a table or desk. They can make an order of objects which is identical or reversed. Later they can draw a picture of the order in regular or reverse order.

Place three objects on a table in this order:

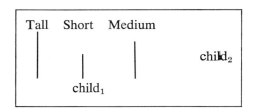

Use objects such that when the child is positioned at child$_2$, he cannot see the short object. Ask, "Where is the short one?" Reach down between the tall and medium objects and pick it up. The child will begin to observe that order is the same regardless of his relative position.

Enclosure.   Set up an electric train on a circular or oval track;[1] run it

---

[1] This track is an example of a simple closed curve. Mathematical characteristics and classification of curves are discussed in the programmed section cf this chapter.

around as in the left diagram. Then place a book or object in a position which hides part of the track as in the right diagram. Ask, "Can the train go

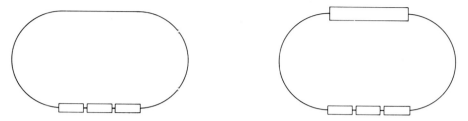

around now?" This will help the child see that the track is closed even though it *does not appear to be.*

In addition to exploration of topological properties, children can be afforded many opportunities to explore their three-dimensional environment. These manipulations are intuitive learning experiences. Children learn concepts of "roundness," "flatness," "edge," "corner" and other concepts through the sense of touch. They cannot define nor even discuss *curved surfaces, flat surfaces, edges* or *vertices* but they have experiences upon which these concepts can later be built.

> The children in nursery school, kindergarten, and first grade should have many experiences with handling models of geometric objects, tracing outlines with their fingers and hands and drawing them, if they are to construct an adequate mental representation of the objects. Showing and telling is not enough. Just to "see" and be "told" is not to abstract and understand. The child must form his own mental constructs based on his own physical action on the objects. Children like to discuss models of these shapes that they see in the physical world such as a cardboard box, a stop sign, or railroad crossing sign (1:185).

This point of view is strongly supported by Flavell who states:

> These spatial representations are built up through the organization of *actions* performed on objects in space, at first motor actions and later, internalized actions which eventuate in operational systems. Our adult representation of space is thus said to result from active manipulations of the spatial environment rather than from any immediate "reading off" of this environment by the perceptual apparatus. For example, we eventually come to "see" objects as together or separated in space, much less as a function of past visual enregistrations of their proximity or separation than from past actions of placing objects together and separating them (2:328).

Concrete materials are needed to allow young children to explore, compare and contrast. Through such *actions* they develop a concept of space. Visual perception is apparently inadequate. Great quantities of tactile and kinesthetic reinforcement are needed.

Grades One, Two, Three, Four—Intuitive Notions of Euclidean Space

By the time most children are in grade two, they have attained the reversibility of operations necessary to explore geometric shapes in greater detail. Using fixed points on shapes as reference points, children can trace them to get the "feel" (sensory-motor action) of various shapes. They can begin to discriminate more sharply various quadrilaterals which exhibit various characteristics of parallelism, angle size and proportion.

Symmetry. Children can explore line symmetry by using mirrors. If a mirror is placed at an angle to a picture, the picture and its mirror image exhibit line symmetry. Another way in which children can easily make sym-

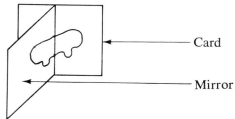

Card

Mirror

metric pictures is by dabbing paint or ink on a sheet of paper and folding it. The crease is the line of symmetry just as the intersection of the card and mirror was the line of symmetry in the first example. Children can be encouraged to bring or name objects which exhibit line symmetry including butterflies, animals and leaves.

Intuitive Exploration and Classification. Considerable experience at classification is provided. Children are stimulated through activities of the following type.

Bring to class several objects of various sizes and shapes which include cylinders, cones, pyramids, cubes, spheres, and right rectangular prisms. Think of some which you might bring. This would be an excellent exercise for you right now. It will help you get the feel for observational experiences. A sample list is on the next page.

The first type of exploratory experience is a tactile, visual experience in which children take various three-dimensional shapes and describe similarities and differences. If presented with a cone and a pyramid, for example, they might describe them as both have a flat side, both have an edge, both have a "point," both are "slanted," and other relations such as texture and color. What are some possible responses for cone and cylinder?

Before you begin the second type of exploration, you need some words to describe what you are about to do. All the solids listed in the preceding paragraph have exactly one surface. Each solid has an inside, an outside and a

> *Sample Models*
>
> 1. Cylinder—canned goods, dowel rods, filmstrip container, un-sharpened pencil
> 2. Cone—ice cream cone, funnel, "witch's hat"
> 3. Pyramid—scale model of pyramid
> 4. Cube—playing blocks, cardboard box
> 5. Sphere—ball, balloon, orange
> 6. Right rectangular prism—most boxes, domino, large gum eraser, book, door, filing cabinet

boundary or surface which can be intuitively thought of as its "shell" or "skin."

In Euclidean geometry an *edge* is a straight line segment. In this discussion, an edge may be curved. Whenever a curve is broken (bends abruptly rather than curves), consider it two or more edges. Examples:

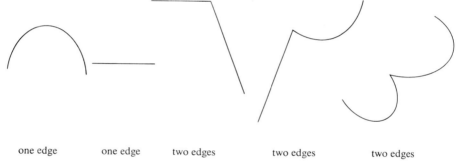

| one edge | one edge | two edges | two edges | two edges |

A cube has twelve edges: four on the top, four on the bottom and four which are vertical.

This discussion will consider *partial surfaces*. A partial surface is bounded by edges. If two locations can be connected without crossing an edge, they are on the same partial surface. A cube has six partial surfaces: a top, a bottom, and four sides.

For the purposes of this discussion, a *vertex* is the intersection of two or more edges. A cube has eight vertices: the "corners." Each of the vertices on a cube is formed by the intersection of three edges.

Children will define edge, partial surface and vertex intuitively, through manipulation. They might think of an edge as "a place where I feel an abrupt change when I move my finger over an object." They might think of a vertex as a "pointed place" on the solid, and they might think of a partial surface as a "smooth part which has a boundary."

Classify the following and then compare your responses with those listed on the next page.

Shape	Number of Edges	Number of Partial Surfaces	Number of Vertices
Cube			
Cone			
Cylinder			
Right rectangular prism			
Sphere			
Square pyramid			
Triangular pyramid			

Attempts to define edges and surfaces usually lead to circularity of definition and provide an excellent opportunity to discuss primitive notions or undefined terms in mathematics.

When children are exploring vertices and edges, they can construct three-dimensional models from two-dimensional cut-outs as pictured here. Such

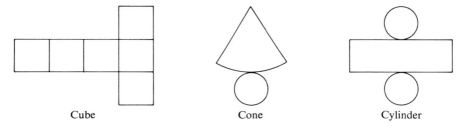

Cube   Cone   Cylinder

experiences will enhance spatial perception and relate two- and three-dimensional experiences.

Exploration of solids leads naturally into study of two dimensions (plane figures) as attention is directed to flat partial surfaces. Common polygons such as square and rectangle are classified. Another very interesting and challenging activity which gives further experience in development of spatial perception is to imagine "cuts" on solids. How many edges and surfaces are on the solid remaining when a corner is cut off a cube? (15, 7) What is the shape of the cross-section of a cylinder cut obliquely top to bottom (exactly one end is cut on the diameter)? (Trapezoid)

Children in primary grades are exposed to the names of various three-dimensional shapes and intermediate level children name, describe and classify them.

When children explore common three-dimensional shapes, they can bring in models, make models or describe shapes which have certain sets of characteristics. For example, think of shapes which satisfy these criteria. Examples are listed on the next page. Think of a shape which has each of the following:

a. 0 edges

b. 1 edge

c. 2 edges

d. 3 edges

e. 4 edges

f. 5 edges

g. 6 edges

h. 20 edges

i. 0 partial surfaces

j. 1 partial surface

k. 2 partial surfaces

l. 3 partial surfaces

m. 4 partial surfaces

n. 5 partial surfaces

o. 6 partial surfaces

p. 20 partial surfaces

q. 0 vertices

r. 1 vertex

s. 2 vertices

t. 3 vertices

u. 4 vertices

v. 5 vertices

w. 6 vertices

x. 20 vertices

y. 1 edge; 2 surfaces

z. 3 edges; 2 vertices

Shape	Edges	Partial Surfaces	Vertices
Cube	12	6	8
Cone	1	2	0
Cylinder	2	3	0
Right rectangular prism	12	6	8
Sphere	0	1	0
Square pyramid	8	5	5
Triangular pyramid	6	4	4

Various combinations can be explored mentally and through manipulations. Records can be kept. Children can be challenged to see if clay models can be made which satisfy given specifications. The relations can be of increasing difficulty with each succeeding grade level. Such exploration will help youngsters conceptualize space through sensory-motor contacts, discover relations and classify. While children in primary grades should explore at an intuitive level, children in the intermediate grades can be provided opportunities to verbalize relationships.

Grades Five and Six—Euclidean Geometry and Sets

As the child moves through the various grades of the elementary school, he encounters more structured aspects of classification. Further, he is able, after about eleven or twelve years of age, to conceptualize space as a set of points and can conceptualize subsets of space. At this time the curriculum should provide many associations between arithmetic and geometry through set theory as recommended by the Cambridge Conference.

Some Possible Responses

a. ellipsoid, sphere
b. hemisphere, cone
c. cone fulcrum, cylinder
d. quartersphere, orange section
e. cylinder with a wedge in the top, cone cut vertically
f. sphere with 5 "slices" removed
g. half-cylinder
h. pyramid with 10-sided base
i. impossible
j. sphere
k. hemisphere
l. cylinder
m. triangular pyramid

n. square pyramid
o. pyramid with pentagonal base (5 sides)
p. pyramid with 19-sided base
q. sphere
r. a cone with a "raindrop" base

s. quarter sphere
t. half a cone
u. half a cylinder
v. square pyramid
w. pentagonal pyramid
x. 19-sided pyramid
y. hemisphere
z. quarter-sphere

The implications of child development patterns are clear. The formal aspects of sets of points probably should be deferred to grades five and six. Teachers of grades two through four can certainly provide *many* intuitive exploratory experiences relative to concepts, such as point, line and ray, providing readiness for more formalized, abstract treatment at higher grade levels.

It is most interesting that not until a youngster is eleven or twelve or almost ready to leave the elementary school can he grasp the idea of unlimited in number. And yet we arbitrarily introduce the line as a set of points in the primary grades. Until this stage the youngster cannot perform the abstract operation of thought which allows the subdivision or separation of the whole indefinitely thus visualizing the line as an infinite set of hypothetical points (1:162).

If Piaget is correct it is a purely rote exercise to talk of lines as sets of points in the primary grades. In so doing the new math becomes as rote as the old math. Children begin to parrot definitions for rays, line segments, triangles, etc. They are not ready for such concepts. Logically space can be considered in terms of sets of points, so can lines and rays, but not psychologically before eleven or twelve years of age (1:169).

The materials in the following programmed section stress the set relations of geometry based on infinite sets of points. The material is appropriate for most fifth- and sixth-graders, and the ideas build upon intuitive definitions and concepts of the K–4 curriculum.

Study the following list of objectives before you proceed. Many frames have questions to which you should respond. Answers are on the second page following the question frame.

Some Basic Concepts of Geometry

Objectives

After completing this unit the student will be able to:

(1) Name or label lines, line segments, rays, points, and polygons with proper notation.
(2) Write equations representing the union and intersection of sets of points.
(3) Label curves as simple or not simple.
(4) Label curves as open or closed.
(5) Distinguish between common shapes and their interiors.
(6) Determine the number of disjoint sets of points in a given plane figure.
(7) Draw Venn diagrams representing relations between types of triangles and quadrilaterals.
(8) Describe methods of reinforcing geometric concepts verbally, manually, visually, and kinesthetically.
(9) Name common items which can be used as models for geometric concepts.

Materials Needed

1. A piece of string or yarn.
2. Small box, ball or other spherical item, cone-shaped item, can or cylindrical jar, block or cubical object, pyramidal object   *Or* set of small geometric models such as those available through Houghton-Mifflin Company.
3. Clay or similar malleable substance such as Play Doh (desirable but not essential).

G–1

Hold your pencil in your hand, lead-end up. Imagine that the pencil point is as sharp as possible. The present position of that pencil point is a *location* with respect to the environment. Now move your hand; the pencil is now in a new location. Similarly, the pencil point is in a new location. In the discussion which follows, *point* can loosely be used synonomously with *location*. *Point* is an undefined term. People talk about points in a way that indicates an *intuitive agreement*. One would have difficulty trying to *define* a point. Try it.

CONTINUE TO G–2.

G–2

If you said a point is a dot, then what is a dot? If you said a point is a location, then what is a location?

In languages, one must start somewhere. Can you imagine trying to learn the meaning of a German word by using only a German dictionary? You would have to know at least one German word, and probably more, to learn the meaning of other German words. Similarly, in mathematics one must know (accept an intuitive notion of) some primitive or basic concept(s) to be able to learn or define new ones. A point is such a primitive notion or "given" in mathematics.

To facilitate conceptualization of geometric concepts, this discourse will intuitively equate *point* with *location*.

CONTINUE TO G–3.

G–3

Using the intuitive definition cited, translate and answer these questions:

(a) What is the set of *all* points?

(b) How many points are on a line segment one inch in length?

(c) What is the set of points all of which are six inches from a given point?

SEE ANSWER FRAME (G–3).

Space is the set of *all* points (locations).

Such a notion of points as locations can be used to develop an intuitive idea of the concept with children. There are many points inside a circle as seen by placing the "locater" (pencil tip) in many different positions or there are many points (locations) inside a tin can as evidenced by the movement of the pencil within the can.

Pretend for a moment that space is made up of exactly three points (locations). Call them A, B, and C. How many subsets* of space are there? What are they?

   * See Appendix A if you are rusty on set concepts.

SEE ANSWER FRAME (G–4).

Notice that *every set of points is a subset of space.*

    (a) Draw a sphere about 3″ in diameter. How many points are in the sphere?

    (b) Place two distinct (different) dots inside the sphere. Label them A and B, and assume they are points. (They describe locations.) Connect them with a straight segment. (Notice that you must "know" what *straight* means. *Straight* is another intuitively defined term which in Euclidean space is used synonomously with "the shortest distance.") You have drawn *line segment AB.*

Why is line segment AB a subset of the set of points inside the sphere?

SEE ANSWER FRAME (G–5).

Set B is a subset of A if all the members of B are in A.

Example: A = {Jim, Bill, Mary}
            B = {Jim, Mary}
            C = {Tom, Mary}
            D = {Jim, Bill}

Every member of B is in A so B is a subset of A.
Every member of C is *not* in A so C is *not* a subset of A.
Every member of D is in A so D is a subset of A.

CONTINUE TO G–7.

G-7

A line segment is a set of points. Every point on the straight path between A and B belongs to the set of points which form line segment AB, denoted

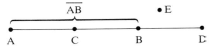

$\overrightarrow{AB}$ or $\overline{AB}$. C belongs to the set; D and E do not. A line segment has many locations so a line segment has many points.

As you recall, a subset is a set which is contained in a given set. When one set of points is a subset of another set of points, all the points of the former are contained in the latter. Look at line segment CD, $\overline{CD}$. All the points on $\overline{BD}$ are also points on $\overline{CD}$ so $\overline{BD}$ is a subset of $\overline{CD}$. How many subsets of $\overline{AD}$ can you name if you think of the universal set of line segments? There are eight.

SEE ANSWER FRAME (G-7).

G-8

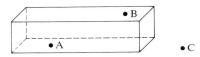

Look at your box or box-shaped solid. There is a set of points inside the box (rectangular solid). Let A and B be points in the box. Let C be a point outside the box. If K = {points in the box}, then {A,B} is a set of points both of which are in K. Hence, {A,B} is a subset of K. Now the line segment connecting A and B is a set of points (locations) all of which are also *inside* the box (belong to K). Thus the line segment AB is a subset of K.

$$\overline{AB} \subset K$$

CONTINUE TO G-9.

(G-3)

(a) What is the set of *all* (locations)?
  Answer: space, everywhere, the universe

(b) How many (locations) are on a line segment one inch in length?
  Answer: an uncountable or endless number.
  Imagine those locations at $\frac{1}{2}, \frac{1}{4}, \frac{1}{8}, \frac{1}{16}, \frac{1}{32}, \cdots$
  This series constitutes an infinite set of positions on a number line.

(c) What is the set of (locations) all of which are six inches from a given (location)?

  Assume your pencil is six inches long. Hold one end in your hand at a fixed position. Now move the other end around with your other hand. Where are all the locations? A ball or sphere? Yes.

CONTINUE TO G-4.

There are eight subsets of space.

Space = {A, B, C} —Every set is a subset of itself, you will recall.

   ∅ —The null or empty set is a subset of every set.

  {A}
  {B}
  {C}
 {A, B}
 {B, C}
 {A, C}

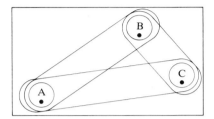

CONTINUE TO G–5.

(a) There are uncountably many points in the sphere.

(b) 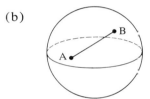

The inside of the sphere is a set of points (locations). All points (locations) on line segment AB are also points (locations) in the sphere so the set of points on AB make up a subset of the set of points inside the sphere. This follows from the definition of a subset.

If this is very clear to you, go to G–10.

If you wish to explore the idea of subsets further, read on . . .

CONTINUE TO G–6.

Line segment AB is denoted $\overline{AB}$ or $\overleftrightarrow{AB}$ and is read "line segment AB." Line segments have two end points, i.e., a "starting" and a "stopping" place. A line segment is a set of points. If S = Space = {set of all points} then $\overline{AB}$ is a subset of S or $\overline{AB} \subset S$. A line segment is a finite portion of a line.

What are some "models" which can be used to represent line segments in elementary school instruction?

SEE ANSWER FRAME (G–9).

(G–7)

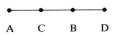

A   C   B   D

All the points on $\overline{AC}$ are on $\overline{AD}$ so $\overline{AC} \subset \overline{AD}$.

All the points on $\overline{CB}$ are on $\overline{AD}$ so $\overline{CB} \subset \overline{AD}$.

Also, $\overline{AB} \subset \overline{AD}$, $\overline{CD} \subset \overline{AD}$, $\overline{BD} \subset \overline{AD}$, $\overline{AD} \subset \overline{AD}$ since every set is a subset of itself, and $\emptyset \subset \overline{AD}$ since the empty set is a subset of every set. Finally, the union of two line segments, $\overline{AC} \cup \overline{BD}$, is a subset.

CONTINUE TO G–8.

G–10

A *line* has endless length. To denote this, line AB is represented by $\overleftrightarrow{AB}$. It is called "line AB." The concept of line is undefined but is intuited as endless in both directions. A and B are distinct (separate) points, and the line which passes through them continues in both directions indefinitely.

What are some models for lines?

What is the relation between $\overline{AB}$ and $\overleftrightarrow{AB}$?

SEE ANSWER FRAME (G–10).

G–11

No, $\overleftrightarrow{AB} \not\subset \overline{AB}$ because every point on $\overleftrightarrow{AB}$ is *not* on $\overline{AB}$.

You will recall that set A and set B are *disjoint* if they have no elements in common.

   (a)   When are two lines disjoint?

   (b)   When are two distinct (different) lines *not* disjoint?

   (c)   Do lines have to be parallel to be disjoint?

SEE ANSWER FRAME (G–11).

G–12

A *ray* can loosely be thought of as a "half line." It has a starting point but continues indefinitely in a straight path in some direction from that point. A ray which starts at A and passes through some other point, B, is called "ray AB" and is denoted $\overrightarrow{AB}$.

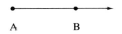

If A, B, C are different points which lie in a straight line, but not necessarily in that order, what three figures can you get when you put $\overrightarrow{AB}$ and $\overrightarrow{AC}$ together?

SEE ANSWER FRAME (G–12).

G–13

(a) There are *three* names for this ray. What are they?

(b) There are *two* names for this *line segment*. What are they?

(c) There are *six* names for this *line*. What are they?

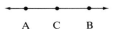

SEE ANSWER FRAME (S–13).

(G–9)

Primary grades should emphasize intuitive notions without the point concept:

1. A taut rope held by two children
2. The intersection of two walls or the ceiling and a wall
3. The edge of a book or table
4. A straightedge
5. A board or thin strip of wood
6. A straw
7. Your piece of string or yarn drawn tightly, etc.

Intermediate grades should emphasize the notion of points:

1. Infinite number of rational numbers on a number line segment
2. A series of dots with greater and greater number
3. Use a pegboard to "fill in" dots (pegs)

CONTINUE TO G–10.

G–14

As with points, lines, and line segments, rays do not exist except in the mind of man. *Models* of rays are used to help build an intuitive notion of the concept. The concept of ray in mathematics is not unlike the use of the word *ray* in everyday language. Name some examples of teaching aids which can be used with children to develop this concept.

SEE ANSWER FRAME (G–14).

(G–10)

Models: 1. The horizon
2. Place a box on the table with two balls of yarn to be pulled out by two children in opposite directions; imagine them walking forever.
3. Railroad (straight) with a little imagination
4. Center line on a straight highway

$$A \qquad B$$

$\overline{AB}$ is a subset of $\overrightarrow{AB}$ since all the points (locations) on $\overline{AB}$ are also points (locations) on $\overrightarrow{AB}$.

Is $\overleftrightarrow{AB}$ a subset of $\overline{AB}$?

CONTINUE TO G–11.

(G–11)

(a) Two lines are disjoint when they have no points (locations) in common.

(b) When they *cross,* i.e., when they intersect, they have a point in common.

(c) No. Hold two pencils like the letter "X" but do not let them touch. They are not parallel, and they are disjoint. Such lines are said to be skew lines.

CONTINUE TO G–12.

(G–12)

There are two rays, $\overrightarrow{AB}$ and $\overrightarrow{AC}$.
Both rays start at **A**.

Since C is different from A and B but is on a straight line with them, either

(1) A is not between B and C   a ray

or

(2) A is between C and B   a line

CONTINUE TO G–13.

(G–13)

(a) The ray *starts* at A.

    $\overrightarrow{AC}$ $\overrightarrow{AB}$ $\overrightarrow{AD}$

(b) A and B are the endpoints.

    $\overleftrightarrow{AB}$ $\overleftrightarrow{BA}$

(c) Any pair of distinct points determine the position of the line.

    $\overleftrightarrow{AC}$ $\overleftrightarrow{AB}$ $\overleftrightarrow{CB}$
    $\overleftrightarrow{CA}$ $\overleftrightarrow{BA}$ $\overleftrightarrow{BC}$

CONTINUE TO G–14.

G–15

How are you coming? Can you do these?

(a) Draw a picture which has $\overleftrightarrow{AB}$ as a subset of $\overrightarrow{AC}$, B $\neq$ C.

(b) Draw a picture which does *not* have $\overleftrightarrow{AB}$ as a subset of $\overrightarrow{AC}$.

Remember: Every element of a set has a *different* name. There cannot be *two*
           points with the same name.

SEE ANSWER FRAME (G–15).

(G–14)

1. Flashlight beam
2. Beam from a headlight on a car
3. The sun's rays
4. Place a ball of yarn in a box. Have a child walk away while pulling the end of the skein through a hole in the box. Imagine that he walks and walks . . .
5. Line of sight or vision from the eye, etc.

CONTINUE TO G–15.

G–16

$\overline{AB}$ is a set of points.

$\overrightarrow{AC}$ is a set of points.

One set is a subset of another when all the members of the first set are members of the second.

Thus, $\overline{AB}$ is a subset of $\overrightarrow{AC}$ when all the points (locations) on $\overline{AB}$ are also points (locations) on $\overrightarrow{AC}$.

In this diagram, $\overline{AB}$ is a subset of $\overrightarrow{AC}$:

In this diagram, $\overline{AB}$ is again a subset of $\overrightarrow{AC}$:

Remember: Ray AC does not stop at C; it continues indefinitely.

CONTINUE TO G–17.

G–17

Consider this diagram:

Answer "yes" or "no" to each of the following statements:

    (a) $\overline{BC}$ is a subset of $\overline{AD}$, i.e., $\overline{BC} \subset \overline{AD}$.

    (b) $\overline{AB}$ is a subset of $\overline{AC}$, i.e., $\overline{AB} \subset \overline{AC}$.

    (c) $\overline{AC}$ is a subset of $\overline{BD}$, i.e., $\overline{AC} \subset \overline{BD}$.

    (d) $\overline{AB}$ and $\overline{CD}$ are disjoint.

    (e) $\overline{AB}$ and $\overline{BD}$ are disjoint.

SEE ANSWER FRAME (G–17).

Hopefully, you are beginning to see that lines, line segments and rays are sets of points.

Express each of the following verbally. What do they mean?

(a) $\overleftrightarrow{AB} \cup \overleftrightarrow{CD}$

(b) $\overleftrightarrow{AB} \cap \overleftrightarrow{CD}$

(c) $\overleftrightarrow{AB} \cap \overleftrightarrow{CD} = \emptyset$

(d) $\overrightarrow{AB} \cup \overrightarrow{AC} = \angle BAC$
  (Study this one!)

Remember: Union consists of all elements in *either* or *both* sets. Intersection is only those elements which are in *both* sets.

SEE ANSWER FRAME (G–18).

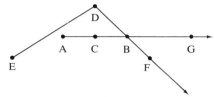

Answer the following questions relative to the figure above. The first two are done for you. Assume A, C, B and G are collinear (lie on the same line).

(a) $\overleftrightarrow{ED} \cap \overleftrightarrow{AC} = \emptyset*$

(b) $\overleftrightarrow{DB} \cap \overleftrightarrow{AC} = B$

(c) $\overleftrightarrow{AC} \cup \overleftrightarrow{CB} = ?$

(d) $\overleftrightarrow{AC} \cap \overleftrightarrow{CB} = ?$

(e) $\overrightarrow{ED} \cap \overleftrightarrow{CB} = ?$

(f) $\overrightarrow{AC} \cap \overrightarrow{CB} = ?$

(g) $\overrightarrow{BF} \cup \overrightarrow{BG} = ?$

(h) $\overrightarrow{BF} \cap \overrightarrow{BG} = ?$

* There are no points which are on *both* ED and AC.

SEE ANSWER FRAME (G–19).

(a)

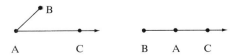

Since $\overleftrightarrow{AB}$ is a subset of $\overrightarrow{AC}$, all the points on $\overleftrightarrow{AB}$ must be on $\overrightarrow{AC}$. This is true when B is any point on $\overrightarrow{AC}$. Either B is between A and C or C is between A and B.

(b) $\overleftrightarrow{AB}$ and $\overrightarrow{AC}$ have a common endpoint, A. If B is on $\overrightarrow{AC}$, $\overleftrightarrow{AB}$ is a subset of $\overrightarrow{AC}$ as indicated above. Hence, B is some point (location) *not* on $\overrightarrow{AC}$.

Examples:

IF THIS IS CLEAR, GO TO G–19, OTHERWISE CONTINUE TO G–16.

G–20

You have been exploring one-dimensional figures in three-dimensional space. If you think of three-dimensional space as the familiar heighth, length and width, then the one-dimensional figures discussed have only length. Lines, angles, line segments and rays have no width or heighth. They have only length. The point, which respesents a location, has no dimension.

Still another set of points of one dimension is the curve. Such a path in three dimensions might be the flight path of a fly or an airplane. A spiral, too, would be such a curve.

This concludes our exploration of one-dimensional figures in three-dimensional space.

CONTINUE TO G–21.

G–21

Pause a moment for review of an important point:

The one-dimensional figures just discussed do not exist, just like numbers do not exist. Numerals are names for numbers; they help you think, talk and express relations about abstract numbers through symbolization. Since lines, points and rays do not exist, you draw pictures or look at things "like" lines in the real world to promote thought processes.

Numbers help you classify, describe and explore your environment to "make sense" of it even though numbers do not exist in the same sense in which a chair is said to exist. Similarly, points, lines, line segments and rays allow you to classify, describe and explore your environment so that you may understand its interrelationships. These concepts are the building blocks for the next area of study, one-dimensional figures in two-dimensional space.

CONTINUE TO G–22.

(G–17)

 (a) Yes, all the points on $\overleftrightarrow{BC}$ are on $\overleftrightarrow{AD}$.

 (b) Yes, all the points on $\overleftrightarrow{AB}$ are on $\overleftrightarrow{AC}$.

 (c) No, all the points on $\overleftrightarrow{AC}$ are *not* on $\overleftrightarrow{BD}$.

 (d) Yes, $\overleftrightarrow{AB}$ and $\overleftrightarrow{CD}$ have *no* points in common.

 (e) No, $\overleftrightarrow{AB}$ and $\overleftrightarrow{BD}$ have point B in common.

CONTINUE TO G–18.

(a) Line segment AB *union* line segment CD is the set of all points on $\overleftrightarrow{AB}$ and all points on $\overrightarrow{CD}$.

(b) Line segment AB *intersect* line segment CD is the set of all points which are on $\overleftrightarrow{AB}$ which are *also* on $\overrightarrow{CD}$.

(c) Line segment AB *intersect* line segment CD is the empty set. The two segments have *no* points in common.

(d) Ray AB *union* ray AC is the angle with the starting point as the vertex.

CONTINUE TO G–19.

Study these carefully.

(a) $\overleftrightarrow{ED}$ and $\overrightarrow{AC}$ have no points in common.

(b) $\overleftrightarrow{DB}$ and AC have point B in common.

(c) $\overline{AB}$; $\overline{AC}$ and $\overline{CB}$ together make $\overline{AB}$.

(d) C; $\overline{AC}$ and $\overline{CB}$ have only point, C, in common.

(e) $\emptyset$; $\overleftrightarrow{ED}$ and $\overline{CB}$ have no points in common.

(f) $\overrightarrow{CB}$; all the points on $\overrightarrow{CB}$ are on $\overrightarrow{AC}$.

(g) $\angle$ FBG; all points on $\overrightarrow{BF}$ and on $\overrightarrow{BG}$ make the angle.

(h) B; the two rays, $\overrightarrow{BF}$ and $\overrightarrow{BG}$, have point B in common.

CONTINUE TO G–20.

So far you have considered the set of *all* points (locations) which was called *space*. Now the discourse will be restricted to a subset of space called a *plane*. A plane is like a wall that has unending length and width but is the thickness of one point. It is like an endlessly large table top. As you have probably guessed, *plane* is another undefined term. You may already have an intuitive notion of the concept.

A plane divides space into three sets of points. All the points in space are on:

    1. one side of the plane (A)
    2. the other side of the plane (B)
    3. on the plane (C)

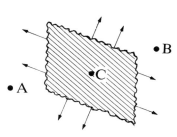

This is a situation similar to being in room A, room B or in the doorway.

The three sets of points are disjoint, i.e., no two of the three sets have a point in common.

CONTINUE TO G–23.

Consider now only the set of points *on* a plane. Since the plane is two-dimensional, all the one-dimensional figures explored can be related to this subset of space. All lines, line segments, rays and points are subsets of planes. Every such figure can be placed on some plane.

However, some *curves* cannot be placed on a single plane. Imagine a spiral in three dimensions like a spring. Only one spiral of the curve or part of a spiral can be placed on *one* plane. In the ensuing work on a plane, only curves which can be placed on *one* plane will be considered.

Take your pencil and move it about on a piece of paper. You have just drawn such a curve (model).

CONTINUE TO G-24.

Two definitions:

> A *closed* curve is one which is not broken; it stops where it starts.
> A *simple* curve is one which passes through no point more than one time.

Can you classify these as closed-simple, closed-not simple, open-simple, open-not simple?

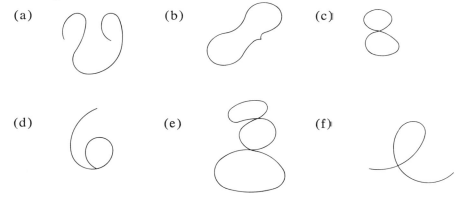

(a)　　　　　　　(b)　　　　　　　(c)

(d)　　　　　　　(e)　　　　　　　(f)

SEE ANSWER FRAME (G-24).

A *simple-closed curve* divides (partitions) the plane into three disjoint sets of points. Draw one and decide what (where) they are.

A numeral "8" divides (partitions) a set into *four* disjoint sets of points. Where are they?

SEE ANSWER FRAME (G-25).

No point on the interior (inside) is on the boundary or exterior (outside).

No point on the boundary is on the interior (inside) or exterior (outside).

No point on the exterior (outside) is on the boundary or interior (inside).

(a) How can you help children explore these concepts?

(b) How can you tell if two points, A and B, are in the same of two or more disjoint sets of points?

SEE ANSWER FRAME (G-26).

Which of the four types of curve is each of the following?

(1) A circle?
(2) A square?
(3) A triangle?
(4) A rectangle?
(5) A line segment?
(6) A line?

Into how many disjoint sets of points does each of the above divide (partition) the plane?

SEE ANSWER FRAME (G-27).

Polygons are simple-closed curves. This is a characteristic of polygons but is *not* a definition.

What else is known of polygons? They are made up of line segments.

Definition: A *polygon* is a simple-closed curve which is the union of line segments.

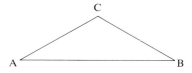

$$\triangle ABC = \overline{AB} \cup \overline{BC} \cup \overline{CA}$$

A *regular polygon* is one with sides of equal length and angles of equal measure.

CONTINUE TO G-29.

G–29

In kindergarten and primary grades, geometric shapes are explored primarily through visual discrimination. Early experiences with circles, squares, rectangles and triangles are common. Teachers use many models of various colors and sizes to help children discriminate *shape* as an independent characteristic of objects.

You have seen that a rectangle is the union of four line segments with special characteristics. Draw a picture of $\overline{AC} \cup \overline{CD} \cup \overline{DG} \cup \overline{GA}$ to form a rectangle. Divide the rectangle into six equal parts.

SEE ANSWER FRAME (G–29).

(G–24)

    (a) open-simple

    (b) closed-simple

    (c) closed-not simple

    (d) open-not simple

    (e) closed-not simple

    (f) open-not simple

Study the definitions if you missed one or more.

CONTINUE TO G–25.

(G–25)

Inside (Interior)
Outside (Exterior)
Curve (Boundary)

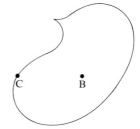

What does it mean to say they are *disjoint?*

Two interiors
One exterior
One boundary

CONTINUE TO G–26.

(a) 1. Use a rope or piece of string on the floor. Ask children to stand inside, on, outside.

2. Relate to penned animals (inside, outside, on-the-fence).

(b) A and B are in the same of two or more disjoint sets if they can be connected without leaving the set. Study these:

A. Yes   B. Yes   C. No   D. Yes   E. No   F. No

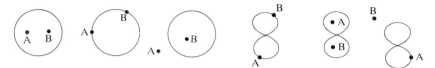

CONTINUE TO G–27.

1. *Circle*—simple-closed curve—3 disjoint sets
2. *Square*—simple-closed curve—3 disjoint sets
3. *Triangle*—simple-closed curve—3 disjoint sets
4. *Rectangle*—simple-closed curve—3 disjoint sets
5. *Line segment*—simple-opened curve—2 disjoint sets
6. *Line*—simple-opened curve—3 disjoint sets (above, below and on)

Squares, triangles and rectangles are all simple-closed curves. They are all polygons. What might you conclude?

CONTINUE TO G–28.

Think!

Q: What is a rectangle?
A: *Four line segments* end to end which form a special simple-closed curve.

Q: What is a line segment?
A: A set of points.

Q: What is a rectangle?
A: The *union of sets of points which form four line segments.*

Q: If you had one of the diagrams shown, did you divide this set of points into six equal sets?
A: No!

Try it again before you look.

SEE ANSWER FRAME (G–30).

(G–29)

If your rectangle looks like this, you are correct.

If you divided it like this:　　　or this

or this　　　or this

you are wrong!

CONTINUE TO G–30.

G–31

In elementary school textbooks on the market today, children are asked to shade half a rectangle or square or circle. They may take a blue crayon and color half of the set of points:

As the mathematican defines it, a circle is a set of points equidistant from a given point. Shade half a circle.

SEE ANSWER FRAME (G–31).

G–32

Whether it is simply an unnamed curve, a circle or a polygon, a simple-closed figure is the set of points contained in its boundary. (The notion is loosely related to perimeter.) The interior points and the boundary together make a *region*. The region is loosely related to area. Shade $\frac{1}{6}$ a circular region. Suggest models which correspond to the mathematical definitions of these concepts:

（a） circle
（b） rectangle
（c） circular region
（d） rectangular region

SEE ANSWER FRAME (G–32).

The models suggested provide opportunities for children to make good visual discriminations of the mathematical concepts. **Caution:** note that felt materials or cardboard objects, while useful, should never be used by themselves. If children acquire the concepts without relating them to the real world where they may be used, *transfer* will be minimal. Children should be afforded many opportunities to explore the environment and perhaps to bring objects and pictures to the classroom for discussion and sharing. Through such activities, children will learn to recognize models easily and skillfully.

How can you reinforce the concept of *circle* kinesthetically?

SEE ANSWER FRAME (G–33).

These concepts help children understand the environment. Through classification they can structure the environment and begin to make informal, and later formal, study and comparison of similarities, differences and relationships between various classes and objects. Certain geometric figures have characteristics and behave in certain ways which help children solve problems and understand their surroundings.

Triangles are rigid, for example. Rectangles, which are not rigid, can be made rigid by adding a diagonal which makes two triangles. The Pythagorean Theorem is useful in work with problem solving involving right triangles as in the triangle on the right.

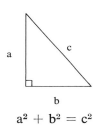

$$a^2 + b^2 = c^2$$

CONTINUE TO G–35.

The rectangle is the set of points which constitute the *boundary*. If you divided the boundary (perimeter) into six equal parts, you are correct.

In common language, this distinction is not made. People use the word *rectangle* to refer to the inside (interior) as well as the shape. However, the distinction made in mathematics between the shape and its inside (interior) is an important one.

CONTINUE TO G–31.

G–35

Informal exploration and classification of the primary grades gives way to an extended vocabulary and formal classification in the intermediate grades. How many kinds of triangles can you name? Separate them by *angles* and *sides*. That is, some triangles have a special name because of relations between their angles and others have special names because of relations between their sides.

SEE ANSWER FRAME (G–35).

(G–31)

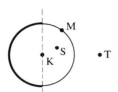

M is a point on the circle; S, K, and T are not.

This is very much in agreement with the Euclidean concept of a circle as a set of points equidistant from a given point. In other words, if K is the center, all the points on the circle are the same distance (radius) from K.

CONTINUE TO G–32.

(G–32)

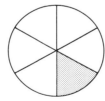

(a) Ring
Hula hoop
Tire (without the wheel)
Clock (frame)
Tin can with ends cut out

(b) Window frame
Picture frame

(c) Coin
Clock *face*
Plate
Saucer
Tin can lid
Round hassock

(d) Picture
Book
Front of a refrigerator
Desk top
Window shade
Domino

CONTINUE TO G–33.

(G–33)

The essential characteristic is *muscular movement* which gives the "feel of" circularity.

Activities such as these can be used:

1. Cut the ends out of a tin can and trace the rim
2. Trace circles with a pencil or fingertip
3. Have children form a circle and move clockwise
4. Cut a sandpaper circular model and have the child trace it

CONTINUE TO G–34.

G–36

Venn diagrams can be used to express the relations.

Let U = {triangles}

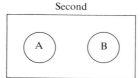
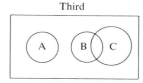

First, draw set A, the set of scalene triangles.

Second, determine where the equilateral triangles are. Are there any in A?
No. Therefore, they are all outside A (set B)

Third, where are the isosceles triangles?
Are any in A? No.
Are any in B? Yes.
Are *all* isoceles in B? No. (set C)

Draw a Venn diagram for the triangles classed by angle relations. Draw another one which relates squares and rectangles.

SEE ANSWER FRAME (G–36).

G–37

Make a Venn diagram which represents the relations between these figures:

Triangles	Polygons
Squares	Curves
Parallelograms	Rectangles

Hint: "Curves" is the universal set since all the others listed are special curves.

SEE ANSWER FRAME (G–37).

(G–35)

Sides

Scalene—no sides congruent

Equilateral—all sides congruent

Isosceles—two sides congruent

Angles

Acute triangles—all angles less than 90°

Obtuse triangles—one angle more than 90°

Right triangles—one angle 90°

Equiangular triangles—all angles equal

CONTINUE TO G–36.

(G–36)

A = {acute triangles}

B = {obtuse triangles}

C = {right triangles}

D = {equiangular triangles}

R = {rectangles}

S = {squares}

All equiangular triangles are acute. All squares are rectangles.

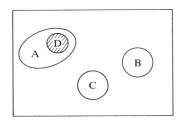   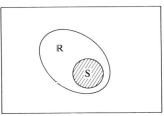

CONTINUE TO G–37.

(G–37)

The largest set is *curves,* so let the Universal set be the set of curves. All the other figures are special curves.

1. Place T = {Triangles}
2. Place S = {Squares} No squares are triangles so the sets are disjoint.
3. Place P = {Parallelograms} All squares are parallelograms so S ⊂ P.
4. Place Y = {Polygons} All triangles, parallelograms are polygons.
5. Place R = {Rectangles} All squares are rectangles, and all rectangles are parallelograms.

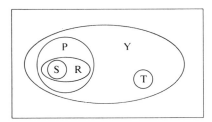

Universal set = U = {curves}

Make up a problem of your own and diagram it.

THE END.

Geometry Self-Test

1. Represent the following with proper notation:
    A. A line which passes through two distinct points, A and B
    B. A line segment with endpoints at A and B
    C. A line segment which starts at M, ends at N and passes through C, i.e., C is between M and N
    D. A ray which starts at A and passes through a different point, B
    E. A ray which starts at B and passes through a different point, A
    F. A ray which starts at M and passes through two distinct points, N and R

2. Use the figure at the right for the next set of questions:
    A. Write an equation which says that $\overline{AB}$ and $\overline{BC}$ together form $\overline{AC}$.
    B. Write an equation which says that ray AB and ray AD form an angle.
    C. Write an equation which says that a triangle is formed by three line segments.

    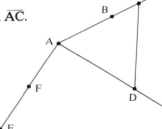

    D. Write an equation which says that ray AD and line segment AF have only one point in common.
    E. Write an equation which says that line segment BC and line segment EF have no points in common.
    F. What is $\overrightarrow{AC} \cup \overrightarrow{BC}$?
    G. What is $\overrightarrow{AC} \cap \overrightarrow{BC}$?
    H. What is $\overrightarrow{AD} \cap AC$?
    I. What is $\overrightarrow{AB} \cup \overline{BC}$?
    J. What is $\overrightarrow{AB} \cap \overline{BC}$?

3. Decide whether each of the following is simple or not simple, closed or not closed:

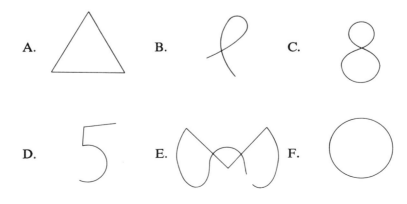

A.   B.   C.

D.   E.   F.

4. A. Draw a circle and shade half the region.
   B. Draw a square and shade half the square.
   C. Shade half a triangular region.
   D. Shade half a triangle.

5. Determine the number of disjoint sets of points in each of these figures:

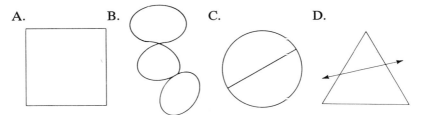

6. Draw Venn diagrams representing the relation between:
   A. Triangles (T), Scalene Triangles (S) and Isosceles Triangles (I)
   B. Polygons (P), Rectangles (R), Parallelograms (L)
   C. Polygons (P), Triangles (T), Squares (S)
   D. Curves (C), Polygons (P), Closed Curves (5)
   E. Polygons (P), Parallelograms (L), Squares (S), Triangles (T), Right Triangles (R), Isosceles Triangles (I)

Answers to Geometry Self-Test

1. A. $\overleftrightarrow{AB}$

   D. $\overrightarrow{AB}$ or $\overrightarrow{AB}$

   B. $\overline{AB}$ or $\overrightarrow{AB}$

   E. $\overline{BA}$ or $\overrightarrow{BA}$

   C. $\overline{MN}$ or $\overrightarrow{MN}$

   F. $\overrightarrow{MN}$ or $\overrightarrow{MR}$

2. A. $\overline{AB} \cup \overline{BC} = \overline{AC}$

   B. $\overrightarrow{AB} \cup \overrightarrow{AD} = \angle DAB$

   C. $\overline{AD} \cup \overline{DC} \cup \overline{CA} = \triangle ADC$

   D. $\overline{AD} \cap \overline{AF} = A$

   E. $\overline{BC} \cap \overline{EF} = \{\ \}$

   F. $\overrightarrow{AC}$

   G. $\overrightarrow{BC}$

   H. A

   I. $\overrightarrow{AB}$

   J. $\overline{BC}$

3. A. simple, closed
   B. not simple, not closed
   C. not simple, closed
   D. simple, not closed
   E. not simple, not closed
   F. simple, closed

4. A.

   B.

   C.

   D.

5. A.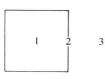

   B.

   C.

   D.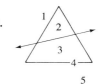

6.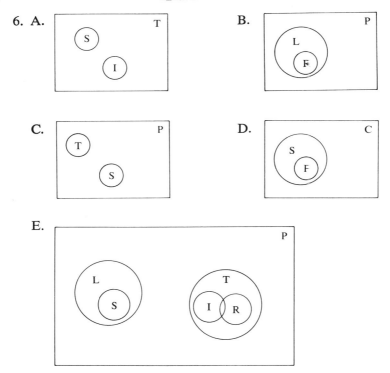

Discussion and Projects

1. What other materials, commercial or homemade, can be used to teach basic concepts of geometry such as point, line, curve, ray, triangle, cube and cone?

2. Suggest other discovery activities, both pure and guided, which can be used relative to geometric concepts. What pure discovery activities can evolve from shapes or models of line segments and points? What guided discovery activities can be used to help children discover differences and similarities between shapes and solids or union and intersection of sets of points?

3. Write behavioral objectives at the concrete (manipulation), semi-concrete (diagrams and pictures) and abstract (written work) level for topics of your choice in primary or intermediate grades.

4. Write evaluation items which seek to measure pupil performance of the objectives cited in the previous question.

5. What topics of geometry can be used as primary or intermediate grade enrichment?

6. How can an overhead projector be used to teach concepts of geometry?

7. How can Tinkertoys and geoboards be used to teach concepts of geometry?

Additional Teacher Education Resources

Filmstrips

> *Modern Mathematics: Geometry—Sets, Rays, Angles, Figures,* Society for Visual Education.
> *Polygons,* Popular Science (5H–5).
> *Topology,* Stanley Bowman (8042)

Overhead Projector Transparencies—3M Company

> Math No. 1, *Plane and Solid Figures*
> Math No. 2, *Unions, Intersection of Lines and Planes*

Kit

> *Mathset—Geometry,* Scott, Foresman & Co.

Bibliography

1. Copeland, Richard W. *How Children Learn Mathematics.* New York: The Macmillan Company, 1970.

2. Flavell, John H. *The Developmental Psychology of Jean Piaget.* New York: Von Nostrand Reinhold Company, 1963.

3. *Goals for School Mathematics.* Boston: Houghton Mifflin Company for Educational Services Incorporated, 1963.

4. Lovell, Kenneth, *The Growth of Understanding in Mathematics: Kindergarten through Grade Three.* New York: Holt, Rinehart and Winston, Inc., 1971.

5. Moredock, H. Stewart, "Geometry and Measurement," Chapter IV, *Mathematics Education,* Sixty-Ninth Yearbook of the National Society for the Study of Education. Chicago: The University of Chicago Press, 1970.

6. Vigilante, Nicholas J. "Geometry for Primary Children: Considerations," *The Arithmetic Teacher* (October 1967), 14:453–59.

APPENDIX

Basic Set Concepts

The notion of set permeates the K–6 curriculum, and set-related concepts form an integral and important part of teacher-education mathematics preparation programs. The ideas are few in number, but they are powerful in the strength of continuity and structure they provide to the curriculum. If you are unfamiliar with the terminology of set language, you would do well to study these pages carefully. If you have already encountered basic set ideas elsewhere, these pages will provide a quick summary and review.

The appendix is presented in three sections. Section one deals primarily with basic definitions and notation of sets and elements; section two presents concepts of set operations and schematic representations; and section three relates sets to numbers and distinguishes between equal and equivalent sets.

Basic Definitions and Notation

What is a set? The concept *set* is undefined. However, people agree at the intuitive level that a set is simply a *group of things.* The group or collection may consist of letters of the alphabet, people, numbers, animals, books, dishes or any combination of things. Sets are usually denoted by capital letters: set A, set B, set C. When letters are used to identify *elements,* they are generally in lower case.

The objects which belong to a set are called the *elements* or *members* of the set and the Greek letter *epsilon,* ϵ, is used to denote membership. Thus, if $\triangle$ is a member of set A, you can write $\triangle \, \epsilon \, A$ which is read "triangle is an element of set A" or "triangle is an element of A." If an element does *not* belong to a set, $\notin$ is the appropriate symbol. Thus, if k is not an element of set T, you write $k \notin T$.

Sets can be described in at least three ways. Each of these uses braces. If set A has elements 0, 1, 2, 3, 4, 5, 6, 7, 8, 9, A can be represented by listing all the elements: A = {0, 1, 2, 3, 4, 5, 6, 7, 8, 9}. Set A can also be represented by describing its elements: A = {all digits in base 10}. Finally, A can be described mathematically: A = { x | x ϵ W, x < 10}, "|" is read "such that"; the statement says, "set A consists of all x such that x is a whole number and x is less than 10." Some other examples:

$$A = \{\triangle, 4, \tfrac{1}{2}, \square\}$$
$$B = \{all \ people \ with \ brown \ eyes\}$$
$$C = \{x \mid x \ \epsilon \ W; 6 < x < 10\} = \{7, 8, 9\}$$

Some sets have an uncountable number of elements. Consider the set of whole numbers; they begin with zero and continue forever. Such a set which is uncountable is called an *infinite set* and can be represented by establishing a pattern and then placing three periods to indicate the pattern is continued, e.g., W = {0, 1, 2, 3, 4, . . .}.

Other examples of infinite sets are "all even whole numbers" or "all odd whole numbers" or "all fractions":

$$A = \{0, 2, 4, 6, 8, 10, . . .\}$$
$$B = \{1, 3, 5, 7, 9 . . .\}$$
$$C = \{\tfrac{a}{b} \mid a \ \epsilon \ W, b \ \epsilon \ W, b \neq 0\}$$

Sets which are countable are *finite sets.*

When all the elements of set B are in set A, B is said to be a *subset* of A, $B \subseteq A$. If there is at least one element in A which is *not* in B, B is said to be a *proper subset* of A, $B \subset A$. (Note the similarity to less than or equal to, $\leq$, and less than, <.) In the previous paragraph, you can see that $A \subset W$ since all even whole numbers are whole numbers and there is at least one whole number which is *not* an even number. Can you explain why $A \subseteq A$? . . . Because every element of A is an element of A. Every set is a subset of itself.

If M = { }, M is said to be the *empty set* or *null set*. The empty set can also be denoted by the Greek letter *phi,* $\emptyset$: $\emptyset$ = { }. The empty set is a subset of *every* set. Let S = {a, b}. Set S has four subsets: { }, {a}, {b}, {a, b}.

Several new terms have been defined in this brief passage. Try these exercises before proceeding to the next section. The answers are given at the end of this appendix.

Exercises

1. Write a mathematical statement which says that
   A. set N consists of Bill, Joe, Kay
   B. set P consists of all multiples of 3 which are whole numbers (represent *three* ways)
   C. set L contains Ford, Chevy, table, dog

2. Write the *eight* subsets of 1.A. above.

3. Write the mathematical statement which says that
   A. Bill is in set N
   B. cat is not an element of set L
   C. 17 is a whole number

4. Tell whether the following are finite or infinite sets:
   A. all the people in New York City
   B. the letters of the alphabet
   C. people with brown hair
   D. multiples of 5

5. What are the elements of these sets? Write them a different way:
   A. $L = \{ x \mid x = 2w, w \in W \}$
   B. $E = \{x \mid 10 < x < 12, x \in W\}$
   C. $T = \{x \mid 8 < x < 9, x \in W\}$

Set Operations

In the first section your attention was focused on a single set each time. Now you will consider more than one set. Consider set A and set B:

$$A = \{1, 3, 5, 7\} \qquad\qquad B = \{2, 4, 6, 8\}$$

There is no element in set A which is in set B; A and B have no common elements. A and B are said to be *disjoint* sets. Disjoint sets have no common elements. If the set of women in the Bridge Club is disjoint with the set of women in the Garden Club, there is no woman who belongs to both clubs.

When working with two or more sets, it is customary to indicate the "super set" from which they were drawn, this "super set" is called the *universal set* or simply the *universe*. The universe is the set of which all the sets of a given discourse are subsets. If $A = \{1, 3, 7\}$ and $B = \{2, 5, 8, 9\}$, the universal set, U, could be

$$U = \{1, 2, 3, 5, 7, 8, 9\}$$
$$or \quad U = \{\text{digits of base } 10\}$$
$$or \quad U = W.$$

In the classroom, a common universe is $U = \{\text{people in this room}\}$. Then Bill $\in$ U if Bill is in the room, and Bill $\notin$ U if Bill is not in the room. If M =

{a, b, c} and N = {c, g, z} then one possible universe is U = {letters of the alphabet}.

Addition can be an operation on the set of whole numbers, 2 + 3 = 5, and division can be an operation on the set of whole numbers, 16 ÷ 8 = 2. A number operation pairs numbers with another number according to some rule. Thus, the pair 2 and 3 are assigned to 5 by the rule of addition and the pair 16 and 8 are assigned to 2 by the rule of division. Two elements of a set are paired with another element of a set. Operations can be performed on sets, too.

Operation of Set Union.   Given two sets A and B in a defined universe, U, the *union* of A and B is a set all the members of which are in A or B. The operation union is denoted ∪; A ∪ B is read "A union B." Thus, if A = {1, 2, 3} and B = {4, 5, 6} then A ∪ B = {1, 2, 3, 4, 5, 6}. If A = {a, b, c} and B = {b, e, k} then A ∪ B = {a, b, c, e, k}. *Elements of a set are not repeated.* A Venn or Euler (pronounced "oiler") diagram can be used to represent set union. Let the rectangular region represent the universal set, U, and let the circular regions represent sets A and B as indicated on the left. Then, A ∪ B is represented by the shaded portion of the diagram on the right.

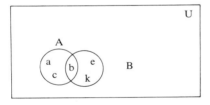 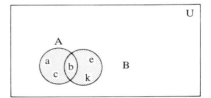

When two sets are disjoint, the Venn diagrams do not contain overlapping circular regions. For two sets A and B, if x ∈ A or x ∈ B then x ∈ A ∪ B.

Let A = {1, 2, 3, 4}
Let B = {a, b, c, d}
Then A ∪ B = {1, 2, 3, 4, a, b, c, d}

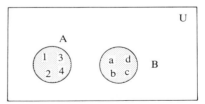

Operation of Set Intersection.   Given two sets A and B, the *intersection* of A and B is the set which contains only those elements which are members of *both* A and B. The intersection of A and B is denoted A ∩ B and is read "A intersection B" or "A intersect B." If A = {1, 2, 3} and B = {2, 4, 6} then A ∩ B = {2}. In the following diagram, let the rectangular region represent the universal set, U, and the circular regions sets A and B. Then the shaded portion of the figure on the right is A ∩ B. If x ∈ A *and* x ∈ B,

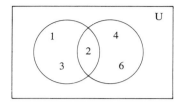 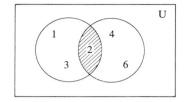

then x ε A ∩ B. When two sets are disjoint, their intersection is the empty set.

Let A = {1, 2, 3}
Let B = {a, b, c}
Then A ∩ B = ∅ = { }

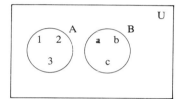

Operation of Set Product or Cross Product.   Given two sets A and B on a defined universe, the set product or cross product of A and B, A × B, is a set of *ordered pairs* in which the first member of the ordered pair is an element of A and the second member of the ordered pair is an element of B. If (a, b) ε A × B then a ε A and b ε B.

The cross product of two sets is a set of ordered pairs which collectively represent all the ways in which elements of the two sets can be paired. If A = {1, 2} and B = {3, 4, 5} then A × B = {(1, 3), (1, 4), (1, 5), (2, 3), (2, 4), (2, 5)}. There are six different ordered pairs which can be named by using an element of A as the first member and an element of B as the second member.

Suppose Bill has two fishing rods, one which is aluminum and one which is fiberglass. He also has four flies; they are red, blue, yellow and green. What are the combinations of fishing gear?

$$\text{Rods} = R = \{a, f\} \qquad \text{Flies} = F = \{r, b, y, g\}$$
$$\text{Gear} = R \times F = \{(a, r), (a, b), (a, y), (a, g), (f, r),$$
$$(f, b), (f, y), (f, g)\}$$

Bill has eight combinations of fishing gear; the cross product has eight ordered pairs.

Notice that A × B ≠ B × A. The number of ordered pairs is the same but the ordered pairs are not identical. (a, b) = (c, d) only if a = c and b = d. If S = {x, y} and T = {m, n, r} then S × T = {(x, m), (x, n), (x, r), (y, m), (y, n), (y, r)} and T × S = {(m, x), (n, x), (r, x), (m, y), (n, y), (r, y); n(S × T) = 6*, n(T × S) = 6*; n(S × T) =

---

* n(T) is explained in the next section.

$n(T \times S)$ but $S \times T \neq T \times S$ since the ordered pairs are not identical.

Exercises

1. Let A = {a, b, c, d}   B = {b, d, g, k}
   A. What is A ∪ B?
   B. What is A ∩ B?
   C. Draw an Euler diagram
2. Let A = {Bill, Mary, Alice}   B = {Tom, Judy, Harry}
   A. What is A ∩ B?
   B. What is A ∪ B?
   C. Draw a Venn diagram
3. Let A = {1, 2, 3, 4, 5}, B = {1, 3, 5, 7}, C = {2, 4, 6}

Find:

A. A ∪ B	F. B ∩ C	K. C × B
B. A ∪ C	G. A ∩ B	
C. B ∪ C	H. A ∩ B ∩ C	
D. A ∪ B ∪ C	I. Draw a Venn diagram	
E. A ∩ C	J. B × C	

Equal and Equivalent Sets, and Number

Two sets are *equivalent* when their elements can be placed in one-to-one correspondence.   If A = {1, 2, 3, 4}

and B = {a, b, c, d} then set A and

set B are equivalent sets because each element in one set can be matched with a distinct element in the other set. Obviously, every set is equivalent to itself. One way to determine equivalence is to place the elements in correspondence; if the sets are finite, you can count the number of elements. If you get the same number of elements in both sets, you know they are equivalent.

Two sets are *equal* when they have the same elements. A = B if every member of A is a member of B and every member of B is a member of A. Let A = {a, b, c, d, e} and B = {e, b, d, c, a}. *A = B because they have the same elements*. Equal sets are always equivalent.

Example: Here are three people and some of their names: Mr. James Jackson—Jack—James—Jim—Mr. Jackson; Mrs. William Corley—Mrs. Corley—Jane—Jane Ellen; Dr. Robert Strong—Dr. Strong—Robert—Bob—Mr. Strong.

> 1. Let U = {The three *people* in the world whose names are Mr. James Jackson, Mrs. William Corley and Dr. Robert Strong}
> A = {James, Jane Ellen}
> B = {Mrs. William Corley, Jim}

A is equivalent to B because the elements can be placed in one-to-one correspondence. Further, A = B because the same two people are in both sets.

2. Let U = {the set of *names* of Mr. James Jackson, Mrs. William Corley and Dr. Robert Strong}

Now A ≠ B because the name "James" is not in both sets. The sets *are* still equivalent.

Example: Here are three numbers and some of their names:

$$\text{Three—III, 3, 2 + 1, 7 − 4}$$
$$\text{Two—2, 1 + 1, 5 − 3, II}$$
$$\text{One—I, 0 + 1, 1, 10 − 9}$$

1. Let U = {all counting numbers}

A = {1, 1 + 1, III}

B = {2, 3, 2 − 1}

A is equivalent to B, A ~ B, because the sets can be placed into one-to-one correspondence. Further, A is equal to B, A = B, because *both sets contain the same numbers, one*, two and three.

2. Let U = {the names for counting numbers} now A is still equivalent to B, A ~ B. However, A ≠ B. A and B do *not* contain the same *names*!

In elementary school, when you use sets to establish number properties of sets you are nearly always working with *equivalent* sets. The number *three* is a quantitative property of sets which have three elements, i.e., the elements can be placed into one-to-one correspondence with this set: {1, 2, 3}.

The number property of a given set is represented by $n(A)$, read "n of A" or "the cardinal number of set A." Thus if A = {a, b, c, d}, then $n(A) = 4$. If B = {○, □, △}, then $n(B) = 3$. The answer to the question, "How many?" is referred to as a *cardinal number*. The cardinal number of set A is four; the cardinal number of set B is three.

When disjoint sets are combined (union), the corresponding operation on their cardinal numbers is addition.

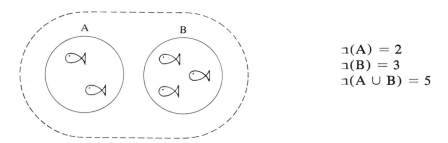

$$n(A) = 2$$
$$n(B) = 3$$
$$n(A \cup B) = 5$$

Try the following exercises to reinforce these concepts. Read the booklet listed at the end of the appendix if you desire additional information and/or reinforcement.

Exercises

1. Let U = {counting numbers} = {1, 2, 3, 4, . . .}, A = {2, 4, 6},
   B = {1 + 1, 4, $\frac{12}{2}$}, C = {1, $\frac{6}{2}$, 5}, D = {1, 3, 5, 7, . . .}.
   A. Which pairs of sets are equivalent?
   B. Which pairs of sets are equal?
   C. What is the cardinal number of each set? (Use proper notation.)
   D. What is n(A ∪ C)?
   E. What is n(A ∪ B)?
   F. What is n(A ∩ D)?
   G. What is n(C ∩ D)?

2. Let U = {*names* for counting numbers}. Answer A through G in
   the previous question.

Answers to Exercises

Section I

1. A. N = {Bill, Joe, Kay}
   B. P = {0, 3, 6, 9, 12, . . .}
      P = {all whole numbers which are multiples of 3}
      P = {x | x = 3w, w ε W}
   C. L = {Ford, Chevy, table, dog}

2. {Bill}, {Bill, Joe}, {Joe}, {Bill, Joe, Kay}, {Kay}, {Bill, Kay}, { },
   {Joe, Kay}

3. A. Bill ε N
   B. cat ∉ L
   C. 17 ε W

4. A. finite   C. finite
   B. finite   D. infinite

5. A. L = {0, 2, 4, 6, . . .}
   B. E = {11}
   C. T = ∅ = { }

Section II

1. A. A ∪ B = {a, b, c, d, g, k}
   B. A ∩ B = {b, d}

   C.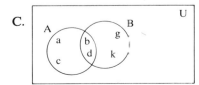

2. A. $A \cap B = \emptyset$
   B. $A \cup B = \{\text{Bill, Mary, Alice, Tom, Judy, Harry}\}$

   C.
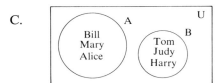

3. A. $A \cup B = \{1, 2, 3, 4, 5, 7\}$
   B. $A \cup C = \{1, 2, 3, 4, 5, 6\}$
   C. $B \cup C = \{1, 2, 3, 4, 5, 6, 7\}$
   D. $A \cup B \cup C = \{1, 2, 3, 4, 5, 6, 7\}$
   E. $A \cap C = \{2, 4\}$
   F. $B \cap C = \emptyset$
   G. $A \cap B = \{1, 3, 5\}$
   H. $A \cap B \cap C = \emptyset$

   I.
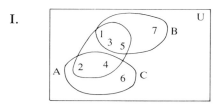

   J. $B \times C = \{(1, 2), (1, 4), (1, 6), (3, 2), (3, 4), (3, 6), (5, 2),$
      $(5, 4), (5, 6), (7, 2), (7, 4), (7, 6)\}$
   K. $C \times B = \{(2, 1), (4, 1), (6, 1), (2, 3), (4, 3), (6, 3), (2, 5),$
      $(4, 5), (6, 5), (2, 7), (4, 7), (6, 7)\}$

Section III

1. A. Equivalent: $A \sim B$, $A \sim C$, $B \sim C$. Also, each set is equivalent to itself.
   B. Equal: $A = B$. Also each set is equal to itself.
   C. $n(A) = 3, n(B) = 3, n(C) = 3, n(D) = $ infinite
   D. $n(A \cup C) = n\{2, 4, 6, 1, \frac{6}{2}, 5\} = 6$
   E. $n(A \cup B) = n\{2, 4, 6\} = 3$ (A and B have the same elements!)
   F. $n(A \cap D) = n\{ \} = \emptyset$
   G. $n(C \cap D) = n\{1, 3, 5\} = 3$

2. A. Same as above
   B. Equal: none, except each set is equal to itself
   C. Same as above
   D. Same as above
   E. $n(A \cup B) = 5$ (Five different *names*.)
   F. Same as above
   G. $n(C \cap D) = n\{1, 5\} = 2$

Additional Teacher Education Resources

I. *Filmstrip*
   The Language of Sets, Society for Visual Education (A557–1)

II. *Booklet*
   Sets, Booklet Number 1, Topics in Mathematics for Elementary School Teachers, National Council of Teachers of Mathematics

Glossary

Accommodation. The process of change *within* to conform to or accept new data. Example: When new information is in conflict with existing beliefs, old beliefs may be altered to coexist with new data.

Adaptation. The successful achievement of a balance between assimilation and accommodation. When the organism successfully integrates the new and the old without distorting either, adaptation occurs.

Angle. The union of two rays which have a common starting point.

Assimilation (intellectual). The process of changing data to a form which can be "taken in." Example: Reality is often altered through perception to agree with existing beliefs.

Common Multiple. k is a common multiple of m and n if k = a(m) and k = b(n) for some counting number(s) a and b. Example: 24 is a common multiple of 3 and 4 because 24 = 8(3) and 24 = 6(4).

Cone. A solid formed by connecting all the points of a simple closed curve to a given point not on the same plane.

Cone, Right Circular. The solid generated by revolving a right triangle about one of its legs.

Curve. Undefined. Can be thought of as a path or the set of points which constitute a path.

Cylinder, Right Circular. A solid generated by revolving a rectangle about one of its sides.

Denominator. The part of a fractional numeral which is written below the line. In $\frac{4}{7}$, 7 is the denominator. If $\frac{4}{7}$ is related to four parts of seven, the denominator indicates the number of parts in the *whole*.

Diagnosis. Evaluation *after* instruction to determine the needs of individuals and groups relative to further development and practice of skills, concepts and generalizations.

Digit. Each of the symbols used to write numerals in the decimal system: 0, 1, 2, 3, 4, 5, 6, 7, 8, 9.

Ellipse. An oval. A plane figure every point of which is a fixed distance-sum from two points called the foci. If the foci are F_1 and F_2 and A and B are on the ellipse then $AF_1 + AF_2 = BF_1 + BF_2$.

Ellipsoid. A solid generated by revolving an ellipse about its major or minor axis (lines of symmetry).

Equilibration. An internalized process by which the individual achieves transition from one level of cognitive development to another, higher level.

Expanded Notation. A numeral is expressed as the sum of the place value components: $267 = 200 + 60 + 7$ *or* $267 = 2 \times 100 + 6 \times 10 + 7 \times 1$

Fact. Used in addition, subtraction, multiplication and division to denote equations in which two of the three members, a, b and c, are digits and the third is a whole number; $a + b = c$, $a - b = c$, $a \times b = c$, $a \div b = c$.

Greatest Common Factor. k is the greatest common factor of p and q if k is the largest number which will divide p and q evenly Example: 2, 3, 6 are common factors of 24 and 30; 6 is the greatest common factor of 24 and 30.

Individualized Instruction. A system of instruction which attempts to meet the unique needs of individuals including rate of learning, social needs, emotional needs and cognitive needs.

Least Common Multiple. The least common multiple of s and t is z if z is the *smallest* multiple of s which is also a multiple of t. Example: Multiples of 5: 5, 10, *15,* 20, 25, *30;* Multiples of 3: 3, 6, 9, 12, *15,* 18, 21, 24, 27, *30.* 15 and 30 are common multiples of 5 and 3; 15 is the *least* common multiple.

Measure. To find the number of times a specified unit is contained in another, unknown, quantity as to find the number of *feet* in an *unknown length* or to find the number of *ping pong balls* in a *jar*.

Modes of Instruction. General methods of instruction which vary in learner involvement, content structuring, strategy sequencing, reinforcement strategies and plans for motivation.

Multiple. x is a multiple of y if $x = m(y)$ for some counting number, m, and whole numbers, x and y. Example: 18 is a multiple of 3 because 18 = 6(3).

Nonterminating Decimal. A decimal which cannot be represented by a finite number of digits without the use of an ellipsis; some repeat (have a period) and some do not. Examples: .3333 . . . , .62146214 . . . , .676776777 . . .

Non-Unit Fraction. A fractional numeral which has a numerator which is *not one*.

Numeration. A method of assigning a number to a numeral. Hence, in *decimal numeration,* 13 is thirteen, and in *base six numeration,* 13 is nine.

Numerator. The part of a fractional numeral which is written above the line, e.g., in $\frac{4}{7}$, 4 is the numerator. When $\frac{4}{7}$ is related to $4 \div 7$, the numerator corresponds to the dividend.

Objective. A statement of a desired pupil behavior to be exhibited as a result of instruction.

One-Dimensional Figure. A figure which has only length, e.g., line, line segment, ray.

One-to-one Correspondence. A matching of each element of set A with exactly one member of set B and each member of set B with exactly one element of set A.

Open Curve. A curve which is not continuous; does not stop where it starts.

Organization. The structure within which cognition occurs. The total framework within which a person's intellectual functions take place.

Partial Product. Part of the product. In the product 24 × 7, 28 is part of the product, 168, and 140 is part of the product, 168. Hence, 28 and 140 are called *partial products.*

$$\begin{array}{r} 24 \\ \times 7 \\ \hline 28 \\ 140 \\ \hline 168 \end{array}$$

Partial Sum. Part of the sum. In the sum 36 + 27, 13 is part of the sum, 63, and 50 is part of the sum, 63. Hence, 13 and 50 are called *partial sums.*

$$\begin{array}{r} 36 \\ 27 \\ \hline 13 \\ 50 \\ \hline 63 \end{array}$$

Place Value. The characteristic of some number systems which gives digits or symbols values which vary in accordance with the position within a numeral. Example: In 489, the digit 8 is eight tens or 80. In 849, the digit 8 is eight hundreds or 800.

Preassessment. Evaluation *prior to* instruction to determine the extent to which individuals and groups have already attained planned objectives.

Pre-operational. Pertaining to experiences occurring *before* work on number operations of addition and subtraction.

Prism.   A solid with parallel, congruent, polygonal bases and sides which are parallelograms.

Pyramid.   A solid formed by a polygon and the triangles which have the sides of the polygon as bases and have as a common vertex a point not in the same plane as the polygon.

Readiness, Experiential.   The extent to which an individual has had a set of appropriate experiences which allow him to understand (attach meaning to) a new learning experience.

Readiness, Maturational.   The extent to which a child has achieved advancement through stages of intellectual development which make it possible for him to achieve new insights and understandings formerly beyond his grasp.

Rectangle.   A quadrilateral with two pairs of congruent line segments and four right angles.

Sequence.   The instructional plan. A set of learning activities designed to teach a concept, skill or generalization.

Seriation.   A series based on some qualitative or quantitative differences in the seriated items as in short to tall, light to heavy, young to old, light green to dark green.

Sphere.   A solid generated by revolving a circle about its diameter.

Square.   A quadrilateral which has four congruent line segments and four right angles.

Subtraction.   The inverse of addition. If $2 + 3 = 5$ then $2 + \square = 5$ and $\square + 3 = 5$ or $5 - 2 = \square$ and $5 - 3 = \square$.

Symmetry, Line.   A figure possesses symmetry with respect to a line, ℓ, if the half figure on one side of ℓ is the mirror image of the other. The two parts must be congruent.

Terminating Decimal.   A decimal which can be represented by a finite number of digits without the use of an ellipsis. A decimal whose fraction equivalent will eventually yield a remainder of zero upon successive division. Examples: .12367, 8.21, .1008794.

Topology.   A system of geometry which relates to those properties of figures which remain unchanged when the figures are deformed in a specified way.

Triangle.   A simple closed curve formed by the union of three line segments.

Index

---

* Page numbers in italic indicate locations of definitions.

** When a double asterisk precedes an entry, that entry can be found in the Glossary, pp. 483–86.